REGION Volume 5, Number 4, 2018

Quality and Inequality in Regional and Urban Systems

Special Issue edited by **Karima Kourtit**, **Peter Nijkamp**, and **Roger Stough**

Table of Contents

Editorial

Articles

Part A: *Creativity and Knowledge as Enabling Factors of Spatial Economic Growth*

Part B: *Structure and Change in Regional Dynamics*

Part C: *Spatial Mobility and Economic Disparity Effects*

This special issue on "Quality and Inequality in Regional and Urban Systems" is edited by Karima Kourtit (KTH Royal Institute of Technology, Stockholm, Sweden; Adam Mickiewicz University, Poznan, Poland), Peter Nijkamp (KTH Royal Institute of Technology, Stockholm, Sweden; Tinbergen Institute, Amsterdam, The Netherlands; Adam Mickiewicz University, Poznan, Poland), and Roger Stough (George Mason University, Fairfax VA, USA). With the exception of the editorial, all contributions to this special issue have already been published in earlier issues of REGION, for the sake of immediate exposure of the content.

- *Effective Clusters as Territorial Performance Engines in a Regional Development Strategy – A Triple Layer DEA Assessment of the Aviation Valley in Poland* by Karima Kourtit, Peter Njkamp and Soushi Suzuki was originally published in vol. 4, no. 3, 39–63.

- *Creativity, Community and Growth: A Social Geography of Craft Beer* by Neil Reid and Jay D. Gatrell was originally published in vol. 4, no. 1, 31–49.

- *Built Environment, Creativity and Social Art: Recovery of Public Space as Engine of Human Development* by Anna Onesti was originally published in vol. 4, no. 3, 87–118.

- *Research Infrastructure, Networks of Science and Regional Development – The Case of Oskarshamm* by Folke Valfrid Snickars and Ulf Karlsson was originally published in vol. 4, no. 3, 119–131.

- *Panel Data Models of New Firm Formation in New England* by Jitendra Parajuli and Kingsley E. Haynes was originally published in vol. 4, no. 3, 65–76.

- *Urban Concentration and Spatial Allocation of Rents from Natural Resources: Zipf's Curve Approach* by Tomaz Ponce Dentinho was originally published in vol. 4, no. 3, 77–86.

- *Regional Public Stock Reductions in Spain: Estimations from a Multiregional Spatial Vector Autorregressive Model* by Miguel A Márquez, Julian Ramajo and Geoffrey Hewings was originally published in vol. 4, no. 1, 129–146.

- *Towards an Integrated Evaluation Approach for Cultural Urban Landscape Conservation/Regeneration* by Francesca Nocca and Luigi Fusco Girard was originally published in vol. 5, no. 1, 33–51.

- *Regional Spanish Tourism Competitiveness. A DEA-MONITUR approach* by Juan Carlos Martín, Cira Mendoza and Concepción Román was originally published in vol. 4, no. 3, 153–173.

- *Territory and Sustainable Tourism Development: a Space-Time Analysis on European Regions* by João Romão, João Guerreiro and Paulo M. M. Rodrigues was originally published in vol. 4, no. 3, 1–17.

- *Spatial mismatch, wages and unemployment in metropolitan areas in Brazil* by Ana Maria Bonomi Barufi, Eduardo Amaral Haddad was originally published in vol. 4, no. 3, 175–200.

REGION, The journal of ERSA / Powered by WU
ISSN: 2409-5370

ERSA: http://www.ersa.org
WU: http://www.wu.ac.at

Editorials

REGION

The Journal of ERSA
Powered by WU

Volume 5, Number 4, 2018, E1–E5
DOI: 10.18335/region.v5i4.257

journal homepage: region.ersa.org

Editorial:
Quality and Inequality in Regional and Urban Systems

Karima Kourtit[1], Peter Nijkamp[2], Roger Stough[3]

[1] KTH Royal Institute of Technology, Stockholm, Sweden; Adam Mickiewicz University, Poznan, Poland
[2] KTH Royal Institute of Technology, Stockholm, Sweden; Tinbergen Institute, Amsterdam, The Netherlands; Adam Mickiewicz University, Poznan, Poland
[3] George Mason University, Fairfax VA, USA

Received: 2 September 2018/Accepted: 17 September 2018

Abstract. In the aftermath of both ongoing globalisation (with both widening and deepening effects on countries, regions and cities) and structural changes resulting from the 2008 economic recession, regions and cities in our world are confronted with a different arena of players, performances and institutions. The challenges are formidable and numerous. Many regions and cities seem to resort to their indigenous strength, without much regard to other players in the field. This has enormous consequences for the competitive behaviour and profile of regional and urban actors but has at the same time deep impacts on the distribution of wealth, income and employment over and within countries, regions and cities. There is indeed much evidence that disparities among regions and in cities are increasing in this new force field.

This special issue of REGION makes a solid scientific attempt (i) to map out the spatial consequences of recent transitions in growth trajectories of countries or regions, and (ii) to trace policy strategies and design effective policy information, to cope adequately with these new challenges. The present special issue does so by highlighting the new force field of regional and urban dynamics from three angles in the context of spatial quality and inequality. These will be briefly sketched below.

1 Introduction

Economies have always had to adjust to the impact of external and internal disequilibrating forces. So, there is nothing new, in general, that the disequilibrating impact that globalization and technological transformation are creating in the functioning of national and regional economic systems. However, it is the speed that these changes are occurring and thus tossing the operation of economic systems into turmoil that is creating new challenges out of the ordinary continuous adjustment and adaptation. When globalization is coupled with information, communication and new telecommunications (ICT) technological change, then the speed of change is accelerated. This speed is not only fast but also continuous, thus resulting in a need to constantly anticipate new developments and at the same time adjust to the newest stressors. The papers for this special edition are presented as a package of some of the consequences of high speed, continuous change and adaption in the face of these changes.

This special edition is presented in three parts. The first considers the role of knowledge and creativity, on the one hand, as drivers of change and, on the other, as factors in the continuous adjustment process. New knowledge in the age of ICT and globalization driven change help to create new ideas and transform them through innovation at an ever-increasing rate into viable and productivity enhanced organizations in both the public and private economic milieu. While serving as major sources of economic growth, knowledge, ICT and globalization also contribute to the adjustment process via new economic planning, policy and management techniques.

Part A: Creativity and Knowledge as Enabling Factors of Spatial Economic Growth

In the first part of this edition, four papers explore the role of these factors in driving and adapting to change. The first paper examines the concept of effective economic clusters and their role in producing economic growth and dynamic adjustment. The second considers the evolution of the craft beer industry as an endogenous growth model or force in the context of regional growth dynamics. Next, there is a paper that advocates the role that art and culture play in reconfiguring the built environment and an impact that this may have on regeneration of society and economy in urban settings. Finally, the fourth paper provides the analysis of how a local community is becoming a R&D and science driven urban economic center, but without a university. These four papers follow in Part A under the heading of creativity and knowledge as enabling factors of spatial economic growth.

> **Kourtit, K., P. Njkamp and S. Suzuki (2017) "Effective Clusters as Territorial Performance Engines in a Regional Development Strategy – A Triple Layer DEA Assessment of the Aviation Valley in Poland", REGION, 4(3), 39-63.**

This paper introduces the concept of effective clusters which are viewed as economic-technology clusters possessing spatial economic synergy, local and region concentration of industry and supporting territorial capital. It is argued that these clusters are center pieces of sustainable territorial performance strategies. A case study focused on one of the most vibrant high technology clusters in Poland, the Dolina Lotnicza Aviation and Aerospace cluster located in the Podkarpackie Region in Southwest Poland. The analysis is multi-level with a benchmark analysis of 25 counties, a comparison of performance of the Dolina Lotnicza cluster with the benchmark analysis, and an efficiency analysis using a super efficiency DEA model of the 16 Polish administrative regions. The case study is used to evaluate the argument that effective clusters are core territorial performance enhancing engines. The findings support the effective cluster concept.

> **Reid, N. and J.D. Catrell (2017) "Creativity, Community and Growth: A Social Geography of Craft Beer", REGION 4(1), 31-49.**

This paper uses the craft beer industry as a vehicle to examine the non-economic growth drivers in emerging industries. Two case studies serve to better understand how the values of entrepreneurs and local firms fit into the way work, place and creativity contribute to the production of growth. Also, the meaning of creativity relative to the craft beer industry is explored and examined. Finally, the results produce a hypothesis that views creativity as a significant factor in niche and emerging industries.

> **Onesti, A. (2017) "Built Environment, Creativity and Social Art: Recovery of Public Space as Engine of Human Development", REGION, 4(3), 87-118.**

The thesis of this paper is that the recovery of public space configured by art and culture and shared with the local community with an inclusive approach, contributes to regenerate creativity, restructuring the relationships among people, communities and landscape. The author argues that this lays the foundation for a creative and regenerative approach. The paper is erected on interpretive analysis and has three major objectives. First is to produce empirical evidence on the relationships among art, heritage and community.

Second, the aim is to develop a methodology for soliciting, integrating and supporting the regeneration of relationships in the town of Torre Annunziata, a case study. And third, the aim is to show the potential of new planning tools.

> **Snickars, F.V. and U. Karlsson (2017) "Research Infrastructure, Networks of Science and Regional Development – The Case of Oskarshamm", REGION, 4(3), 119-131.**

This paper examines how the Oskarshamm region in Sweden appears to have become an R&D center with a wide-ranging scientific network without a university. The Oskarshamm region became the locus along with other places such as Lund, Hamburg and Kiruna of analyses in search of a final location for the internment of nuclear waste. These studies concluded that Oskarshamm was one of the most likely disposal sites. Infrastructure and social network analysis were used to estimate the resulting changes in scientific and infrastructure capacity of Oskarshamm. Over time the analysis of the Oskarshamm site built a strong base of scientific human capital and cooperation between scientists and industry there. The paper focuses on the accumulation of scientific know-how and industry/science cooperation in Oskarshamm as a development that enhanced its technological and scientific infrastructure and thus its regional development capacity.

Part B: Structure and Change in Regional Dynamics

Part B has four papers that relate to economic and spatial structure and their relationship to regional dynamics and vice versa. The first paper examines the correlates of new firm formation in the New England Region of the U.S. and concludes that some of these correlates support prevailing theory and beliefs, but some provide evidence of contradicting conclusions. A second paper examines the relationship between urban concentration and the ownership of natural resources in countries and concludes that the spatial distribution of ownership of resources positively influences urban population densities. The third paper examines the impact of the 2008 global recession on capital stocks in the autonomic regions of Spain and finds that yields of the post 2008 remaining capital are so low in some regions that regional growth has declined significantly. Finally, the last paper in Part B considers a set of indicators for evaluating the role of the cultural urban landscape's contribution to sustainable development and thus contributes to the debate on the future of sustainable development policies and programs.

> **Parjuli, J. and K. Haynes (2017) "Panel Data Models of New Firm Formation in New England", REGION, 4(3), 65-76.**

This study examines the determinants of new firm formation at the county level (1999-2009) in New England, USA. A panel data spatial econometric analysis finds that human capital and population density are positively associated with single unit firm births in both counties and their neighboring counties. Population growth rate also has a significant positive effect on new firm formation with most occurring in spillovers flowing from a growing county to its neighbors. Firm births are negatively affected by the ratio of large/small firms and unemployment rate both within counties and its neighbors. However, no significant impact is found from levels of local financial capital and personal income growth. The paper is of interest, because it tests and challenges some prevailing conclusions about the determinants of new firm formation.

> **Denthino, J.P. (2017) "Urban Concentration and Spatial Allocation of Rents from Natural Resources: Zipf's Curve Approach", REGION, 4(3), 77-86.**

Concern in this paper is with the hypothesis that the dependence level of a country on natural resources may positively influence the level of urban concentration. Analysis of a group of countries using a Zipf curve approach shows that countries with a higher level of urban concentration have higher levels of income coming from natural resources and education expenditures, while public expenditures on health and foreign direct investment (FDI) contribute to spatial redistribution. The paper concludes that the spatial distribution of property rights over resources and related rents influence urban concentration densities.

Marquez, M.A., J. Ramajo and G.J.D. Hewings (2017) "Regional Public Stock Reductions in Spain: estimations from a Multiregional Spatial Vector Autoregressive Model", REGION 4(1), 129-146.

Following the 2008 global recession, public investment in Spain fell, so severely in some regions that they have not been able to replenish depreciated capital. This study models the interdependencies among the Autonomic Regions of Spain using a multiregional specification. The results show that global decreases in public investment have a major and homogeneous effect on the output of all regions. However, regions vary in terms of their public capital stock responses.

Nocca, F. and F.G. Girard (2018) "Toward an Integrated Evaluation Approach for Cultural Landscape Conservation/Regeneration", REGION, 5(1), 33-51.

This paper observes and describes the international debate focused on the need for a new paradigm for defining sustainable development policies and programs. Further, the debate has moved the concept of development toward a more futuristic and cultural perspective and is expected to add a focus on adopting a role for cultural heritage in the new paradigm. The paper first discusses potential indicators that could be used to evaluate the ability of the cultural urban landscape's contribution to sustainable development. A multi-dimensional approach for empirical analysis and for measuring the effects of the cultural urban landscape on sustainable development in general and more specifically on its conservation and regeneration is proposed at the end of the paper.

Part C: Spatial Mobility and Economic Disparity Effects

Part C has three papers that focus on aspects of spatial mobility and economic/income disparity impacts in 21st century economies. The first two papers focus on competitiveness and sustainability of the tourism industry in Spain and the NUTS 2 regions of the European Union, respectively. The last paper examines wage and employment spatial mismatch developments in the metropolitan areas in Brazil. The first paper examines competitiveness performance of the autonomous regions of Spain and concludes that poorer performing regions should consider changes in how their destination businesses operate in such areas, for example, in marketing and enhancing service quality. Next, a second study on a space/time analysis of NUTS 2 regions concludes that dynamics in the tourism industry often have positive competitiveness effects and tend to ameliorate the negative impacts of interregional competition. The final paper of Part C examines the spatial mismatch problem and hypothesis for Brazil. The analysis finds that there is little evidence supporting this hypothesis when the measure is job opportunities. However, when the metric used for the analysis is wages, they find that the mismatch problem is stronger in large metropolitan regions and for low income workers.

Martin, J.C., C. Mendoza and C. Roman (2017) "Regional Spanish Tourism Competitiveness", REGION, 4(3), 153-173.

This paper relates an analysis of the regional tourist competitiveness performance of the autonomous regions of Spain using superior DEA Efficiency modeling to produce a performance ranking of the regions' efficiency (that is, their competitiveness). Madrid and La Rioja regions have a high level of competitiveness, while the more interior regions of Spain are less competitive. The study concludes that the lagging regions should examine practices of their destination management organizations and take corrective action.

Romano, J., J. Guerreio and P. Rodrigues (2017) "Territory and Sustainable Tourism Development: Space Time Analysis on European Regions", REGION, 4 (3), 1-17.

This paper examines the role of resource and culture assets in tourism supply and sustainability. Using advanced spatial econometric analysis of data for the European NUTS 2 regions, it is found that natural resources do not have an expected positive effect on tourism competitiveness. Further, regions with abundant natural resources often have developed unsustainable mass forms of tourism with low value added and with little benefit for host communities. The analysis also supports a conclusion that spatial autocorrelation exists and that spillovers from tourism dynamics tend to have a positive effect on tourism competitiveness and thus to offset negative effects of competition among regions.

Barufi, A.M. and E.A. Haddad (2017) "Spatial Mismatch: Wages and Employment in Metropolitan Areas of Brazil", REGION, 4(3), 175-200.

This paper examines the hypothesis that a lack of accessibility to job opportunities may affect an individual's prospects in the labor market, especially for low-skilled workers. This is more commonly called the spatial mismatch hypothesis. Analysis finds that there is little evidence that this hypothesis holds for residents of metropolitan areas of Brazil. However, there is support for the hypothesis, when the labor market measure used is wages. Further, when wages are used, the impact is higher for large metropolitan regions and for low-skilled workers.

All in all, we may conclude that a thorough analysis of spatial quality and inequality in a geographically heterogeneous world calls for advanced statistical and econometric techniques. Such a diversified toolbox is a sine qua non for a better understanding of spatial complexities in a dynamic and open world economy.

Articles

Part A:

Creativity and Knowledge as Enabling Factors of Spatial Economic Growth

REGION

The Journal of ERSA
Powered by WU

Volume 4, Number 3, 2017, 39–63
DOI: 10.18335/region.v4i3.166

journal homepage: region.ersa.org

Effective Clusters as Territorial Performance Engines in a Regional Development Strategy – A Triple-Layer DEA Assessment of the Aviation Valley in Poland

Karima Kourtit[1], Peter Nijkamp[2], Soushi Suzuki[3]

[1] KTH Royal Institute of Technology, Stockholm, Sweden; Adam Mickiewicz University, Poznan, Poland (email: karima.kourtit@abe.kth.se)
[2] KTH Royal Institute of Technology, Stockholm, Sweden; Tinbergen Institute, Amsterdam, The Netherlands; Adam Mickiewicz University, Poznan, Poland (email: pnijkamp1@gmail.com)
[3] Hokkai-Gakuen University, Sapporo, Japan (email: soushi-s@lst.hokkai-s-u.ac.jp)

Received: 29 September 2016/Accepted: 18 May 2017

Abstract. In the past decades, a new concept has been introduced in the regional development literature, viz. economic-technological clusters. A wealth of studies has been published on the conceptual, operational and policy foundation, and relevance of this concept, especially in relation to previously developed regional growth concepts, such as industrial districts, industrial complexes, or growth centers. In the present paper, clusters will be regarded as the spatial foci of sustainable territorial performance strategies and synergetic actions by both public and private actors. This paper aims to address the relevance of cluster concepts for an effective regional development policy, based on the notion of territorial capital. It does so by introducing a new concept, viz. effective cluster, in which spatial-economic synergy, local/regional concentration of industry, and the supporting role of territorial capital are regarded as the main determinants of a highly performing cluster in a given territory. The effective cluster concept will be illustrated and tested on the basis of a field study on the aviation and aerospace cluster 'Dolina Lotnicza' in the Podkarpackie region in South-East Poland. This is one of the most vibrant high-tech clusters in the country. Rather than providing a critical assessment of the specific development strategy of the Podkarpackie region, this study will show the added value of a new general conceptual framework based on effective clusters. A novel approach based on a triple-layer architecture will be adopted here, viz. a quantitative comparative analysis of the 16 Polish 'voivodships' (main administrative regions in the country, at a NUTS-2 level), a benchmark analysis of the 25 counties ('powiats') within the Podkarpackie voivodship (at a NUTS-4 level), and an effective industrial cluster analysis on the basis of the individual aviation firms located in the Podkarpackie region. In each step, an extended Data Envelopment Analysis (DEA), characterized by a merger of a Slack-Based Measure (SMB) and a super-efficiency (SE) DEA model, will be used in order to achieve an unambiguous ranking of the various regions or relevant Decision Making Units (DMUs) in the area concerned. The study will employ an extensive database based on field work among the individual actors in the cluster, in combination with a broadly composed territorial-capital database for the areas under study. The paper will be concluded with some strategic policy lessons.

1 Introduction: Aviation as a Smart Specialization

Over the past decades, regional development policy has sought to remove the deficiencies in the economic structure of less developed regions through the development of effective infrastructures and the use of appropriate knowledge and innovation systems. Clearly, modern regional development policy seeks to exploit often the economic potential of promising – though not necessary lagging – regions through the creation of accessible transport and communication systems and the transmission of advanced knowledge among actors (see Acz et al. 2009). An important intervening opportunity for an effective use and dissemination of knowledge among actors is formed by social capital (see Westlund 2006). Against this background, regions in an advanced knowledge economy and an open systems' network may act as an economic and technological engine for accelerated knowledge-based spatial development.

Nowadays, there is an increasing awareness that regions should exploit their competitive advantage through a focus on those cognitive activities in which the regions concerned have a proven excellence. This has prompted the notion of smart specialization. The rationale of this concept is based on the idea that in an open world, regions and industries have to compete for the most efficient market strategy, so as to maximize their revenues through a specialization in the most productive or efficient activities. Consequently, regional clusters of industries should not engage in a broad and unfocussed portfolio of industrial or service activities, but should rather seek to optimize their market position on the basis of a smart choice of a limited number of specialized industries (see Batabyal, Nijkamp 2015), such as medical technology, nanotechnology, or environmental technology.

A good example of regional smart specialization is formed by the airline industry. Aviation is a rapidly growing industry world-wide. For example, it is sometimes argued that in the decades to come at least 30,000 new aircraft would have to be built so as to meet the rising demand of mobile people. In the light of this large-scale global development, this dynamic offers, of course, a great opportunity for regional development, provided a proper aviation specialization is strived for from a place-based perspective.

Central and Eastern Europe has a long-standing tradition in the development of aircraft and related products, in particular the Czech Republic, Romania, and Poland. After the fall of the iron curtain, these countries have aimed to employ the historical roots of their former strong aviation industry as an anchor point for developing new regional spearheads in the aerospace industry (see for a review Bochniarz 2007). One of the regions which has in recent years played an active role in the redevelopment of a modern aviation sector is the Podkarpackie region in the South-Eastern part of Poland. It has heavily invested in new infrastructures, advanced knowledge, and international linkages so as to build up a modern aerospace industry. To emphasize the smart aviation specialization in this region, it has in recent years been baptized as the Aviation Valley (see Kaszuba 2012).

The smart specialization in aerospace activities in a given region is based on the assumption that this knowledge-intensive and innovation-driven activity may form a cornerstone for new advanced activities in the area concerned. This modern cluster specialization may generate high revenues, many new jobs, and a high international profile. This calls of course for a thorough (mainly quantitative) assessment of all relevant effects of such an aviation cluster. A good example of such an impact study, on the Boeing aviation cluster in Washington State (USA), can be found in CAI (2013) and Sommers et al. (2008). Additionally, in recent years, various studies in Europe have been carried out on the (regional-) economic significance of the aviation sector. Some interesting examples can be found in a study for the European Commission (ECORYS 2009), and in a study on aviation networks (Zuliani, Jalebert 2005). A policy-oriented study on the regional aerospace cluster policy in Europe can be found in Schönfeld, Jouaillec (2008).

It goes without saying that in the light of the economic and cognitive importance of high-quality regional aviation initiatives, proper decisions have to be taken on the choice of the portfolio of activities, on the skill levels needed, on the necessary infrastructural provisions, and on the set of innovation strategies needed to ensure the highest performance of the cluster concerned.

In the light of the previous observations, this paper aims to assess the success factors of the Polish Aviation Valley by seeking to arrive at a relative performance ranking of key actors, by using a 3-stage Data Envelopment Analysis (DEA), for an effective cluster constellation to be evaluated in three successive steps: (i) a comparative evaluation of the performance of the Podkarpackie region in South-East Poland vis-à-vis the other main administrative regions ('voivodships'); (ii) a comparative evaluation of the performance of the 25 counties ('powiats') in the Podkarpackie region that are the home base of the various firms in the Aviation Valley in Podkarpackie; and (iii) a comparative evaluation of the micro performance of the most important aviation business firms in this cluster on the basis of detailed interview information from these firms. The methodological toolbox for this triple-layer assessment comprises in particular: principal component analysis (PCA) and Data Envelopment Analysis (DEA).

The present study is organized as follows. After this introductory section, Sections 2 and 3 will, respectively, be devoted to a conceptual exploration and a concise description of the economic backgrounds and the current cluster position of the above mentioned Aviation Valley in Poland. In Section 4, we will present the methodological backgrounds of our territorial performance model, followed by a description of the database collected and employed for our research purposes. In Section 5, the operational model will be treated in the form of a comparative benchmark analysis of the constituents of the triple-layer architecture, where territorial capital data will be used as input for the DEA. The subsequent section (Section 6) will be devoted to a description and interpretation of our results, while the final section will offer concluding remarks, in particular on policy lessons for the Aviation Valley.

2   Territories and Production Units in Clusters

Regional development is not 'manna from heaven', but the result of deliberate smart strategic choices, decisions, and actions of stakeholders in a given area. It is based on an effective policy effort – both public and private – to shape attractive conditions for accelerated sustainable growth in a geographically concentrated area (see Andersson et al. 2016). The achievement of such a goal needs the fulfilment of various prerequisites: economies of density of activities, multi-tasking synergy of smart development strategies, and existence and exploitation of internal and external network liaisons among all relevant actors (see for an overview Capello, Nijkamp 2009).

In the rich history of regional development policy a variety of instrumental concepts has come to the fore: industrial districts, growth poles, growth centers, geographical clusters, development axes, industrial complexes, special economic zones, high-tech parks, etc. Despite a diversity in meaning and scope of such spatial growth concepts, they all served to enhance the economic performance of the area concerned, with a view to formulating and implementing solid strategies in order to improve its socio-economic competitive profile and to reduce spatial disparities in a regional or (inter)national arena through various forms of scale and agglomeration advantages (Nijkamp 2016).

Countries, regions, and municipalities all over the world are exposed to the challenge and opportunity to improve continuously their position and to optimize their socio-economic performance, by economizing on the use of critical (internal and external) resources to enter a more promising – though also more risky – competitive spatial-economic environment in a globalizing system. Such a performance may comprise: welfare, socio-economic well-being, income, safety, employment, economic growth, (inter)national recognition, social cohesion, sustainable development, and so forth. It should be noted here that there is in general no unambiguous and measurable performance measure for such territories, in contrast to industrial organizations, where nowadays KPIs (key performance indicators) act as signposts for company strategies. Clearly, some attempts at designing such systematic information have been made in recent years. For example, in an urban context, the notion of XXQ (maximum quality of a city) has recently been advocated as an overarching policy objective including in particular economic, social, and ecological performance indicators of a city (see Nijkamp 2008, Kourtit 2014, 2015).

It seems plausible that any territory in the form of an interlinked spatial entity (country, region, municipality) seeks to optimize its relative position in a balanced way in order to achieve the highest possible quality of welfare, living, and working in this area (see Nijkamp 2008, Kourtit 2014, 2015), as compared to others. These 'others' may be the direct neighbors in the vicinity, but they may also be found at the international stage (see for instance, the competition between global world cities such as New York, London, Paris, or Tokyo) (we refer here, for example, to Kourtit et al. 2013, Arribas-Bel et al. 2013). Regions in our world may be assumed to maximize their contribution to – and share in – the total 'performance production' at a global scale, or at least within a given relevant continent or country. This performance[1] may be measured on a multidimensional and even multilevel scale – including e.g., GDP per capita, employment, public facilities, socio-economic equality, and ecological quality as well as critical network elements – as part of a so-called 'Territorial Performance Index'(TPI), which may act as crucial location factors and drivers for various actors across geographical units (see also Camagni 2009). Such a TPI is clearly a latent variable and may be the result of either competitive strategies or cooperation initiatives, or both, with regard to players in the same domain (see also Healy, Cote 2001). In this context, Kaasa, Part (2008) argued that "an individual's achievements would be higher, if he or she competed and cooperated with others through different networks and common value systems" (p. 5). This also holds for territories (countries, regions, cities, etc.) which may be seen as multi-tasking production units, often in liaison with other territories.

In the light of the previous observations, we will assume in the present paper that each territory has a TPI which can be produced or created through a smart combination of various productive inputs, in particular, Human Capital (HC), Infrastructural Capital (IC) and Social Capital (SC) (see also Becker 2009, De la Fuente, Vives 1995, Heckman 2000, Ravikumar, Glomm 1992, Rodriguez-Pose, Fratesi 2004). The TPI production function is thus shaped through at least three distinct – but often mutually connected – production factors. The welfare of regions is thus critically dependent on its resource use (Nijkamp 2016). The blend of these three categories of production inputs will be coined here 'Territorial Capital' (TC).

'Territorial Capital' is a new concept that has received much policy attention in the past decade (see OECD 2001, European Commission 2005). It takes its starting point in the unifying concept of a region which unites various productive forces (capital, labor, infrastructure, knowledge, innovation, resources, or social capital) that act as jointly operating production factors so as to increase regional productivity and efficiency and to sustain socio-economic growth. It may be defined as the set of geographically and locally bounded critical assets, amenities, and conditions that provide the competitive advantages of places and their uniqueness and attractiveness through an efficiency-enhancing contribution to sustainable growth (Camagni 2009). TC is thus not only geographically bounded, but also functionally related to a regional system (in material, social, technological, cultural, and cognitive terms). This idea was inspired by the seminal contributions of Camagni (2002, 2009) , Camagni, Capello (2011, 2013, 2015), Capello et al. (2011), Caragliu (2015), Fratesi, Perucca (2014), and Perucca (2014). This idea has first been introduced as an operational tool in the regional development literature by Camagni (2002) and has been followed by various subsequent empirical territorial capital studies (see for a survey, amongst others, Capello et al. 2011). The three constituents of TC can be briefly described as follows:

- Human capital (HC): knowledge, training, education, R&D, learning-by-doing strategies, creativity, innovativeness, entrepreneurial attitude.

- Infrastructural capital (IC): physical transport and communication facilities, connected networks, energy grids, water facilities, ICT, digital information and moni-

---

[1]The 'performance' concept already has a long history in industrial management and business economics. In general terms, this concept can be defined as: 'a person's achievement under test conditions' (Oxford Encyclopaedic English Dictionary). However, in productivity and efficiency studies, this concept is defined much more broadly and refers to a systematic operational measurement – often in comparison with relevant actors – of the relevant economic achievement position of an actor or corporate organization (see also Kourtit 2014, 2015, p. 16). The latter meaning will also be adopted in our study on the aviation and aerospace cluster in the Podkarpackie region in South-East Poland.

toring systems.

- Social capital (SC): communication networks, business alliances, incubators, socio-cultural cohesion strategies, cooperation programs, knowledge spillover networks, voluntary organizations (NGOs, etc.).

The smart combination of these productive resources by a region leads to the unifying concept of a 'resourceful region', as advocated in Nijkamp (2016). It is clear that HC, IC, and SC are compound and multidimensional latent vectors, which can only indirectly be observed through measurable indicators (see Section 4). They determine in combination the TPI for each relevant area. In this context, an interesting research question with important regional policy implications concerns the effectiveness of enhancing and improving the regional cluster performance – of both the actors individually and the region as a whole – in producing a desired result on the basis of a smart (innovative and sustainable) use of territorial capital in the area concerned.

In our study we will provide an empirical test of this concept for the Podkarpackie region (voivodship) in South-East Poland. We will address in particular the question: "which territorial capital assets play an efficient role in the mechanism of an effective cluster in the Aviation Valley in this region?" This calls for a triple-layer analysis: (i) a comparative performance analysis of the Podkarpackie region in Poland as the home basis of aviation activities; (ii) a detailed spatial analysis of the counties ('powiats') in Podkarpackie, as the counties ('powiats') in this region are rather heterogeneous and offer different territorial capital assets, and (iii) a comparative study at the firm level to identify the attractiveness factors in the various counties for the individual firms in the Aviation Valley.

3 The Aviation Sector in Poland

3.1 Transformation of the aviation industry in Poland[2]

The airline sector (aviation sector) has over the past decades turned into one of the most dynamic, rapidly growing and high-tech oriented industries in the world, mainly as a consequence of deregulation and intense competition in this sector (see e.g. Adler, Golany 2001, Berechman, de Wit 1996, Burghouwt, Huys 2003, Button 2002, Nijkamp 1996). The demand drivers and the supply conditions of modern aviation have been extensively examined in the literature, in particular, the pricing and routing scheduling, as well as the airport operations. Less attention has been paid to the production and location aspects of aircraft and aircraft equipment and services. The latter – mainly manufacturing – issue has in recent years become an important component of modern regional cluster analysis and policy. Poland has historically been an important center of airplane production, until this sector collapsed after the fall of the iron curtain. Against the background of a dedicated regional policy, the aviation production sector has recently become one of the spearheads of policy support for the Aviation Valley in the Podkarpackie region in South-East Poland.

The history of the Polish aviation industry dates back to the 1930s, when several aviation companies were established in the Central Industrial Area (Centralny Okręg Przemysowy (COP)) in Poland. The transformation of the economic system in Poland in the early 1990's opened new possibilities for the – traditionally strong – Polish aviation industry, but created also several new obstacles that could have slowed down or even stopped its favorable development, if not bypassed effectively. One of the most important strategic decisions was outlining and deciding how the industry should be privatized by choosing and convincing strategic investors (companies which would provide significant investment capital) and by considering and implementing alternative methods of ownership transfer. It was essential to plan how the industry would enter into international cooperative agreements, while showing strength and competitiveness. Market opportunities existing at

---

[2]The authors wish to thank Zbigniew Bochniarz, Emilia Barbara Sieńko-Kułakowska, Grzegorz Pisarczyk and Waldemar Ratajczak for their great contribution to this section on the transformation and sustainable development of the aviation industry in Poland.

the time indicated that Poland could take advantage of well-established aviation industry facilities and of past achievements, and build up a competitive advantage, particularly in the light-aircraft market. The historical presence of human capital and industrial engineering traditions in the Podkarpackie region – dating back to the pre-WWII period – helped to encourage a revitalization of the aviation industry.

3.2 Sustainable development of the aviation industry in Poland

3.2.1 A sketch of the industry

The expansion of the Polish aviation industry after the transformational period in the 1990s appears to depend strongly on a combination of expansion of international industrial cooperation and foreign direct investment (FDI). As a result, the industry had a rich export offer in terms of advanced aviation products (or rather, sub-assemblies, components, parts, and equipment) for export to e.g., the USA, Venezuela, Indonesia, Italy, Greece, Canada, Spain, Germany, South Korea, and Vietnam. This led to a new and creative revival of industrial spirit and organization. Operating plants in this area are specialized in the production of aircraft components and services (high-tech, training, and executive services), helicopters, gliders, sub-assemblies (aluminum, composite, GRFP), and accessories. Over 140 businesses appeared to operate in 2015 in the Polish aviation and aviation-related sector, with approx. 1 billion EUR in annual sales, and 24,000 employees in total. The majority of these activities are composed of small and medium-sized businesses (SMEs), while companies are partly owned in some cases by foreign investors; there is also a small number of businesses that are owned by the National Treasury in Poland. The majority of the aviation facilities in Poland is located in the South-Eastern part of the country, mainly in a few existing clusters, in which the Aviation Valley in Podkarpackie is the most prominent one.

The biggest foreign investors in the Polish aviation industry are General Electric, United Technologies Corporation, EADS CASA, Pratt & Whitney Canada, Goodrich, Hispano Suiza, and Avio (see Figure 1). The production potential of these businesses is high, mainly due to the quality of the products offered (thanks to a long-standing experience on how to treat materials, casting, mechanics, and electronics) and competitive labor costs. The currently existing network cluster of production and service companies supported by R&D centers have the potential to cooperate in fulfilling and referring orders of replacement parts and complete products for the aviation sector. Thanks to the contribution of companies to R&D, collaboration with research centers and universities, participation in foreign projects, human capital, and the strongly developing clusters, the aviation sector is one of the most innovative ones in the whole Polish economy (see also Ratajczak 2008).

The growth of the aviation industry would not have been possible without qualified human capital. Every year over 11,000 engineers graduate from Polish technical universities, while about 650 graduates have a major in aviation. A highly developed university education system and on-the-job training systems, combined with a rich tradition of excellence, are factors that greatly improve the quality of aviation sector personnel, as is witnessed by the Triple-Helix constellation around the Rzeszow area. Additionally, thanks to new initiatives (such as AERONET), the aviation sector has achieved a close cooperation between industry, government, and educational institutions, serving the common goal of better preparing personnel, for example, by designing specialized educational programs and offering qualified majors to adequately fit the needs of the job market. Clearly, industry-university-policy interfaces appear to be a critical success factor for the growth of the aviation sector in Poland. For a strategy analysis of this phenomenon we refer to Kourtit, Nijkamp (2017).

3.2.2 The Aviation Valley: the Dolina Lotnicza cluster

The Polish aviation industry's prospects for economic and technological advancement are particularly dependent on strategies for effectively operating modern industrial aviation clusters. A promising role model for such a strategy may be found in the Aviation

Source: Internal documents from the Aviation Valley (Dolina Lotnicza) cluster and Marshall Office
Notes: Encircled areas are aviation regions in Poland, in which the Aviation Valley in the South-East is the dominant one

Figure 1: The aviation industry in Poland

Valley (Dolina Lotnicza) cluster in this country. This cluster contains over 100 innovative manufacturing businesses responsible for a large number of aviation products such as components, major assemblies, and sub-assemblies for jet engines, gliders, and helicopters, produced for some of the most important aviation manufacturers and users in the world. Companies in the Aviation Valley are also responsible for the manufacturing of finished products for final clients. Many of the companies in the cluster work together to fulfill their project's tasks in an efficient way, while also a number of businesses complete their entire manufacturing process using only their own resources and offering their products directly to the market. The Aviation Valley represents nowadays about 90% of the aviation industry in Poland. Associated partners are worldwide leaders in their respective fields, such as Pratt & Whitney, Sikorsky, Agusta Westland, Hispano Suiza Polska, Goodrich, MTU Aero Engines, Hamilton Sundstrund, and a dozen of small and medium-sized businesses (see again Figure 1).

A critical challenge in developing this cluster was to bring also small and medium-sized businesses with a commercial link to aviation into the cluster, including those with Polish and foreign investment sources. Through the flow of – and access to – new technologies, these businesses are able to achieve ambitious cooperative goals in the cluster. The realization of such industrial processes means essentially a shift of various activities in the value chain towards the center of the cluster. Experiences from other big clusters indicate that such undertakings lead to effective and high synergy and to measurable economic benefits. The Aviation Valley in Poland has indeed managed to include a large number of critical market and technological leaders among its cluster participants, who continue to bring their added value into the cluster. Consequently, a characteristic of the Aviation Valley cluster is the emergence of a fully developed value chain, as depicted in Figure 2 which shows the structure of the cluster (see also Kaszuba 2012).

The various R&D, production, and market operations in the Aviation Valley cluster have been a model of cooperation between industry and research in Poland. For example, aviation manufacturers meet regularly with representatives of the best Polish technical universities and research centers that have partnered with them. It is noteworthy that among the businesses originating from the Polish aviation industry, only a few large companies (e.g., PZL Mielec, EADS PZL, PZL-Świdnik) produce final goods. Small and medium-sized businesses operate mainly in a cooperative and/or subcontractor role, producing only specific elements of the airframe and equipment of airplanes, or building specialized aircraft parts. However, subcontractors and suppliers are not the only small businesses which play an important role. There are also other small firms that build their own aviation designs, including technologically advanced small aircraft and gliders.

Source: Internal documents from the Aviation Valley (Dolina Lotnicza) Cluster and Marshall Office
Notes: Companies divided by employment level (scale on the left axis)

Figure 2: The structure of the Aviation Valley (Dolina Lotnicza) cluster in Poland

The total sales of all businesses in the aviation sector in Poland have been steadily rising, with the Podkarpackie region as the uncontested leader. The sector has been growing drastically, with sales even quadrupling in the years 2003-2008. This dynamic development is closely linked to foreign investments, as the majority of sales are the result of supplying foreign companies which own or contract these Polish manufacturers.

It is also clear that the presence of and access to an advanced knowledge base in the Podkarpackie area – in particular, higher education institutes – play a critical role in supporting new technology industries (see Calzonetti, Reid 2013). R&D plays a critical role in the success of the Polish aviation industry in general and of Dolina Lotnicza in particular. As a world-class cluster, it has a main goal to conduct advanced academic R&D as well as establishing innovative solutions in the field of aviation engineering (European Aeronautics 2001). Clearly, the Polish aviation industry does currently not yet participate in large-scale manufacturing of passenger planes. This has significant implications for the development of a new model of cooperation with the few world leaders shaping their global supply chain. It influences also the scientific and technological research of the Polish aviation industry and forces it to retain its competitive niche position (Baczko 2011). It is noteworthy that also the Polish job market may be strengthened in the future by a highly qualified workforce able to develop, design, and build high-quality and highly innovative aviation subcomponents and complete products. We will now address the framing of the critical success factors and conditions for this creative aviation development in this region in Poland.

4 A Triple-Layer DEA Model for the Aviation Valley

4.1 Introduction

The notion of an industrial cluster has gained much popularity over the past two decades (see Porter 1990). Recent contributions to cluster concepts and policies can be found inter alia in Asheim et al. (2006), Kasabov, Sundaram (2016), and Scholl, Brenner (2016). As mentioned in Section 1, a cluster may be seen as a complement to earlier concepts from the regional-economic growth literature, such as industrial districts, industrial corridors, growth centers, or development axes (see also a recent contribution by Gibson et al. 2013, Nijkamp 2016). The Aviation Valley – called Dolina Lotnicza in Polish – is a rapidly growing industrial cluster, but needs still further development, in terms of both widening and deepening. In order to become an 'effective cluster' – well anchored in the region on the basis of cooperative strategies ('social capital') and through advanced cognitive and technological applications – in a regional development context, new initiatives are needed, based on entrepreneurship, leadership, and good governance at local and regional levels.

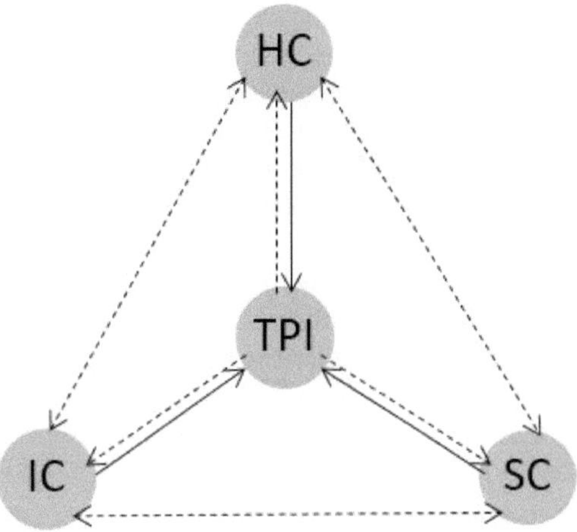

Source: Authors' design

Figure 3: Scheme of the TPI production function (positive externalities for effective cluster performance)

The basic idea of an effective cluster – sketched out in Figure 3 – is that it enhances economic performance of each cluster participant and of the cluster as whole through a smart combination of human, social, and infrastructural capital[3]. Such a cluster is thus driven by positive externalities and may be seen as a flagship for successful regional development.

The Polish aerospace cluster contains more than 100 firms and at present over 1 billion EUR annual revenues, with a concentration in Podkarpackie. This flagship project hosts all major global aviation manufacturers, but still needs a further strengthening and more synergy in order to become an effective and efficient industrial agglomeration, as highlighted in the seminal writings of Marshall, Isard and Porter, to mention only a few.

Industrial clusters are often spontaneously emerging, thematically oriented industrial concentrations, but they may also be the result of dedicated policy decisions to favor a certain industrial concentration in a given region. In both cases, there is a need for informed stimulating policies so as to maximize cluster benefits through innovativeness, productivity increase, and smart specialization. In the specific case of the Aviation Valley, there has been a long tradition of aerospace activities which have been an undercurrent for a rejuvenation of this sector in the past decades after the fall of the iron curtain. Clearly, there is also a need for applied statistical and econometric techniques for testing, understanding and assessing a cluster's performance.

The aim of the present section is to design a systematic and operational framework to provide an original analysis of the cluster achievement data, based on the above mentioned triple-layer architecture, by using an extended and stepwise Data Envelopment Analysis (DEA) to position these regions (voivodships), counties (powiats) and firms on the basis of their relative performance, i.e. by relating their multiple outputs to multiple inputs in the context of an effective cluster to be attained through a balanced mix of HC, IC, and SC, next to the business achievements of individual cluster participants and of the cluster as whole (see also Kourtit, Nijkamp 2013a). We will now offer the design of a conceptual model for an effective cluster assessment in our analysis (see Figure 3).

Figure 3 sketches out the central research aim of the present paper: the assessment of the territorial performance of an advanced industrial area (i.e., an effective cluster) as a function of its human, infrastructural, and social capital provisions (i.e., its total

---

[3]A comprehensive definition of an effective cluster is: "A geographical and tangible concentration of advanced economic, technological and social activities – both private and public – in a given region, that is driven by synergy coming from network of actors committed (social capital) and usually supported by public policy in order to enhance the cluster performance (in particular, competitiveness, innovation, shared values and trust) – of both the actors individually and the region as a whole – on the basis of a smart (innovative and sustainable) use of territorial capital in the area concerned" (www.effectiveclusters.eu).

territorial capital). The validity and relevance of this TPI methodology will now be tested by means of an application to the Aviation Valley in the Podkarpackie region in South-East Poland, which aspires to become a leading high-tech region in the field of the aviation industry in Europe. We will test our conceptual TPI model on the basis of a triple-layer and a (super-efficient) DEA model using a wide array of empirical data on this Aviation Valley and the territorial capital of the region and of the constituent areas concerned.

It is thus clear that Territorial Capital (TC) is a basket of areal productive assets in an effective cluster composed of Human Capital (HC), Infrastructural Capital (IC), and Social Capital (SC). These three constituents make up the production inputs for the Territorial Performance Index (TPI) in our Data Envelopment Analysis (DEA). Given the large multidimensional databases, the use of a multivariate statistical analysis is a necessary tool in the triple-layer approach in our study so as to obtain a systematically structured database.

4.2 Principal Component Analysis (PCA)

Our triple-layer database contains a wide variety of important statistical factors which determine the quantitative performance of a DMU, at each of the three levels of our analysis (voivodship, powiats and firms). This set of multiple indicators contains at each level an extensive set of multicollinear variables, so that it would be hard to draw straightforward and unambiguous conclusions on the underlying causal mechanisms. Therefore, it was necessary to apply a multivariate analysis – in this case, a principal component analysis – to identify uncorrelated and mutually independent factors, which can be used as proxies for the determinants of regional growth.

In the particular case of detailed statistical information on the 16 voivodships in Poland, we have a broad and detailed annual database (population, labor market, economic variables, etc.) on all voivodships and powiats. Clearly, this leads to a case of multicollinearity in our data. To avoid statistical biases, we used a principal component analysis (PCA), so that we are able to distil from a multicollinear data set a new set of transformed and independent variables that do not suffer from multicollinearity. The next step in our triple-layer analysis was to apply a DEA to each of the three constituents of our database.

4.3 Data Envelopment Analysis (DEA)

DEA has become an established method in management sciences and industrial organization theory to assess the efficiency of complex organizations, often referred to as Decision Making Units (DMUs). It finds its origin in activity analysis and multiple objective programming, and aims to identify in a comparative sense the relative efficiency of DMUs on the basis of their output versus input ratios, in multiple dimensions. So, DEA is essentially a generalized productivity analysis.

The standard DEA model was developed by Charnes et al. (1978) (usually abbreviated as the CCR model). This model – and its many variants and extensions – has found thousands of applications in the scientific literature over the past decades. We refer here to various overview publications, such as Charnes et al. (1994), Zhu (2003), Färe et al. (1998), Ray (2004), Cooper et al. (2006), Zhu, Cook (2007), Suzuki, Nijkamp (2016a,b), Susuki, Nijkamp (2017), and Suzuki et al. (2010, 2015).

The result of a DEA analysis is normally a ranking of DMUs according to their degree of output efficiency. In this way, it is not only possible to find the position of each individual DMU on the efficiency ladder, but also to find out which inputs should be changed, so as to obtain a more efficiently operating organization. There is a great variety of DEA models, starting from the basic CCR model originally developed by Charnes et al. (1978). Over the past decades, a whole range of adjustments and revisions have been implemented, so as to cope with weak elements, limitations, or specific needs of DEA model applications (see Susuki, Nijkamp 2017). We will use here an adjusted version of a standard DEA model, namely a Slack-Based Measure (SBM) – in a triple-layer architecture – to identify the relative efficiency of voivodships, powiats and aviation business firms in Poland, in order to draw conclusions on the success conditions of the aviation sector in this country and its regions and counties.

In the context of the triple-layer constellation of smart or effective cluster policy in Poland, the so-called Slack-Based Measure (SBM) model turned out to provide a meaningful tool for performing a DEA analysis at three consecutive levels of DMUs, viz. voivodships, powiats, and enterprises. The SBM model was initially developed by Tone (2001) and has found various interesting applications in the literature.

The main distinction between the standard CCR model and the SBM model is related to a radial type projection model and non-radial type model, respectively. A shortcoming of the radial model is a neglect of slacks in computing the efficiency score. Consequently, the radial type model may lead to a biased and overestimated efficiency score. In contrast, the non-radial type models including SBM are able to deal with a slack presence. Hence, an SBM model can improve the overestimation problem.

We will next, in the application of the triple-layer SBM DEA model, include one more extension, viz. the concept of super-efficiency. In the standard DEA model, DMUs located on the efficiency frontier are all equally efficient and hence receive an efficiency score of 1. In many cases, it is desirable to make a further distinction among these efficient firms with an equal score of 1. This has prompted the notion of super-efficiency (SE), through which an unambiguous ranking of DMUs can be achieved (see Tone 2001). We will present here the results of a combined SBM-SE model in our DEA of the Aviation Valley in Poland.

In our empirical DEA application, we will use the (transformed PCA) data on HC, IC, and SC as inputs for a DEA exercise in each of the three stages, while we will use the TPI as output (or performance indicator), based on the architecture of our model sketched in Figure 3. In conclusion, we position PCA and DEA in the context of our triple-layer explanatory model for the performance of relevant DMUs in the aviation industry in the Polish Aviation Valley.

4.4 Conceptual framing of territorial performance in DEA

4.4.1 Architecture of the model

The constituents of the Territorial Performance Index (TPI), viz. HC, IC, and SC, have been outlined in previous sections, based on the schematic presentation in Figure 3. We will, in the present subsection, integrate these building blocks into a more comprehensive TPI framework, by first extending the basic Figure 3 with the most prominent functionalities of the three capital categories under consideration (see Figure 4).

The functional-causal linkages among HC, IC, and SC can be used as the building blocks for a more comprehensive operational model that maps out the total factor productivity (TFP) of the determinants of regional development. A schematic presentation of this model can be found in Figure 4.

It should be added, that next to these contextual capital assets from the business environment in the region, the territorial performance of a region is also determined by the business efforts and subsequent performance actions of private firms in the cluster. The latter category may comprise KPIs of the private sector in the region under consideration. We will now describe in slightly more detail the various explanatory constituents in our TPI production function.

4.4.2 Human Capital

Human capital has become an important topic in economic research since the seminal contributions of Schultz (1961) and later on by Becker (2009). It is nowadays seen as a crucial factor for economic growth and efficiency. Human capital (HC) comprises the personal characteristics and cognitive skills of people who share the responsibility for regional development in a given area. HC is a multi-dimensional concept which includes inter alia: cognitive skills, training facilities, educational programs, advanced knowledge use, R & D expenditure, technical support programs, creativity, human health

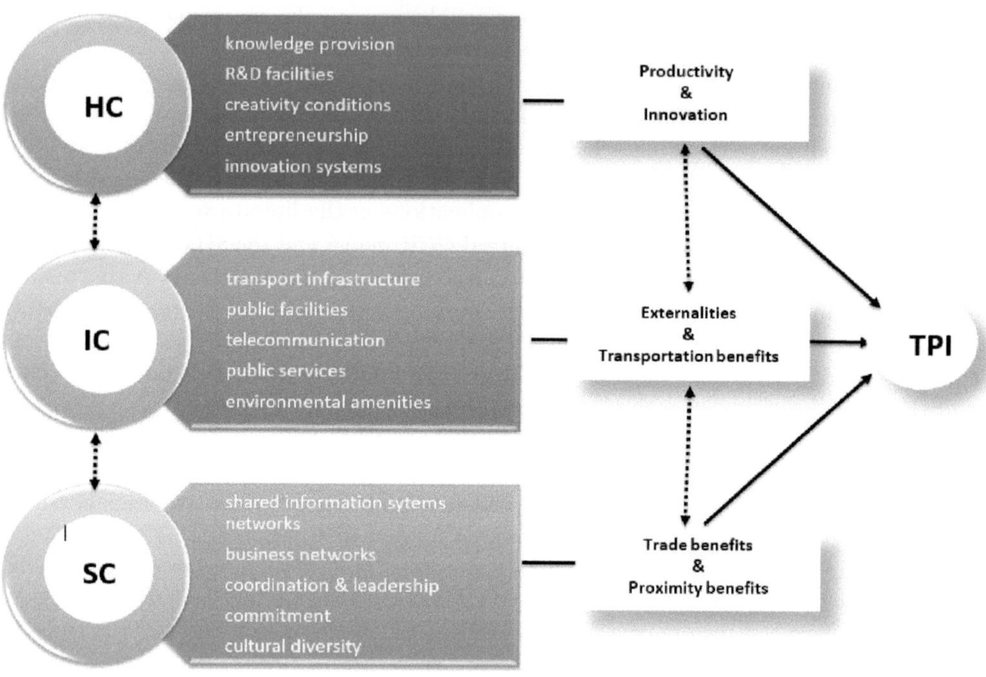

Source: Authors' design

Figure 4: A comprehensive representation of the TPI model

conditions, learning experiences, organizing capacity, innovativeness, open innovation systems, entrepreneurship, etc.

4.4.3 Infrastructural Capital

Infrastructure is often regarded as a prominent factor in regional-economic development, in both developed and developing economies (Aschauer 1989, Bröcker, Rietveld 2009, Elburz et al. 2015). Infrastructural capital (IC) refers to the necessary physical and material conditions in the form of public or collective goods that shape or induce the welfare of a country or region. Infrastructure may be instrumental in accelerating economic growth and mitigating spatial disparities. It may adopt various forms, e.g., land transport infrastructure, air and water transport facilities, public amenities and telecommunication. Examples are: roads, streets, parking facilities, railways, railway stations, public transport facilities, airports, runways, ports, energy grids, telecommunication facilities, public services (e.g. health care), environmental amenities, tourist and recreational facilities, etc. The assessment of the impact of IC on regional development calls generally for a broad multidimensional impact model (see e.g., for a general survey and meta-analytical synthesis Celbis et al. 2015).

4.4.4 Social Capital

Social capital is a more recent concept in economic research. It found its origin in sociological research and was first advocated by Hanifan (1916), who described social capital as: "Those tangible assets [that] count for most in the daily lives of people: namely goodwill, fellowship, sympathy, and social intercourse among the individuals and families who make up a social unit" (p. 130). Later on, it was further popularized inter alia by Jacobs (1961), Bourdieu (1981), Coleman (1988) and Fukuyama (2001).

Putnam (1993) offers a more contemporaneous definition: "Social capital refers to features of social organization, such as networks, norms, and trust, that facilitate coordination and cooperation for mutual benefit" (p. 35). Social capital plays a critical role in

Table 1: The multivariate database (reduced into a single-period database with two independent factors by means of a PCA) for the 16 voivodships in Poland[5]

Regions	INPUTS		OUTPUT
	HC	IC	GDP
ŁÓDZKIE	15.24383785	17.76018463	101423
MAZOWIECKIE	59.36306148	1	364513
MAŁOPOLSKIE	27.573995	17.73570387	128009
ŚLĄSKIE	35.9421777	37.32693562	207104
LUBELSKIE	9.357115528	13.42869107	65845
PODKARPACKIE	7.993997384	12.56609439	65365
PODLASKIE	3.351309907	6.687236914	37601
ŚWIĘTOKRZYSKIE	5.554316221	17.32539808	40047
LUBUSKIE	1	11.88567379	36940
WIELKOPOLSKIE	22.30567904	18.32329266	161485
ZACHODNIOPOMORSKIE	9.306254571	13.49000607	62463
DOLNOŚLĄSKIE	22.36283317	14.45307287	140901
OPOLSKIE	4.482978925	20.22856136	35130
KUJAWSKO-POMORSKIE	10.08726379	18.42180737	74515
POMORSKIE	18.02637696	11.99428224	95701
WARMIŃSKO-MAZURSKIE	2.997127294	12.4321011	45008

Source: Source: Authors' own calculation using data from the Statistical Office in Rzeszow (2014)

regional development through the following channels: cooperation among actors, information sharing, trust and honesty, open communication channels, network connectivity, acceptance of coordination or leadership, socio-economic links, cultural bonds and bridges, social commitment, respect for others' values, duty performance, reliability, etc. It goes without saying that the measurement of social capital in an operational explanatory framework is fraught with many difficulties and needs usually the consideration of many variables.

After this description of concepts and data we will now proceed with our analysis and present the database for our triple-layer DEA applications.

5 Information Collection

5.1 Statistical databases

A wealth of statistical information has been collected on regional development in Poland and in the Podkarpackie region, the home base of the Aviation Valley[4]. These data concerned in the first stage the determinants and characteristics of regional welfare in each of the 16 voivodships in Poland in a detailed manner. This macro-regional exploration led to the composition of an extensive multivariate database, with more than 70 indicators comprising five-grained information on the components of Territorial Capital (TC), systematically subdivided into Human Capital (HC), Infrastructural Capital (IC), and Social Capital (SC) (according to the framework in Figures 1 and 2). This multivariate database on HC, IC, and SC indicators was next transformed into a structured database containing two independent factors by means of a principal component analysis (PCA). The endogenous variable employed here (i.e., TPI) is GDP per capita (see Table 1), which is assumed to be determined by the two main components in this table.

The input factors – represented here as two independent vectors after a multivariate

---

[4]The database for the Aviation Valley study in Poland has been collected in the framework of a research project Effective Clusters – Basis for Innovation and Source of Sustainable Regional Development. The authors wish to thank Krzysztof Kaszuba for his advice on the sources of secondary data, Emilia Barbara Sieńko-Kułakowska and Grzegorz Pisarczyk for their great assistance in collecting primary data, and Waldemar Ratajczak for advice on the various research steps. The detailed source data are contained in the relevant background documents for this project.

Table 2: The multivariate database (reduced into a single-period database with 3 independent factors by means of a FPCA) for the 25 powiats in the Podkarpackie region

| POWIATS | INPUTS | | | OUTPUT |
	SC	IC	HC	Average monthly gross wages and salaries (zl)
BIESZCZADZKI	823.34	12.18	84.54	3237.17
BRZOZOWSKI	964.54	59.7	84.66	2964.62
JASIELSKI	713.27	66.86	121.14	3038.82
KROSNIENSKI	954.48	74.88	66.34	2887.05
SANOCKI	584.01	23.32	92.91	3078.45
LESKI	480.87	41.48	121.76	3283.39
M.KROSNO	578.93	281.42	266.59	2980.59
JAROSLAWSKI	535.03	75.96	131.29	3328.63
LUBACZOWSKI	513.1	36.96	93.7	2951.96
PRZEMYSKI	1423.3	43.62	57.41	3036.69
PRZEWORSKI	647.76	87.34	86.93	2931.78
M.PRZEMYSL	487.39	237.84	174.27	3325.5
KOLBUSZOWSKI	939.97	68.46	62.57	2929.58
LANCUCKI	613.6	135.86	97.73	2890.03
ROPCZYCKO-SEDZISZOWSKI	586.34	72.52	103.49	3138.68
RZESZOWSKI	962.87	100.36	74.59	3070.98
STRZYZOWSKI	525.57	62.96	75.23	2786.37
M.RZESZOW	1168.8	343.04	232.39	3859.86
DEBICKI	711.79	89.38	103.39	3165.79
LEZAJSKI	686.66	69.5	104.19	3146.29
MIELECKI	717.79	82.04	114.9	3329.68
NIZANSKI	746.86	61.32	70.86	2890.57
STALOWOWOLSKI	650.9	92.46	122.86	3360.58
TARNOBRZESKI	828.56	81.6	78.74	3326.4
M.TARNOBRZEG	536.3	145.88	153.09	3200.51

Source: Source: Authors' own calculation using data from the Statistical Office in Rzeszow (2014)

transformation from HC, IC, and SC – are the control variables to achieve an output value. Consequently, this data set from stage 1 can be used for an efficiency evaluation by means of DEA.

In the next (meso) layer, viz. the level of the 25 'powiats' (counties) within the Podkarpackie region, a similar approach was adopted, which led again to the composition of three independent factors from SC, IC, and HC, acting as drivers of regional welfare in these counties, while again output or GDP per capita (in terms of average monthly gross wages and salaries) was used as the dependent TPI variable (see Table 2).

Given the rich database at a county level in the Podkarpackie region, in this case the multivariate statistical PCA was separately applied to each of the multidimensional constituents of the HC, IC, and TC indicators in the respective area.

In the third and last (micro) layer, an extensive database was collected on the drivers and perceptions of the individual firms based in the Aviation Valley and located in different powiats in Podkarpackie. This database was the result of semi-structured and often time-consuming detailed interviews with the top managers of these firms, as well as with many other stakeholders. The firms under consideration were both large firms and SMEs. We will now offer a concise description of the elements of the latter database (see also Table 3).

The interview questions covered a wide range of business activities, such as industrial products, forward and backward linkages, service provision, employee types and size, profitability conditions, growth figures, HRM, management structures, links with local

Table 3: Database on drivers and perceptions of individual firms based in the Aviation Valley and located in different powiats in the Podkarpackie voivodship

FIRMS	FA1OU	FA2OU	SC	IC	HC	F1I	F2I
AT1	3	5	650.9	92.46	122.86	2	3
BE2	5	4	1168.8	343.04	232.39	5	4
CA3	4	4	536.3	145.88	153.09	4	3
HE3	2	3	962.87	100.36	74.59	5	2
HI4	5	4	586.34	72.52	103.49	3	4
MA5	5	6	717.79	82.04	114.9	5	3
MT6	5	4	962.87	100.36	74.59	3	4
PZ6	6	6	717.79	82.04	114.9	5	5
TH7	6	4	650.9	92.46	122.86	4	5
TR8	5	6	613.6	135.86	97.73	5	4
UT9	5	3	578.93	281.42	266.59	4	3
WS10	6	6	1168.8	343.04	232.39	5	4
ZM11	5	5	1168.8	343.04	232.39	5	4
AD12	5	5	939.97	68.46	62.57	3	4
AE13	5	6	578.93	281.42	266.59	4	5
AE14	5	6	717.79	82.04	114.9	4	5
AI15	5	5	962.87	100.36	74.59	4	4
AR16	5	0	1168.8	343.04	232.39	3	6
AS17	5	5	1168.8	343.04	232.39	4	4
BM18	4	5	962.87	100.36	74.59	4	5
BO19	5	6	717.79	82.04	114.9	5	4
BR20	6	6	613.6	135.86	97.73	4	5
C021	4	3	1168.8	343.04	232.39	3	4
EL22	5	6	1168.8	343.04	232.39	4	4
EU23	5	5	717.79	82.04	114.9	4	5
FI24	4	1	939.97	68.46	62.57	3	3
FL25	5	5	717.79	82.04	114.9	4	5
FO26	1	5	686.66	69.5	104.19	1	1
GU27	5	6	586.34	72.52	103.49	5	4
HA28	5	5	717.79	82.04	114.9	2	2
IN29	5	6	650.9	92.46	122.86	3	5
IW30	5	6	650.9	92.46	122.86	4	5
KA31	5	0	717.79	82.04	114.9	3	5
MA32	3	5	1168.8	343.04	232.39	3	3
MA33	4	5	717.79	82.04	114.9	3	4
MC34	5	5	962.87	100.36	74.59	4	3
ME35	4	5	962.87	100.36	74.59	3	5
MI36	5	5	578.93	281.42	266.59	2	2
NO37	6	5	1168.8	343.04	232.39	4	4
PO38	4	3	650.9	92.46	122.86	3	3
PO39	5	5	962.87	100.36	74.59	4	5
PZ40	5	5	711.79	89.38	103.39	2	4
RE41	6	6	717.79	82.04	114.9	5	6
R042	5	5	717.79	82.04	114.9	2	4
SE43	6	5	525.57	62.96	75.23	4	4
SP44	4	3	717.79	82.04	114.9	3	4
TW45	5	4	962.87	100.36	74.59	3	1
UN46	4	5	711.79	89.38	103.39	4	4
WA47	5	5	717.79	82.04	114.9	3	5
WI48	6	6	578.93	281.42	266.59	4	4
WS49	4	2	578.93	281.42	266.59	3	3
WY50	5	5	586.34	72.52	103.49	2	3
ZE51	5	5	962.87	100.36	74.59	3	4
ZP52	5	6	717.79	82.04	114.9	5	6

Source: Authors' own calculation using data from interviews in Podkarpackie Voivodship, powiats and gminas (2014) and data of different powiats in the Podkarpackie voivodship from the Statistical Office in Rzeszow (2014)
Notes: Firm names are strictly confidential and therefore anonymized; FA1OU: General growth; FA2OU: Export and revenues; F1I: Strong network and innovation sources; F2I: Cooperation and competitiveness

authorities, cluster linkages, internationalization, etc. The interviews were organized for four distinct groups of business entities of the most important firms and agencies located in the Aviation Valley. We will provide a brief account of these interviews.

The first group consists of large companies which are the main producers for the global airline industry and are closely linked with their parent companies abroad. The second group comprises small and medium-sized companies with a production profile that is partly related to the airline industry and that is linked in a supply chain to large aviation companies in the region. The third group of interviewees addressed institutions of a supporting nature for the aviation business, e.g., universities, consultation and certification institutions, agencies for regional development (all members of the so-called Aviation Valley Association); these organizations are linked to other members of the Aviation Valley Association by providing advisory, training and certificate services, and by jointly carrying out R&D projects. Finally, the last group of interviewees is composed of companies and institutions of a varying legal or administrative status as well as of local and regional authorities related to the Aviation Valley Association, with an external common value chain; examples of such participants are inter alia: institutions with various levels of education – mostly colleges and universities – , banks and financial institutions, local administrations at various levels, other smaller clusters operating in the region, training and consulting companies, and so forth.

As mentioned above, four different types of surveys were designed, while also in-depth survey questions adjusted to specific classes of respondents were added. Clearly, this research task contained a multiplicity of appropriate survey questions geared towards each group of respondents so as to make a comprehensive diagnosis for all respondents in the Aviation Valley whenever possible. In the case of the first two groups of business firms, the survey questions were similar, so that it was possible to compare results which are common to every surveyed company within the cluster, so as to arrive at a consistent interpretation of the results. Our survey questions were designed in a flexible and open way, so that a wide range of specific planning issues for the region could be addressed. Questions were grouped according to a systematic typology of topics, so that the analysis of various questions could provide systematic information on the scope of the research. Clearly, the survey among business firms is to be treated anonymously and its results are used here as summary data without any possibility to identify individual companies which answered particular questions. A total of 55 companies – members of the cluster – took part in the survey.

The primary sources of statistical information were thus supported and complemented by confidential survey research conducted on a group of general companies/institutions cooperating in and with the Aviation Valley Association. The choice of respondents was conditioned by the range of cooperation and the cluster's influence on its economic and technological environment. Therefore, among the institutions and companies interviewed were: (1) financial institutions (banks, insurance companies, support institutions), (2) institutions related to environmental protection and ecology (including informal associations), (3) local government agencies, (4) political parties, (5) energy power companies, (6) transport and logistics companies, (7) local marketing and PR institutions, (8) non-governmental organizations, (9) other local clusters, (10) schools and training institutions, (11) government agencies supporting the cluster activities, and (12) others, e.g., service companies dealing with quality management, human resources management, provision of telecommunication services, and so forth.

The above survey encompassed in total 35 service institutions operating in the Aviation Valley Association environment. It was directed to a total of 73 potential respondents. The response rate for this survey was 48%. The specific results from the group survey questions concerned: general knowledge about the Aviation Valley Association, evaluation of cooperation intensity between the respondent and the cluster (and its members), barriers in the area of business connections, potential motives for entering the cluster, affiliation with other cluster structures and its benefits, evaluation of strategic operations, and marketing and communication of the Aviation Valley Association. Moreover, there were also questions concerning the evaluation of the potential of the region to attract new firms, to further develop a company or the cluster as a whole, or to get access to sources of development funding or institutional information on who should take action for concrete sustainable development initiatives.

And finally, there were also demographic questions concerning basic information about the human resource profile of the company interviewed.

5.2 In-depth interviews and participatory research

The field research was based on multiple sources of information, from several stakeholders, individual cluster members, local experts, etc. In-depth interviews with cluster participants were also held; they were a crucial element of the field research. An in-depth interview is essentially a communication exercise with a respondent conducted on the basis of a pre-specified mental scenario. Interviews were conducted by persons especially trained for this aim as part of the project, while the interviewer was an active and qualified participant in the communication, in order to gather meaningful strategic and operational information. In-depth interviews are an alternative to focus-group interviews. Due to the specific aim of the project and the diversity of respondents, direct in-depth interviews were chosen. They provide in general a better feeling of ease among interviewees. This is especially important when it comes to issues related to trust evaluation and cooperation between representatives of other companies and institutions within the cluster.

For the sake of comprehensiveness of the research issues, respondents in the cluster were chosen according to following criteria: hierarchal position in the company or institution surveyed, membership of the Aviation Valley Association, and involvement in operations initiated by the Aviation Valley Association. The interviews were carefully prepared in advance, while relevant information about the aim of the project and of the research and about the nature of the questions to be raised during the interview was provided. For representatives of big companies, small and middle-sized companies, and institutions of the business environment who were members of the cluster, similar questions were prepared.

Finally, the aim of the participatory research was to engage representatives of the cluster members in the decision processes and to help in shaping the cluster's development policy. The aim of this action research was to gain knowledge about the future business environment, and strategic knowledge oriented towards the solution of pressing problems. Both aims are interrelated and therefore, it was necessary to engage participants in the organization, as well as in the formulation of strategic conclusions regarding the diagnosis of their collective interests and their connections. The aim of engaging key actors of the cluster in participatory research was also to create awareness of essential issues for these actors, and to show that their voice counts, so that they have a real impact on what is going to happen in the cluster's future. Such research may become a catalyst of proactive involvement, and may create the foundation of establishing participatory mechanisms in the cluster.

6 Results of a Triple-Layer DEA Benchmark Analysis in the Podkarpackie Region in Poland

The predominant aim of our research is now to assess the relative economic performance of Polish regions, of counties inside the main region concerned (Podkarpackie), and of individual firms in the Aviation Valley on the basis of an efficiency (or productivity) analysis by means of a DEA (see Figures 3 and 4). In our empirical application we will use the above presented extensive database on Polish regions, counties, and individual actors in the aviation cluster, in combination with the rich performance database for the Podkarpackie region in Poland. We are seeking to achieve a ranking of agents in the triple-layer architecture based on a comprehensive set of indicators and aim to assess the efficiency (or productivity) of the different layers of agents in the context of an effective cluster performance, by examining more carefully the ratio between multi-attribute outputs and multi-attribute inputs of each layer. As mentioned, data envelopment analysis (DEA) is an appropriate tool in this context. Thus, our study aims to provide a critical analysis of the performance data of DMUs in the triple-layer architecture of the Aviation Valley by using an SBM model and a super-efficient (SE) DEA approach, respectively, to position

Table 4: SBM-SE scores of 16 NUTS-3 Voivodships of Poland

Nr.	DMU Voivodship	Score	Nr.	DMU Voivodship	Score
1	DOLNOŚLĄSKIE	0.561	9	PODKARPACKIE	0.755
2	KUJAWSKO-POMORSKIE	0.636	10	PODLASKIE	0.995
3	ŁÓDZKIE	0.592	11	POMORSKIE	0.443
4	LUBELSKIE	0.626	12	ŚLĄSKIE	0.477
5	LUBUSKIE	1.730	13	ŚWIĘTOKRZYSKIE	0.469
6	MAŁOPOLSKIE	0.388	14	WARMIŃSKO-MAZURSKIE	0.849
7	MAZOWIECKIE	19.195	15	WIELKOPOLSKIE	0.768
8	OPOLSKIE	0.385	16	ZACHODNIOPOMORSKIE	0.582

Source: Authors' own calculation

Table 5: SBM-SE scores of 25 NUTS-4 Powiats of Podkarpackie in Poland

Nr.	DMU Powiat	Score	Nr.	DMU Powiat	Score
1	bieszczadzki	1.390	13	m.Przemysl	1.003
2	brzozowski	0.687	14	m.Rzeszow	0.642
3	debicki	0.908	15	m.Tarnobrzeg	0.727
4	jaroslawski	1.012	16	mielecki	0.708
5	jasielski	0.693	17	nizanski	1.082
6	kolbuszowski	1.062	18	przemyski	0.628
7	kroSnieNski	0.711	19	przeworski	0.757
8	lancucki	0.679	20	ropczycko-sedziszowski	0.628
9	leski	0.637	21	rzeszowski	0.649
10	lezajski	0.404	22	sanocki	1.038
11	lubaczowski	0.788	23	stalowowolski	1.039
12	m.Krosno	1.011	24	strzyzowski	0.811
			25	tarnobrzeski	0.434

Source: Authors' own calculation

these DMUs unambiguously on the basis of their relative performance. The empirical results of the SBM-SE model based on the triple-layer approach will now be presented in Tables 4-6 for each of the three layers concerned.

We will offer here a concise interpretation of the findings in these tables. As far as Table 1 is concerned, it turns out that there are only 2 super-efficient voivodships on the NUTS-3 level in Poland, with a clearly prominent position for Mazowieckie, situated in the central-eastern part of Poland. There is quite some variation among the efficiency outcomes of the non-efficient voivodships in Poland. It is noteworthy that the efficiency of the Podkarpackie region – which is the region addressed in our study – does not differ significantly from the Wielkopolskie region which is a rather strong region in the Western part of Poland dominated by Poznan. Thus, the Podkarpackie region is performing rather well, despite its peripheral location. This may be seen as a promising sign for future development efforts.

On the next layer of powiats (NUTS-4 regions or counties) within the Podkarpackie region, we observe quite a few (8) super-efficient areas. They are scattered all over the Podkarpackie voivodship, which means that the efficiency performance of these counties offers a balanced geographical picture, except for these powiats that are external border regions (e.g., to Ukraine). This finding is interesting, as the aviation industry in the Podkarpackie region is not concentrated in one point location, but shows a broadly dispersed cluster pattern all over this region. Apparently, the benefits of this strategy accrue to a wide group of counties in the voivodship. The relatively low score of Rzeszow has to do with the fact that the city itself does not have a strong industrial base, since most aviation activities are located in a wide radius around the city.

Table 6: SBM-SE scores of 55 firms in the Aviation Cluster in Podkarpackie in Poland

Nr.	DMU Firms	Score	Nr.	DMU Firms	Score
1	AD10	1.016	28	MA39	0.710
2	Ae11	1.007	29	MC27	0.731
3	Ae35	0.829	30	Me14	1.000
4	Ai20	0.844	31	MI52	0.316
5	AR4	1.000	32	MT30	0.744
6	AS48	0.502	33	No50	0.475
7	AT40	0.559	34	Po15	0.960
8	BE42	0.601	35	Pol43	0.691
9	BM8	1.049	36	PZ19	0.927
10	Bo21	0.916	37	PZ45	0.646
11	BR17	0.793	38	Re16	0.967
12	CA13	1.001	39	Ro47	0.640
13	CO38	0.476	40	SE7	1.032
14	EL48	0.493	41	Sp28	0.775
15	Eu32	0.857	42	Th18	0.862
16	Fi3	1.053	43	Tr12	1.008
17	FL33	0.857	44	TW51	0.498
18	Fo36	0.347	45	Un29	0.830
19	GU5	1.088	46	UT9	1.022
20	HA53	0.396	47	Wa31	0.800
21	He2	1.529	48	Wi26	0.582
22	Hi34	0.767	49	WS25	0.613
23	In24	0.805	50	WS46	0.540
24	IW23	0.816	51	Wy49	0.545
25	KA1	1.000	52	Ze41	0.714
26	Ma22	0.887	53	ZM44	0.581
27	Ma37	0.456	54	ZP6	1.040

Source: Authors' own calculation

Finally, the efficiency scores for the firms in the aviation industry shows an interesting pattern. There is apparently a set of 16 super-efficient firms, and a broad distribution of less efficient firms. As mentioned, details on these anonymized firms cannot be provided, but there is also a fair balance between small and large firms. It is also interesting to observe that there are a limited number of very inefficient firms with rather low scores. Consequently, for specific enterprises in this aviation cluster there is much scope for improving their business performance. It is also noteworthy that the geographic distribution of efficient and inefficient firms over the various powiats is rather balanced.

The overall conclusion from our triple-layer DEA model application is that on all levels of decision-making – ranging from individual business firms in the aviation cluster through counties (which provide the direct geographical location area for these firms) to the level of voivodships charged with official regional policy competences – there is still much scope for socio-economic performance improvement. The Podkarpackie region has in the past decade demonstrated a great potential in enhancing its competitive position as an effective aviation cluster (see Kaszuba 2012), but there is undoubtedly more room for strengthening its position.

It should be added that in a deterministic DEA model these findings are of course numerically correct, but that in policy practice such accurate and ambitious adjustments by DMUs may sometimes be hard to achieve. Nevertheless, this information is indicative for the direction and intensity of necessary policy handled in a region, powiat, and firm so as to become more efficient in a competitive environment. In conclusion, there is a need for an intensified policy effort to achieve and strengthen the socio-economic vitality and efficiency of the aviation actors in the triple-layer architecture in Poland.

7 Policy Lessons

Regional development policy aims to cope with the challenge of spatial disparities. It is based on a smart combination of various critical capital assets in a region which functionally and spatially interact and which yield synergetic economic opportunities and promising challenges for innovation and progress. The present study regards sustainable territorial performance – as a manifestation of regional development – as the overarching principle for competitive advantages and economic growth in a system of regions, which is particularly induced by territorial capital, comprising human capital, infrastructural capital, and social capital. In the long-standing tradition of regional development policy, a wide variety of effective facilitators or drivers of accelerated spatial growth has been distinguished, for instance, industrial districts, growth poles, growth centers, industrial complexes, special economic zones, communication axes, and so forth.

Regional development calls for an active involvement of stakeholders or agents (DMUs) at different institutional levels. Awareness of the actual position of a DMU on the achievement ladder is a sine qua non for performance improvement. The Aviation Valley cluster in the Podkarpackie region in South-East Poland offers a good example of a dedicated but complex regional development effort; it is not only a fascinating and pioneering cluster policy experiment, but offers also a great opportunity for designing and implementing innovative and effective cluster research initiatives and for building strong business networks and creating 'collective buying power'. It is indeed a miraculous and encouraging phenomenon that a less privileged and peripheral territory like the Podkarpackie region is able to act as a seedbed for a broad portfolio of advanced aviation activities, not only with a great economic spinoff for the area concerned, but also with significant spillovers to the rest of the country and of Europe, and in various cases even with a world-wide outreach.

The Podkarpackie voivodship and its powiats are confronted with a great many challenges, notably geographic isolation, far-reaching demographic transformations, complex force fields in this part of Europe, unequal social participation, and ever-rising mobility trends. These multi-faceted challenges may be turned into new opportunities, in particular in such concerns as advanced business and environmental facilities, knowledge-intensive and creative strategies for socioeconomic well-being and prosperity (see Kourtit, Nijkamp 2013b) with a strong need for intensified policy efforts, and availability of a strong and dedicated workforce in high-tech engineering.

The general challenge is to improve the competitive high performance of the Podkarpackie region, to strengthen and stimulate its constituent powiats, and to improve further the attractiveness of the Aviation Valley as a sustainable high-quality place to work and live, and to incorporate technology and innovation in overall sustainable developmental strategies so as to make the Valley a seedbed for global frontrunners for future development. The notion of a territorial performance index (TPI) has proven its relevance and applicability in our research.

In this context, strong and fit-for-purpose territorial capital may create a strong Aviation Valley, in particular, through strengthening information and knowledge facilities, advancing institutional support systems, fostering fruitful business networking initiatives, recruiting new talents on the labor market, favoring high-skilled job opportunities and establishing a sufficient and effective venture capital system (see Kourtit, Nijkamp 2013b, Kourtit 2015). All such effective cluster conditions are critical success factors for a promising living, working, and business environment in the Aviation Valley. A mixture of advanced process, product and service innovation initiatives, advanced labor force concentrations, socio-cultural initiatives, interconnected public facilities, and geographic knowledge synergy may be regarded as the constituents of a successful regional creative and innovation system that forms the basis for an effective aviation cluster.

In our applied empirical case study on the Aviation Valley in the Podkarpackie region in Poland, we have focused our attention in particular on the quality of human capital, social characteristics, and on infrastructural amenities synergy from the perspective of an effective cluster against the background of social and economic dynamics at different scale levels, on the basis of the TPI model. Clearly, the aim of our analysis was not to offer a critical review of current official development policies and implementations in the region concerned. We have rather addressed the information base and the conceptual framing of the strong and weak points in this area, with a particular view to regional, local, and industrial detail.

At the level of Polish voivodships, the regions Mazowieckie and Lubuskie are found to be efficient (with efficiency scores equal to 1) based on our DEA model. This "efficiency" means that these two regions can produce a large amount of economic performance (outputs), with the use of relatively small amount of inputs (territorial capital). This result may be confronted with relatively highly inefficient regions, such as Małopolskie, Świętokrzyskie and Opolskie. The Podkarpackie region is found in a middle position with a trend to improve its performance.

At the next spatial scale, viz. of powiats, the most efficient powiats in the Podkarpackie region in Poland are Bieszczadzki, Sanocki, Leski, Lubaczowski, Przemyski, Kolbuszowski, Strzyzowski and Tarnobrzeski. These powiats appear to offer new opportunities for social and economic synergy as a result of a strong county attractiveness and the presence of broadly based public and private facilities. There is obviously also a great opportunity for advanced growth initiatives and improvement strategies of lower performing powiats. Apparently, territorial capital is very supportive for high aviation industry performance.

Finally, by looking at the third stage for efficient firms in the Aviation Valley in the Podkarpackie region in Poland, we can by means of our DEA model identify the firms with a maximum level of efficiency, which from our analysis turns out to comprise 16 firms. These firms may be labelled the 'high performing firms' among our sample of 55 high-tech firms in the Aviation Valley. These 'high performing firms' are able to exploit their high socio-economic and technological performance even more, as they have strongly established business resources that underscore the importance of territorial capital.

In conclusion, a strategic view on a high performing region, country, or firm may be used as an effective approach to identify important and smart KPIs (key performance indicators) that are involved to maximize the creative, innovative, and technological potential of the agent concerned. The triple-layer design of our research, addressing three types of actors with distinct competences, has proven to be a valuable methodological departure for an effective cluster analysis of the Aviation Valley in Poland. This approach may provide untapped opportunities for knowledge-based institutional, geographically-focused, and cultural and business activities, that are needed in order to stay ahead of the fierce competition and to advance continuously the high socio-economic achievement potential.

Clearly, any DEA study – including ours – is a comparative benchmarking analysis of the efficiency – or the broad economic performance – of various stakeholders or actors (e.g., regions, agencies, firms). The reasons why some actors have an exceptional performance in comparison to others in the same sample call for further specific case research. The same holds for all other DMUs who want to improve their performance position on the achievement ladder. It should be added that a sensitivity analysis using another DEA method, viz. the CCR model, leads to largely the same result, so that our findings seem to be rather robust and consistent. It should be added that essentially a wide array of DEA variants could have been applied (such as BCC, Malmquist indices, etc.), but that would have led to a different study. For more details on this option we refer to a recent study by Susuki, Nijkamp (2017).

The overall conclusion is that the Aviation Valley in the Podkarpackie region in Poland has unique opportunities and a rich scope for further improvement and development and may act as a catalyst for welfare improvement in this territory.

References

Acz Z, Braunerhjelm P, Audretsch D, Carlsson B (2009) The knowledge spill-over theory of entrepreneurship. *Small Business Economics* 32: 15–30. CrossRef.

Adler N, Golany B (2001) Evaluation of deregulated airline networks using data envelopment analysis combined with principal component analysis with an application to Western Europe. *European Journal of Operational Research* 132[2]: 260–273. CrossRef.

Andersson M, Klaesson J, Larsson JP (2016) How local are spatial density externalities? Neighbourhood effects in agglomeration economies. *Regional Studies* 50[6]: 1082–1095. CrossRef.

Arribas-Bel D, Kourtit K, Nijkamp P (2013) Benchmarking of world cities through self-organizing maps. *Cities* 31: 248–257. CrossRef.

Aschauer DA (1989) Is public expenditure productive? *Journal of Monetary Economics* 23: 177–200. CrossRef.

Asheim B, Cooke P, Martin R (2006) *Clusters and Regional Development: Critical Reflections and Explorations.* Routledge, London

Baczko T (2011) Report on innovativeness of the aviation sector in Poland in 2010. http://issuu.com/inepan/docs/ang_pdf_raport_okladki

Batabyal A, Nijkamp P (2015) *The Region and Trade: New Analytical Directions.* World Scientific Publishing, New York

Becker GS (2009) *Human Capital.* University of Chicago Press, Chicago. CrossRef.

Berechman J, de Wit JG (1996) An analysis of the effects of European aviation deregulation on an airline's network structure and choice of a primary West-European hub airport. *Journal of Transport Economics and Policy* 30[3]: 251–274

Bochniarz Z (2007) Strategic issues of financing sustainable development in transforming economies: The case of Central Europe. In: Xiaowen J, Ebben J (eds), *Entrepreneurial Strategy Innovation and Sustainable Development.* Sichuan University Press, Chengdu, China, 1029–1049

Bourdieu P (1981) Décrire et préscrire. note sur les conditions de possibilité et limites de l'efficacité. *Actes de la Recherche en Sciences Sociales* 38[1]: 69–73. CrossRef.

Bröcker J, Rietveld P (2009) Infrastructure and regional development. In: Capello R, Nijkamp P (eds), *Handbook of Regional Growth and Development Theories.* Edward Elgar, Cheltenham, 152–281. CrossRef.

Burghouwt G, Huys M (2003) Deregulation and the consequences for airport planning in Europe. *disP-The Planning Review* 39[154]: 37–45. CrossRef.

Button K (2002) Debunking some common myths about airport hubs. *Journal of Air Transport Management* 8[3]: 177–188. CrossRef.

CAI – Community Attributes Inc. (2013) Washington State Aerospace Industry. Community Attributes Inc. (CAI), Seattle, Washington

Calzonetti FJ, Reid N (2013) The role diversities in supporting new technology industries through commercialisation spin-off activities. *Studies in Regional Science* 43[1]: 7–23. CrossRef.

Camagni R (2002) On the concept of territorial competitiveness: sound or misleading? paper presented at the ERSA conference 2002, European Regional Science Association, http://www-sre.wu.ac.at/ersa/ersaconfs/ersa02/cd-rom/papers/518.pdf

Camagni R (2009) Territorial capital and regional development. In: Capello R, Nijkamp P (eds), *Handbook of Regional Growth and Development Theories*. Edward Elgar, Cheltenham, 118–132. CrossRef.

Camagni R, Capello R (2011) *Spatial Scenarios in a Global Perspective: Europe and the Latin Arc Countries*. Edward Elgar, Cheltenham. CrossRef.

Camagni R, Capello R (2013) Regional competitiveness and territorial capital: A conceptual approach and empirical evidence from the European Union. *Regional Studies* 47[9]: 1383–1402. CrossRef.

Camagni R, Capello R (2015) Rationale and design of EU cohesion policies in a period of crisis. *Regional Science Policy and Practice* 7[1]: 25–49. CrossRef.

Capello R, Caragliu A, Nijkamp P (2011) Territorial capital and regional growth: Increasing returns in knowledge use. *Tijdschrift voor Economische en Sociale Geographie* 102[4]: 385–405. CrossRef.

Capello R, Nijkamp P (2009) *Handbook of Regional Growth and Development Theories*. Edward Elgar, Cheltenham. CrossRef.

Caragliu A (2015) The economics of proximity. PhD dissertation, VU University, Amsterdam

Celbis G, Nijkamp P, Poot J (2015) Infrastructure and trade: A meta-analysis. *REGION* 1[1]: 25–64. CrossRef.

Charnes A, Cooper WW, Lewin AY, Seiford LM (1994) *Data Envelopment Analysis: Theory, Methodology and Applications*. Kluwer, Boston. CrossRef.

Charnes A, Cooper WW, Rhodes E (1978) Measuring the efficiency of decision making units. *European Journal of Operational Research* 2: 429–444. CrossRef.

Coleman JS (1988) Social capital in the creation of human capital. *The American Journal of Sociology* 94: 95–120. CrossRef.

Cooper WW, Seiford L, Zhu J (2006) *Handbook of Data Envelopment Analysis*. Kluwer, Boston. CrossRef.

De la Fuente A, Vives X (1995) Infrastructure and education as instruments of regional policy. *Economic Policy* 20: 11–54

ECORYS (2009) Competitiveness of the EU aerospace industry. Rotterdam

Elburz Z, Nijkamp P, Pels E (2015) Public meta-analysis. Discussion paper, Department of Spatial Economics, VU University, Amsterdam

European Aeronautics (2001) Meeting society's needs and winning global leadership. Report of the group of personalities, http://www.acare4europe.org/sites/acare4europe.-org/files/document/Vision%202020_0.pdfm

European Commission (2005) Territorial state and perspectives of the European Union. Scoping document and summary of political messages, Brussels, Belgium

Fratesi U, Perucca G (2014) Territorial capital and the effectiveness of cohesion policies: An assessment for CEE regions. *Investigaciones Regionales* 29: 164–191

Färe R, Grosskopf S, Russell R (1998) *Index Numbers*. Kluwer, Boston

Fukuyama F (2001) Social capital, civil society and development. *Third World Quarterly* 22[1]: 7–20. CrossRef.

Gibson MD, Kundu S, Satish M (2013) Dispersion model evaluation of PM2.5, NOx and SO2 from point and major line sources in Nova Scotia, Canada using AERMOD Gaussian plume air dispersion model. *Atmospheric Pollution Research* 4: 157–167. CrossRef.

Hanifan LJC (1916) The rural school community centre. *Annals of the American Academy of Political and Social* 67[1]: 130–138. CrossRef.

Healy P, Cote S (2001) The wellbeing of nations: The role of human and social capital, education and skills. Oecd, paris

Heckman JJ (2000) Policies to foster human capital. 54[1]: 3–56. CrossRef.

Jacobs J (1961) *The Death and Life of Great American Cities*. Random House, New York. CrossRef.

Kaasa A, Part A (2008) Human capital and social capital as interacting factors of economic development: Evidence from Europe. IAREG, Estonia, working paper IAREG WP 2/04. CrossRef.

Kasabov E, Sundaram U (2016) Conceptualizing clusters as dynamic and path-dependent pools of skills. *Regional Studies* 50[9]: 1520–1536. CrossRef.

Kaszuba K (2012) Aviation cluster 'aviation valley' - case study. Report, Rzeszow School of Business, Rzeszow, Poland

Kourtit K (2014) Competiveness in urban systems - studies on the 'urban century'. VU University, Amsterdam, The Netherlands

Kourtit K (2015) The 'new urban world' - economic-geographical studies on the performance of urban systems. Adam Mickiewicz University, Poznan, Poland

Kourtit K, Nijkamp P (2013a) In search of creative champions in high-tech spaces: A spatial application of strategic performance management. *Journal of Regional Science* 53[5]: 749–777. CrossRef.

Kourtit K, Nijkamp P (2013b) The new urban world - The challenge of cities in decline. *Romanian Journal of Regional Science* 7[2]: 9–28

Kourtit K, Nijkamp P (2017) A multi-layer analysis of effective clusters in regional development policy: A case study on Poland. Public administration and regional studies (forthcoming)

Kourtit K, Nijkamp. P, Suzuki S (2013) Exceptional places: The rat race between world cities. *Computers, Environment and Urban Systems* 38: 67–77

Nijkamp P (1996) Liberalization of air transport in Europe: The survival of the fittest? *Swiss Journal of Economics and Statistics* 132[3]: 257–278

Nijkamp P (2008) XXQ factors for sustainable urban development: A systems economics view. *Romanian Journal of Regional Science* 2[1]: 1–34

Nijkamp P (2016) The resourceful regions: A new conceptualisation of regional development strategies. *Journal of Regional Research* 36: 191–214

OECD (2001) OECD territorial outlook. OECD, Paris

Perucca G (2014) The role of territorial capital in local economic growth: Evidence from Italy. *European Planning Studies* 22[3]: 537–562. CrossRef.

Porter ME (1990) *The Competitive Advantage of Nations*. MacMillan, London. CrossRef.

Putnam R (1993) The prosperous community. *The American Prospect* 13[4]: 35–42

Ratajczak W (2008) Impact of Poland's integration with the European Union on the socio-economic status of Polish regions. *Moravian Geographical Reports* 16[1]: 2–15

Ravikumar B, Glomm G (1992) Public versus private investment in human capital. *Journal of Political Economy* 100[4]: 818–834. CrossRef.

Ray SC (2004) *Data Envelopment Analysis: Theory and Techniques for Economics and Operations Research.* Cambridge University Press, Cambridge

Rodriguez-Pose A, Fratesi U (2004) Between development and social policies. *Regional Studies* 38: 97–113

Schönfeld T, Jouaillec F (2008) The regional aerospace cluster policy in Europe. Paper presented to the 26th International Congress of the Aeronautical Sciences. http://-www.icas.org/ICAS_ARCHIVE/ICAS2008/PAPERS/628.PDF

Scholl T, Brenner T (2016) Detecting spatial clustering using a firm-level cluster index. *Regional Studies* 50[6]: 1054–1068. CrossRef.

Schultz Th (1961) Investment in human capital. *American Economic Review* 51[1]: 1–17

Sommers P, Beyers WB, Wenzel A (2008) Industry cluster analysis for Washington State, workforce development areas. Washington State Workforce Board, Seattle, Washington

Statistical Office in Rzeszow (2014) Podkarpackie voivodship – subregions, powiats, gminas, podkarpackie voivodship. http://rzeszow.stat.gov.pl/publikacje-i-foldery/roczniki-statystyczne/wojewodztwo-podkarpackie-podregiony-powiaty-gminy-2014,4,11.html

Susuki S, Nijkamp P (2017) An evaluation of energy-environment-economic efficiency for Asian countries: A proposal for a time-series target-oriented DFM model in data envelopment analysis. In: Batabyal A, Nijkamp P (eds), *Regional Growth and Sustainable Development in Asia.* Springer, Singapore (forthcoming). CrossRef.

Suzuki S, Nijkamp P (2016a) An evaluation of energy-environment-economic efficiency for EU, APEC and ASEAN countries: Design of a target-oriented DFM model with fixed factors in data envelopment analysis. *Energy Policy* 88: 100–112. CrossRef.

Suzuki S, Nijkamp P (2016b) Preference elicitation in generalized data envelopment analysis: In search of a new energy balance in Japan. In: Shibusawa H, Sakurai K, Mizunoya T, Uchida S (eds), *Socioeconomic Environmental Policies and Evaluations in Regional Science.* Springer, Singapore, 601–618. CrossRef.

Suzuki S, Nijkamp P, Rietveld P (2015) A target-oriented data envelopment analysis for energy-environment efficiency improvement in Japan. *Energy Efficiency* 8[3]: 433–446. CrossRef.

Suzuki S, Nijkamp P, Rietveld P, Pels E (2010) A distance friction minimization approach in data envelopment analysis: A comparative study on airport efficiency. *European Journal of Operational Research* 207: 1104–1115. CrossRef.

Tone K (2001) A slacks-based measure of efficiency in data envelopment analysis. *European Journal of Operational Research* 130: 498–509. CrossRef.

Westlund H (2006) *Social Capital in the Knowledge Economy: Theory and Empirics.* Springer, Berlin, Heidelberg

Zhu J (2003) *Quantitative Models for Performance Evaluation and Benchmarking.* Springer, Berlin. CrossRef.

Zhu J, Cook W (2007) *Modeling data irregularities and structural complexities in data envelopment analysis.* Springer, New York

Zuliani JM, Jalebert G (2005) L' Industrie Aeronautique Européenne. *L' Espace Geographique* 34[2]: 117–144

REGION

The Journal of ERSA
Powered by WU

Volume 4, Number 1, 2017, 31–49
DOI: 10.18335/region.v4i2.144

journal homepage: region.ersa.org

Creativity, Community, and Growth: A Social Geography of Urban Craft Beer

Neil Reid[1], Jay D. Gatrell[2]

[1] University of Toledo, Toledo, OH, USA (email: neil.reid@utoledo.edu)
[2] Bellarmine University, Louisville, KY, USA (email: jgatrell@bellarmine.edu)

Received: 15 July 2016/Accepted: 10 March 2017

Abstract. To better understand the non-economic drivers of growth in emerging industries, this paper examines the craft beer industry. Specifically, the paper will review two examples – the Black Cloister Brewing Company in Toledo, OH and Louisville's 3rd Turn Brewery – to understand how the values of entrepreneurs and local firms that are situated at the nexus of work, place, and creativity promote growth. Further, the paper will consider the socio-cultural meaning of creativity relative to the craft beer industry and the many ways in which the concept of innovation traditionally used by economic geographers to understand growth can be better understood within the context of creativity in select niche industries. In doing so, the paper represents a conceptual shift away from the linear process of innovation towards the more holistic notions of creativity, as well as community.

1 Introduction

> *Creativity is thinking up new things. Innovation is doing new things.*
> Theodore Levitt

The American craft beer industry has experienced significant growth in recent years. In November 2015, the number of craft breweries in the United States reached 4,144 eclipsing the previous high of 4,131 in 1873 (Brewers Association 2015d). This growth is particularly impressive considering that as recently as 2011 there were only 2,004 craft breweries in the United States (Brewers Association 2015b). Based on recent data, the growth is showing no signs of slowing down. Indeed, new breweries are opening at a rate of more than two per day and there are over 1,500 new breweries currently in the planning stages (Brewers Association 2015a). As a result, craft breweries now command a 12.2% share of the U.S beer market by volume and 21% by sales (Brewers Association 2015a, 2016a). Growth of the industry has been driven by consumer demand for alternatives to the beer that is produced by America's two mega-brewers – Anheuser-Busch and Miller Coors[1]. Yet, as we will explore, the growth of the craft beer industry – particularly at the local scale – may not simply be a desire for something different – or niche markets – but an industry intentionally embedded within a complex collection of non-economic

---

[1] On October 10 2016, a merger between Anheuser-Busch InBev and SABMiller was finalized. To comply with U.S. anti-trust regulations the combined company agreed to sell its stake in MillerCoors. MolsonCoors, who already had a 42% ownership stake in MillerCoors, purchased the remaining 58%. The purchase makes MolsonCoors the world's third largest brewing company (Nurin 2016, Svaldi 2016).

values and drivers – specifically creativity and a sense of community – that coincides with
a passion for beer.

2   The US Beer Industry: From Macro to Micro

In order to appreciate the scale and scope of the disruptive force of craft beer on the broader
U.S. brewing industry, it is essential to understand the historical context – specifically
insofar as the sector has long been dominated by a few large macro-brewers with a
narrow, or thin, collection of analogous beers. For example, the product line portfolio
of Anheuser-Busch and Miller Coors is dominated by the American pale lagers (think
Budweiser, Bud Light, Miller Lite, Coors) whose taste profiles are bland, undifferentiated,
and unimaginative (Choi, Stack 2005). Anheuser Busch readily admits that over the
years they have tinkered with the recipe of their signature Budweiser in order to make it
less bitter and pungent, thereby making it more palatable to a larger and larger segment
of the American population (Ellison 2006). The emergence of American beer as a bland
homogeneous product is the result of the interplay of a number of events and trends
that occurred in American society during the 20th century. These include Prohibition,
the emergence and widespread adoption of refrigeration and packaging technologies, the
utilization of television as a medium for mass marketing, the creation of national brands,
consumer demand for homogenous products, brewery consolidation, and the emergent
dominance of the mass production system that allowed brewers to realize economies
of scale (Choi, Stack 2005, Tremblay, Tremblay 2009). For the large brewers, as their
product became increasingly homogeneous, creativity was primarily restricted to the
branding and marketing of their product lines (Imarenezor 2016, Monloss 2016).

While homogenous product lines produced by macro-brewers dominated the market
throughout the 21st century, the seeds of disruption were sown in February 1978 with the
legalization of home brewing and the subsequent state by state legalization of microbreweries and brewpubs. California and Washington were the first states to legalize brewpubs
in 1982, with Oregon following the next year, 1983 (Fallows 2010). By 1995, brewpubs
were legal in 45 states and the District of Columbia (Acitelli 2015). Today, they are legal
in all 50 states. Home brewing is critical to the growth and success of the American
craft beer industry. An estimated 1.2 million Americans brew beer at home. The two
million barrels of beer that they produce on an annual basis represents approximately
1% of all the beer brewed in the United States. (American Homebrewers Association
2016). An estimated 90% of commercial craft brewer started out as home brewers. The
websites of craft breweries are replete with stories of their founders starting off as home
brewers (brewing beer in their basement, garage, or kitchen) and at some point making
the decision to commercialize their hobby (Alonso 2011, Calagione 2011, Grossman 2013,
Magee 2014). The home garage, kitchen, or basement is to the craft beer industry what
the business incubator is for a high-tech start-up company.

The emergence and growth of the American craft beer industry is a clear indicator
that increasing numbers of Americans are demanding more diversity in terms of their beer
choices. They are no longer satisfied with drinking beers such as Budweiser or Miller Lite.
The Brewers Association recognizes over 150 different styles of beer (Brewers Association
2015a), many of which are now produced commercially by American craft breweries. The
result is that the American consumer now has an amazing variety of beers to choose from.
This demand for craft beer is driven by a number of factors. One of these is neo-localism
– the "deliberate seeking out of regional lore and local attachment by residents (new and
old) as a delayed reaction to the destruction in modern America of traditional bonds to
community and family" (Shortridge 1996, p. 10). As a result, there is a growing demand
in the United States for products that have a strong connection with the community or
region within which consumers reside. In concrete terms, neo-localism is manifested in
the increasing numbers of farmers markets (Cone 2012), community supported agriculture
initiatives (Galt et al. 2012), and community gardens (National Gardening Association
2014) across the United States. Craft beer, it has been argued, is yet another indicator
of the strength of the American neo-localism movement. Schnell, Reese (2003, p. 66)
suggest that "the explosive growth of microbreweries indicates a desire on the part of

an increasing number of Americans, brewers and consumers alike, to reconnect with the cities or the towns in which they live, to resurrect a feeling of community tied to a specific landscape". Indeed there is evidence that "successful microbreweries are geographically focused, often producing specialized products with a strong local flavor" (Wesson, Nieva de Figueiredo 2001, p. 400). These are inherently local niche markets with limited range[2].

Based on market research, demand for craft beer appears to be driven primarily by the millennial cohort – young Americans between the ages of 21 and 34 (Crowell 2013, Duva 2014). Millennials have been characterized as "confident, liberal, upbeat, and open to change" (Pew Research Center 2010, p. 1). Millennials have higher levels of educational attainment than previous generations, prefer experimentation over brand loyalty, and are willing to pay more for a product that they perceive to be of higher quality (Pew Research Center 2010, Gilman 2014, Rotunno 2014). In making purchasing decisions an overwhelming majority of millennials ($>80\%$) prefer to buy from companies that support solutions to specific social issues, while feeling that there is too much power concentrated in the hands of a few big companies (Winograd, Hais 2014). These values suggest a good match with craft brewers. Craft beer costs, on average, twice as much as macro-beer yet this does not seem to be squelching demand. Higher quality inputs are a significant contributor to the higher price point enjoyed by craft beer (Satran 2014). While large brewers engage in extensive philanthropy (e.g., see Anheuser-Busch 2016) craft breweries, because of their small size, are able to connect with their local communities in very customized and intimate ways. These include not only supporting local charities but also by making their brewery space available for community events and activities (Kirchenbauer 2014, The Beer Professor 2015). Craft breweries donate an average of $3.25 for every barrel of beer that they brew; the corresponding figure for Anheuser-Busch is only 35 cents per barrel (Herz 2014, Shilton 2016). Many craft breweries are also aggressively engaged in environmental initiatives designed to minimize their impact on the environment (McWilliams 2014, Schultz 2015, Ceres 2016). Environmental sustainability efforts include investing in renewable energy, waste recapture, recycling, and sustainable sourcing. As a result of these, and other, differences between craft and macro-brewers, we examine how the emergence of commercial craft brewing represents a departure from prior economic geographies and reflects a new social geography that is embedded with an emerging discourse on creativity, place, and values.

3 Theoretical Framework: Towards Creativity

Innovation has long been of interest to economic geographers. Indeed, geographies of high tech innovation, the spatial dynamics of innovation, and accounts of innovative places conceptually fueled much of the literature throughout the late-1980s and 1990s (Scott 1988, Storper, Walker 1989, Florida, Kenney 1990, Malecki 1991, Saxenian 1994, Lyons 1995, Audretsch, Feldman 1996, MacPherson 1997). Researchers focused on proximity and knowledge production, high tech corridors, and the diffusion of products and processes across space. This initial emphasis on innovation and technology gave rise to an explicit interest in science and technology inputs (such as engineering degrees) and the role of higher education in the development and deepening of the spatial division of labor.

Concomitantly, geographers sought to investigate sectors, including the service sector, which supported high-tech growth. These studies examined metropolitan regions and specific specialized industries (like so-called producer services) to understand the scale and scope of spatial interactions that define innovative communities, industries, and sectors (O hUallachain, Reid 1991, 1993, Markusen 1996). Eventually, geographies of innovation went micro and began to seek an understanding of the relationship between firm growth, knowledge production, and production systems on the ground and across space. In all of these studies, the research clearly demonstrated that the spatial division of labor and associated hierarchies, as well as "specialization", were well articulated, deepening, and that the cleavage between core and periphery was expanding.

---

[2] There are a small number of craft breweries (~ 135) that have expanded beyond local markets and have a regional footprint of several dozen states (Reid, Gatrell 2015). These breweries represent $\sim 4\%$ of the total brewery count.

Over time, geographies of innovation and the narratives of high tech growth came to dominate more applied economic development research, as well as the practice of economic development. As a result, communities across the U.S. and world sought to become the next "Silicon Valley", "Silicon Alley", or the "Silicon Forest". The emergence and expansion of science and technology driven growth was supported in large part by the popularity of Porter's Competitive Advantage of Nations (Porter 1990) and the so-called cluster approach. While Porter noted the existence of non-technological clusters – and Hayter (2000) has identified commodities-based clusters – the policy emphasis was almost exclusively on high tech growth and industries as communities struggled to revitalize local economies (i.e. Porter 1990, Scott 1993, Kaufman et al. 1994). Yet, the question of place always seemed to complicate innovation on the ground not only in peripheral regions with limited and often under-skilled labor markets, but also in larger metropolitan areas. In short, the 1990s and early 2000s illustrated that innovation couldn't be engineered in a global economy driven by the pernicious forces of uneven development per se – hence something else may have been driving the success of communities and differentiating places.

3.1 Beyond Linear Innovation Systems: Place & The Creative Class

Given the shortcomings of Porterian economic development, the spatial dynamics of neoclassical innovation models proffered by economists, and the explosion of research into the importance of the service sector, economic geography needed a new concept that reflected the intangible often-place based uncertainties that promote growth. Enter the abstract notion of "creativity" – innovation's non-linear socio-cultural and squishy partner and the creative class. Unlike innovation systems that could arguably be relocated or re-engineered, creativity as a concept and practice is inherently embedded in place and reflects a more holistic collection of socio-spatial relationships that are more cultural and historical – than a simple economic model. And these unique social-cultural relationships serve to define the creative class across space. The core of the creative class comprised elites, consumers, and leaders who shared progressive values and who drove urban revitalization in "hip" cities, established and emerging, across America.

According to Florida (2012), it is the creative class that drives and maintains the economic engine of cities vis-à-vis not only economic production; but the "squishy" concept of values. Like Supreme Court Justice Potter, Florida's new explanation for high growth regions boiled down to "I know it when I see it". The basic thesis asserted that urban growth and labor markets reinforce one another and highly articulated urban centers are anchored by a collection of elites that foster progressive values and an openness to new ideas and social change that attracts and retains talent. Florida's "creative class" was simultaneously a factor which explained production, consumption, and social change. Like any good economist, Florida and his colleagues asserted that the creative class could be modeled and as such quasi-quantitative indices such as the "bohemian index", "gay index", and "diversity index" proliferated the literature – and the popular media. Like the cluster before it, the "creative class" became a recipe that could be used to understand the comparative dynamics of economic development across space and gave rise to a full range of public policy initiatives – and associated progressive values.

Borrowing from Florida, we believe that emerging research on the "creative class" and progressive values has the potential to be an interesting and important conceptual development. That is, values can be used to explain economic development – and specifically a consumption driven model of development which deviates considerably from prior production centered frameworks like clusters. Moreover, the notion of the creative class is an attractive one, resonates with public discourses, and doesn't correspond to a single industry (i.e., specialization no longer dominates the discussion) and indeed economic diversification, entrepreneurism across multiple sectors, and niche industries were now as important as identifiable agglomerations such as "gun belt". In short, the new narrative could be used to revitalize the Rust Belt as well as explain the robust economies of tourist communities from Key West to Jackson Hole. Yet, the creative class doesn't explain creativity per se – it simply suggests you'll know it when you see it.

The purpose of this paper is to expand on the concept of creativity within a specific defined industrial niche. In contrast to work which emphasizes places, creativity as a concept can be examined by exploring a single industry – craft beer – that is closely associated with local markets, neighborhoods, and neo-localism (Flack 1997, Wesson, Nieva de Figueiredo 2001, Schnell, Reese 2003). Further, we assert that creativity is not synonymous with innovation or necessarily a process. Rather, creativity reflects a shared collection of socio-cultural relationships that might reside in place – or across a common industry, such as craft beer. For that reason, creativity is a highly contextualized set of values, interactions, and practices[3].

3.2 Space v. Place: Towards a Theory of Creativity & Community

As we have argued elsewhere, the everyday geographies of communities, culture, and politics of place are important to understanding the waxing and waning economics of localities (Gatrell, Reid 2002). To that end, we believe creativity – as a value – can be a useful framework which emphasizes niche local markets and entrepreneurism.

So what is the relationship between creativity and economic development from the perspective of geographers and regional scientists? Simply put – discussions of creativity and development extend from the Marxist concept of "creative destruction" as embodied in the classic work of Schumpeter (1942) (see also Scott 2006). In concrete terms, "creative destruction" asserts that the process of innovation in product and process is an ongoing regime that serves to eclipse the relevance of existing processes and products in the market place and can be used to explain capitalism's inherent spatial contradiction – uneven development (Smith 1984). While rooted in a Marxian reading of economics, "creative destruction" is not creativity per se. For that reason, we believe researchers have struggled to identify proxies, like patents, trademarks, industrial research, university research dollars and so on, to understand creativity in place.

More recently though, Törnqvist's The Geography of Creativity (Törnqvist 2011) provided researchers with a hybrid account of technological innovation that models the diffusion of technology across space and time, as well as the unique role 'special places' have played in fostering the innovation and creativity. Törnqvist's work echoes Scott (2006) insofar as creativity is a broader phenomenon embedded within social networks that are productive, consumption oriented, and symbolic. Yet, we would argue both Scott and Törnqvist are bound by the limited conceptualization of creativity as synonymous with technological innovation.

Unlike innovation, "creativity", as a spatial practice, gives meaning to place, production, and consumption – and the resulting "cultural" politics of local economic development (McCann 2002, Gatrell, Reid 2002, 2005). In the process, as Scott (2006) recognized – but framed differently - the practices associated with creativity serve to structure a "creative field" comprised of specific locational attributes and "geographically-differentiated webs of interaction" (Scott 2006, p. 3) that promote entrepreneurial activities – and enable entrepreneurs and creators to thrive. The classic example of so-called webs of interaction would be the growth, expansion, and sustained innovation observed in Silicon Valley. In the case of craft beer though, we are interested in understanding the values driven nature of the sector that resides at the nexus between creativity, community, and growth. Indeed, the local craft beer industry exists within a framework, or creative field, informed by shared experiences that drive economic development, transform neighborhoods, and may signal the potential to develop a new socio-cultural explanation for economic growth.

4 Craft Beer: Creativity as a Value

While the long-term viability of any business depends upon generating a profit there are some business owners for which non-financial returns enter into the calculus of their business model (Walker, Brown 2004). Such firms engage in what is termed satisficing behavior; in other words they are not driven by the maximization of profits. In contrast to a purely economic framework, satisficing behavior appeals to and obtains personal

---

[3] Hence, the notion that a "Creative Class" exists may within and between places be a misnomer. Rather, the discussions surrounding the creative class may reflect geography of progressive politics as it has become embedded within the U.S. urban hierarchy.

"value" from Maslow's hierarchy of needs (Maslow 1954). Specifically, Maslow (1954) proposes that other factors (such as physiological, safety, belonging, esteem, and self-actualization) influence behavior, motivate individuals, and inform decisions. In the business context, satisficing behavior occurs "when a firm's profit equals the managers' minimum acceptable or 'satisfactory' level and they then knowingly sacrifice additional profit in the pursuit of these higher order needs" (Kaufman 1990, p. 42). In the case of the craft beer industry, "belonging", "esteem", and/or achieving a firm's full creative potential (i.e., self-actualization) may take precedent over simple ROI. As these higher-order needs are non-monetary in nature they have been referred to as "psychic income" (Thurow 1978).

The idea that craft brewers engage in satisficing economic behavior has been hinted at by a number of researchers and writers. Wesson, Nieva de Figueiredo (2001, p. 392) observed that craft brewers are "often motivated by a love of brewing as by profits" while Day (2015) has described them as "astonishingly un-businesslike"[4]. A study of nascent craft brewers in Alabama concluded that "while the ultimate goal of brewers may be running a profitable operation, lifestyle or personal factors also appear to be important" Alonso (2011). Thurnell-Read (2014) examined the higher-order needs that seem to be valued by craft brewers in England. Among the brewers interviewed by Thurnell-Read there was "a sense of reward and satisfaction found in the production of what is perceived to be a product distinguished by the skills, passion and care deployed in its production." The brewers spoke of enjoying the creative process of making beer, the satisfaction they derived for being responsible for the final product, and the respect they felt from seeing customers drinking and clearly enjoying beer that they had brewed. These feelings were in sharp contrast to the boring, stressful, repetitive, and unfulfilling work that they had experienced in their previous jobs – descriptions that call to mind Marx's use of the adjectives alienation and estrangement to describe the worker's "relationship to the products of his labor" (Marx 1959, p. 30). In the documentary, Beer Wars (2010), Greg Koch, CEO of Stone Brewing Company, states that "I do not care how much beer we make. I only care how we make it". For the British, the selection of ingredients that go into their beer is driven by a desire to maximize product quality. Keeping down production costs is not part of the calculus.

Craft brewers also have a strong attachment to place. The ownership of craft breweries is ordinarily "local" – and entrepreneurial home brewers who decide to commercialize their hobby almost always do so in the place in which they live. The place often becomes a critical part in the identity of the brewery. The name of the brewery and the name of the beers that they produce often reflect local landmarks, historical figures, landscapes, historical events etc. (Flack 1997, Schnell, Reese 2003, Fletchall 2016). While most of the ingredients used by the breweries, with the exception of the water, are imported there is a growing interest in using more locally-grown ingredients. While three states (Idaho, Oregon, and Washington) grow 96% of the hops harvested in the U.S. there has, in recent years, been an expansion of hop growing outside of this core region. Driven by demand from craft brewers for local hops the plants are now grown in over 25 states (George 2016). While it is still the exception this has resulted in a small number of breweries producing beer made with all local ingredients. For example, in 2016 Boiler Brewing Company in Lincoln, Nebraska brewed a beer, appropriately named Nebraska Native, using all Nebraska ingredients (Matteson 2017). Examples such as this have been the catalyst for discussions around whether the concept of terroir has a place in the world of craft beer (Draft Magazine 2011, Bolden 2015). The connection that craft beer has with local places can be connected with the broader desire among growing numbers of people for food products that are locally-produced. As noted by Trubek, Bowen (2008, p. 24) "there is a growing movement that counters our placeless relationship to food and responds to increasing consumer demand for products that incorporate new dimensions of quality." Craft beer, made with high quality ingredients, by a brewer that lives locally,

---

[4]As craft beer has become a big business, global beer makers have sought to access craft and local markets through the strategic acquisition of micro-brewers, as well as larger regional craft brewers. Consequently, it could be argued that the current explosion of craft breweries – and the firm lifecycle – may be akin to the technology start-ups of the mid-1990s that enable small scale organizations to leverage modest novelty into sizable financial gains.

and with whom you can in all probability have a conversation with when you visit a local brewery is attractive to growing numbers of Americans.

Craft brewers are not only intimately connected to the product they make but also to the customers who drink their beer. These drinkers tend to be primarily millennials. A recent study by Mintel (2013) showed that 50% of older millennials (aged 25-34) drink craft beer compared with only 36% for the general population. Mike Stevens and Dave Engbers who founded Founders Brewing Company in Grand Rapids, Michigan note that "we don't brew beer for the masses. Instead, our beers are crafted for a chosen few, a small cadre of renegades and rebels who enjoy a beer that pushes the limits of what is commonly accepted as taste. In short, we make beer for people like us" (Founders Brewing Company 2016). The idea that craft brewers make beer for people like themselves should come as no surprise. People who make craft beer also drink craft beer.

The opportunity to be creative is valued by many craft brewers and is manifest in a number of different ways. Water, hops, barley, and yeast are the four basic ingredients that go into making beer. While the macro-brewers have a standard recipe upon which their beers are brewed craft brewers have creatively experimented with different types and combinations of these basic ingredients. Take hops for example. There are over one hundred different varieties of hops (Hopunion 2016). Different hops have different characteristics and the types and combinations used will influence both the flavor and aroma of the beer. In addition to different hop varieties craft breweries also use different hopping regimes that impact the flavor/aroma profile of their beer. Thus by adding hops at different stages of the brewing process (dry-hopping versus late-hopping) quite distinctive flavor/aroma profiles can be obtained (Schönberger, Kostelecky 2011). A number of craft brewers also engage in the practice known as wet-hopping which involves adding fresh hops (as opposed to say pelletized hops) that are delivered to the brewery within 48 hours of being picked (Vandenengel 2014). The plethora of hop varieties and the choice of different hopping regimes has been the catalyst for considerable creativity among craft brewers and have been credited with promoting new scientific research related to hops (Schönberger, Kostelecky 2011).

Beyond the four basic ingredients craft brewers are using their creativity to incorporate other ingredients into their beers. The list of these additional ingredients is almost endless and includes cacao, mango, cucumbers, tea and even bull testicles (All About Beer Magazine 2013, 2015a,b,d,e). Brewers are also working creatively to brew beers that no longer exist. Dogfish Head Brewery in Milton, Delaware have worked with Dr. Patrick McGovern an archaeologist at of the University of Pennsylvania Museum in Philadelphia to recreate a number of what they term ancient ales. These are ales whose recipes have been found in ancient tombs or derived from chemical analysis of ancient pottery (Dogfish Head 2016).

With so many craft breweries producing so many different styles of beer a major challenge facing many brewers is getting the consumer to notice and purchase their particular beers rather than all the others that are available. One way some craft brewers have addressed this challenge is to have creatively designed eye-catching packaging and labeling. A number of craft breweries hire brand consultants to assist them with the design of customized packaging and labels (American Craft Beer 2015). Brooklyn Brewery's iconic logo was designed by the celebrated New York graphic designer Milton Glaser (Agger 2013). In 2015 Arcadia Brewing Company of Kalamazoo, Michigan held a contest in which they invited local artists to submit label designs for their aptly named Art Hops brew (Mah 2016). On the other hand, some breweries opt for in-house design teams. In 2015 Ninkasi Brewing Co. of Eugene, Oregon announced the establishment of an artist-in-residence program whereby selected artists work with the brewery's in-house design and marketing team in the development of designs for new packaging and labeling (All About Beer Magazine 2015c).

5 Creativity, Passion, and Growth: Two Examples

As suggested above, economic geography's understanding of place, growth, and creativity have evolved over the past twenty years. As part of this evolution, the research suggests the scale of the analysis increasingly focuses on micro-level socio-economic contexts with special attention being paid to non-economic drivers of local growth. In an effort to understand the rescaling of local economic development, we believe the explosion of craft beer, as an industry, and the perspective of entrepreneurs active in this space are emblematic. For that reason, we examine two cases: The Black Cloister Brewing Company and 3rd Turn Brewing. The breweries were chosen because they are located in the cities in which the authors reside. This gave the authors easy access to the owners and staff for interview purposes and also allows them, through frequent visits as customers – a.k.a. participant-observation, to attain a feel for the atmosphere of the respective breweries. Likewise, the authors' insider knowledge as residents provide access to more local information resources and an understanding of the broader craft beer sector as it exists today and has developed over time in Toledo and Louisville. Additionally, both case studies are decidedly local insofar as the owners were homebrewers, intentionally invested in their home communities, and explicitly seek to create business that reflect a sense of place combined with business practices that are community centered.

5.1 The Black Cloister Brewing Company

The Black Cloister Brewing Company (BCBC) opened its doors in Toledo, Ohio in March 2015. The brewery is located in an 1874 structure that had been vacant since the 1970s in the heart of downtown Toledo (Cunningham 2015a). The brewery has the capacity to brew 1,000 barrels of beer per year which places it within the largest 1,000 craft breweries in the United States in terms of production volume. The CEO and Founder of Black Cloister is Tom Schaeffer. Schaeffer has an interesting background in that he is an ordained and practicing Lutheran Pastor. His Church, Threshold has its Sunday worship at the Black Cloister. Like many craft brewery owners Tom started out as a home brewer and was the founder of the local homebrew club, the Glass City Mashers (Brewers Association 2015c). Tom is also a certified Cicerone (the beer industry's equivalent of a wine sommelier).

Schaeffer (2016, personal interview, February 29) talked about the role that creativity plays at the Black Cloister, although he did so in quite different and distinctive ways. Schaffer began by talking about the role that creativity can play in helping old industrial cities like Toledo recover from the vagaries of the Great Recession of 2007-09. Toledo was particularly hard hit by the economic downturn and has since struggled to recover (Treanor, Costello 2015). In Schaeffer's opinion the retention and nurturing of creative workers is essential to Toledo's economic recovery and growth. Schaeffer notes that the Black Cloister has supported local creative businesses. The huge 50 foot mural that adorns the back wall of the brewery's tap room was designed by a local design and build studio, Graphite Design + Build, while the beer mugs that are given to members of the brewery's Mug Club are manufactured by a local glass blowing studio, Gathered Glassblowing studio. Both businesses are a few minutes' walk from the brewery. Schaeffer's mention of the importance of creative workers and industries resonates with the work of Richard Florida and his colleagues on the role of the creative class in economic development (Florida 2012, Lee et al. 2010). Additionally, in a highly informative paper on the economic history of Boston between 1630 and 2003, Glaeser (2006) emphasizes the importance of maintaining skilled workers during times of economic adversity. Boston was able to do that throughout its history whereas in cities like Detroit better educated, skilled, and creative workers abandoned the city. The most creative cities in the country, Schaefer noted, have a flourishing craft beer scene. This assertion is supported by Fallows (2016) who suggests that the existence of craft breweries in an indicator of a healthy and successful community. Other key characteristics of a healthy and successful community according to Fallows (2016) include a focus, by local residents, on working together, often in public-private partnerships to address local challenges, the existence of an identifiable civic champion, a compelling civic story, a vibrant downtown, the existence of a research university, a community college that is valued by and which serves the local community, elementary and secondary schools that have an element of experimentation about them, openness to outsiders, and a longer-term vision of what the community will look like in the future.

To Schaeffer creativity and brewing are linked. Brewing is very much a creative process. He makes a distinction between producing and creating beer. Producing beer is a process that Anheuser-Busch and Miller-Coors engage in. He recalled a conversation that he had with someone who had been a manager at a major brewery. The people there were hired to do a job, to produce beer, and not to engage in any creative thinking or production. Schaeffer also talks about the outcome of the creative process – the beer itself. There are times when he has made the decision to discard an entire batch of beer, not because there was anything wrong with it per se but because it did not match the intended flavor profile. The beer was perfectly fine (to use industry terminology there were no "off flavors") and could have been sold, at a significant profit, in the brewery's tap room. However, to have sold beer that did not match the intended flavor profile would have, in Schaeffer's opinion compromised the brewery's (and the brewer's) integrity. On some occasions, rather than discard beer, they have been able to sell it to a nearby distillery (Toledo Spirits) who have used it to produce, for example, hop-flavored whiskey. Even when it has been possible to sell a batch of beer to the distiller the brewery is making pennies on the dollar.

Head Brewer, Shannon Fink (2016, personal interview, February 9), had a rather serendipitous path into the world of professional brewing. She was a nurse for eleven years, a job that she disliked intensely. She found it unrewarding, stressful, emotionally draining, and overloaded with paperwork. In contrast, she describes her work environment at the brewery as "Zen-like". When asked to identify something that she disliked about working as a brewer she visibly struggled to identify anything and simply stated that she was "living the dream". Indeed, Fink enjoys the process of brewing so much ("It makes me happy" she stated) that on her days off she brews beer at home. Like Schaeffer, Fink started out as a home brewer. She had been introduced to home brewed beer by a nursing colleague and very shortly thereafter was brewing her own beer on her back patio. She was also educating herself by reading as many books about beer and brewing as she could lay her hands on. While her training and experience in nursing meant that she had a solid background in science, Fink also has an artistic streak. She taught herself how to draw in charcoal. She loved the one art course that she took in college. Her father, in fact, encouraged her to pursue her passion for art beyond college but Fink felt that there was no money to be made in art – until she entered the world of commercial brewing. She was a member of the local home brewing club that Schaeffer had founded and when the Black Cloister was close to opening he encouraged her to apply for one of the brewer's positions. Fink describes the brewing process as a "perfect marriage of art and science" (Cunningham 2015b). It is the creative process that she finds most rewarding – the opportunity to take ingredients and create a unique beer, a process of which she never tires. In recalling her days as a home brewer Fink described herself as being like a "mad scientist", always experimenting with different types and quantities of ingredients. Fink did not rely on reading books and trial-and-error to improve her brewing skills. She is also a graduate of the American Brewers Guild Craftbrewer's Apprenticeship Program, a 28-week program that focuses on brewing science and includes a five weeks of practical experience in the form of an internship at a craft brewery. It was after completion of this program that Schaeffer promoted Fink to the position of Head Brewer.

Fink also spoke about the satisfaction that she feels when she sees customers enjoying the beer that she has brewed. She often sits incognito at the Black Cloister's bar. Both Schaeffer and Fink talked about the role passion plays in the industry. Fink noted that much of the work that she does is not creative. She may, for example, spend an entire day cleaning various pieces of equipment. The job is also, at times, physically demanding as 50lb bags of malted barley have to be carried from one part of the brewery to another. But it her passion for the creative task of making beer that makes the less glamorous parts of the job worthwhile. Schaeffer spoke of the important part passion plays in the hiring of new employees. As part of the interview for a position at the Black Cloister interviewees are asked to talk passionately about a topic for five minutes. It can be any topic (it does not need to be beer). Schaeffer reckons that if an individual cannot talk passionately for five minutes on a topic about which they claim to be passionate then the probability is low that they will be able to talk passionately with customers about the brewery's beer. Knowledge of beer is less critical. As Schaeffer noted he can teach employees about beer; he cannot teach them to be passionate. As a result Schaeffer has listened to passionate monologues from interviewees on a variety of topics from dog parks to human genome sequencing.

5.2 3rd Turn Brewing

3rd Turn Brewing is located in Louisville, Kentucky. Like many craft beer firms, 3rd Turn's story is a familiar one that extends from an individual passion for beer and home brewing to a desire to create something meaningful – an experience and a product – in a local community (or place) that reflects the values and shared history of the owners. Opening in September 2015, the taproom initially focused 100% on guest taps. The micro-brewery served its first own commercial beer, a stout, in late-December. Going forward, 3rd Turn will continue to feature regional guest taps from more established Kentucky brewers such as Against the Grain, Apocalypse, Monnik, Beer Engine, and Country Boy. While many breweries limit outside pours, the owners are committed to celebrating the community of beer that has developed across the state and the Kentuckiana region. The tap room – is just that – a tap room. While no food is available for sale, the owners partnered with local restaurants for delivery, welcomes carry-ins (or potlucks), and the place serves as a gathering place.

3rd Turn was founded by three partners (Brian Minrath, Dale Shinkle, and Greg Hayden), each now on their third career. Despite an unintentional allusion to their personal narratives, the brewery was named for Churchill Downs' Third Turn and positions the brand squarely within the local history (Hayden et al. 2015, personal interview, December 22). Indeed, the name leverages local knowledge of Louisville insiders as the brand refers to a particular in-field location at Churchill Downs where residents can enjoy the derby which has now become an elite event for out-of-town guests and affluent locals. In this sense, the brewery, like many craft beer firms, builds on the well-established themes of neo-localism and explicitly appeals to a niche place-based market. Further, the vision of 3rd Turn blends the values of community insofar as the brewery owners sought "to create a space where J'Town [a community in metropolitan Louisville] residents and other East Enders" can enjoy beer "in a community setting." (Rothgerber 2016, p. 43).

What makes 3rd Turn's story interesting is that the endeavor represents an explicit and intentional desire on the part of Shinkle, Hayden, and Minrath, as well as Ben Shinkle (head brewer and Dale's brother), to re-vision their lives as entrepreneurs and to create something meaningful for their families and hometown. Lifestyle, values, and meaning-making drive their entrepreneurism. For example, Dale and Greg are both chemists who've been friends since college and both subsequently pursued careers in business as a CPA and safety planner, respectively (Hayden et al. 2015, personal interview, December 22). It was in the corporate world that Greg met their third partner, Minrath. As of early 2016, Greg was the only founder that had transitioned to full time at the brewery to pursue his passion and new career. In the case of Ben, Greg, and Dale, the 3rd Turn venture permitted them to take their hobby to the next level. While Ben is the head brewer, 3rd Turn specializes in the scaled up recipes developed by the former chemists – in particular Greg – that serve as the foundation of the production system. To that end, Greg and Dale's passion for chemistry and beer continues to inform their work – and each speaks of esters, sugars, and active yeast with a passion that reflect their desire to create "something new".

In terms of their beer, 3rd Turn explores and creates beers that intentionally reside outside of the traditional style guide. For example, the team created a hefe gerst based on a Ukrainian Steam Beer that uses barley as the primary grain (Shinkle 2016, personal interview, February 27). With a current annual maximum production capacity of roughly 2,000 barrels, the goal is to create unique beers in much smaller quantities that will be served primarily at the tap room – as well as on guest taps across Kentucky and southern Indiana[5]. The theme of creativity and collaborating with the community also

---

[5] In late December 2016, 3rd Turn announced a planned expansion and new facility in nearby Crestwood, KY located in Oldham County. The new "farm" location will permit the firm to expand production.

extends to their "mug club". Like many tap rooms, 3rd Turn has implemented an annual membership program and the mugs are handcrafted by a local artist in residence, Fong Choo – a faculty member at nearby Bellarmine University which is also Dale and Greg's alma mater. The individual nature of the ceramic mugs makes 3rd Turn unique and reflects the owner's desire to seek inspiration, foster community, and develop collaboration in non-traditional arenas. Like BCBC, 3rd Turn is operationalizing creativity broadly and deploying everyday strategies that reinforce economic development and themes from the "creative class".

Beyond creating beer, the owners clearly value community, hard work, collaboration, and fun. However, they understand business too. Indeed, site selection was a lengthy process that included working with local officials in multiple locations in suburban Louisville to identify an underserved market (think intervening location). As a result of their efforts, they chose a location – a former Moose Lodge that was once a church – which enabled 3rd Turn to be the first brewery located beyond the outer belt – miles away from other more stablished local competitors – many of whom have pours available on 3rd Turn taps.

6 Discussion

Craft brewers and beer drinkers are part of a broader local movement that increasingly redefines, or perhaps reframes, local economic development. Or put another way, the values-oriented entrepreneurs driving the craft brew industry see themselves as engines of community-building at the micro-scale. In doing so, craft brewers become "change agents". As change agents, brewers and breweries are often the anchor of revitalizing neighborhoods and spur further capital investment. In both of the case studies, the firms intentionally located in more marginal or transitional areas and the breweries are adaptations of prior uses. Moreover, the realities of the craft brewers – and the micro-spaces which they occupy are instructive as their success depends heavily on their ability to leverage creativity (product, marketing, and brand identity) in a very dense marketplace (Mann 2016).

According to Julia Herz, craft beer program director for the Brewers Association, craft "brewers are not just opening up businesses to run a profit; they have a different version of the American Dream – one where you can use your brewing as a platform for improving your community." (Shilton 2016). Craft breweries both contribute to and benefit from agglomeration economies. In an increasing number of cases these agglomeration economies are buttressed by geographic concentrations of locally-owned, often, creative businesses. Indeed, breweries are sometimes seen by policy makers as one of the critical elements of economic growth and neighborhood revitalization (City of Louisville 2014, Loosemore 2016). Indeed, the location of the vast majority of craft breweries in Louisville coincides with revitalizing (arguably artistic or bohemian) urban districts such as Portland (Against the Grain production, Falls City), NuLu (Against the Grain, Akasha and Goodwood), and Germantown (Monnik). To that end, the city of Louisville has specifically targeted the craft beer industry as a critical element of growth in select neighborhoods and a working group has proposed a bike-able "beer trail" similar to the successful bourbon trail (City of Louisville 2014). In the case of Toledo's Black Cloister Tom Schaeffer noted the geographically proximate glass blowing and build and design studios that have contributed to the ambience that he is trying to create for his customers.

In another corner of Ohio, the Great Lakes Brewing Company has been credited with being a catalyst in the socio-economic revitalization of the Cleveland's Ohio City neighborhood. In the late nineteenth and early twentieth century Ohio City was a bustling industrial neighborhood with docks, mills, foundries, distilleries, and bottling works (Ohio City Neighborhood 2016c). By the end of the Second World War, however, the neighborhood was in decline. Pat and Dan Conway, who founded the Great Lakes Brewery in 1986, have been described as the "beer men who became the unlikely leaders of the neighborhood's revival" (Alexander 2013). Today, Ohio City is a vibrant, ethnically diverse neighborhood (34% of its 9,000 residents are African American and 23% are Hispanic) that is teeming with small locally-owned businesses. These include other breweries, restaurants, bicycle shops, book stores, a glass blowing studio etc. (Ohio City

Neighborhood 2016b,d). Since 2005, the crime rate has fallen approximately 25% and real estate values have doubled. It has been rated as the second most walkable neighborhood in Cleveland (Ohio City Neighborhood 2016a).

Like Ohio City, Denver's Lower Downtown (LoDo) neighborhood is another that has benefited from the establishment of a craft brewery. In this case it is the Wynkoop Brewery. Like Ohio City, Lower Downtown Denver was once a bustling neighborhood and a major industrial area that drew its sustenance from the Union Pacific rail yard. By the early twentieth century LoDo was in decline as the railroad's importance as transportation medium decreased. It was not until the late-1980s that LoDo started to witness a revival and the Wynkoop Brewery played a key part in that process. "LoDo's characteristics make it an ideal site for the downtown's restaurant and entertainment center. The Wynkoop was the pioneer which laid the foundation for this vision's realization, which then became an anchor for the broader development of LoDo" (Weilar 2000, p. 175). Today, much like Ohio City, the area is thriving and is home to some of the best restaurants, galleries, shops and boutiques in the city, as well as a dozen or so craft breweries. Compared with Ohio City, however, the LoDo neighborhood is not as demographically diverse; 80.4% of its population is white. Out of 32 Denver neighborhoods it is the 27th in terms of the share of non-whites in its population (Statistical Atlas 2015).

As the discussion suggests, local craft brewers are critical "place-makers" and contribute to the overall sense of place associated with Millennial driven urban revitalization.[6] This is a process and a relationship that is well-established and shows little sign of slowing down. At the same time this has been very much an organic process with home brewers making the choice to commercialize their hobby and in so doing making an incremental contribution to local economic development. However, as we have seen in the Louisville case, the growth of craft brewing has caught the attention of policy makers with the result that some communities are starting to think strategically about how to foster and nurture the industry. This includes enacting legislation to make the regulatory environment friendlier to the industry (Bragg 2016).

7 Conclusion

While it may be too much to say that the craft beer industry has disrupted the broader beer industry there is no doubt that its emergence has impacted in a significant way the large multi-national brewing companies. Faced with increased competition from craft brewers in the United States, Anheuser-Busch and SABMiller finalized a $100 billion merger in 2016. This merger provides unprecedented economies of scale and, at a time when its share of the U.S. market is declining, gives Anheuser-Busch access to growing markets in Africa and Latin America (Brown 2016). Craft beer's emergence in the United States may now be actively re-scaling economic development and reconfiguring traditional explanations of economic growth. While growth may be a by-product of craft beer entrepreneurs, the evidence suggests the drivers and decisions of entrepreneurs are nuanced, more local, and often reside outside of the simple arithmetic of ROI. While no doubt all entrepreneurs seek to maximize their investment, non-economic drivers such as creativity, community, and even a passion for brewing are critical to the success of craft firms. Indeed, the success of the firms themselves is largely dependent upon the creativity of brewers and the neighborhoods (or communities) within which they are embedded.

While the notion of values-driven entrepreneurism may not necessarily be new (e.g., Ben & Jerry's or Hobby Lobby), the experience of the craft beer industry is unique as the framework that drives the sector may be signposting the emergence of new hybrid models of economic development that account for place, community, creativity, and growth. As the two cases illustrate, the industry at the local scale appears to have been driven – in part – by non-economic drivers and that these drivers are inherently scaled, as well as experienced, at the everyday world of neighborhood communities. More importantly, and

---

[6] While craft brewing was popular before the appearance of the so-called millennial cohort research and data suggest that the millennials are the key demographic that have driven growth of the industry more recently. Recent market research shows that 57% of people who drink craft beer on a weekly basis are millennials, compared with 24% and 17% for Gen Xers and Baby Boomers, respectively (Brewers Association 2016b).

not surprisingly, the language of craft brewers parallels that of the creative class and reflects the shifting consumption patterns and lifestyle of a now established millennial cohort.

References

Acitelli T (2015) When brewpubs started booming. *All About Beer Magazine*, February 11. http://allaboutbeer.com/when-brewpubs-started-booming/

Agger M (2013) I love Brooklyn Brewery. *The New Yorker*, March 5. http://www.newyorker.com/culture/culture-desk/i-brooklyn-brewery

Alexander D (2013) Beer entrepreneurs fuel comeback of struggling Cleveland neighborhood. *Forbes*, November 26. http://www.forbes.com/sites/danalexander/2013/11/26/beer-entrepreneurs-fuel-comeback-of-struggling-cleveland-neighborhood/#14cc94c3574f

All About Beer Magazine (2013) Join all about beer for a beer tasting with Wynkoop Brewing Co. *All About Beer Magazine*, March 29. http://allaboutbeer.com/news/beer-tasting-with-wynkoop-brewing-co/

All About Beer Magazine (2015a) Cucumber beers: stars of the summer? *All About Beer Magazine*, August 13. http://allaboutbeer.com/cucumber-beers/

All About Beer Magazine (2015b) Founders Brewing Co. announces first backstage series beer of 2016: 'mango magnifico'. *All About Beer Magazine*, January 25. http://allaboutbeer.com/news/founders-brewing-backstage-series-2016-mango-magnifico/

All About Beer Magazine (2015c) Ninkasi Brewing Co. announces artist in residence program. *All About Beer Magazine*, June 26. http://allaboutbeer.com/news/ninkasi-brewing-co-announces-artist-in-residence-program/

All About Beer Magazine (2015d) Stone brewing re-releases stone 12th anniversary bitter chocolate oatmeal stout. *All About Beer Magazine*, January 25. http://allaboutbeer.com/news/stone-12th-anniversary-bitter-chocolate-oatmeal-stout/

All About Beer Magazine (2015e) Tea: an untapped beer ingredient? *All About Beer Magazine*, April 23. http://allaboutbeer.com/tea-an-untapped-beer-ingredient/

Alonso AD (2011) Opportunities and challenges in the development of micro-brewing and beer tourism: A preliminary study from Alabama. *Tourism Planning & Development* 8[4]: 415–431

American Craft Beer (2015) The art of branding craft beer. *American Craft Beer*, February 18. http://americancraftbeer.com/item/the-art-of-branding-craft-beer.html

American Homebrewers Association (2016) Homebrewing stats. http://www.homebrewers-association.org/membership/homebrewing-stats/

Anheuser-Busch (2016) Serving our communities with pride. http://www.anheuser-busch.com/betterworld/community.html

Audretsch D, Feldman M (1996) R&D spillovers and the geography of innovation and production. *The American Economic Review* 86[3]: 630–640

Beer Wars (2010) Dir. Anat Baron. Ducks in a Row Entertainment Corporation. DVD

Bolden E (2015) Can craft beer truly express a sense of place? *Punch*, July 9. http://punchdrink.com/articles/can-craft-beer-express-terroir-with-rogue-farms-wolves-and-people-brewery/

Bragg V (2016) New bill proposed to help attract more craft breweries to Virginia. *WSET.com*, January 8. http://wset.com/news/local/new-bill-proposed-to-help-attract-more-craft-breweries-to-virginia

Brewers Association (2015a) Brewers association reports big gains for small and independent brewers. July 27. https://www.brewersassociation.org/press-releases/brewers-association-reports-big-gains-for-small-and-independent-brewers-2/

Brewers Association (2015b) Number of breweries. https://www.brewersassociation.org/-statistics/number-of-breweries/

Brewers Association (2015c) Tom Schaeffer. https://www.brewersassociation.org/profile/-tom-schaeffer/

Brewers Association (2015d) The year in beer: U.S. brewery count reaches all-time high of 4,144. December 2. https://www.brewersassociation.org/press-releases/the-year-in-beer-u-s-brewery-count-reaches-all-time-high-of-4144/

Brewers Association (2016a) Small and independent brewers continue to grow double digits. March 22. https://www.brewersassociation.org/press-releases/small-independent-brewers-continue-grow-double-digits/

Brewers Association (2016b) Today's craft beer lovers: Millennials, women and hispanics. August 15. https://www.brewersassociation.org/communicating-craft/understanding-todays-craft-beer-lovers-millennials-women-hispanics/

Brown L (2016) A-B InBev finalizes $100b billion acquisition of SABMiller, creating world's largest beer company. *Chicago Tribune*, October 11. http://www.chicagotribune.com/business/ct-megabrew-ab-inbev-sabmiller-merger-20161010-story.html

Calagione S (2011) *Brewing Up A Business: Adventures In Beer*. John Wiley & Sons, Hoboken, NJ

Ceres (2016) Brewery climate declaration. http://www.ceres.org/declaration/about/climate-declaration-campaigns/brewery#breweries

Choi DY, Stack MH (2005) The all-american beer: A case of inferior standard (taste) prevailing. *Business Horizons* 48[1]: 79–86. CrossRef.

City of Louisville (2014) Mayor's local brewery workgroup report. City of Louisville, Louisville, KY. http://louisvilleky.gov/sites/default/files/mayors_office/pdf_files/-mayors20beer20report20201420ver202.pdf

Cone T (2012) Number of US famers markets surges. *USA Today*, August 3. http://usatoday30.usatoday.com/news/nation/story/2012-08-03/farmers-markets-increasing/56727330/1

Crowell C (2013) Craft beer consumer stats: How will they affect your business plan? *Craft Brewing Business*, May 3. http://www.craftbrewingbusiness.com/business-marketing/craft-beer-consumer-stats-how-will-affect-your-business-plan/

Cunningham B (2015a) Black Cloister Brewing Co. taps opening date. *Toledo Blade*, February 26. http://www.toledoblade.com/Peach-Weekender/2015/02/26/Black-Cloister-Brewing-Co-taps-opening-date.html

Cunningham B (2015b) Black Cloister's Fink is head of the class. *Toledo Blade*, September 24. http://www.toledoblade.com/Peach-Weekender/2015/09/24/Black-Cloister-s-Fink-is-head-of-the-class.html

Day P (2015) How the craft beer revolution started. *BBC News*, December 30. http://www.bbc.com/news/business-35120401

Dogfish Head (2016) Ancient ales. http://shop.dogfish.com/ancientales

Draft Magazine (2011) The dirt on terroir. *Draft Magazine*, July 26. http://draftmag.com/the-dirt-on-terroir/

Duva N (2014) Elitism, or something else? Millennials and the war on big beer. *CNBC.com*, November 8. http://www.cnbc.com/2014/11/07/why-those-elitist-millennials-hate-big-beer.html

Ellison S (2006) After making beer ever lighter, Anheuser faces a new palate. *Wall Street Journal*, April 26. http://www.wsj.com/articles/SB114601602889736048

Fallows J (2010) Jimmy Carter: Not the king of beers? (updated). *The Atlantic*, August 19. http://www.theatlantic.com/politics/archive/2010/08/jimmy-carter-not-the-king-of-beers-updated/61599/

Fallows J (2016) Eleven signs a city will succeed. *The Atlantic*, March. http://www.theatlantic.com/magazine/archive/2016/03/eleven-signs-a-city-will-succeed/426885/?.utm_source=SFFB

Fink S (2016) Personal interview. Toledo, OH, February 9

Flack W (1997) American microbreweries and neolocalism: "Ale-ing" for a sense of place. *Journal of Cultural Geography* 16[2]: 37–53. CrossRef.

Fletchall AM (2016) Place-making through beer-drinking: A case study of Montana's craft breweries. *Geographical Review* 106[4]: 539–566. CrossRef.

Florida R (2012) *The Rise of the Creative Class, Revisited.* Basic Books, New York

Florida R, Kenney M (1990) Silicon Valley and Route 128 won't save us. *California Management Review* 33[1]: 68–88. CrossRef.

Founders Brewing Company (2016) History. http://foundersbrewing.com/history/

Galt RE, O'Sullivan L, Beckett J, Hiner CC (2012) Community supported agriculture is thriving in the central valley. *California Agriculture* 66: 8–1. CrossRef.

Gatrell J, Reid N (2002) The cultural politics of local economic development: The case of Toledo Jeep. *Tijdschrift voor Economische en Sociale Geografie* 93[4]: 397–411. CrossRef.

Gatrell J, Reid N (2005) Placing economic development narratives into emerging economic spaces: Project Jeep, 1996-1997. In: LeHeron R, Harrington J (eds), *New economic spaces: New economic geographies.* Ashgate, Aldershot

George A (2016) 2016 world harvest report U.S. hops. *The New Brewer* November/December: 64–69

Gilman HR (2014) How millennials' use of social networks explains their politics. *Brookings Tech Tank*, November 24. https://www.brookings.edu/blog/techtank/2014/11/24/how-millennials-use-of-social-networks-explains-their-politics/

Glaeser EL (2006) Reinventing Boston: 1630-2003. *Journal of Economic Geography* 5: 119–153. CrossRef.

Grossman K (2013) *Beyond the pale: The story of the Sierra Nevada Brewing Co.* John Wiley & Sons, Hoboken, NJ

Hayden G, Shinkle D, Shinkle B (2015) Personal interview. Jeffersontown, KY, December 22.

Hayter R (2000) *Flexible Crossroads: The Restructuring of British Columbia's Forest Economy.* UBC Press, Vancouver, BC

Herz J (2014) Craft brewers' 2014 charitable donations top $71m. *Brewers Association* https://www.brewersassociation.org/communicating-craft/craft-brewers-contribute-millions-to-local-causes/

Hopunion (2016) A hop for every flavor and style. https://www.hopunion.com/hop-varieties/

Imarenezor C (2016) Super Bowl 50: Anheuser-Busch returns to commercial lineup for 28th year. *Vibe*, January 16. http://www.vibe.com/2016/01/super-bowl-50-anheuser-busch/

Kaufman A, Gittell R, Merenda M, Naumes W, Wood C (1994) Porter's model for geographic competitive advantage: The case of New Hampshire. *Economic Development Quarterly* 8[1]: 43–66. CrossRef.

Kaufman BE (1990) A new theory of satisficing. *The Journal of Behavioral Economics* 19[1]: 35–51. CrossRef.

Kirchenbauer H (2014) Philanthropy is alive and well in the craft beer industry. *San Diego Troubadour*, June. http://sandiegotroubadour.com/2014/06/philanthropy-is-alive-and-well-in-the-craft-beer-industry/

Lee SY, Florida R, Gates G (2010) Innovation, human capital, and creativity. *International Review of Public Administration* 14[3]: 13–24. CrossRef.

Loosemore B (2016) Falls City announces new bottled beers. *The Courier Journal*, March 1. http://www.courier-journal.com/story/life/food/spirits/beer/2016/03/01/falls-city-announces-new-bottled-beers/81158592/

Lyons D (1995) Agglomeration economies among high technology firms in advanced production areas: The case of Denver/Boulder. *Regional Studies* 29[3]: 265–278. CrossRef.

MacPherson A (1997) The role of producer service outsourcing in the innovation performance of New York state manufacturing firms. *Annals of the Association of American Geographers* 87[1]: 52–71. CrossRef.

Magee T (2014) *So you want to start a brewery? The Lagunitas story.* Chicago Review Press, Chicago, IL

Mah L (2016) Art Hops beer and logo design make debut at Friday night Art Hop. *Mlive*, January 9. http://www.mlive.com/entertainment/kalamazoo/index.ssf/2016/01/art_hops_beer_and_logo_design.html

Malecki E (1991) *Technology and Economic Development: The Dynamics of Local, Regional, and National Change.* Longman, New York, NY

Mann D (2016) Five funny names in Louisville beer – and why brewers come up with them. *Louisville Business First*, February 1. http://www.bizjournals.com/louisville/news/2016/02/01/five-funnynames-in-louisville-beer-and-why-brewers.html

Markusen A (1996) Sticky places in slippery space: A typology of industrial districts. *Economic Geography* 72[3]: 293–313. CrossRef.

Marx K (1959) *Economic and philosophical manuscripts of 1844.* Progress Publishers, Moscow

Maslow AH (1954) *Motivation and Personality.* Harper & Row, New York, NY. CrossRef.

Matteson C (2017) Boiler brewing company tackles Nebraska-made beer. *Lincoln Journal Star*, January 11. http://journalstar.com/lifestyles/food-and-cooking/boiler-brewing-company-tackles-nebraska-made-beer/article_bfe16c27-b68d-50d2-a90a-fa13fda7ff89.html

McCann E (2002) The cultural politics of local economic development: Meaning making, place-making, and the urban policy process. *Geoforum* 33[3]: 385–398. CrossRef.

McWilliams J (2014) The ecological creed of craft beer. *Conservation*, http://conservation-magazine.org/2014/03/sustainable-practices-in-craft-brewing/

Mintel (2013) The rise of craft beer in the US – craft beer sales have doubled in the past six years and are set to triple by 2017. January 23. http://www.mintel.com/press-centre/food-and-drink/the-rise-of-craft-beer-in-the-us-craft-beer-sales-have-doubled-in-the-past-six-years-and-are-set-to-triple-by-2017

Monloss K (2016) How Budweiser ditched its old look and crafted a new visual identity. *Adweek*, January 24. http://www.adweek.com/news/advertising-branding/how-budweiser-ditched-its-old-look-and-crafted-new-visual-identity-169144

National Gardening Association (2014) *Garden to Table: A 5-year Look at Food Gardening in America*. National Gardening Association, Williston, VT

Nurin T (2016) It's final: AB InBev closes on deal to buy SABMiller. *Forbes*, October 10. http://www.forbes.com/sites/taranurin/2016/10/10/its-final-ab-inbev-closes-on-deal-to-buy-sabmiller/#3155e6f137d6

O hUallachain B, Reid N (1991) The location and growth of business and professional services in American metropolitan areas, 1976-1986. *Annals of the Association of American Geographers* 81[2]: 254–70. CrossRef.

O hUallachain B, Reid N (1993) The location of services in the urban hierarchy and regions of the United States. *Geographical Analysis* 25[3]: 252–267. CrossRef.

Ohio City Neighborhood (2016a) About the neighborhood. http://www.ohiocity.org/about

Ohio City Neighborhood (2016b) Demographics. http://www.ohiocity.org/demographics

Ohio City Neighborhood (2016c) History. http://www.ohiocity.org/history

Ohio City Neighborhood (2016d) Neighborhood guide. http://www.ohiocity.org/guide

Pew Research Center (2010) Millennials: Confident. Connected. Open to change. Pew Research Center, Washington, D.C.

Porter M (1990) *The Competitive Advantage of Nations*. Basic Books, New York, NY. CrossRef.

Reid N, Gatrell JD (2015) Brewing growth: Regional craft breweries and emerging economic development opportunities. *Economic Development Journal* 14[4]: 4–12

Rothgerber H (2016) Better beer through Bellarmine chemistry. *Bellarmine Magazine*, Winter. http://www.bellarminemagazine.com/better-beer-through-bellarmine-chemistry/

Rotunno T (2014) The BMW of beer: Brewery crafts luxury approach. *CNBC*, May 3. http://www.cnbc.com/id/101636905

Satran J (2014) Here's how a six-pack of craft beer ends up costing $12. *HuffPost Taste*, September 12. http://www.huffingtonpost.com/2014/09/12/craft-beer-expensive-cost_n_5670015.html

Saxenian A (1994) *Regional Advantage: Culture and Competition in Silicon Valley and Route 128*. Harvard University Press, Cambridge, MA

Schaeffer T (2016) Personal interview. Toledo, OH, February 9

Schönberger C, Kostelecky T (2011) 125th anniversary review: The role of hops in brewing. *Journal of the Institute of Brewing* 117[3]: 259–267. CrossRef.

Schnell SM, Reese JE (2003) Microbreweries as tools of local identity. *Journal of Cultural Geography* 21[1]: 45–69. CrossRef.

Schultz K (2015) Drink your way to sustainability with these climate-conscious microbrews. *Yes! Magazine*, April 3. http://www.yesmagazine.org/planet/drink-your-way-to-sustainability-with-these-climate-conscious-microbrews

Schumpeter JA (1942) *Capitalism, Socialism and Democracy*. Harper & Row, New York. CrossRef.

Scott A (1988) *Metropolis*. University of California Press, Berkeley, CA. CrossRef.

Scott A (1993) The new southern California economy: Pathways to industrial resurgence. *Economic Development Quarterly* 7[3]: 296–309. CrossRef.

Scott A (2006) Entrepreneurship, innovation, and industrial development: Geography and the creative field revisited. *Small Business Economics* 26[1]: 1–24. CrossRef.

Shilton AC (2016) Craft beer vs. Budweiser: How small brewers are winning back the neighborhood. *Yes! Magazine*, March 2. http://www.yesmagazine.org/new-economy/craft-beer-vs-budweiser-how-small-brewers-are-winning-back-the-neighborhood-20160302

Shinkle D (2016) Personal interview. Jeffersontown, KY, February 27.

Shortridge JR (1996) Keeping tabs on Kansas: Reflections of regionally based field study. *Journal of Cultural Geography* 16[1]: 5–16. CrossRef.

Smith N (1984) *Uneven Development*. Blackwell, Cambridge, MA. CrossRef.

Statistical Atlas (2015) Race and ethnicity in Lodo, Denver, Colorado. Cedar Lake Ventures, Inc. http://statisticalatlas.com/neighborhood/Colorado/Denver/Lodo/Race-and-Ethnicity

Storper M, Walker R (1989) *The Capitalist Imperative*. Blackwell, Cambridge, MA

Svaldi A (2016) Molson Coors claims all of MillerCoors, making home-grown brewer the third largest in the world. *The Denver Post*, October 11. http://www.denverpost.com/-2016/10/11/molson-coors-claims-millercoors/

The Beer Professor (2015) Community space. December 29. http://www.thebeerprofessor.com/?.p=1573

Thurnell-Read T (2014) Craft, tangibility and affect at work in the microbrewery. *Emotion, Space, and Society* 13[1]: 46–54. CrossRef.

Thurow LC (1978) Psychic income: Useful or useless? *The American Economic Review* 68[2]: 142–145

Treanor C, Costello B (2015) The Toledo metropolitan statistical area. *Economic Trends* September 3. https://www.clevelandfed.org/newsroom-and-events/publications/economic-trends/2015-economic-trends/et-20150903-the-toledo-metropolitan-statistical-area.aspx

Tremblay VJ, Tremblay CH (2009) *The U.S. Brewing Industry*. The MIT Press, Cambridge, MA

Törnqvist G (2011) *The Geography of Creativity*. Edward Elgar, Northampton. CrossRef.

Trubek A, Bowen S (2008) Creating the taste of place in the United States: can we learn from the French? *GeoJournal* 73[1]: 23–30. CrossRef.

Vandenengel H (2014) The fresh flavors of wet hop ales. *All About Beer Magazine* 35[5]. http://allaboutbeer.com/article/wet-hop-beer/

Walker E, Brown A (2004) What success factors are important to small business owners? *International Small Business Journal* 22[6]: 577–594. CrossRef.

Weilar S (2000) Pioneers and settlers in Lo-Do Denver: Private risk and public benefits in urban redevelopment. *Urban Studies* 37[1]: 167–179. CrossRef.

Wesson T, Nieva de Figueiredo J (2001) The importance of focus to market: A study of microbrewery performance. *Journal of Business Venturing* 16[4]: 377–403. CrossRef.

Winograd M, Hais M (2014) How millennials could upend Wall Street and corporate America. *Governance Studies at Brookings*, May. https://www.brookings.edu/wp-content/uploads/2016/06/Brookings_Winogradfinal.pdf

The Journal of ERSA
Powered by WU

Volume 4, Number 3, 2017, 87–118
DOI: 10.18335/region.v4i3.161

journal homepage: region.ersa.org

Built environment, creativity, social art: The recovery of public space as engine of human development

Anna Onesti[1]

[1] University of Napoli Federico II, Naples, Italy

Received: 11 September 2016/Accepted: 5 September 2017

Abstract. The paper is a part of a comprehensive research aimed at operationalizing HUL approach and experimenting it in the buffer zone of Pompei, mainly in Torre Annunziata (Italy), and is based on the recognition of art and cultural heritage as tools for "managing the change" of landscape. The proposed thesis is that the recovery of public space, configured by art and culture and shared with local community according to an inclusive approach, contribute to regenerate creativity, reconstructing the relationships between people, communities and landscape. This lays the foundations for a "creative environment" and regenerative, concived as a prerequisite of development. In this process, art is a driver which acts on the creativity of local residents, stimulating their critical thinking, open-mindedness and design capacity, and leading them to accept diversity as an opportunity. Focusing on theories and on the empirical analysis of a best practice, MAAM Museum in Rome, this paper has three main objectives: to produce empirical evidence on the relationship between art, heritage and community relationships; to make transferable and replicable in other contexts, such as Torre Annunziata, the process experienced at MAAM; to develop a methodology able to soliciting, integrating and supporting the regeneration of relationships in the town of Torre Annunziata.

1 Introduction

Population growth and migration, climate change and energy resources, economic crisis and social inequality, cultural globalization and rapid growth of ICTs are global processes affecting both people and places. The "New Urban World" (Nijkamp, Kourtit 2012) calls for a deeper reflection on the strategies to implement, by acting locally, with the aim of safeguarding and promoting human wellbeing and human dimension of development. As UNESCO recommendation pointed out, "Urban growth is transforming the essence of many historic urban areas. Global processes have a deep impact on the values attributed by communities to urban areas and their settings, and on the perception and realities of their inhabitants and users" (UNESCO 2011, art. 17).

Despite the inability of many local policies to face new global challenges, all around the world there is an increasing number of bottom-up experiences in which artistic practices activate the change in degraded or abandoned spaces and urban areas, giving shape to new urban landscapes. Slums, abandoned factories, degraded public spaces, historical centers become a testing ground for new forms of synergies between different actors, artists, foundations, cultural associations, third sector organizations, professionals and citizens. From street art to site-specific installations, from poetry to theater up to "live" works, artistic experience, shared with local communities, become instrument to regenerate both the system of relations between people, which supports the definition of community, and the process of interaction between people and built environment. New forms of patronage, alternative to the public, are emerging and new institutions, legal bodies, associations and foundations arise in order to manage the process of change. Spread throughout the world, these practices are shaping a 'geography of change' (Fondazione Pistoletto 2003), in which art is an instrument of investigation, understanding and change of reality.

It is not just the empirical evidence which underlines the "social" function of art and cultural heritage. By the Faro Convention (Council of Europe 2005b), the European Community recognized that cultural heritage is the fundamental element that characterizes and holds together a community. Through the notion of heritage community (Article 2 b), Faro Convention demonstrates that "by valuing and wishing to pass on specific aspects of the cultural heritage, in interaction with others, an individual becomes part of a community" (Council of Europe 2005a, art. 2). Consistent with the focus definitively on people and "their constantly evolving values, beliefs, knowledge and traditions" (Council of Europe 2005b, art. 2, paragraph a), cultural heritage assumes the widest possible sense, as it can be intended "as a continuing process, of creating, constructing, using and changing heritage" (Fairclough et al. 2014, p. 11). In this framework, promoting cultural heritage protection is a "central factor in mutually supporting objectives of sustainable development, cultural diversity and contemporary creativity" (Council of Europe 2005b, art. 5, paragraph e).

Supporting the principles introduced by Faro Convention, UNESCO Recommendations on Historic Urban Landscape (UNESCO 2011) interpret conservation as a strategy to achieve a balance between urban growth and life quality on a sustainable basis (art. 3) and consider cultural diversity and creativity as key assets for human, social and economic development (art. 12). The definition of tools to implement HUL approach, prompted by UNESCO (2011, art. 24), becomes crucial not only in order to protect the landscape, but above all to build a new "human" development on a local basis, which is consistent with new Millennium goals (United Nations 2015). Operationalizing HUL approach means, therefore, to contribute to achieve the United Nations Sustainable Development Goals and, in particular, the "urban" one (Goal 11) and to make "inclusive, secure, resilient and sustainable cities" (Fusco Girard 2014).

The paper is part of a comprehensive research aimed at operationalizing the HUL approach and experimenting it in the buffer zone of Pompei, mainly in Torre Annunziata (Italy) (Fusco Girard et al. 2016) and focuses on the contribution of art and cultural heritage for "managing the change" of landscape. The proposed thesis is that the recovery of public space, configured by art and culture and shared with local community according to an inclusive approach, contributes to regenerate creativity, reconstructing the relationships between people, communities and landscape. This lays the foundations for a "creative environment" (Törnqvist 1983, Santagata 2009) and regenerative (Fusco Girard 2014), conceived as a prerequisite for development. In this process, art is a driver which acts on the creativity of local residents, stimulating their critical thinking, open-mindedness and design capacity, and leading them to accept diversity as an opportunity.

Focusing on theories and on the empirical analysis of a best practice, such as MAAM Museum in Rome, this paper has three main objectives: to produce empirical evidence on the relationships between art, heritage and community; to make transferable and replicable in other context, such as Torre Annunziata, the process experienced at MAAM; to develop a methodology able to soliciting, integrating and supporting the regeneration of relationships in the town of Torre Annunziata.

2 The beauty of HUL

HUL approach introduces the "principle of relationality" (Fusco Girard 2013) as a new holistic and integrated vision, which links tradition and modernity, past and present, present and future in a systemic/circular and synergistic perspective of development, centered on human beings. This approach outlines a new cultural perspective for urban initiatives, which enhances relationships and interdependencies between the different aspects and the whole and compares universal values and local identities (D'Auria, Pugliese

2013). The historic urban landscape, "world of men and things", can be interpreted as a complex adaptive system with two interacting subsystems: built environment (Ciribini 1979) and heritage community (Council of Europe 2005b). Communities act on built environment through a sedimented intangible cultural capital, making use of and enhancing local resources. In turn, built environment causes relational impacts on communities, regenerating both social ties and their relationships with environment.

This link between cultural production, daily needs and behaviours of people is very strong in Italy: for describing the intangible cultural capital of the community we just say "cultura materiale" ("material" culture), whereas other countries use the term "intangible", focusing more on non-material dimensions (Cuccia, Santagata 2003). Built environment is the tangible expression par excellence of the communities that have shaped it. It reveals in material forms the system of values, exhibiting the processes that, over time, shaped it (Bouchenaki 2003): to meet their needs and to adapt the performance of built heritage – local communities continuously change the landscape (Fontana 2012, Viola 2012), choosing what to preserve and what to change, in a dynamic equilibrium between past and future (Caterina 2012). At the same time, communities are shaped by the built environment which, through its spatial organization and its relationship with nature and climate, defined their structural attributes, influencing the behavior of both individuals and community. The reciprocal interaction between places and communities has produced long-lasting co-evolutionary dynamics (Magnaghi 2012), which in turn created the extraordinary diversity of Italian landscapes. The "co-evolutionary" relationship between community and built environment and the relationship between place and community are both elective relationships of care, feeding, maintenance and culture-expressive: people belong to a territory as they belong to a culture . There can be no landscape without a cultural perspective, allowing the harmonious coexistence of different elements, also very distant in time (Bonesio 2012). As landscape is the creation of a community as a whole, its conservation is related to the reconstruction of community and it is an essential element of local self-sustainable development (Magnaghi 2010).

2.1   The meaning of beauty

"Beauty" has been defined as the set of attributes which man enjoys without desiring to possess them (Eco 2005), going beyond daily needs to express the making of sense and avoiding the fear of passing (Givone 2012). These attributes of beauty makes it ontologically a "common ownership" good which everyone should use without any exclusive claim (Rodotà 2012).

Beauty is not a mere embellishment of reality, but a structural data, which comes from the diversity and plurality of interconnected elements (Fusco Girard 1989). The beauty of landscape derives from the synthesis of different dimensions. Communicating that some criteria/attributes are satisfied at the highest levels, and each element is interconnected to the other, the landscape transfers a sense of wholeness, of fulfillment. In this sense, beauty becomes the main indicator of "proper functioning" of landscape as a complex ecosystem: in the case of a natural landscape, beauty refers to the perfect functioning of the ecosystem, in the case of a built landscape, it shows the link between place and communities, the harmony between nature and man (Fusco Girard, Nijkamp 2005).

A significant contribution to a definition of complex beauty is owed to the theories of the philosopher Arnold Berleant, who pointed out that the loss of human scale in the cities have an aesthetic character, in a sense not limited to visual aspects. As beauty has a synesthetic character, negations of beauty are not only in the transformations which invasively modify scenes and urban views, but also in traffic flows that invade the cities (aesthetic intrusion), in the presence of excessive sound and color (aesthetic distortion), in poor quality of living (aesthetic deprivation), linked to bad sunlight exposure, in unrestrained lifestyle, in the excess of food and consumption (aesthetic depravity). Adopting Schiller's theory (1794 in Berleant 2004) who places the aesthetic experience at the basis of morality, Berleant sees beauty as a source, a sign and a standard of human value. For changing landscape, it is necessary an aesthetic knowledge, meaning the ability to perceive landscape through all the senses, a kind of re-creation, that implies the need to retrace the creative process generating the element which we enjoy (Berleant

2004). Whereas, landscape acts on humans as a field of forces, which establishes an absolute reciprocity relation, so that the user is an integral part of it.

The influence of beauty in physical regeneration, moral and spiritual landscapes and sites have been explicitly recognized by UNESCO since 1962. Beauty contributes to the cultural and artistic life of people but must be harmonized with the needs of communities, their evolution and the rapid development of technical progress (UNESCO 1962). Where settled communities are able to recognize, protect and "produce" beauty issues rather than individual interests, territory has a greater ability to magnetize economic investment, stimulating the new economic activities. A beautiful landscape then becomes a driving factor of economy (Greffe 2005), when the community perceives its value and activates to preserve it. In a circular dynamics, the beauty of the landscape in turn increases the feeling of belonging, the sense of community (Fusco Girard, Nijkamp 2005), and encourages maintenance processes, which result in the conviction that "it is good to" take care of the place. Putting the beauty of the landscape in the center of the transformation process has a double meaning. On the one hand, it means preserving historical beauty, while maintaining efficiency in dynamic processes that shaped the built environment over time as a complex ecosystem. On the other hand, it means reversing the degradation processes and closing the loop between resources and landscape features, enabling new relationships between place and community.

It becomes necessary to "redesign aesthetic of existence", to move beyond the void of appearances, to rethink the unique space of poiesis, its not transitory, its form, its essence, to approach art, not retaining to the past, but saying modernity opposed to conformism (Trione 1996).

2.2 Measurable relationships of landscape

The interactions between community and built environment can be measured by a system of indicators, which allows not only to make communicable and sharable design and selection criteria, but also to determine causal links between heritage and society, while improving the forecasting ability and choice of everyone involved. It allows us to analyze the results of already tested practices, identifying weaknesses to be improved and strengths to be proposed; thereby it facilitates the construction of new tools to support decision making regarding the implementation of UNESCO (2011) recommendations.

The set of indicators must describe the different relationships which feed the landscape system and can be so classified:

1. actions of people on built environment through intangible cultural capital;

2. relations between physical attributes of built environment;

3. influences of built environment on people;

4. internal relationships of heritage community (social capital);

5. relationships of landscape with external environment.

It is interesting to note that there is a close interaction between every single set of indicators in our framework, as every set is both effect of the previous set and cause of the next one. The process of empowerment activated is a regenerative process of development, capable of activating new circular processes, that in turn can face social and physical degradation.

The first series of indicators describes the way in which community is related to built environment through strategies and actions aimed at caring the built environment and at continuing the creative process of landscape production (Magnaghi 2010). In the existing literature, built environment indicators are mainly insufficient and must be improved (Lynch, Mosbah 2017). Indicators related to the attitude of people towards the built environment are useful in order to prove with facts their place-attachment and to make it measurable.

As pointed out by some researchers (Brown et al. 2003, Eshelman, Evans 2002), maintenance and "home personalization" reveal place attachment, whereas observed incivilities (vandalism, litters and graffiti, ...) predict lower place attachment. The relationship between people and place can be measured also through the attitudes to pro-environmental behaviour (Sanchez, Lafuente 2010, Dunlap et al. 2000), that are strongly linked to values and identity (Gatersleben et al. 2014). Some indicators related to actions of people on built environment have been highlighted in a study aimed at measuring sustainability progress at local level in the United States (Lynch, Mosbah 2017).

Indicators as care, maintenance, recovery and reuse of existing buildings, care and cleanliness of public space and lack of vandalism (Ipsos MORI 2015, Campos, Oliveira 2016), recycling and saving water, saving energy are effective in evaluating the relationship between people and place without resorting to a psychometric approach (Lynch, Mosbah 2017). This paper suggests how to integrate existing indicators with new ones, that better describe the way in which local community acts on the built environment. We suggest to enrich existing literature with new indicators (see Appendix A) as reuse of built heritage, production of site specific art work, integration of art in public spaces, use of public space for artistic activities, rate of local materials and technologies, rate of bioclimatic design solutions, lack of vandalism.

The second kind of indicators describes physical changes produced by the actions of people on place, understood as changes to the structure of the built environment system. This kind of indicators has been mainly studied in the field of visual indicators (Ipsos MORI 2015, Tveit, Sang 2014, Campos, Oliveira 2016), as they are able to describe how much and why a particular place attracts people and activities. Landscape preferences are basically linked to nine visual concepts: naturalness, stewardship, complexity, imageability, visual scale, historicity, coherence, disturbance, ephemera and security (Tveit, Sang 2014). Although our framework excludes some items that are contained elsewhere, indicators related to built environments already proposed in existing literature, as size and quality of public spaces, length of pedestrian paths, preservation status of old buildings, presence of green and open spaces closed to traffic, harmony in dimensional characters (lack of dimensional misalignments in heights), are useful to describe changes in the relationships with the built environment. Aiming to relate built environment to health, an early study conceived by the City Wellbeing Program in Australia (Paine, Thompson 2016) proposes a framework of indicators related to the quality and attributes of built environment, which are very useful in describing internal relationships of built environment system.

Whereas indicators which describe actions of community on built environment and its changes are quite easy to measure, as they can measured mainly through physical dimensions, it is much more difficult to measure the influence of built environment on community and the changes of its internal relations.

Although it is still unclear whether and under what conditions cultural heritage produces beneficial effects on economic development and social community, many areas of impact have been highlighted (D'Auria, Monti 2013).

Starting from research on social capital conducted by Putnam (Putnam et al. 1993, Better Together 2004) and in parallel by Matarasso (1997), it was possible to dissolve the dilemma of whether heritage is "use or ornament". But nevertheless the link between cultural heritage and sustainable development, while described in detail, is still mainly committed to a framework of indicators mostly perceptual and descriptive, based on surveys, interviews, narrative arguments, which cannot determine the causal links between heritage and social growth (Cicerchia 2015).

Earlier studies (CHCFE 2015, HLF 2015) highlight the ability of heritage (and landscape) to enhance both personal and social development. A significant contribution to the identification of social impacts of heritage comes from some studies on the impacts of art on people and communities (Brown 2006, Bollo 2013, Brown, Novak-Leonard 2007, Carnwath, Brown 2014). This field of studies pointed out that cultural participation produces personal and social impacts, not only during the cultural event or immediately afterwards, but also long after the event. In fact, the changes in our beliefs, skills and attitudes rarely are perceived during cultural participation, as they require a sedimentation time before they manifest themselves. The extended impacts, that manifest themselves through behaviors and concrete actions, need a long time (Carnwath, Brown 2014) and can culminate in other similar impacts. Just cumulative impacts generate significant results in terms of sense of belonging, mindedness, mental health and well-being.

Aiming at describing the influence of built environment on people, individual impacts of heritage can result in three main areas of impact: learning, skills and personal development; improved physical and mental health; cultural activity and well-being (HLF 2015), which increases the level of satisfaction with their lives. Indicators can be distinguish in three relative subcategories. The first one includes indicators as participation in lifelong learning; attending of upper school; students level of literacy and numeracy; level of ICT competencies; specialization in the high knowledge intensity. The second one includes health indicators as life expectancy and healthy life at birth; age-standardised cancer mortality rate (19-64 years old) and mortality rate for dementia and related illnesses (people aged 65 and over); life expectancy without activity limitations at 65 years of age; stress condition. The last one, related to cultural participation, includes involvement of disadvantaged people; incidence of knowledge workers on employment; social and civic participation; voluntary activities.

The systemic structure of social community makes social impacts of heritage more important than the sum of individual impacts. As it improves personal development, in turn heritage induces the improvement of interpersonal relationships. In literature, social impacts of heritage on community relate to three areas of impact: greater interaction between people, that hence the strengthening of social capital; a deeper sense of collective identity, linked to sense of place; enhanced levels of awareness and understanding between particular groups, with a positive effect on community cohesion (HLF 2015).

A significant attempt to make measurable social impacts of heritage on community has been experienced by Dzialek (2014), which, in studying the link between social capital and economic development in different regions of Poland, has brought a number of indicators derived from statistical studies, to three independent components, "formal bridging social capital", "informal bonding social capital" and "informal bridging social capital", stressing the distinction between bonding social capital and bridging social capital (Putnam 2000).

Recently two additional forms of social capital have been added: linking capital, which describes the ability to connect in a vertical direction, and it is the basis of participation around a shared project of individuals with interests and levels of responsibility also very different from each other (Szreter, Woolcock 2004) and can be considered a vertical bridge between powers and asymmetric means (Prior, Tavano Blessi 2012); bracing social capital (Rydin, Holman 2004), used to describe a combination of bridging and bonding capital, but with more attention to the combination of weak and strong bonds in networks. Bracing social capital can be a valid descriptor of hybrid processes of social innovation (Holman, Rydin 2013).

Of special interest are the studies conducted since 2010 by CNEL and ISTAT to measure "fair and sustainable wellbeing" (ISTAT 2015), which integrates indicators of economic, social and environmental measures. The initiative follows the international debate, stimulated by the Stiglitz-Sen-Fitoussi Commission and the international initiatives of the OECD, to measure the progress of societies beyond the PiL (Cicerchia 2015).

This study, that provides every year new data, proposes many useful indicators, able to describe the impact of built environment on the community and the relationships of landscape as a complex system.

The impacts of heritage on community can be expressed as changes in conditions or internal relations, encouraging dialogue between persons not belonging to the same social circle, stimulating acceptance diversity, openness, helping the understanding of different ideas. This type of phenomenon is described through indicators that measure the relatedness of the community and mainly to the presence and density of local associations of various kinds (sports, cultural or social). Other indicators describe the transformation of bridging social capital in bonding social capital and creative growth of the community through the development of cooperative and synergistic initiatives, linked by "working together", which become the glue of society and the engine of attractiveness and competitiveness of the local economy.

The last set of indicators describe the exchanges of information and people with the external environment of landscape as an open system. The possibilities to exchange are deeply influenced by the connections to the global network (Cohen 2014), that are described through indicators as intensity of use of internet, Wifi coverage, smartphone penetration. The ability of local system to exchange information is described by indicators as numbers of start-up, research intensity, propensity for patenting, rate of technological innovation in the production system, rate of innovation of the product / service of the national production system. As art can be considered a form of communication, the exchange of artworks and products of cultural and creative industries production can be odd as indicators of exchange with external environment too. The second kind of external relationships, that describes the exchange of people, can be measured through indicators as new residents, tourists and visitors, artists, that focus on the presence of foreign people, and on the number of exchange between local community and tourists or artists, that measure more deeply the effective possibilities of change. Last set of indicators provides a final comparison of landscape attractivity through measuring web exposure, popularity index web, prizes and awards. The whole set of indicators is listed in the Appendix A.

The proposed system of indicators, graphically represented on urban maps, leads to a multicriteria approach (Cerreta et al. 2014) for assessing the spatial diffusion of sustainable and human development (Fusco Girard, De Toro 2007, Cerreta, De Toro 2012).

3   Art for the beauty of HUL

3.1   From personal wellbeing to community empowerment

The observation of the multitude of bottom-up initiatives, through the driving force of art, is producing significant results both as recovery of places and regeneration of relationships. Understanding the process by which the individual relationship between person and art contributes to activating a system of relations with the built environment and between people can lead to outline a strategy for urban regeneration processes. Artistic experience is generally a personal emotional experience, which results in a direct relationship between the artistic input and who receives it; from personal emotional experience art enhances wellbeing, also linked at making sense and satisfacting identity needs. From the personal relationship and well-being, art develops an attitude of respect, care, antithetical to the degradation dynamics that characterize the urban spaces. So, the relationship with artwork becomes an attitude of care towards a heritage which is recognized as a common good. Furthermore, sharing the same experience and the same sense of affection, people pass from feeling extraneous in the city to becoming a member of a community (heritage community) (Council of Europe 2005b) whose members recognize the same landscape as cultural heritage. So, a social relationship between people which share the same artistic experience is produced from individual relation between human and artwork. From the regeneration of relations between community and built environment it is possible to activate new virtuous development processes, linked to symbiosis between people/place and synergies between people. The ability of individuals to develop self-identity and autonomous cultural models is reflected in the production capacity of landscape, linked more and more at its ability to offer intangible components. So, art contributes to local development, as it acts on people, influencing their behaviours and openness and stimulating their learning capacity and attitude to innovation (Sacco et al. 2015).

The reconstruction of relations between individuals, community and place, driven by art, lays the foundation of a "creative environment" (Santagata 2009), in which productive synergies and regenerative are activated. These conditions are the requirements of sustainable local development (De Rita, Bonomi 1998, Ciapetti 2010), which relies on the empowerment of local communities and on their ability to produce cultural heritage, managing the change of landscape. In Italy, the white paper of creativity (Santagata 2009) proposes a local development model based on creativity and culture as engines of growth that respects the "grammar of sustainability", as it seeks not only to pass on to future generations infrastructure and cultural resources, but also to preserve equity and defend cultural diversity (Bertacchini, Santagata 2012).

The recognition of the link between creativity, innovation and local development (UNCTAD 2008) suggests to enhance the creativity of people, which is linked to the

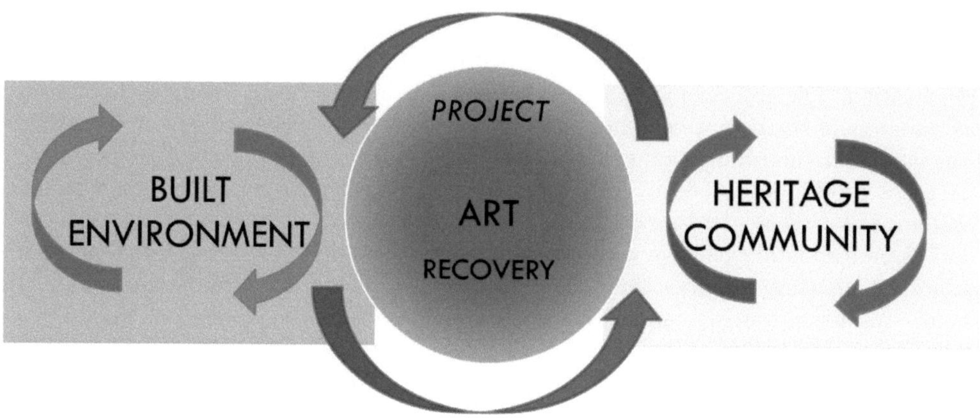

Figure 1: The contribution of art in reactiving the systemic functioning of landscape (Picture: Anna Onesti)

ability to find new and useful combinations between different elements (Poincaré 1906). Creativity of local people is fundamental in building a "creative environment", which is a milieu able to producing and disseminating projects regardless of their scope, either cultural, social, environmental and economic (Greffe 2015). Starting from the consideration that it is possible to distinguish certain activities which play a key role in producing an intrinsic motivation for creative thinking, Sacco, Segre (2009) pointed out the link between creative activities and cultural-led local development, recognizing different "rate" of creativity in human activities. Passing from supercore creativity to creativity, external aims grow up and intrinsic creativity decreases. Art, identified as super-core creativity, has a special function in the relationship between community and built environment, because it contributes to the construction of a new critical knowledge, able to recreate communities. An additional function is performed by the recovery of built heritage, creativity-core activities, which spreads and connects with the built heritage soliciting creative effects from art (see Figure 1).

The art manufacturing process, as well as the recovery of built environment, are both creative activities which, shared with local communities, stimulate individual and collective creativity. While they feed material culture, enhancing planning and designing capacity of local community and putting in relation old place and new technologies, they contribute to regenerating social capital, nurturing both bonding and social capital and building bracing capital. With the transition from personal emotions to community belonging, art contributes to producing new value creation circuits, linked to sharing capacity and cooperative, which in turn introduces new forms of wealth creation. This determines the regeneration of relationships, intended as social capital of community, physical capital of built environment and capacity to change the landscape, in a virtuous regenerative and self-sustaining cycle. As a final outcome, the art determines choral harmony, which generates a field of attractive forces in the landscape. The "beauty" of the landscape, which can be understood as a reflection of an ecology ecosystem between community and built environment, become the main indicator of this harmony. So, it's possible to argue that art contributes to the beauty of landscape not as a decoration but as structural process that guides local communities in the recovery of relationships. Through signs, forms, actions, gestures, the artist invents relationships. Every new artwork is a proposal for how to inhabit a common world (Bourriand 1998).

3.2 A practice: the MAAM, Museum of Other and Elsewhere, in Rome

On March 2009 a group of about 200 people, mainly immigrants, with the support of an organization for the right to housing, occupied an abandoned factory of about 20 thousand square meters in the eastern suburbs of Rome. Few months later, Giorgio De Finis, anthropologist, art curator and filmmaker, with the filmmaker Fabrizio Boni, proposed to the occupants to make a documentario, called "Space Metropoliz", showing the preparation of a surreal journey to the Moon, the only place available for them. The movie Space Metropoliz (released in 2014) became an opportunity to engage artists and scientists in working with Metropoliziani, teaching them about the moon and building the rocket. At the end of shooting, Metropoliz hosted many artworks, strictly related to the place, and the inhabitants of Metropoliz, feeling "protected" by art, asked to continuing the "game". With more than 500 artworks site-specific and more of 400 artists involved, today they shape Museum of Other and Elsewhere of Metropoliz, one of the most important cultural institutions of Rome (De Finis 2015). MAAM is a new kind of museum, real museum (Pietroiusti 2015) in which people live, taking care of their heritage. Flavours, colours, sounds, art works, historic industrial heritage are integrated in a strange harmony, which confuses art and life in a unique mixed city.

Passing from an "utopia of escape" (to the moon) into an "utopia of reconstruction" (Mumford 1922), MAAM demonstrates that art can be instrumental to build community values, not only interpersonal ones but also interethnic, transforming a disenfranchised group into a heritage community (Council of Europe 2005b). MAAM is recognized by the community as a common good and has established a symbiotic relation between inhabitants and place.

The process through which the art becomes driver of endogenous development can be glances by the following model, that becomes also the reading scheme of the MAAM experience:

- Art as game, Space Metropoliz. The film, presented out of competition at the Venice Film Biennial in 2014, introduces art as both a Trojan to penetrate into the occupied factory and a relational device to liberate the imagination of people and to free them from the burden of everyday life. Intended as a game which makes men free (Schiller 1793 cited in Berleant 2004), art returns to artistic dimension a context without any chance for redemption. Imagining a different world gives Metropoliziani the hope to improve their lives and to build a better future.

- Art as an utopia, a project of change. Passing from Space Metropoliz to MAAM Museum, art guides the transition from an utopia of escape to an utopia of reconstruction (Mumford 1922). Instead of telling the journey of Metropoliziani to the moon as "a happy ending", MAAM shows the physical and social recovery of Metropoliz, which is closer to architects than to artists. Integrating people needs and spacial quality, art contributes to rethink the world and contributes to regenerate social institution and urban community, starting from the recovery of public space, with places for socializing.

- Art as knowledge and communication. Art is instrumental both in learning about the moon and in exhibiting Metropoliz to Romans. As first artworks of MAAM, Gian Maria Tosatti realized a large telescope and placed it on top of the tower, with the collaboration of local inhabitants in cutting, assembling and welding the metal. In a similar way, Hogre made a big sign , with a height of 30 m, which points the way to the moon. As a new urban landmark, these two artworks mark the landscape, referring an idea of art as an ethical sign, which binds matter and thought (Leroy-Gourhan 1964, Lukàcs 1975).

- Art as a barricade. At MAAM, art continuously produces not only cultural values, but also economic, recognized outside, which protect the community from forced eviction and the site from destruction. The demolition of the factory, which would be necessary to the realization of the building complex originally planned, would look more and more like the serious destruction of an artistic valuable collection of hundreds of works recognized by the art system.

- Art as relational system, connecting human activities. At MAAM, art has also another aim: to avoid the enclave effect and open the gates of Metropoliz to the city, sewing together two extremes of the contemporary city, the art museum, the highest place par excellence, and the slum, the lowest and degraded. The attractive power of the art collection of MAAM creates a stream of visitors, who never would have

Table 1: actions on built environment

Maintenance and recovery activities	Diffused in the site	
Artworks	500	
Production of films	2	
Exhibitions	Venere degli stracci by M. Pistoletto held in 2015	
Art gallery	1 (Pinacoteca Domestica Diffusa. Diffused exhibition of artworks in houses)	
books production	3	
Workshop for self-construction	2 (with Facoltà di Architettura Roma Tre 2011; kids rock supported by Commons Camp and Studio Superfluo, 2015)	Figure 2: Local people contributing to the maintenance of artworks

come into contact with this type of community. In this way, art puts in relations Metropoliz to Roma and Tor Sapienza neighborhood, contributing to explain the housing crisis and the serious situation of tens of thousands of people deprived of basic civil rights: school, medical care and voting. Art is in the MAAM a meeting and reporting system to look at others without prejudice.

- Art as a real museum, a new landscape. It develops the idea of a "real" museum (Pietroiusti 2015), an object that exists, has a current consistency in the order of things, concerns facts and existing people, in opposition of the contemporary art museums, unreal objects, seemingly imposed. MAAM can be intended as "place of the Muses", center of knowledge, a place where human activities are connected, as it has been theorized and experimented by Michelangelo Pistoletto (2003).

3.3 Relational indicators at MAAM

The abandonment and degradation that characterized this site before were so strong that social capital had zero value and social dynamics were stationary. In this sense, we can suppose that the social and cultural growth of these communities had no other origin than the process of "recovery" under study.

MAAM can be considered an avant garde for its highly experimental and innovative character, far from ordinary and institutional contexts. For this feature, it can not be replicated elsewhere as it is, but is very useful in order to understanding the relationships that the recovery of public space configured by social art can activate between people, place and community and the processes of involvement of local communities.

Although it was born in an illegal context, free from international policies, MAAM is first of all an approach to local development that, starting from the recovery of public space, acts not only on both physical space but on local people too, as it transforms them in a high quality place and a heritage community strictly linked. MAAM offers a possible answer to some question proposed by United Nations with SDGs as it unconsciously relates to the urban goal, that points out the necessity to make cities more inclusive, secure, sustainable and resilient. MAAM can be considered a good practice for scientific interest because, aiming to rebuild a micro community through the recovery of public space, it tests an innovative tool that although externally-led, as it is a cultural and architectural project, since its birth continuously incorporates community in each phases of development. It is interesting to stress that MAAM came from a specific request of people lived in Metropoliz that, after experimenting the power of art in protecting them

Table 2: Internal relationships of built environment

Urban garden	1
Playroom	1
Schoolroom	1
Sport equipment	2 (football field and basket playground)
Meeting room	1
Piazza	1
Restaurants	1(Cucina Meticcia Metropoliz)

Figure 3: MAAM is part of the skyline of Roma suburbs

Table 3: Internal relationships of heritage community

Local community-culture	200
Local community-people	200
Local community-public	200
Involved disadvantaged people	200
Children involved	70
Afterschool programs	daily
Sport associations	Football team
Sports	Weekly tournment of football; Tournament "Mediterraneo antirazzista"
Educational workshops	1
No profit organizations	2

Figure 4: Art workshop for children in the MAAM ludoteca (playing room)

against forced eviction, proposed to de Finis to continue the "game of art".

Inhabitants of Metropoliz approve every artistic proposals, interact with artists (see Figure 1), sometimes providing material help in building artworks, but never replace artists. MAAM is not an experience of co-design or co-recovery, as it doesn't comes from a local community project, but from a cultural and social project based on community needs and daily shared with them (see Figure 2). MAAM is also supported by third sector organizations and by scholars and cultural associations: in its implementation it proposes a new comprehensive participatory dynamics, which clearly outlines the role and responsibilities of each actor (see Figure 3). Although developed out of the institutional framework, MAAM is an example of hybrid tools for local development through the recovery of public space.

At MAAM art, that is mainly for local people, becomes from a protective barricade a common good, inseparable from the built environment, as people increasingly link their identity to Metropoliz (i.e. they say they are Metropoliziani) and become more and more empowered in place care and management (see Figure 4). Through MAAM museum people of Metropoliz are becoming a heritage community (Council of Europe 2005b), as a social organization that establishes a system of relations and interrelations and adopt a language of its own, through which it communicates with the external environment.

Interactions of people from different countries, ethnicities, social and cultural conditions makes cultural diversity the core elements of MAAM. Although at MAAM art is for

Table 4: Relationships between landscape and external environment

Residents	200
Tourists	Not available
Exchanges tourists/ local community	Open every Saturday
Exchanges artists/local community	Daily
Start-ups	1
Research projects	1
Artworks for export	It is not provided for the production of artworks for sale, just once for self-financing)
Film production	1
New collaborative activities	1 (catering company of local women)
Urban activities	4 (Carnevale a Tor Sapienza; maintenance of urban public space; Free school of Italian for foreigns; La via dell'arte project (artistic path between metro station and MAAM)
Technological innovation for artistic production	3 artworks
Facebook likes	15325
Google	17800 (researching "museo dell'altro e dell'altrove di Metropoliz")
prizes and awards	premio internazionale Marisa Giorgetti. Sezione diritti umani; Institutional recognized in the list of the museums in Rome

Figure 5: The gateway to MAAM

residents, it attracts more and more visitors and it is counted on official Rome website site among main art museums.

Experimenting the proposed framework of relational indicators at MAAM is very useful in order to both understanding and checking the systemic impacts of art on people and place and to testing the application of the framework into a real context.

The first set of indicators (see Table 1), related to the actions of people on built environment, shows very interesting results, as at MAAM more than 500 artworks site specific have been produced (De Finis 2017). Also many cultural events have hosted at MAAM, and are characterized by the strictly integration between cultural activities and public space. This process is accompanied by many maintenance and recovery works and by the reuse of many abandoned space, that are mainly done by local people.

This first set of indicators suggests that art is driver on a new attitude towards built environment.

In turn, this process changes the internal relations of built environment, as it creates new available spaces and new internal paths. The second set of indicators (see Table 2) shows new collective set of spaces: urban garden, playroom, restaurant, meeting room, square and sport equipment.

The third set of indicators (see Table 3) reveals the impact of the process on local people (not only adults but also children and young people) through measuring their active participation to culture and their involvement in the management of Metropoliz. This process of social involvement in turn causes the growth of new collective forms of social capital that, although informal, highlights the production of both bonding and bridging capital. Whereas the first one describes the growth of strong relationships between people, and can be considered the glue of MAAM, the second one refers to weak links between different people, and can be considered the source of MAAM artistic and cultural force. Although the observation of the case study is still too limited in time in order to demonstrate that the MAAM communities is becoming a heritage community (Council of Europe 2005b), it is noticeable that it is going to build a creative milieu, a social science and cultural context, that is an essential precondition of sustainable development.

The last set of indicators (see Table 4) shows the relationships for MAAM and its external environment through the exchange of knowledge, people and materials. It is interesting to highlight that in the absence of sponsorships and a commercial promotion, MAAM fame was mainly achieved by speaking through the network and unconventional channels. The increasing number of visitors and cultural tourists identifies MAAM as a creative approaches for heritage-based sustainable development (D'Auria 2009). The results achieved at MAAM, expressed in terms of increased relations, synergies and attractiveness, suggest to consider it a best practices. All data refer to 2016.

3.4 Towards an hybrid approach: creative crossovers and "living lab"

The experience of the MAAM can be interpreted as a cultural project, an experiment of social art, which proposes a new dynamic and participatory approach, where the role and responsibilities of everybody are quite clearly outlined. Intended as an example of a cultural project, MAAM paves the way to a public space design aimed at producing cultural crossovers, as systematic methodologically predictable social effects. Cultural crossovers are the effects intentionally produced by the hybridization of art and culture with the most varied sectors, opposite to alternative spillovers, accidental and episodic effects of cultural policy (Sacco, Sciacchitano 2015).

MAAM suggests a process of embeddedness that we propose to implement in different and more ordinary context. In order to make the experience of MAAM replicable and transferable elsewhere, after decoding the process of empowerment of communities through artistic experience, it is necessary to test its "model" in a laboratory context through field testing. Laboratory experimentation allows us to identify cause/effect relationships and to produce empirical evidence about the role of art as a driver of human development.

Live experimentation of the proposed approach requires operational hybrid tools able to meet bottom-up approach of participatory processes with top-down scientific approach and to bring experimentation into a systematic and structured framework of innovation.

Cities are opposite of scientific laboratories that are distinctly and purposefully created to be separate from the lived world in order to manipulating variables and testing hypotheses. Through laboratorization it is possible to set boundaries where controlled experiments can take place and be recorded, in order to transform events/experiments into facts/knowledge. The real world can function as a laboratory, since it adhere to life 'as it is really lived' (Evans, Karvonen 2014). In order to produce laboratory knowledge and make communicable and sharable causal links, it's necessary both to set material, institutional and conceptual boundaries to the testing field and, through measurable indicators, to provide a richness of data that allows statistical patterns to emerge.

An useful tool for hybrid approaches are Living Labs, that were developed in the 90's within MIT, Massachusetts Institute of Technology, with the aim of making knowledge, experiences and daily needs of people the starting point of innovation. Defined by the European network ENoLL (www.www.openlivinglabs.eu) as "user-centred, open innovation ecosystems based on a systematic user co-creation approach integrating research and innovation processes in real life communities and settings", Living Lab is both an approach and an arena (Schliwa 2013) and is characterized by three main features:

1. being confined in a geographically or institutionally bounded space;

2. making social and/or material alterations aimed to conducting intentional experiments;

3. incorporating iterative learning into the process.

Living labs have been exploited as an effective tool in the transitional phases from spontaneous collaboration practices to the empowerment of local communities for local development as they represent a model of territorial innovation based on social economy and community governance (Concilio 2013).

Living lab seems to be a very effective tool that supports the recovery of public space, making it a social innovation and culture-driven tool. As testing arena, Living lab can coincide with public space, that in turn through live experimentation becomes place of social innovation. As place where social processes mainly happen and have a social balancing attitude (Caterina 2013), public spaces become the testing arena for an approach to recovery that actively involves and embeds the whole community.

4   Case study: HUL of Torre Annunziata

The paper focuses on the town of Torre Annunziata, in the Vesuvius area, a case study particularly relevant because it documents a productive landscape (Tempesta 2009), characterized by the symbiosis of a local community dedicated mainly to the production of pasta for food use and a built environment configured for its production (Viola et al. 2014).

Since the nineteenth century, a lot of pasta factories (102 pasta factories; 1.678 employees) prospered thanks to climate attributes (continuous ventilation and good sun exposure), infrastructure (a canal from Sarno river and an industriousness seaport) and the special knowledge of the pasta drying process, imported by a community from Amalfi (Abenante 2011). The urban landscape changed according to the production process; ground floors and basements of residential buildings housed productive uses; a strong link characterized the continuity of public spaces and spatial elements, open up on the street in order to airing and drying pasta and moving raw materials and finished products (Diano 2015). The built environment was configured as a bioclimatic system, which used natural ventilation and rainwater harvesting to facilitate the manufacturing and drying process of pasta production (Napolitano 2015). Airflows, cooled and purified in the transition from green areas, were conveyed into the buildings by means of special architectural concept (Pinto, Viola 2015).

The "quartiere murattiano", Murat district (see Figure 6), developed along two main streets, Via Mazzini and via Oplonti, and bordered by Via Murat and Corso Umberto, hosted the largest concentration of pasta factories, with over one hundred pasta factories in the early twentieth century (Pinto, Viola 2015). Today there is a single pasta factory, the only heir of the local tradition, which preserves a collective memory. The buildings for the production of pasta, arranged along a green area, which favored the ventilation of buildings, have been transformed by various actions that together have altered the character of the area, as well as the green band has been parceled and occupied by a series of poor quality buildings.

The study of Murat district is especially important for knowing dynamics and relationships of the urban landscape system.

The beauty of Torre Annunziata, main indicator of the harmony between communities and built environment, declined with the collapse of pasta production, caused by the interaction of different external pressures. The decommissioning of pasta factories broke the relations between communities and built environment: local community is less and less able to change the built environment and, in turn, built environment produces less and less relational impacts on the community (see Figure 7).

4.1   Relational indicators in Torre Annunziata

In order to understand the systemic functioning of Torre Annunziata landscape, it is useful to measuring relational indicators through the proposed framework. Using the data provided by official sources, integrated with some data derived from on-site analysis, it is possible to have a rather complete picture of the situation (see Appendix B).

The first area of indicators, describing the actions of people on built environment, shows a very critical picture: many are the buildings in mediocre or poor conditions and the index of deterioration is significant, although there is a fairly consistent use of historic buildings.

Place attachment of local community is hard to find: streets and public space are very dirty and there are no public art installations or cultural event, except for the religious

Figure 6: View from buildings roofs in Murat district with Sorrento and its coast in the background

feast Madonna della Neve (Our Lady of Snow), whose procession goes through the center of the town.

The effects of this behaviour on built environment internal relations is obvious, as the second area of indicators shows. In Torre Annunziata there are no public space available for local community and the public green space in the town is very low; incidental contacts between people are blocked more than favored along the streets, that serve only as a park and transit site for cars. All this happens despite the area being subject to legal protection constraints due to the presence of cultural heritage and historic landscape as Oplonti site. These indicators highlight the quality of built environment as a potentiality to improve. Other potentialities are in the bioclimatic functioning of many buildings (ventilation, water recycling system) that, although not in use, can be recovered in order to minimize the consumption of resources.

The influence of built environment on people is very weak: participation in lifelong learning, rate of adults with high school diploma or degree, rate of young people with university education and specialization in the high knowledge intensity are low in Torre Annunziata and lower in Murat district. In turn, the incidence of people not engaged in education, employment or training is quite high. Although they refer to the whole metropolitan area, health indicators as life expectancy at birth and age-standardized cancer and dementia and related illness mortality rate show a low level of well-being. Social participation of people is quite low, as participation rate in election indicators highlight. Volunteers rate and non-profit employees rate are similarly very small, showing low participation of the population in the community social life.

All this results in the scarcity of relationships of heritage community, with few social cooperatives and non-profit organizations.

At the end of our analysis, the last set of indicators, that describes the relationships between landscape and external environment, highlights the whole system criticality. The exchanges of information are very poor as indicators as propensity for patenting, patent impact in innovation sectors reveal. The exportation of art and cultural and creative industries production, that can be considered a form of exchange of information, is virtually zero. The only significant exportation of high quality goods is related to the pasta produced by the only still active pasta factory, that exports its products in USA,

Figure 7: Buit environment and local community decay in Torre Annunziata

UK, France, Spain, Germany, Austria, Greece, Emirates, Japan, Australia.

The exchanges of people, both residents and visitors, are very poor too: demographic variation shows shows a loss of 4490 units from 2001 to 2011 and tourist flow is almost nil, with the exception of visitors to Oplonti archaeological site, which only stay for the time of the visit. Last set of indicators, that provides a final comparison of landscape attractivity by travel reviews on web (TripAdvisor) definitively highlights a very low attractivity of Torre Annunziata and mostly of Murat district.

The whole set of indicators related to Torre Annunziata is listed in Appendix B.

4.2 What of MAAM is replicable in Torre Annunziata?

The recovery of built heritage, while necessary, is not enough to improve the quality of landscape and activate a new development, unless it is not accompanied by the reactivation of local communities and the recovery of their ability to relate to the built environment. This awareness calls for a reflection on cultural and social dynamics capable of contributing to the process of empowerment of local communities.

In order to reactivating the systemic functioning of Torre Annunziata landscape and improving its "beauty", it is necessary to recovery the creativity of its local community, which leads to regenerating the system of relations between people, communities and environment. In order to activating this process, the study suggests to use art as a driver.

We can argue that, first of all, it is replicable the founding idea of MAAM that art, even though cannot bring people on the moon, it can help people to build the moon here on Earth (De Finis 2015), contributing to get people to think differently and to make public space available for the whole community.

It is also replicable the idea that art can be the driver for building a creative milieu, which is the requirement for local development. It's useful to underline that art cannot be considered the characteristic vocation of a place, but the structural element which drives the development and characterizes every place. MAAM is also replicable as a cultural project, in which the physical recovery of public space, configured by art, is instrumentally used to produce social and cultural crossovers: the recovery of public space, as place of relationships, is able to produce social crossovers, depending by both the architectural/artistic design choices and the process of empowerment of local community. MAAM is not a project of self-recovery, but it is a project strongly focused on the need of marginalized communities who occupy the building, which is shared each day.

Though it is impossible to replicate the experience of MAAM, it is possible to reply the process of empowerment, through which art involves local community: it starts from suggesting art as game, an embedding process by which local community can be involved in an utopia, project of the change. This model is based on art as knowledge disposal and produces a barricade, a system of new values able to protect people and place from external influences, and a relational system, which supports the exchange of information between people. At the end, art makes a new landscape, a real museum, intended as "place of Muses", a place of reproduction of cultural and social values. In its practical implementation, this approach leads to test new forms of landscape management, based on the recognition of public space as a commons.

4.3 Attributes and value of art in three different scenarios

For the development of Torre Annunziata, three different scenarios have been proposed in the PRIN research project (Fusco Girard et al. 2016) developed from Department of Architecture of University of Napoli Federico II: productive networks, touristic hub and centre of sustainable consumption and production. A way to compare them is comparing the meaning of art in each one (see Figure 8).

The first scenario, productive network, sees Torre Annunziata as a place of typical production, strictly linked to tourism. This scenario can include the production of artworks and crafts. The production of art is limited at tourists as customers and art is intended as a private good to take away and is supported by traditional economy, market driven. Art is here instrumental in adding economic values and could produce social spillovers linked to the involvement of local artisans. The second scenario, touristic hub, sees Torre Annunziata as a resort area with accommodation and playground facilities instrumental to increasing residence time of tourists. This scenario can include art both as big event and temporary occurrence and as decoration of touristic places. Art is only for tourists and is intended as a foreign art, imported in order to satisfy the market demand. Art is supported by traditional economy and is a potential source of gentrification. It is instrumental in adding economic values and nurturing local attraction capacity, but it can produce social spillovers, linked to the interaction between residents and tourists, nurturing the sense of identity.

Although the proximity to heritage site and the beauty of Torre Annunziata landscape suggest to focus on cultural heritage as a source of local economy, tourism is not necessary the right way to pursue it, whereas it is one of the fastest-growing economic sectors in the world. Putting tourism at the centre of local development can produce many distortions, as pointed out by an early study (Romão, Nijkamp 2017, WTO 2017). With considering tourism central in local development processes, the recovery of public space must focus mainly on the needs of tourists and only afterwards on the ones of local community. This approach brings to exploit cultural heritage as an economic asset to be exploited in order to meet touristic demand, with a customer oriented strategy mainly based on a oleographic vision that progressively silks its authenticity, cultural vitality and ability to innovate (Sacco et al. 2015). Landscape and cultural heritage are lever for sustainable development, in both economic and environmental, social and cultural terms (Fairclough et al. 2014) as they are vital resources for the citizens (European Commission 2015).

Furthermore, the process of high and quick development of tourism potentially contributes to the reduction of the importance of other economic sectors, including agriculture and manufacturing. In turn, it produces a negative correlation between the rate of workforce employed in tourism and both tourism competitiveness, levels of productivity, resilience (facing economic crisis in 2007), education of population, investments in R&D and attitude to innovation.

But if tourism is programmed and oriented, it can contribute to local sustainable development as it produce a myriad of interactions between insiders, which daily live the place, and outsiders, which see landscape with different eyes. As it contributes to rediscovering the sense of belonging and in turn to re-activating the bond between people and place, this kind of tourism is able to produce circular relationships with local community. The development of tourism related activities must be shared with local community and followed by the development of other economic sectors, able to integrate knowledge, innovation, qualified human resources and value added.

The third scenario, centre of sustainable consumption and production, sees Torre Annunziata as a node in a network of places dedicated to the production and consumption of local goods, as food and crafts. This scenario does not contrast with tourism, but rather

Figure 8: The contribution of art in the proposed scenarios of development

it contributes to develop integrated economic activity and to improve the relationships of tourists and local people. This scenario relates traditional pasta production to the proximity of archeological sites of Villa di Oplonti and Pompeii ruins. Art is intended as daily, permanent opera, produced locally and site-specific. It is mainly for residents though it is a source of attraction for tourists. This kind of art, called social art, is supported by new types of economy as collaborative and sharing economy and is an aid for facing new urban challenges, which are evident in Torre Annunziata. In the third scenario, art is instrumental in adding economic/cultural values and in engaging people, sharing knowledge, connecting people, designing urban recovery, finding the strength for change. It produces social crossovers as it causes the regeneration of relations and inter-relations between people and built environment. The third scenario seems to be the best solution in order to improve the quality of landscape and activate a new development, driven by the reactivation of local communities and the recovery of their ability to relate to natural and built environment.

4.4 Towards a new beauty: art, recovery, public space

In order to implement the chosen scenario, a priority is "regenerating the beauty" of public space, recognized as a space of social capital par excellence (Bullen, Onyx 1998, Prior, Tavano Blessi 2012) in which to activate a new urban metabolism, based on the circularization processes and linked to the symbiotic / synergy concepts (Fusco Girard 2013). This results in actions directed towards the system of urban open spaces and the system of the semi-public spaces, where the exchanges of information, culture, goods, linked to the production and commercialization of pasta take place. The recovery of the public space proposed focuses both on streets, little squares, degraded areas, and entrance hall, courtyards, terraces and, in particular, the green area located between Via Oplonti and Via Mazzini, which today are partly saturated by superfetations and dilapidated buildings. The regeneration of bioclimatic attributes of buildings and urban fabrics, which were once functional to pasta production, can produce added values for both low energy manufacturing and residential and urban comfort. In this sense, the intervention of recovery, which is characterized by the search for a balance between conservation and innovation, can promote a renewed and fruitful dialogue between innovative approaches and local building culture and to activate new synergies and impulses with effects on local economy (Caterina et al. 2015).

In the process of recovering this area, art assumes, as described, a structural function and researches the physical and symbolic integration with architecture. In the past the relationship between art and architecture, called syncretism, was common; in Italy it's still mandatory to allocate a percentage of the budget of public buildings to "make them beauty" through art works (law nr. 717/1945). To this end, the project of recovery must identify spatial and technical elements to make the sublayer and the background of artworks, symbiotically integrated with architecture. The project provides the installation of sculptures and spatial installations along the open area between buildings which, cleared from accretions and shanties, becomes a path in the green, to be used not only as a place of recreation but also as a slow mobility path. Artworks are also integrated in the street space, configuring the external walls of buildings, especially those with no architectural value, in order to give new meanings to public space and to reconcile differences between new and historical buildings. Although it is mainly focused on the public space, the proposed intervention is completed with the re-use of abandoned buildings by providing, in addition to new production activities, residences and workshops for artists, spread in the urban fabric. The reuse is accompanied by new management mode, providing that, in exchange for their hospitality, the artists are committed to produce and leave some works, whose residents become custodians.

5 Conclusions

The recovery of public space pursues the creativity of local community as a preparatory action to local development and deduces from local community and its sedimented culture the enablers of development.

The recovery process proposed for Torre Annunziata suggests a hybrid approach, in which the "emotional" and community based bottom-up approach with the "rational" and scientific top-down approach are integrated.

In order to operationalise the proposed approach in Torre Annunziata, the paper proposes to use living lab as an hybrid tool able to both experiment in a real field the thesis based on art as driver of development and to really activate new development processes with the empowerment of local communities.

Living Lab is an instrument able to act as an interface between the project and the community in different stages of the process.

Living Lab, implemented in the described area of Torre Annunziata as a real environment, becomes both space of interchange between local knowledge and expert knowledge, way to evaluating relational impacts of the project, place of interaction between institutional actors and new forms of management of common space.

In order to operationalizing the role of art as driver of development, Living Lab assumes the meaning of laboratory of civil aesthetic (Fusco Girard 2012), as a place where to put together artists, designers, citizens, enterprises and associations of the third sector and to produce not only aesthetic values but also social values. The integration between art and built environment, which in the past has always characterized public places, becomes the driver of implementing new forms of communication between culture and communities and regenerating both the material culture, and social capital. Living Lab can be an operational tool for transforming public space into a creative and regenerative environment. In this way, the recovery of public space suggests an alternative/supplementary way to produce wealth and proposes a new idea of economics, as next and cooperative economy, whose core is to participate and to cooperate. It contributes to rebuild a micro-community (or networks of micro-communities), in which economy not only creates but redistributes wealth.

In conclusion, configured by art as driver of development and shared with the local community, the recovery of public space can be proposed as a tool to implement HUL approach, as proposed by UNESCO, and to make cities inclusive, safe, resilient and sustainable. At the same time, the identification of the Living Lab as an auxiliary tool in the implementation of this approach closes the loop with respect to the demand of new operational tools, promoted by UNESCO Recommendations. The approach proposed is also in line with the indications of European Council with regard to participatory governance of cultural heritage (2014/C 463/01) and is consistent with the European Council's conclusion on cultural and creative exchanges to stimulate innovation, economic sustainability and social inclusion (2015/C172/04). In addition, it tracks an operational approach to promote intercultural dialogue and keep the community together through culture in shared public spaces (www.voiceofculture.eu), recognizing that art must be destined to all and not reduced to additional activities for small groups of users.

References

Abenante A (2011) Maccaronari. Ires Campania, Napoli

Berleant A (2004) The aesthetics of art and nature. In: Berleant A, Carlson A (eds), *The Aesthetics of Natural Environments*. Broadview, Peterborough, Ont

Bertacchini E, Santagata W (2012) *Atmosfera creativa. Un modello di sviluppo sostenibile per il Piemonte fondato su cultura e creatività*. Il Mulino, Bologna

Better Together (2004) Bettertogether: The arts and social capital. Saguaro seminar on civic engagement in America, John F. Kennedy School of Government, Harvard University, Cambridge, MA http://www.bettertogether.org/

Bollo A (2013) The learning museum report 3: Measuring museum impacts. http://online.ibc.regione.emilia-romagna.it/I/libri/pdf/LEM3rd-report-measuring-museum-impacts.pdf

Bonesio L (2012) *La questione epistemiologica e il linguaggio. Territorio, luogo, paesaggio*. Firenze University Press, Firenze

Bouchenaki M (2003) The interdependency of the tangible and intangible cultural heritage. 14th ICOMOS General Assembly and International Symposium: 'Place, memory, meaning: preserving intangible values in monuments and sites', Victoria Falls, Zimbabwe. http://openarchive.icomos.org

Bourriand N (1998) *Esthétique relationnelle*. Les presses du réel, Dijon

Brown AS (2006) An architecture of value. *GIA Reader* 17[1]: 18–25

Brown AS, Novak-Leonard J (2007) Assessing the intrinsic impacts of a live performance. Dance Center, Columbia College, Chicago

Brown B, Perkins DD (2001) Neighborhood revitalization & disorder: An intervention evaluation. Final Project Report, National Institute of Justice, Washington, DC, https://www.ncjrs.gov/pdffiles1/nij/grants/196669.pdf

Brown B, Perkins DD, Brown G (2003) Place attachment in a revitalizing neighborhood: Individual and block levels of analysis. *Journal of environmental psychology* 23[3]: 259–271. CrossRef.

Bullen P, Onyx J (1998) Measuring social capital in five communities in nsw: A practitioner's guide. Management alternatives pty limited

Campos A, Oliveira RC (2016) Cluster analysis applied to the evaluation of urban landscape quality. *WIT Transactions on Ecology and the Environment* 204: 93–103

Carnwath JD, Brown A (2014) Understanding the value and impacts of cultural experiences. Arts council England, London

Caterina G (2012) Prefazione. In: Viola S (ed), *Nuove sfide per le città antiche*. Liguori Editore, Napoli

Caterina G (2013) Conservazione, manutenzione e gestione degli spazi pubblici e dei beni architettonici. In: Castagneto F, Fiore V (eds), *Recupero Valorizzazione Manutenzione nei Centri Storici. Un tavolo di confronto interdisciplinare*. Lettera 22, Siracusa, 14–17

Caterina G, Bianchi A, Pinto MR, Viola S, Diano D, Napolitano T, Biancamano PF, Onesti A (2015) A participatory approach for built heritage preservation. Case study: the municipality of Sassano, Italy. In: Amoeda R, Lira S, Pinheiro C (eds), *Proceedings of the 2nd International Conference on Preservation, Maintenance and Rehabilitation of Historical Buildings and Structures*. Porto, Portugal, 463–470

Cerreta M, De Toro P (2012) Urbanization suitability maps: A dynamic spatial decision support system for sustainable land use. *Earth System Dynamics* 3[2]: 157–171. CrossRef.

Cerreta M, De Toro P, Fusco Girard L (2014) Integrated assessment for sustainable choices. *Scienze Regionali* 13[1]: 111–142. CrossRef.

CHCFE (2015) Cultural heritage counts for Europe. CHCFE Consortium, http://www.-encatc.org/culturalheritagecountsforeurope

Ciapetti L (2010) *Lo sviluppo locale.* Il Mulino, Bologna

Cicerchia A (2015) Why we should measure. what we should measure. In: Cicerchia A (ed), *Economia della Cultura.* Rivista dell'Associazione per l'Economia della Cultura, 11–22

Ciribini G (1979) *Introduzione alla tecnologia del design.* Franco Angeli Editore, Milano

Cohen B (2014) Smart city index master indicators survey. Smart cities council, http://-smartcitiescouncil.com/resources/smart-city-index-master-indicators-survey

Concilio G (2013) Innovazione territoriale e living lab. Esperienze e visioni, Cilento Labscape, Working Paper, Napoli

Council of Europe (2005a) Explanatory report to the council of Europe framework convention on the value of cultural heritage for society. Council of Europe treaty series, no. 199, https://rm.coe.int/16800d3814

Council of Europe (2005b) Framework convention on the value of cultural heritage for society (Faro convention). https://www.coe.int/en/web/conventions/full-list/-/conventions/treaty/199

Cuccia T, Santagata W (2003) Adhesion - exit: incentivi e diritti di proprietà collettivi nei distretti culturali, in Diritti, Regole, Mercato. Economia pubblica ed analisi economica del diritto. XV Conferenza SIEP, Pavia

D'Auria A (2009) Urban cultural tourism: Creative approaches for heritage-based sustainable development. *International Journal of Sustainable Development* 12: 275–289. CrossRef.

D'Auria A, Monti B (2013) The guardianship of the landscapes between identification and assessment: Ischia and its lost identity. In: Rezekne Higher Education Institut (ed), *Society, integration, education: utopias and dystopias in landscape and cultural mosaic: visions values vulnerability*, Volume IV. Proceedings of the International Scientific Conference on Society, Integration, and Education Location, Udine, Italy, 165–176

D'Auria A, Pugliese S (2013) The governance of UNESCO cultural landscapes between universal values and local identity: the case of Campania. In: Rezekne Higher Education Institut (ed), *Society, integration, education: utopias and dystopias in landscape and cultural mosaic: visions values vulnerability*, Volume V. Proceedings of the International Scientific Conference on Society, Integration, and Education Location, Udine, Italy, 189–200

De Finis G (2015) *Forza tutt*. La barricata dell'arte.* Bordeaux edizioni, Roma

De Finis G (2017) *Maam. Museo dell'Altro e dell'Altrove di Metropoliz̈città meticcia.* Bordeaux edizioni, Roma

De Rita G, Bonomi A (1998) *Manifesto per lo sviluppo locale.* Bollati Boringhieri, Torino

Diano D (2015) Le pressioni perturbative del sistema insediativo di torre annunziata (NA). *BDC – Bollettino Del Centro Calza Bini* 15[1]: 3960. CrossRef.

Dunlap RE, van Liere KD, Mertig AG, Jones RE (2000) New trends in measuring environmental attitudes: Measuring endorsement of the new ecological paradigm: a revisited NEP scale. *Journal of Social Issues* 56: 425–442. CrossRef.

Dzialek J (2014) Is social capital useful for explaining economic development in Polish regions? 962[2]: 177–193. CrossRef.

Eco U (2005) *Storia della bellezza*. Bompiani, Milano

Eshelman PE, Evans GW (2002) Home again: Environmental predictors of place attachment and self-esteem for new retirement community residents. *Journal of Interior Design* 28[1]: 1–9. CrossRef.

European Commission (2015) Getting cultural heritage to work for Europe. Report of the Horizon 2020 expert group on cultural heritage, Directorate General for Research and Innovation, http://bookshop.europa.eu/en/getting-cultural-heritage-to-work-for-europe-pbKI0115128/

Evans J, Karvonen A (2014) 'Give me a laboratory and I will lower your carbon footprint!' – urban laboratories and the governance of low-carbon futures. *International Journal of Urban and Regional Research* 38: 413–430. CrossRef.

Fairclough G, Dragićević-Šešić M, Rogač-Mijatović L, Auclair E, Soini K (2014) The Faro convention, a new paradigm for socially – and culturally – sustainable heritage action? *Culture* 8: 9–19

Fondazione Pistoletto (2003) Geographies of change. A project by Cittadellarte-Fondazione Pistoletto 2003-2017, http://www.geographiesofchange.net/

Fontana C (2012) Re-tracing the systemic approach in architecture, and developing working tools. Methods, Models, Simulations and Approaches Towards a General Theory of Change. Proceedings of the Fifth National Conference of the Italian Systems Society, Marche Polytechnic University, Italy

Fusco Girard L (1989) Qualità e quantità nello sviluppo urbano. i riflessi sul problema della valutazione. In: Fusco Girard L (ed), *Conservazione e sviluppo: la valutazione nella pianificazione fisica*. Franco Angeli, Milano

Fusco Girard L (2012) Creativity and the human sustainable city: Principles and approaches for nurturing city resilience. In: Fusco Girard L, Baycan T (eds), *Sustainable City and Creativity. Promoting Creative Urban Initiatives*. Ashgate, 55–96

Fusco Girard L (2013) Toward a smart sustainable development of port cities/areas: the role of the 'historic urban landscape' approach. *Sustainability* 5[10]: 4329–4348. CrossRef.

Fusco Girard L (2014) Editorial. *BDC – Bollettino Del Centro Calza Bini* 14[2]: 243–249. CrossRef.

Fusco Girard L, Cerreta M, De Toro P, Pinto MR, Viola S (2016) The PRIN research project. the cultural/historic urban landscape: A resource for urban regeneration and local development. Presentation at "The Science of the City", Advanced Brainstorming Carrefour, Napoli

Fusco Girard L, De Toro P (2007) Integrated spatial assessment: A multicriteria approach to sustainable development of cultural and environmental heritage in San Marco dei Cavoti, Italy. *Central European Journal of Operations Research* 15[3]: 281–299. CrossRef.

Fusco Girard L, Nijkamp P (2005) *Energia, bellezza, partecipazione: la sfida della sostenibilità*. Franco Angeli

Fusco Girard L, Torrieri F (2009) Cultural tourism and strategic evaluations: Towards integrated approaches. In: Fusco Girard L, Nijkamp P (eds), *Cultural Tourism and Sustainable Local Development*. Ashgate, London

Gatersleben B, Murtagh N, Abrahamse W (2014) Values, identity and pro-environmental behaviour. *Contemporary Social Science* 9[4]: 374–392. CrossRef.

Givone S (2012) L'origine della creazione artistica. http://www.arte.rai.it/articoli/givone-lorigine-dellispirazione-artistica-3-di-5/22627/default.aspx

Greffe G (2015) Culture and creativity. In: Kakiuchi E, Greffe X (eds), *Culture, Creativity and Cities*. SUIYO-SHA. Available at https://www.researchgate.net/publication/-301603142_Culture_Creativity_and_City

Greffe X (2005) Culture and local development. OECD, Paris

HLF – Heritage Lottery Fund (2015) Values and benefits of heritage: A research review. Heritage lottery fund, https://www.hlf.org.uk/values-and-benefits-heritage

Holman N, Rydin Y (2013) What can social capital tell us about planning under localism? *Local Government Studies* 39[1]: 71–88. CrossRef.

Ipsos MORI (2015) Beauty and social prosperity survey 2015. Respublica London, https://www.ipsos.com/sites/default/files/migrations/en-uk/files/Assets/Docs/-Polls/ipsos-mori-respublica-topline.pdf

ISTAT (2015) Equitable and sustainable well-being. Project to measure equitable and sustainable well-being 2013-2015, http://www.misuredelbenessere.it/

Leroy-Gourhan A (1964) *Le geste et la parole*. Albin Michel, Paris

Lukàcs G (1975) *Cultura e rivoluzione. Saggi 1919-1921*. Newton Compton Editori, Roma

Lynch AJ, Mosbah SM (2017) Improving local measures of sustainability: A study of built-environment indicators in the United States. *Cities* 60: 301–313. CrossRef.

Magnaghi A (2010) *Progetto locale. Verso la coscienza di luogo*. Bollati Boringhieri, Torino

Magnaghi A (2012) Le ragioni di una sfida. In: Magnaghi A (ed), *Il territorio bene comune*. Firenze University Press, Firenze, Italy, 11–30

Matarasso F (1997) Use or ornament? The social impact of participation in the arts, comedia, stroud. http://www.culturenet.cz/res/data/004/000571.pdf

Mumford L (1922) *Storia dell'utopia* (translated and reprinted 2008 ed.). Donzelli editore, Roma

Napolitano T (2015) Sistema edilizio e risorsa idrica. il caso studio di torre annunziata (na). *BDC – Bollettino Del Centro Calza Bini* 15[1]: 61–70. CrossRef.

Nijkamp P, Kourtit K (2012) The 'New Urban Europe': Global challenges and local responses in the urban century. *European Planning Studies* 21[3]: 291–315. CrossRef.

Paine G, Thompson S (2016) Healthy built environment indicators. City Wellbeing Program, CFRC, UNSW, Australia

Pietroiusti C (2015) Possibili caratteristiche di un museo "reale". In: de Finis G, Benincasa F, Facchi A (eds), *Exploit. Come rovesciare il mondo ad arte*. Bordeaux edizioni, Roma, 737–742

Pinto MR, Viola S (2015) Identità sedimentate e nuova prosperità per il paesaggio urbano produttivo. *BDC – Bollettino Del Centro Calza Bini* 15[1]: 71–91. CrossRef.

Pistoletto M (2003) Il terzo paradiso. 2003–2017, http://terzoparadiso.org/

Poincaré JH (1906) *Scienza e metodo* (translated and republished 1997 ed.). Einaudi

Prior J, Tavano Blessi G (2012) Social capital, local communities and culture-led urban regeneration processes: The Sydney Olympic Park experience. *Cosmopolitan Civil Societies Journal* 4[3]: 78–96. CrossRef.

Putnam RD (2000) *Bowling Alone: The Collapse and Revival of American Community.* Simon and Schuster, New York

Putnam RD, Leonardi R, Nanetti R (1993) *Making democracy work: civic traditions in modern Italy.* Princeton University Press, Princeton

Rodotà S (2012) Il valore dei beni comuni. La repubblica, 5 gennaio 2012

Romão J, Nijkamp P (2017) Spatial-economic impacts of tourism on regional development: challenges for Europe (no. 2017_01). Working paper, University of Evora, CEFAGE-UE (Portugal) http://www.cefage.uevora.pt/en/content/download/6410/76704/version/1/-file/2017_01.pdf

Rydin Y, Holman N (2004) Re-evaluating the contribution of social capital in achieving sustainable development. *Local Environment* 9[2]: 117–133. CrossRef.

Sacco PL, Ferilli G, Tavano Blessi G (2015) *Cultura e sviluppo locale: verso il Distretto culturale evoluto.* Il Mulino, Bologna

Sacco PL, Sciacchitano E (2015) Incroci creativi: due conferenze sulla cultura nel semestre di presidenza lettone dell'Unione Europea. Il Giornale delle Fondazioni, http://www.ilgiornaledellefondazioni.com/

Sacco PL, Segre G (2009) Creativity, cultural investment and local development: A new theoretical framework for endogenous growth. In: Fratesi U, Senn L (eds), *Growth and Innovation of Competitive Regions.* Berlin-Heidelberg, Springer-Verlag

Sanchez MJ, Lafuente R (2010) Defining and measuring environmental consciousness. *Revista Internacional de Sociologia* 68[3]: 731–755. CrossRef.

Santagata W (2009) *Libro Bianco sulla Creatività. Per un Modello Italiano di Sviluppo.* Università Bocconi Editore, Milano, Italy

Schliwa GI (2013) Exploring living labs through transition management. challenges and opportunities for sustainable urban transitions. Masterthesis, Lund University, Lund, Sweden

Szreter S, Woolcock M (2004) Health by association? social capital, social theory, and the political economy of public health. *International Journal of Epidemiology* 33[4]: 650–667

Tempesta T (2009) Economia del paesaggio. In: Boggia A, Festa A (eds), *La valutazione del danno ambientale e paesaggistico.* Villa Umbra-Regione Umbria, Perugia

Trione A (1996) *Estetica e Novecento.* Laterza, Bari

Törnqvist G (1983) Creativity and the renewal of regional life. In: Buttimer A (ed), *Creativity and Context: A Seminar Report.* Gleerup, Lund, 91–112

Tveit MS, Sang AO (2014) Landscape assessment in metropolitan areas-developing a visual indicator-based approach. *SPOOL* 1[1]: 301–316

UNCTAD (2008) Creative economy report. http://unctad.org/en/docs/ditc20082cer_en.pdf

UNESCO (1962) Recommendation concerning the safeguarding of beauty and character of landscapes and sites. http://portal.unesco.org/en/ev.php-URL_ID=13067&URL_DO=-DO_TOPIC&URL_SECTION=201.html

UNESCO (2011) Recommendation on the historic urban landscape. UNESCO World Heritage Centre, Resolution 36C/23, Annex, Paris, France

United Nations (2015) Transforming our world: the 2030 agenda for sustainable development. sustainabledevelopment.un.org

Viola S (2012) *Nuove sfide per le città antiche.* Liguori Editore, Napoli

Viola S, Pinto MR, Cecere AM (2014) Recovering ancient settlements: Approaches to negotiation for collective spaces. Proceedings of 40th IAHS World Congress on Housing, Sustainable Housing Construction, Funchal, Madeira, Portugal

WTO – World Tourism Organization (2017) Tourism highlights 2016 edition. Madrid, UNWTO

A Appendix

Table A.1: Relational indicators

indicators	contents	source
actions on built environment		
Cleanes of public space	Washing and sweeping of public space	Campos, Oliveira (2016)
Care of public space	Maintenance, recovery and management of public space (i.e. conservation of materials of sidewalks, decks, flowerbed, street furniture)	Campos, Oliveira (2016)
Care of public space by citizens	Maintenance, recovery and management of public space by citizens	Revised from Campos, Oliveira (2016)
Care of private buildings	Maintenance and recovery of existing buildings	Revised from Campos, Oliveira (2016), Lynch, Mosbah (2017)
Personalization signs	Family names, initials, ornaments on private buildings	Brown, Perkins (2001)
Use of buildings	Rate of buildings occupacy	Revised from Ipsos MORI (2015)
Reuse of historical buildings	Rate of project of building reuse	Revised from Ipsos MORI (2015)
Art production site-specific	Number of artworks locally produced and destined to remain in situ	Revised from Tveit, Sang (2014)
Public art	Integration of art in public space	new
Art and culture in public space	Rate of use of public space for artistic and cultural activities	new
Pro-environmental behaviours - water	Rate of use of recycling and saving water systems	Revised from Lynch, Mosbah (2017)
Pro-environmental behaviours - energy	Rate of use of renewable energy systems	Revised from Lynch, Mosbah (2017)
Bioclimatic design solutions	Rate of use of bioclimatic design solutions	Revised from Lynch, Mosbah (2017)
Use of local materials	Percentage of local materials and technologies	new
Innovation of local and traditional technologies	Rate of innovation of local and traditional technologies	new
Care of the future	Strategic plans for long-term	Fusco Girard, Torrieri (2009)
Relations between physical attributes of built environment		
Walkability Indices	Number of walking routes with a high walkability score / number of all walking routes (%)	Paine, Thompson (2016)
WalkScore	Rating 1-100 describing easy access to places	Paine, Thompson (2016)
Design of building frontages fostering incidental contact	% dwellings fronting streets or walkways that include opportunities for contact with passers-by (eg. seats on a porch, open windows to living areas)	Paine, Thompson (2016)
Design of common areas in buildings fostering incidental contact	% common areas that include spaces with seats and/or to otherwise linger and talk with neighbours	Paine, Thompson (2016)
Public space accessible to the community	% of open space available with unrestricted access	Paine, Thompson (2016), Fusco Girard, Torrieri (2009)
Contact with nature in public space	Area of public open space including vegetation and/or water / area of all public open space (%)	Paine, Thompson (2016)
Contact with nature in public space	Length of streets containing tree plantings: length of all streets (%)	Paine, Thompson (2016)

Continued on next page

Table A.1 – continued from previous page

indicators	contents	source
Consistency of the historic urban fabric	Share inhabited buildings constructed before 1919 and in excellent or good condition than the total of the buildings.	BES_Istat (9.10)
Cultural heritage	Number of archaeological, architectural and museum surveyed in the information system "Risk Map of Cultural Heritage" (MiBAC) per sq km	BES_Istat (9.1)
Public expenditure on cultural heritage	Municipal government spending allocated to functions related to the culture and to the goods per capita.	BES_Istat (9.2)
Influence of built environment on people		
Participation in lifelong learning	People aged 25-64 who participated in education (formal education) and training (non-formal education) / population aged 25-64 * 100	BES_Istat (2.6)
People with at least upper secondary education	Percentage of people aged 25-64 years having completed at least upper secondary education on total people aged 25-64 years.	BES_Istat (2.2)
Level of literacy	Scores obtained in the tests of functional literacy skills of students in the 2nd class of upper secondary education	BES_Istat (2.8)
Level of numeracy	Scores obtained in the tests of numeracy skills of students in the II classes of upper secondary education	BES_Istat (2.9)
People with high level of ICT competencies	Percentage of people aged 16 years and over who can perform at least 5 over the 6 listed operations on the computer on total people aged 16 years and over.	BES_Istat (2.10)
Specialization in the high knowledge intensity	Employed in high-tech manufacturing sectors and those of services to knowledge intensive / total employees * 100.	BES_Istat (11.6)
Life expectancy at birth	Life expectancy expresses the average number of years that a child born in a given calendar year can expect to live if exposed during his whole life to the risks of death observed in the same year at different ages	BES_Istat (1.1)
Healthy life expectancy at birth	Average number of years that a child born in a given calendar year can expect to live in good health on the assumption that the risks of death and perceived health conditions remain constant	BES_Istat (1.2)
Age-standardised cancer mortality rate (19-64 years old	Mortality rate for cancer (initial cause) by five year age groups for people aged 19-64 years, standardized by the Italian 2001 Census population of the same age groups.	BES_Istat (1.7)
Age-standardised mortality rate for dementia and related illnesses (people aged 65 and over)	Mortality rate for nervous system diseases and psychical and behavioural disorders (initial cause) by five year age groups for people aged 65 years and over, standardized by the Italian 2001 Census population of the same age groups.	BES_Istat (1.8)
Life expectancy without activity limitations at 65 years of age	Average number of years that a person aged 65 can expect to live without suffering limitations in daily activities due to health problems, assuming that the risks of death and disability remain constant over time and equal to those observed in a specific calendar year	BES_Istat (1.9)

Continued on next page

Table A.1 – continued from previous page

indicators	contents	source
Cultural participation	Synthetic indicator of the level of cultural participation based on the aggregation of the following indicators: People who have seen videotapes or DVDs in the past 12 months; Percentage of people in the 12 months before the interview have traveled at least once in Cinema, Theatre, Museums and exhibitions, archaeological sites, monuments, concerts (classical music, opera + Other music concerts); Reading: Percentage of people who read the newspaper at least once a week; Percentage of people who have read at least one book in the 12 months preceding the interview; Percentage of people who read a magazine regularly (weekly or periodic)	BES_Istat (2.11)
Involvement of disadvantaged people	Disadvantaged persons involved	new
Incidence of knowledge workers on employment	Employers with college education (ISCED 5-6) in professions Scientific Technology (ISCO 2-3) / Total employed * 100.	BES_Istat (11.3)
Social participation	Based on the aggregation of the following indicators: a) People aged 14 and over who during the last 12 months have participated in meetings of associations (cultural / recreational, ecological, civil rights, for peace); b) People aged 14 and over who during the last 12 months have participated in meetings of trade unions, professional associations or category; c) People aged 14 and over who during the last 12 months have participated in meetings of political parties and / or have worked free for a party d) People aged 14 and over who pay a monthly fee to a club or periodic / sports club e) People aged 14 and over in the last 12 months took part in meetings or initiatives (cultural, sporting, recreational, spiritual) made or promoted by parishes, organizations / religious groups or spiritual	BES_Istat (5.1)
Civic and political participation	Based on the aggregation of the following indicators: 1) People aged 14 and over who talk about politics at least once a week 2) People aged 14 and over who inform policy at least once a week 3) People aged 14 and over who participated in online consultations or voting on social issues (civic) or political (eg. Urban planning, signing a petition) in the last 3 months 4) People aged 14 and over who have read and posted opinions on social or political problems on the web over the past 3 months	BES_Istat (6.2)
Voluntary activities	People aged 14 and over in the last 12 months worked free for associations or voluntary groups / People aged 14 and over * 100	BES_Istat (5.5)
Local community-people	Percentage of people involved in local community activities over the past two years	Dzialek (2014)
Local community-people	Percentage of people involved in public meeting (rather than in the workplace) in the last year	Dzialek (2014)
internal relationships of heritage community		
Local community-foundations	Average number of foundations, associations and public organizations per 10,000 inhabitants	Dzialek (2014)
Local community-art and culture	Average number of members of the arts, music and other cultural groups for 10,000 inhabitants	Dzialek (2014)
Local community-hobby	Average number of members of interest groups and hobby for 10,000 inhabitants	Dzialek (2014)

Continued on next page

Table A.1 – continued from previous page

indicators	contents	source
Local community-sport	Average number of members of sports and recreational groups for 10,000 inhabitants	Dzialek (2014)
NGOs	Number of non-governmental organizations registered for 10,000 inhabitants	Dzialek (2014)
Charitable Organizations	Number of public charities for 10,000 inhabitants	Dzialek (2014)
Religious organizations	Member of religious organizations and church	Dzialek (2014)
Religious organizations	Members of organizations, associations, parties, committees advise, religious groups, unions and other groups to 100 people	Dzialek (2014)
No profit organizations per 10,000 inhabitants	Number of non-profit organizations / total population * 10,000	BES_Istat (5.9)
Social cooperatives every 10,000 inhabitants	Number of social cooperatives / total population * 10,000	BES_Istat (5.10)
Coworking activities	Number of activities and businesses housed in coworking	new
Number of networks	Number of networked production activities	new
Relationships between landscape and external environment		
Intensity of use of the internet	People 16-74 years who used the internet at least once a week over the 12 months preceding the interview / persons of 16-74 years * 100	BES_Istat (11.7)
Numbers of start-up	Number of start-ups / total enterprises	Greffe
Research intensity	Spending on R&S/GDP *100 (Ocse).	BES_Istat (11.1)
Propensity for patenting	Total number of patent applications the European Patent Office (EPO) per million inhabitants	BES_Istat (11.2)
Rate of technological innovation in the production system	Companies that have introduced technological innovations (product and process), organizational and marketing in the three-year period / total number of companies with at least 10 employees * 100	BES_Istat (11.4)
Rate of innovation of the product / service of the national production system	Companies that have introduced product innovations-service over three years / Total Companies with at least 10 employees * 100	BES_Istat (11.5)
Contemporary art production to a foreign market	Number of works of art produced on-siteand destined to the external market	Fusco Girard, Torrieri (2009)
Cultural and creative industries production	Number of cultural and creative industries production	Revised from Fusco Girard, Torrieri (2009)
New residents	number of people who decide to live and develop their own projects in a place (young)	Greffe
Tourists and visitors	Number of tourists and visitors	Greffe
Exchanges tourists / local community	Events involving the interaction between tourists and locals	new
Exchanges artists / community	Events involving the interaction between artists and locals	new
Web exposure	Number of results available on google	new
Popularity index web	number of groups like facebook, approval rating on tripadvisor, foursquare, etc ..	new
Prizes and Awards	Number of awards granted in the last five years	new

B   Appendix

Table B.2: Existing relationships in Torre Annunziata

indicators	source	metro-area of Napoli	Napoli municipality	municipality	census area	district	year	positive direction
Actions on built environment								
Residential buildings in mediocre or poor condition	ISTAT Ottomila census				459	124	2011	min
Rate of buildings in poor condition	ISTAT Ottomila census			0,3	0,7		2011	min
Rate of buildings in good conservation status	ISTAT Ottomila census			79.8	59.2		2011	max
Index of building degradation	ISTAT			0.2			2011	min
Consistency of occupied historical homes	ISTAT Ottomila census			22.5	41.1		2011	max
Use of buildings	ISTAT Ottomila census			3.1%	10.1%		2011	min
Cleanes of public space (rate 1-5)	on-site analysis				1		2016	max
Art production site-specific	on-site analysis				0		2016	max
Public art	on-site analysis				0		2016	max
Art and culture in public space	on-site analysis				0		2016	max
Annual municipal electricity production from renewable sources (photovoltaic)	GSE			277.91			2016	max
Annual municipal electricity production from renewable sources (photovoltaic)	ispra			0.59			2014	max
Relations between physical attributes of built environment								
WalkScore	www.-walk-score.-com					78	2017	max
Design of building; frontages fostering incidental contact (%)	on-site analysis					80	2015	max
Public space accessible to the community	on-site analysis					0	2015	max
Public green spaces rate	SIT			0.32			2011	max
Contact with nature in public space (1)	on-site analysis					0	2016	max
Contact with nature in public space (2)	on-site analysis					0	2016	max
Consistency of the historic urban fabric	ISTAT BES	38.2					2011	max
Rate of urban areas with protection constraints	MIBACT					1	2011	max

Continued on next page

Table B.2 – continued from previous page

indicators	source	metro-area of Napoli	Napoli munici-pality	munici-pality	census area	district	year	positive direc-tion
Cultural heritage	ISTAT BES			1			2011	max
Influence of built environment on people								
Participation in lifelong learning	ISTAT Ottomila census			4.4			2011	max
Rate of adults with high school diploma or degree	ISTAT Ottomila census			48.6	39.1		2011	max
Rate of young people with university education	ISTAT Ottomila census			18.1	12.2		2011	max
Level of literacy	ISTAT BES		190				2014	max
Level of numeracy	ISTAT BES		191.3				2014	max
Specialization in the high knowledge intensity	ISTAT Ottomila census			32.1	26.4		2011	max
Incidence of people not engaged in education, employment or training (NEET)	ISTAT Ottomila census			24.8	32.7		2011	min
Life expectancy at birth (men)	ISTAT BES		77.6				2013	max
Life expectancy at birth (women)	ISTAT BES		82.4				2013	max
Age-standardised cancer mortality rate (19-64 years old	ISTAT BES		11.1				2013	min
Age-standardised mortality rate for dementia and related illnesses (people aged 65 and over)	ISTAT BES		21.5				2013	min
Participation rate in European elections	ISTAT BES		48.5				2014	max
Participation rate in regional elections	ISTAT BES		61.2				2010	max
Volunteers rate per 100 inhabitants aged 14 and over (%)	ISTAT BES		3				2011	max
Non-profit employees	ISTAT			87			2011	max
Internal relationships of heritage community								
Social cooperatives every 10,000 inhabitants	ISTAT BES		1.3				2011	max
No profit organizations per 10,000 inhabitants	ISTAT BES		18.2				2011	max
Relationships between landscape and external environment								
Propensity for patenting (per 1 million of inhabitants)	ISTAT BES		14.5				2012	max
Patent impact in the High-tech sector (%)	ISTAT BES		23.9				2012	max
Patent impact in the ICT sector (%)	ISTAT BES		24.6				2012	max

Continued on next page

Table B.2 – continued from previous page

indicators	source	metro-area of Napoli	Napoli munici-pality	munici-pality	census area	district	year	positive direc-tion
Patent impact in biotechnology sector (%)	ISTAT BES	20.2					2012	max
Contemporary art production to a foreign market	on-site analysis					0	2015	max
High quality production to a foreign market	on-site analysis					1	2015	max
Demographic variation 2011-2001	ISTAT Ottomila census		-4490				2011	min
Travel reviews	Trip Advisor		1097			0	2017	max
Things to do	Trip Advisor		33			0	2017	max

The Journal of ERSA
Powered by WU

Volume 4, Number 3, 2017, 119–131
DOI: 10.18335/region.v4i3.143

journal homepage: region.ersa.org

Research infrastructure, networks of science and regional development – the case of Oskarshamn

Folke Valfrid Snickars[1], Ulf Karlsson[2]

[1] KTH, Stockholm, Sweden
[2] Linköping University, Linköping, Sweden

Received: 15 July 2016/Accepted: 13 September 2017

Abstract. Final disposal of nuclear waste is a global engineering challenge. The Swedish nuclear industry has consequently spent more than thirty years investigating the best sites and technologies for the final storage of nuclear waste. Universities have been involved as experts in this large-scale R&D activity. This has resulted in a well-documented body of knowledge for supporting relevant decision-making. Simultaneously, as a result, global research infrastructure networks have been developed and consequently more than 140 PhD theses have been produced. Eleven of these PhD holders are now full professors.

Based on earlier work on research infrastructures from Lund, Hamburg, and Kiruna, see for instance Snickars, Falck (2015), we have addressed the question of the role of a technical research infrastructure in the development of the fields of engineering and natural science while simultaneously generating regional development. It has provided an opportunity to empirically study the use of research infrastructure in a specialized technology field. At the same time, this study investigates one municipality's efforts to specialize in research without a university in the vicinity.

Do networks of cooperation differ between research groups and research infrastructures? How can a region build its smart specialization on research infrastructure? How can research equipment once belonging to a company be transformed to a public research infrastructure asset?

Our results indicate that research infrastructures such as the ones in Oskarshamn are powerful creators of international research networks. It is possible, although somewhat difficult in view of scattered systems for data provision, to assess their academic and societal impacts. Engineering research has its own networks of university-industry and industry-university interaction where project-based value is cogenerated dynamically. In this study, we have come some way towards empirically analyzing the networks of research cooperation between industry and university using methods of infrastructure and social network analysis.

1 Introduction

Final disposal of nuclear waste is a global engineering challenge with solutions varying by country since the trading of waste is not generally a politically viable solution as it is in other waste management areas. Research infrastructure networks can potentially be used as a basis for the transformation of test sites to complementary uses. Dynamic micro analysis can be performed since there is an ample supply of data, albeit less than

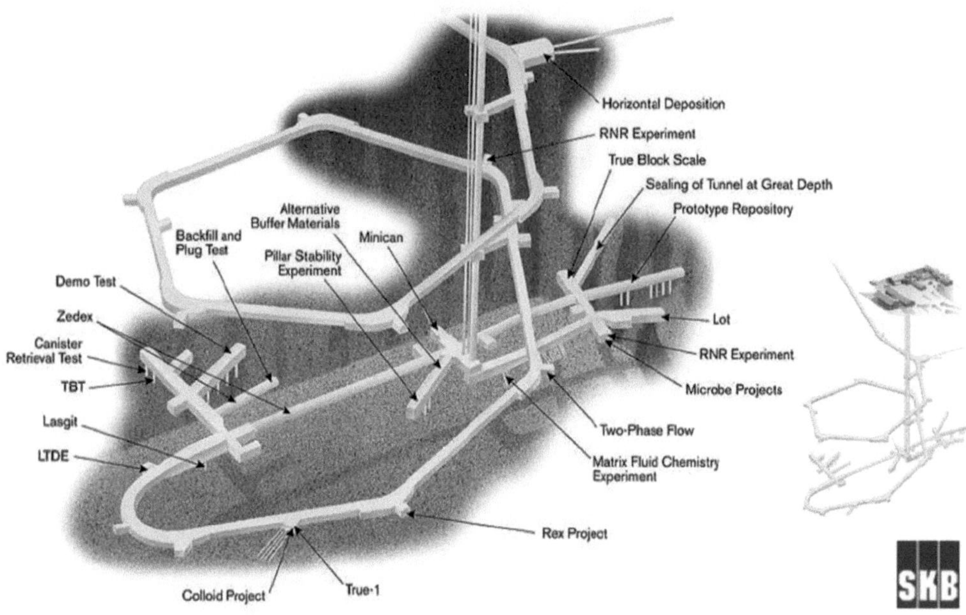

Figure 1: The underground test installations in the Äspö Hard Rock laboratory including names of major experiments

organized. The mutual trading of knowledge between industry and universities involving effective policy schemes can be an interesting spillover mechanism.

Using the Äspö Hard Rock laboratory as a case study, research questions to be addressed in the current paper are as following:

- What quality of science can be generated in an industrial development project?

- How can an experimental research facility belonging to a company be transformed into a public research infrastructure?

- How can a region foster smart specialization through a research infrastructure?

Oskarshamn in southeastern Sweden is the location of one of three nuclear power stations, the primary site for intermediate storage of nuclear waste and the main experimental site for testing technologies for final storage. A decision has been made to store waste in Forsmark northeast of Stockholm for the long-term. National resources are available to assist Oskarshamn in a smooth transformation to another, smarter industrial specialization. The question is, can resources be transformed into new uses in an experimental mine, building on local competence, environmental resources, and international investments in research cooperation?

The core innovation idea is to transform the environment, which is illustrated in Figure 1, to a geosphere laboratory and develop this in the long term as an international research infrastructure in engineering science.

The Äspö laboratory has a depth of some 500 metres and is located on an island within the security zone of the nuclear power plants outside Oskarshamn in a nearby archipelago. Its main mission has been to test the viability and security aspects of storage of nuclear waste. The prototype repository experiment is located in one part of the underground facilities. Other parts are used for the testing of bedrock, and rock drilling properties as well as various environmental experiments to further the understanding of how radioactivity spreads in an underground bedrock environment.

2 The Äspö Hard Rock laboratory in SKB activities

Surveying work began at Äspö in 1986, as the Swedish Nuclear Fuel and Waste Management Company (SKB) wanted to explore the possibility of building an underground laboratory there. This was the beginning of the research and technological development that has taken place in and around Äspö for almost three decades.

It was in its 1986 research, development and demonstration programme that SKB presented the first plans to construct its own underground laboratory. These plans extended from 1987 until 2010 and included for instance detailed studies of natural barriers and their function in a final repository, developing methods and technologies for final disposal as well as demonstrating what its different sections would look like.

The first development measures were already under way before construction of the laboratory had begun. In preparation for, and during construction work, different methods of studying bedrock from the surface were tested. Later the rock was studied in detail in tunnels and shafts. These methods were then used for the comparative site investigations at Forsmark and Oskarshamn before the final choice of Forsmark as the site of the spent fuel repository was made.

The experiments performed at Äspö were collected into a comprehensive database, called Sicada, which now holds the preconditions and results of a 30-year period of experiments, and environmental measurements. The database also comprises information about environmental conditions in the area around the mine itself. It is one of the largest such databases in the world. SKB has also kept track of its research projects which have been organized in a series of three year research and development programmes. There are now around ten programmes in total and documentation on the main results of each programme is currently available.

The activities of SKB can be seen as a large industrial development project. The ultimate goal is to propose a viable and secure technical system to store the nuclear waste in the bedrock forever. A proposal from SKB for this technology is currently being assessed in the Swedish legal system. The assessment will take several years and might lead to a further need for investigations by the Äspö laboratory. The actual depositing of waste is not foreseen to take place before the middle of the 2020s.

The goal of the current paper is to use the publication databases of SKB to estimate some of the scientific and industrial impacts of the research activities at Äspö. The focus will be on publications in a broad sense as they exist in the public databases of SKB. We will characterize the publication patterns reported by SKB in terms of volumes, types of publication, main researchers, and industrial collaboration. In this regard, we will attempt to assess the scientific impact of the work at Äspö for the researchers, and disciplines involved.

We will provide some basic information about SKB as a starting point for the analysis of publication networks. The presentation will concern SKB as a whole, since it is not possible to separate activities at Äspö from other research activities in the company records. Figure 2 illustrates the total production value of SKB across time.

The total production level was about 1.73 billion SEK in the maximum year 2012. The sharp rise in the production level after 2010 has to do with changes in the company accounting. Even if this is the case the yearly resource use is substantial, for instance, in comparison to the volume of resources used for research in a medium-sized technical university.

Figure 3 illustrates the role of research costs in the company across time. We see a steady decline in the yearly allocations to research both in terms of costs and personnel. The share of research personnel was 40 percent in 2000 and had fallen to 22 percent in 2013. The decline in cost terms is even sharper, reflecting the simple fact that SKB has been approaching the end of its research and development programme.

3 Literature review

The analysis is based on earlier work on research infrastructures in Lund, Hamburg, and Kiruna where the emphasis has been on already well-established research infrastructures,

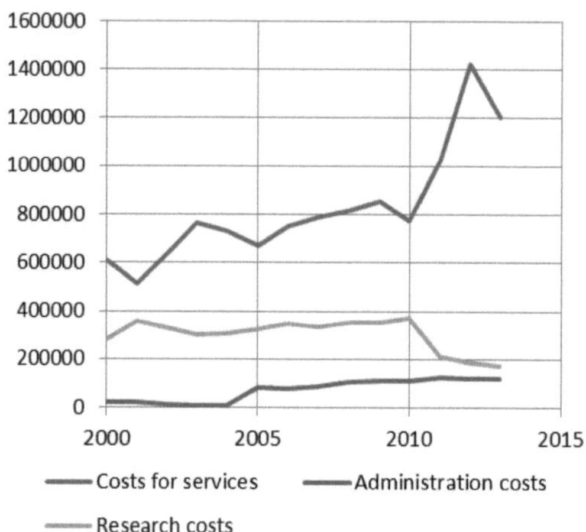

Notes: kSEK current prices

Figure 2: Composition of SKB production system 2000-2013

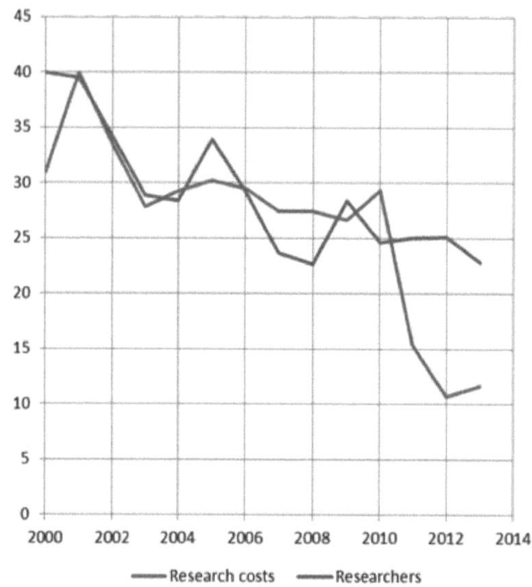

Notes: in percent

Figure 3: Share of resources allocated to research within SKB 2000-2013)

see Falck et al. (2011) and Snickars, Falck (2015). Those studies have formed part of
the input to proposals for new Swedish and EU road maps for research infrastructure
raising the question of the importance of those infrastructures for regional development.
If such effects can be shown this will add both to the scientific value of investments, as
well as the use of EU structural funds and related investment programmes to generate
even broader societal impacts.

The Oskarshamn case provides an opportunity to empirically study the use of research
infrastructure in a highly specialized technology field where activities are performed in a
parallel fashion by university researchers, and development-oriented firms and consultants.
In our earlier studies, the starting point has been basic research in physics and the question
has been whether this research can be proved to have industrial and societal impacts. In
the current study, the starting point is an advanced technological development project in
the nuclear field and a central question has been whether this development project has
had measurable scientific impacts. A further question is how important and lasting the
collaboration has been for the firms, and thus for the impacts on regional development
and growth.

The current case study also provides an opportunity to test contemporary theories on the knowledge industry and its mechanisms for the generation and diffusion of knowledge spillovers and innovations. The work is based on thought models in Mellander, Florida (2007), Andersson, Beckmann (2009), Helmers, Overman (2013) and Batabyal, Nijkamp (2015). The case also provides a challenge to study a municipality's efforts to specialize in research and development without a university in the region or even in the vicinity of the region, see also OECD (2012).

Prior work has largely been focused on externalities between firms, or alternatively university-industry linkages, emphasizing localized knowledge spillover effects and functional regions as arenas for knowledge flows, see also Snickars, Falck (2015). Horlings et al. (2012) argue that the existing literature provides no direct empirical evidence demonstrating that impacts actually occur around scientific research facilities and that there is insufficient evidence to support the claim that such investments will, for instance, attract and retain talent and promote innovation.

Helmers, Overman (2013) is one of the first studies to provide empirical evidence on the relationship between agglomeration and a large-scale scientific research infrastructure. Their study considers agglomerative effects of investments in a so-called synchrotron light source in the United Kingdom, and found that the establishment of the Diamond Light Source in Didcot induced clustering of related research activities and increased the research output of nearby organizations, as well as of organizations that did not utilize the facility.

Rekers (2013) has theoretically portrayed the European Spallation Source (ESS) as an enormous addition to the innovation-based economy of the Öresund region. She argues that the anticipated local benefits associated with ESS are tied to the degree of embeddedness of the facility in regional knowledge networks that facilitate localized learning. However, it is also emphasised that innovative work is inherently uncertain, unanticipated and non-linear, where investments do not directly and predictably lead to successful outputs. The counter-argument is rather that impacts can be proactively created.

Johansson, Quigley (2004) argue that networks may provide some or all of the external utility gains derived from agglomeration since knowledge networks that comprise linkages into the global scientific community enlarge the pool of specialized workers that can be considered as interregional sources of new and diverse knowledge.

The research on the impact and utilization of non-large-scale research facilities appears very limited. Falck et al. (2011) have attempted to explicitly demonstrate how the MAX synchrotron facility in Lund is utilized by researchers across the world and whether there is scope to consider MAXlab as a research infrastructure with regional implications. The main result from this study is that it is not possible to consider MAXlab as a regional research facility without considering the importance of its Nordic, European, and global linkages

The current study can also be conceived through the framework of recent attempts to provide a comprehensive map of the pathways to impact of scientific research, see for instance Snickars et al. (2013). Academic impacts have several interconnecting dimensions. A research project, research program, or research infrastructure, can also generate a wide variety of social and economic impacts. These impacts occur in different time scales but also on different spatial scales. Since research is an activity performed in an open global environment, economic and social impacts may also occur regionally, nationally, and internationally. Snickars, Falck (2015) argue that since the Kiruna-based radar station EISCAT has been for a long time identified as a research infrastructure of international importance, its impacts have surely occurred in the global environment. EISCAT has been selected as a top-priority EU research infrastructure.

4   Research and development outputs

SKB details its plans for continued research and technological developments every third year in a special R&D programme which commenced in the 1980's. The most recent one was released in 2013. In this context, however, we will not deal with the scientific substance

Table 1: Äspö publication pattern by type 1993-2013

| From | 1999 | 2002 | 2005 | 2008 | 2011 | 1999 |
To	2001	2004	2007	2010	2013	2013
Article	13	8	26	4	32	83
Proceedings	22	13	22	1	5	63
Report	113	176	67	52	28	436
Thesis	25	20	23	22	12	102
Total	173	217	138	79	77	684

of this comprehensive research portfolio, but instead concentrate on the networks within science generated by the research, and on the linkages to industrial development activity.

An international review of SKB's research and development efforts was made in 2012, see Nuclear Energy Agency (2012). This review emphasized the importance for SKB to clearly show the chain of events whereby theory is transformed into practice, including how to translate safety analyses into industrial production and application. This work will become increasingly important closer to the start of construction and operation of the final storage facility in Forsmark. The results of this work are currently reviewed and evaluated by the Swedish Radiation Safety Authority (SSM), in a comprehensive licensing process. The NEA review report praises SKB's approach to public outreach work that is described as at the forefront of international practice.

A major part of the research reported in the current paper has been generated by merging publication data from different sources within SKB. The central source of data has been the yearly reports on the publication output from researchers involved in the SKB research programme. These publications consist of both technical reports, proceedings from workshops and conferences, and academic papers published in peer-reviewed journals, see SKB (1994 2014) and SKB (2013).

The composition of these outputs of the research and development projects is summarized in Table 1 which is constructed from yearly reports for the period 1998-2013 and contains some 700 publications. We note that four out of seven of the recorded publications are technical reports and that a rather small number of publications are recorded as articles.

The funding profile of the research done at the Äspö laboratory is shown to decline across time (Figure 2 and 3). This does not necessarily mean that the publication output follows the same pattern. Figure 4 illustrates that the publication level was highest in the period between the end of the 1990s and the middle of the first decade of the 2000s. About 120 publications per year were then produced. The latest ten-year period has exhibited a steady fall in the number of publications as indicated by the relevant yearly reports.

Since research on final disposal is a complex engineering challenge it might be expected that joint publication would be relatively common. Figure 5 illustrates this pattern for the period 1998-2011. We observe that about half of the publications are single-authored with a tendency of this ratio to increase across time. Around one third of the publications have two authors while the share of publications involving three or more authors is one out of five.

We also observe that the share of publications with two authors has remained stable over time. Instead bigger networks of cooperation have been split and more publications have been single-authored. This would seem to indicate that the share of technical reports has also decreased over time as the need for large-scale experimental setups has been reduced.

The total output of PhD degrees has been in the order of seven per year producing a total of 143 dissertations. The PhD degrees have been awarded from a wide set of Swedish and international universities with a focus on the major technical universities in Sweden, especially the Royal Institute of Technology. Four of the dissertations have been produced at non-Swedish universities, see Figure 6.

The dissertations have been an initial part of the career of the persons involved. We

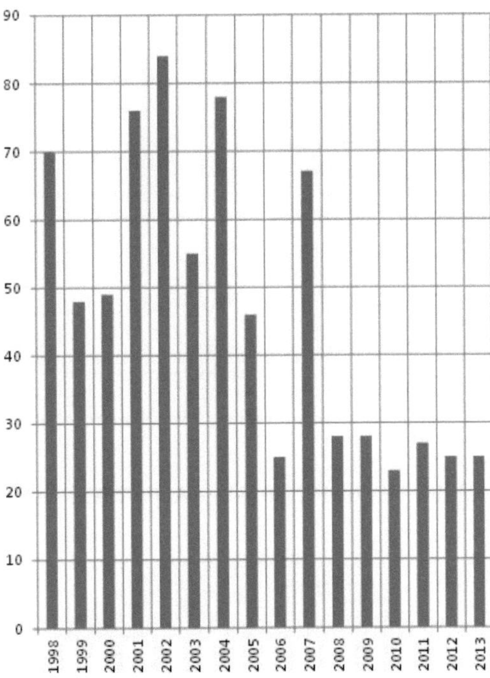

Figure 4: Publications based on experiments at Äspö hard rock laboratory 1998-2013

have followed these careers by tracking down the current affiliation and work title of each of the doctoral students using Äspö as their experimental area, see Figure 7 for an illustration.

In this way, it is possible to characterize an important part of both the academic and the industrial footprint that the Äspö test site has implicitly generated. We will outline the development for dissertations finished during each of the three-year SKB research plans.

We note that eleven of the 143 persons having written their dissertations on results from experimental work performed at the Äspö hard rock laboratory are full professors in 2016. This is somewhat less than one out of ten. Somewhat more than one out of ten has reached director positions in the private or government sector. The bulk of the degree holders have research or management positions. The share of degree holders who are found outside academia increases substantially over time.

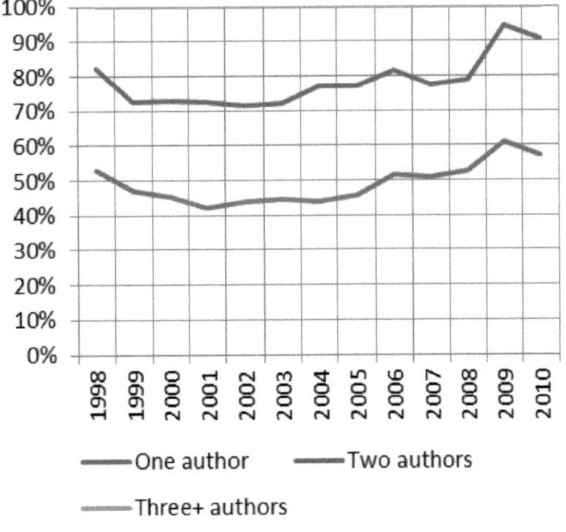

Figure 5: SKB articles according to number of authors across time 1997-2011

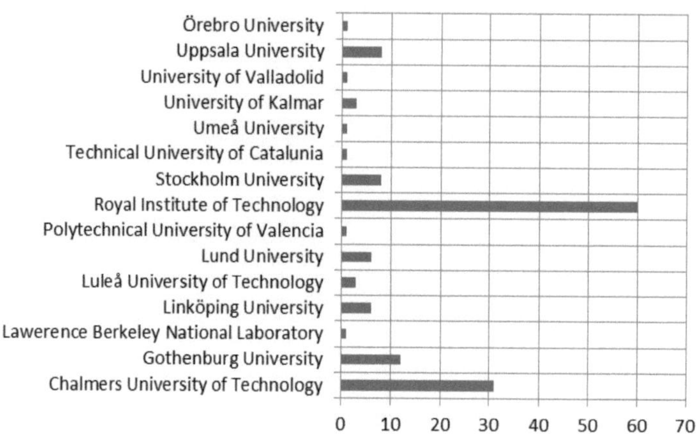

Figure 6: University affiliations of PhDs using Äspö Hard Rock laboratory 1992-2013

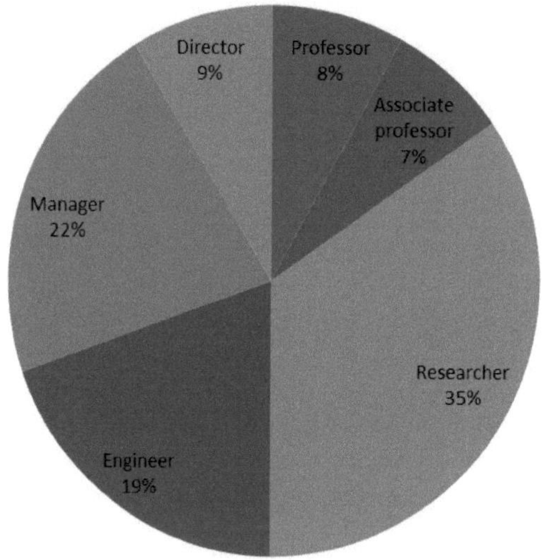

Figure 7: Current work positions for doctoral students using the Äspö hard rock laboratory 1992-2013

One can conclude that an important output of the activities at Äspö has been the production of academic, industrial and management competence for the technology area.

5 Research cooperation and publications

The research and development work at Äspö has been mostly concentrated on testing alternative technologies for the transport, deployment, and storage of nuclear waste. Another focal area has been performing scientific modelling and testing properties of the bedrock in which storage facilities are to be prepared and the waste stored safely for a very long time. For these reasons, documentation of the work has had to be done very carefully so that one can verify results achieved at later points in time.

A comprehensive database, called Sicada, has been set up which also contains systematic measurements of external environmental conditions in the biosphere around Äspö. These arguments indicate that the research and development work has involved a large amount of teamwork, and a large amount of jointly produced publications. However, we have not set up a database for each research project but rather focused on the publications emerging from these projects as they are presented in the yearly reports from SKB.

Figure 8 provides an illustration of patterns of collaboration with non-university organizations as reflected in the publication records from the Äspö hard rock laboratory.

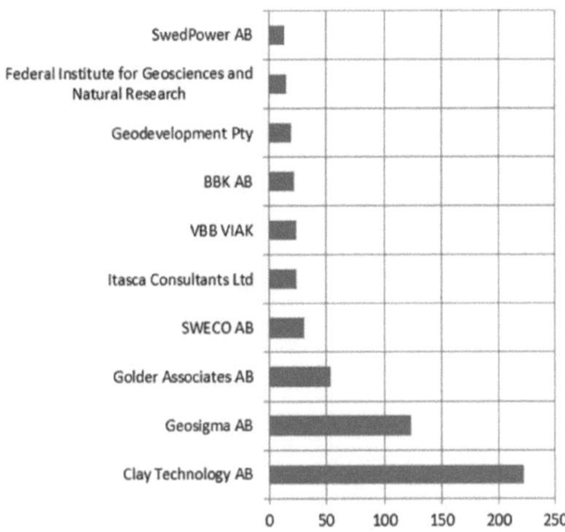

Figure 8: Number of co-authorships involving non-university organizations in publications from Äspö hard rock laboratory 1998-2013

The figure reveals that the most frequently occurring company name is Clay Technologies. It comes as no surprise that this is the company at which two of the leading scientists have been working. The author with the largest number of mentions in the database seems to be working both from his base at Gothenburg University and from his geoengineering consulting company. This observation also holds in a more general sense. It seems that a number of scientists have acted from both university departments and private enterprise platforms in their work at the laboratory.

We can note from the company names shown in Figure 8 that industrial cooperation extends to both Swedish and international companies. Some companies seem to be rather small and very specialized towards the Äspö context. Other networks seem to involve some major Swedish civil engineering consultants who have a specialization in rock mechanics and tunneling.

The pattern observed here is quite different from what may be observed in relation to other research infrastructures. The Äspö case shows that a major technological problem-solving effort can give rise to scientific development, create new academic subjects and provide challenges to existing engineering science.

6   Network analysis of research cooperation

Scientific work depends on the free access to earlier research results. Some publications will be disseminated widely and then effectively function as capital inputs to the ongoing research. The notion of academic impact factors stems from this observation. Highly cited scientists then effectively work as research leaders even if there is no formal connection between the leaders and the followers. In the context of the current case of the Äspö hard rock laboratory we might ask which researchers are the research leaders by analyzing the publication database in terms of patterns of joint authorships. Is it possible to identify subgroups of researchers through the publication analysis?

From the perspective of network theory (Johansson, Quigley 2004), researchers' affiliations are network nodes and co-authorships establishes edges between the nodes. As a result, nodes and edges form pairwise linkages including link-weights for each publication, where linkages indicate joint-publications and link-weights indicates the number of joint-publications between a specific pair. Double back relationships between nodes are controlled for so that each pairwise linkage is unique. The visual exploration of the networks is made using the Gephi software package, see for instance Bastian et al. (2009). The analysis will again be based on publication patterns found in the yearly reports from SKB.

Figure 9 gives an overview of the results. It is obvious that there are groupings of researchers who collaborate with other persons in their fields of science. Some of these

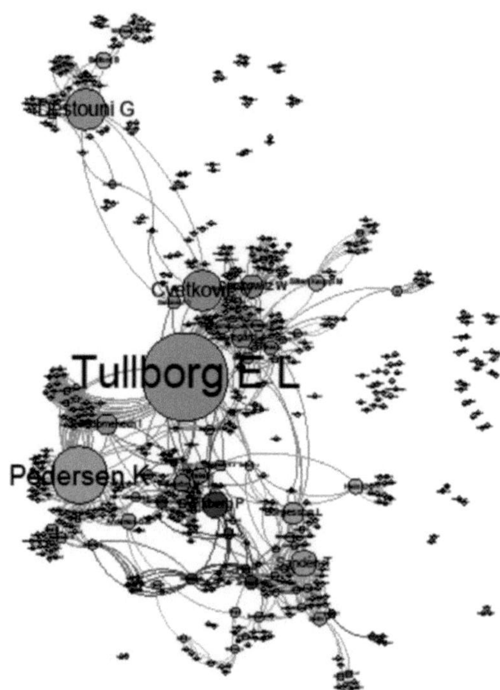

Figure 9: The research network of Äspö-based activities according to SKB yearly reports 1998-2013

groups are independent of the core group, while others are peripheral without belonging to a certain group. In the current case, these are persons who have contributed to the test programmes without having scientific ambitions of their own.

The size and positioning of the persons in the network is determined by the so-called betweenness centrality measure, see Freeman (1977). The indicator measures all the shortest paths between every pair of nodes of the network and then counts how many times a node is on a shortest path between two others. It is a very revealing measure in the case of a network of scientists as it allows us to detect people that occupy an intermediate transfer position between other people or groups.

We note from the figure that some of the researchers who have published the most are not central to the network. Conversely, others stand out as hubs around whom most of the research and development work has emerged during the fifteen-year period investigated. We have partitioned the graph so that those researchers who have the closest affinity in terms of joint publications share the same colour. Seven major groupings have been identified.

Figure 10 shows research networks resulting in academically published articles linked to the Äspö Hard Rock laboratory according to organizational home 1998-2014, see also Falck, Snickars (2017).

As we can see the research activity is characterized by cooperation between researchers from Sweden and other countries. More specifically, among the 90 articles shown in Figure 9 which have been authored by more than 200 persons in more than 70 different research institutions in 18 countries, a small minority do not build on inter-organizational cooperation.

We can conclude that the strategic importance of the Äspö Hard Rock laboratory is not only connected to the task of developing technology for the final disposal of nuclear waste but has also implied strategic research cooperation between researchers in university and industry. This strengthens the position of Sweden as a research nation. The presence of such cooperation accounts for spillover effects in the whole knowledge production system through informal social networks. These effects are not confined to the nuclear industrial networks

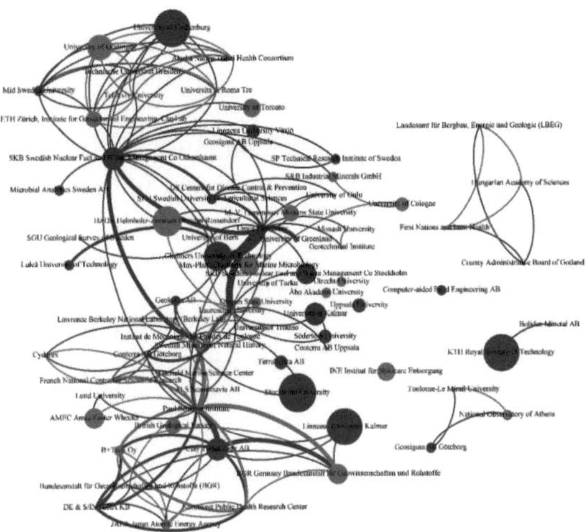

Notes: Blue=Swedish organization, Red=International organization. Node size representsnumber of published articlesto which organiations mentioned have contributed. Link thickness indicates number of coauthored and colour (red/blue/purple) 1998-2014

Figure 10: Research networks resulting in academically published articles linked to the Äspö Hard Rock Laboratory according to organization 1998-2014

From a strategic perspective it is not only the presence and volume of research activities which is important but also how the projects have been organized. Projects involving actors from different organizations provide non-monetary benefits which spill-over within the network. The Äspö Hard Rock laboratory has therefore acted as a catalyst for new engineering science and new engineering practices.

7   Conclusions

This study examines the economic and societal importance of the Äspö hard rock laboratory, including the nature, scale, and spatial configuration of related scientific work and other activities. It demonstrates that the nuclear installations in Oskarshamn may give rise to specialized local labour markets, increased human capital levels, consumption of local goods and facilities, and perhaps also functions as a magnet for highly-skilled professionals. It appears, however, that the Äspö laboratory neither resulted in any substantial clustering of related activities nor has it generated any significant economic effects in the short and medium term. Instead, it contributes to strengthen regional competitiveness and attractiveness in a more general sense, suggesting the economic and societal importance of the Äspö laboratory as a knowledge infrastructure is long term and should be interpreted in a strategic context.

There are additional aspects of Oskarshamn as an important node in the nuclear cluster in southeastern Sweden, which includes several complementary organizations such as the encapsulation plant, the central interim storage facility for spent nuclear fuel, the canister laboratory and the bentonite laboratory. The long-term work of SKB in general and the Äspö laboratory in particular has thus implied a large injection of research funding across time in the region.

Another important aspect of the Äspö laboratory is as an interconnecting infrastructure and organization in value creating knowledge networks with global reach. The gains from these network linkages or global knowledge pipelines relate to transactions of formal and informal knowledge and other advantages including memberships in scientific communities that contribute to renewal and dynamism of local knowledge. These network linkages may imply the same type of external utility gains derived from any agglomeration of similar or dissimilar activities, and can be expected to arise from extra-regional sources of new and diverse knowledge.

However, the related development work needs to carefully consider how to promote a high level of absorptive capacity among organizations with related activities. This is in order to maximize the potential benefits of hosting an advanced scientific research infrastructure and to facilitate localized learning and thus contributing to strengthen the nation and region as well as the city of Oskarshamn in a sustainable way.

In terms of the classification of impacts presented in Snickars et al. (2013) a number of observations can be made. First, the main impacts of the Äspö laboratory stay within the technological system related to nuclear technology. It simultaneously creates worldwide academic advancement through the use of innovative equipment, techniques and technologies in a cross-disciplinary setting. The existence of the infrastructure in southeast Sweden has a positive side-effect for the training and teaching of students at academic levels in several Swedish universities engaged in nuclear-related research and education.

The Äspö laboratory as a part of the SKB system has played a role in creating social and economic impacts but there is no distinct profile outside the energy sector. It is clear that SKB's activities increase public engagement and interest in research related to energy in general and nuclear energy in particular.

The fact that this research has been effectively performed in Oskarshamn clearly adds to the role of southeast Sweden as an energy cluster. This aspect of Äspö could be further promoted through deepened studies of the current type for other infrastructures. The geosphere-related development at Äspö may enhance quality of life in view of its attractiveness for cultural tourism.

In summary, it might be said that there is a clear potential to promote social and economic impacts of the energy sector in Oskarshamn especially if one considers the sector as a whole. In this context, it is interesting to observe that the Äspö laboratory can have a very strong role in the national research infrastructure system in Sweden, and at the European level. It can be related to other research infrastructures at the European level for which Sweden has been selected as the host. This international visibility does not seem to fully penetrate to the level of regional and local decision making. There is room for action for instance in relation to the new policy round within the structural funds.

We conclude by providing answers to the research questions posed in the introduction:

- Research infrastructures as the Äspö Hard Rock laboratory are powerful and productive creators of international research and research networks;

- It is possible although technically somewhat difficult to reveal the academic and societal impacts of Äspö-related research and development which become visible if the perspective in broad enough;

- Engineering research has its own peculiar networks of university-industry interaction where value is cogenerated dynamically which makes it a challenge to specialize in it for a peripheral region.

We have come some way in analyzing the productivity of research cooperation using the case of Äspö as a test area but considerably more work needs to be done both to enhance the quality of the background data and to demonstrate the knowledge valorization chains.

Acknowledgement

We acknowledge economic support from the municipality of Oskarshamn in performing the research reported in the current paper. We also thank SKB library staff for allowing access to project and publication data.

References

Andersson ÅE, Beckmann M (2009) *Economics of knowledge: Theory, models and measurements*. Edward Elgar, Cheltenham

Bastian M, Heymann S, Jacomy M (2009) Gephi: An open source software for exploring and manipulating networks. International AAAI Conference on Weblogs and Social Media

Batabyal A, Nijkamp P (2015) Creative capital in production, inefficiency, and inequality - a theoretical analysis. Paper presented at an international workshop, Tinbergen Institute, Amsterdam

Falck S, Snickars F (2017) Societal benefits of the Äspö hard rock laboratory. Research report, Department of Urban Planning and Environment, KTH

Falck S, Snickars F, Westlund H (2011) Research hubs in the Baltic sea region: An explorative study about research cooperation and the usage of research facilities in physics and life sciences. Research paper, Royal Institute of Technology (KTH) and the Swedish Research Council (VR)

Freeman L (1977) A set of measures of centrality based on betweenness. *Sociometry* 40: 35–41. CrossRef.

Helmers C, Overman HG (2013) My precious! The location and diffusion of scientific research: Evidence from the synchrotron diamond light source. SERC Discussion Papers, SERCDP0131. Spatial Economics Research Centre (SERC), London School of Economics and Political Science, London

Horlings E, Gurney T, Somers A, van den Besselaar P (2012) The societal footprint of big science – A literature review in support of evidence-based decision making. Working paper 1206, Rathenau Instituut, Den Haag

Johansson B, Quigley JM (2004) Agglomeration and networks in spatial economies. *Papers in Regional Science* 83: 1–13. CrossRef.

Mellander C, Florida R (2007) The creative class or human capital? – Explaining regional development in Sweden. Working paper series in economics and institutions of innovation 79, Centre of Excellence for Science and Innovation Studies, KTH. CrossRef.

Nuclear Energy Agency (2012) The post-closure radiological safety case for a spent-fuel repository in Sweden. An international peer review of the SKB license-application study of March 2011. NEA/RWM/PEER(2012)2, OECD, Paris

OECD (2012) Oecd territorial reviews, småland - blekinge. Research report, OECD, Paris

Rekers JV (2013) The european spallation source (ESS) and the geography of innovation. In: Kaiserfeld T, O'Dell T (eds), *Legitimizing ESS: Big Science as a Collaboration Across Boundaries*. Nordic Academic Press, Lund

SKB (1994–2014) Äspö hard rock laboratory annual report 1993-2014. Technical reports

SKB (2013) RD&D programme 2013. Technical report, TR-13-18

Snickars F, Blaus J, Eriksson T, Reitberger G (2013) Economic and social impacts of kth research: A follow-up study of the research assessment exercise 2012. Research report, VINNOVA and KTH

Snickars F, Falck S (2015) Inter-regional trade in research-based knowledge: The case of the EISCAT radar system. In: Batabyal A, Nijkamp P (eds), *The region and trade: New analytical directions*. World Scientific, London, 227–264. CrossRef.

Part B:

Structure and Change in Regional Dynamics

REGION

The Journal of ERSA
Powered by WU

Volume 4, Number 3, 2017, 65–76
DOI: 10.18335/region.v4i3.167

journal homepage: region.ersa.org

Panel Data Models of New Firm Formation in New England

Jitendra Parajuli[1], Kingsley E. Haynes[2]

[1] George Mason University, Arlington, VA, USA
[2] George Mason University, Arlington, VA, USA and Hong Kong University of Science and Technology, Kowloon, HK, China

Received: 10 October 2016/Accepted: 9 August 2017

Abstract. This study examines the impact of the determinants of new firm formation in New England at the county level from 1999 to 2009. Based on the Spatial Durbin panel model that accounts for spillover effects, it is found that population density and human capital positively affect single-unit firm births within a county and its neighbors. Population growth rate also exerts a significant positive impact on new firm formation, but most of the effect is from spatial spillovers. On the contrary, the ratio of large to small firms in terms of employment size and the unemployment rate negatively influences single-unit firm births both within counties and among neighbors. However, there is no significant impact of local financial capital and personal income growth on new firm formation.

1 Introduction

Entrepreneurship is an important component of the US economy. Schramm (2004) suggested that the US is the leading entrepreneurial country in the world. New firms drive innovation and even during recessionary periods entrepreneurs provide impetus for recovery and economic growth. More recently, the US was ranked as the most entrepreneurial nation among 132 countries in the world and it was suggested that the US has entered a new innovation-driven stage of development (Acs et al. 2015).

Although the National Bureau of Economic Research (NBER) noted that the US experienced major economic contractions in 2001 and from late 2007 through mid-2009 (NBER 2009), the rate of new entrepreneurs (i.e., the percentage of adult population becoming entrepreneurs) has not changed abruptly. In 2001, this rate was 0.28% and from 2007 through 2009, it changed from 0.30% to 0.34% (Fairlie et al. 2016). However, such an aggregate index does not reflect the actual variation of entrepreneurial activities at the regional and local level. Moreover, spatial dependence and heterogeneity often mask local spatial patterns and spillovers (see Anselin 1988, LeSage, Pace 2009). This paper argues that while new firm formation is determined by the local characteristics of individual regions over time, it is also important to understand the effect of spatial externalities in firm births. Using fixed effects panel data models, this study examines the impact of the determinants of new firm formation in the high innovation region of New England – Connecticut, Maine, Massachusetts, New Hampshire, Rhode Island, and Vermont. This is done at the county level from 1999 through 2009 in order to capture local effects.

This paper is arranged in the following sections. A theoretical background is presented in the next section (Section 2). Research methodology, data description, and information sources are presented in Section 3. The empirical results are provided in Section 4. Section 5 includes concluding remarks, policy recommendations, and directions for future research.

2   Literature Review

For various reasons, economic activities are not consistent across space and time. Following Marshall, Krugman (1991) argued that businesses agglomerate in a region because of the pooled labor market, production of non-tradable specialized inputs, and the possibility of greater productivity due to information spillovers. Agglomeration (Ellison, Glaeser 1999), area-based policy (Anyadike-Danes, O'Reilly 2005), cluster strategy (Delgado et al. 2010), and regional embeddedness (Dahl, Sorenson 2012) all influence business location decisions and the distribution of economic activities.

Population density is an important determinant of new firm births. According to Reynolds et al. (1994), urbanization and agglomeration are closely associated with population density and new firm formation rates are often positively associated with population density. Audretsch, Fritsch (1994) also found a positive relationship between population density (agglomeration) and new firm births. The percentage of entrepreneurial activity is higher in urban regions that are characterized by high population density (Bosma, Schutjens 2011). However, if a region has already maximized the benefits of urbanization, high population density can have negative impacts as well (Delfmann et al. 2014).

Human capital and entrepreneurship are closely associated with each other (Garvin 1983, Robinson, Sexton 1994, Davidsson, Honig 2003). Fritsch (1992) suggested that new business founders are highly skilled and Armington, Acs (2002) noted the importance of human capital on firm births. Regional variation in new firm formation, especially in the service sector, is contingent upon the availability of college-educated individuals that normally establish and manage new business ventures (Acs, Armington 2004). Likewise, human capital is crucial for innovation and information flow, and hence promotes new firm formation (Lee et al. 2004).

Financial capital is crucial for starting a new business. Personal, informal – acquaintances and angel investors – and/or formal financial institutions, such as banks, are often the sources of investment. Often, new businesses and entrepreneurs reap the benefits of the local financial environment where they were born or have lived for long time periods (Michelacci, Silva 2007, Robinson, Cottrell 2007, Dahl, Sorenson 2012). Sutaria, Hicks (2004) found a positive relationship between local bank deposits per capita and new firm formation. On the contrary, Kim et al. (2006) noted that potential entrepreneurs gain more from human capital and that financial capital is not a necessary condition for entrepreneurial ventures.

Establishment size is equally important for new firm formation. Audretsch, Fritsch (1994) examined the relationship between new firm births and mean establishment size using different frameworks and found both positive and negative association between them. In general, there is a negative association between average firm size and births in a region. That is, the larger the mean size of existing firms, the smaller the rate of new firm formation (Kangasharju 2000, Armington, Acs 2002, Lee et al. 2004). However, Sutaria, Hicks (2004) found that regions with larger firm size have faster firm birth rates.

The effect of unemployment on new firm formation is mixed. For instance, Reynolds et al. (1995) found a positive relationship between unemployment rate and firm births. Unemployed individuals can start new ventures in the earlier stages of unemployment. However, if unemployment persists for a long period, the propensity for self-employment declines (Ritsila, Tervo 2002). While Sutaria, Hicks (2004) found a negative relationship, Fritsch, Falck (2002) concluded that there is no relationship between new firm formation and unemployment. Storey (1991), Audretsch, Fritsch (1994), and Cheng, Li (2010) argued that depending on the type of estimation models, the unemployment rate can have both positive and negative association with new firm births.

Population growth also influences new start-ups. On the one hand, Audretsch, Fritsch

(1994), Davidsson et al. (1994), Guesnier (1994), Kangasharju (2000), and Armington, Acs (2002) noted that regional differences in firm birth rates can be explained by population growth. On the other hand, Sutaria, Hicks (2004) did not find any positive association between population growth and new firm formation and attributed the findings to modeling limitations.

Another predictor of new firm formation is per capita income growth. While Armington, Acs (2002) and Lee et al. (2004) found evidence of a positive effect, Sutaria, Hicks (2004) found no statistically significant effect of per capita income growth on new firm formation.

A number of studies have attested to the existence of spatial and temporal variation of entrepreneurship in the US. For instance, Armington, Acs (2002) suggested that entrepreneurial activities vary considerably across space, but not much over time. Acs, Mueller (2008) indicated that regional characteristics determine start-up rates. Urban, suburban, and rural differences in new business formation are also evident (Renski 2009). Parajuli, Haynes (2017) found that the spatio-temporal distributional patterns of single-unit firm births fluctuate in New England. In essence, whether within clusters, metropolitan areas, or states, new venture growth fluctuates over time and across space (see Guzman, Stern 2015, Morelix et al. 2016). Based on these findings, this study hypothesizes that the determinants of new firm formation influenced single-unit firm births within and across local areas (counties) in New England from 1999 through 2009 – a period covering the "great recession".

Since the effect of individual determinants on new firm formation varies, based on the general findings, it is hypothesized that regions with higher population densities should experience higher firm births. The availability of higher human capital and local financial capital should also be positively associated with new firm formation. However, new firm formation should be negatively associated with the size of the existing firms in terms of employment. As the unemployment rate does not have any consistent effect on new firm formation, it is hypothesized that the relationship between the unemployment rate and new firm births is indeterminate. Finally, higher population growth rate as well as higher per capita income growth rate should be positively associated with new firm formation.

3   Methodology and Data

Unlike pure cross-sectional and time series analyses, the panel data technique offers various advantages, such as ability to control for individual heterogeneity and allows for more variability while reducing the issue of multicollinearity and providing more degrees of freedom (see Baltagi 2005). However, it should be noted that the distribution of a variable of interest – new firm formation – often exhibits spatial heterogeneity and spatial autocorrelation when cross-sectional observations – counties – are spatial units (see Anselin 1988). As the non-spatial panel model will not be able to capture such effects and since spatial interaction effects in the form of spillovers are expected, it is necessary to calibrate spatial panel models that allow one to account for such effects in relation to the new firm formation dynamics.

For a panel of N observations over time T periods with K explanatory variables, a spatial panel regression model that includes spatial effects is (see Elhorst 2003, 2014):

$$Y_t = \rho W Y_t + \alpha \iota_N + X_t \beta + W X_t \theta + u_t \tag{1}$$

where u_t is the error component and is defined as:

$$u_t = \lambda W u_t + \epsilon_t \tag{2}$$

In equations (1) and (2), Y_t is an $NT \times 1$ vector of the dependent variable, ι_N is a $NT \times 1$ vector of the constant terms, X is an $NT \times K$ matrix of the independent variables, β and θ are both $K \times 1$ vector of the coefficients, and ϵ is a $NT \times 1$ vector of error terms that are independent and identically distributed with mean zero and variance σ^2. In addition, W is the spatial weight matrix of size $N \times N$, scalar ρ is the spatial autoregressive term, and scalar λ the spatial autocorrelation term.

The spatial weight matrix, W, describes the arrangement of possible interactions among spatial units. Such matrices could be based on the order of contiguity, inverse distance, or nearest neighbors (see Elhorst 2014). For example, the queen contiguity weight matrix accounts for common edges and vertices of contiguous spatial units with respect to the reference spatial unit. In the case of a non-normalized, first-order queen weight matrix that takes binary values (0 and 1) weight coefficients assume 1 for the commonly shared edges and vertices in the immediate vicinity and 0 otherwise. The weight matrix is generally normalized for the ease of interpretation (see Elhorst 2014). As the spatial panel model takes into consideration spatial interactions based on the spatial weight matrix, in Equation (1), WY_t and WX_t represent the spatially weighted dependent and independent variable in the matrix form, respectively.

Based on the value of ρ, λ, and θ, different types of models can be specified:

- If $\lambda = 0$ and $\theta = 0$: Spatial autoregressive model (SAR)

- If $\rho = 0$ and $\theta = 0$: Spatial error model (SEM)

- If $\lambda = 0$: Spatial Durbin model (SDM)

- If $\lambda = 0$, $\rho = 0$, and $\theta = 0$: Non-spatial model

The global Moran's I statistic given by Equation (3) is used for examining spatial dependence (Bailey, Gatrell 1995).

$$I = \frac{N \sum_{i=1}^{N} \sum_{j=1}^{N} w_{ij}(x_i - \bar{x})(x_j - \bar{x})}{\sum_{i=1}^{N}(x_i - \bar{x})^2 (\sum_{i \neq j} \sum w_{ij})} \tag{3}$$

where w_{ij} is the element of weight matrix W, x is the variable of interest, and $\bar{x}$ is the mean of x.

There are a number of issues that have to be accounted for while calibrating a panel data model. First, the fixed effects model is generally preferred when there is a specific set of cross-sectional observations and the inference is based on them instead of the sample drawn from the population (see Baltagi 2005). Thus, as this study is focused only on New England, the fixed effects models will be adopted. Second, firm births in a county are likely to affect firm births in the neighboring/contiguous counties. That is, there are direct and indirect effects associated with new firm formation and these impacts can be considered in the SAR and SDM techniques. Thus, both SAR and SDM will be calibrated. Based on the log-likelihood and Akaike Information Criterion (AIC), the appropriate model will be selected. Third, as noted earlier, as new firms provide impetus to growth even during recessions (Schramm 2004), rates of new entrepreneurs have not abruptly changed during the observation period (Fairlie et al. 2016), and entrepreneurial activities change more across regions than over time (Armington, Acs 2002), only county-specific effects will be considered. The XSMLE module in Stata will be used for the estimation purpose (Belotti et al. 2016).

Data at the county level used in this study come from three different sources – the Census Bureau (CB), Bureau of Economic Analysis (BEA), and Bureau of Labor Statistics (BLS). The number of single-unit firm births, area (in square miles), public school enrollment, capital deposit (in US dollars) in local commercial and saving institutions, and establishment size in terms of employees are from the CB. Data from the BEA include per capital personal income (in US dollars), population, population growth rate, and per capita personal income growth. The unemployment rate was obtained from the BLS. Table 1 provides the details of variables.

4   Empirical Results

The temporal variations of single-unit firm births (in logarithm) by states in New England and by counties in Rhode Island are shown in Figure 1.

In New England, over the study period, Massachusetts and Vermont experienced the largest and smallest number of single-unit firm births, respectively. In addition, at the state level, new firm formation was generally declining between 2007 and 2009. This

Table 1: Variable details

Variable	Description	Data Source
Dependent in logarithm		
lsub	Logarithm of single-unit firm birth	CB
Independent in logarithm		
lpopden	Logarithm of population density	BEA and CB
lpubenrpc	Logarithm of public enrollment per capita	BEA and CB
lfincappc	Logarithm of per capita deposit in local commercial and savings institutions	
lestratiol	Logarithm of the ratio of establishments with 50 or more employees to establishments with less than 10 employees	CB
luempr	Logarithm of unemployment rate	BLS
Independent in non-logarithm		
popgr	Population growth rate	BEA
perincgr	Per capital personal income growth rate	BEA

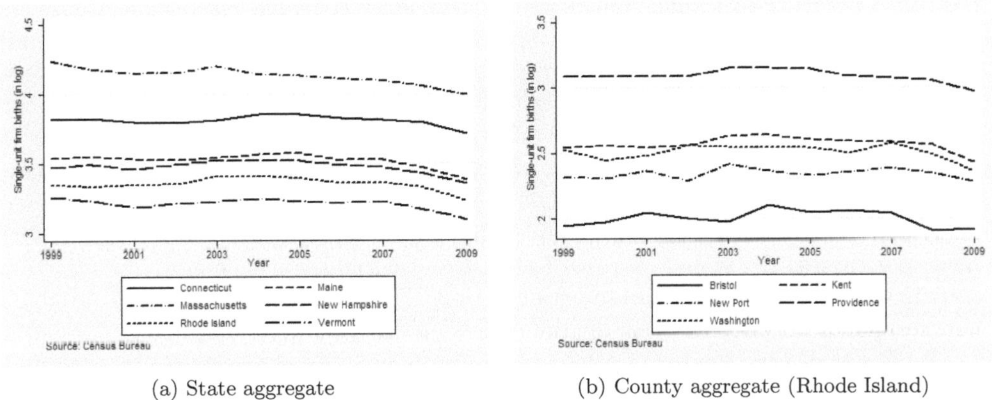

(a) State aggregate   (b) County aggregate (Rhode Island)

Figure 1: Temporal variation of single-unit firm births

corresponded with the bottoming out of the great recession. As shown in Figure 1b, such a trend was also observable at the county level within a state.

The spatial distributions of single-unit firm births (in logarithm) in 1999 and 2009 in New England are shown in Figure 2.

The estimated values of two non-spatial regression models – pooled and fixed effects panel – with the logarithm of single-unit firm births as the dependent variable are shown in Table 2.

In order to select the appropriate model between the pooled and fixed effects model, the F-statistic is used. The null hypothesis is that the intercept term (individual effects) is constant across all counties (i.e., the model is "poolable") and the alternative hypothesis is that the intercept term varies across counties (see Baltagi 2005). The F-statistic for degrees of freedom $F(64, 643)$ is equal to 204.67 with $p < 0.000$. This suggests that, at 5% significance level, the null is rejected and the fixed effects model is chosen. Further, log-likelihood and AIC values also suggest that the fixed effects model is appropriate compared to the pooled model.

As the unit of observations is not randomly selected, the fixed effects estimation makes sense. It should also be noted that the observation period is short and hence unit root analysis of individual time series is often not effective (see Baltagi 2005).

The non-spatial fixed-effects panel model suggests that for the 65 counties in New Eng-

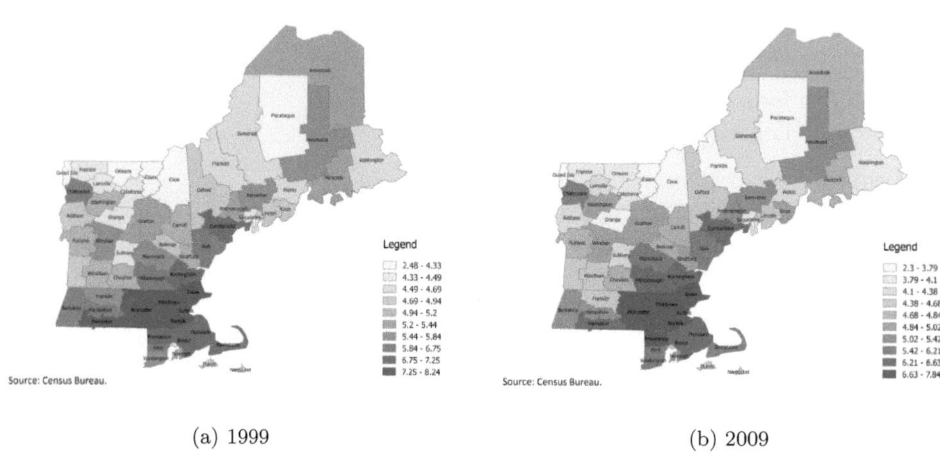

(a) 1999   (b) 2009

Figure 2: Spatial variation of single-unit firm births in 1999 and 2009

land[1] over the period of observation (1999–2009), controlling for other factors, population density, public enrollment, and personal income growth have a statistically significant positive correlation with single-unit firm births. On the contrary, establishment size and unemployment rate have a significant negative association with new firm formation while holding other variables constant. County level financial capital and population growth rates were not significantly associated with firm births.

Before calibrating the spatial fixed-effects panel models, the Moran's I statistics for all variables across the study period are calculated. The global Moran's I statistics based on the first-order queen contiguity weight matrix are presented in Table 3.

Except for the human capital variable, that is, the logarithm of public school enrollment per capita, the global Moran's I statistic of variables are generally positive and statistically significant in each observation period. The results imply that each variable is autocorrelated in space and that spatial dependence exists.

Table 4 shows the estimated values of the fixed effects SAR and fixed effects SDM in which the logarithm of single-unit firm births is the dependent variable. Based on the log-likelihood and AIC values, the preferred model is the fixed effects SDM.

In the fixed effects SDM, the spatial dependence associated with single-unit firm births (ρ) is positive and statistically significant and suggests that new firm formation is spatially endogenous with respect to individual counties. Population density and public school enrollment per capita are both statistically significant and positively associated with single-unit firm births. Establishment size ratio is also statistically significant, but negatively associated with new firm formation.

Note that the SDM estimates are not interpreted as partial derivatives as in the classical regression technique. This is because a change in an explanatory variable in a county can impact single-unit firm births in other neighboring counties based on the spatial weight matrix (here, the queen contiguity matrix). Instead, the direct, indirect, and total effects as shown in Table 5 are interpreted (see LeSage, Pace 2009).

Population density has a positive direct and indirect impact on single-unit firm births. The difference between the coefficient estimate (0.945) and the direct effect estimate (1.109) is 0.164, which reflects a positive feedback to a county itself. That is, an increase in population density results in an increase in the number of new firms within a county. The spatially lagged coefficient of population density is not significant, but the indirect effect is positive and statistically significant and has a magnitude that is almost twice the magnitude of the direct effect. This suggests a large spillover resulting from the population density of a county to nearby counties. The total impact is 3.220 and statistically significant. Thus, ceteris paribus, a 10 percent increase in population density would result in more than a 32 percent increase in new firm formation and that about 1/3

---

[1] Although there are 67 counties in New England, this study only considers 65 contiguous counties.

Table 2: Non-spatial regression models

	Pooled	Fixed effects panel
Intercept	6.068***	
	(16.27)	
lpopden	0.397***	1.215**
	(20.72)	(3.48)
lpubenrpc	0.424*	0.304***
	(2.23)	(3.88)
lfincappc	0.234***	0.002
	(4.44)	(0.08)
lestratiol	0.839***	-0.315***
	(13.18)	(-5.25)
luempr	0.017	-0.266***
	(0.21)	(-8.18)
popgr	0.036	0.013
	(0.95)	(1.28)
perincgr	0.016†	0.007**
	(1.82)	(2.82)
Log-likelihood	-650.004	444.674
AIC	1316.008	-873.348
Observation	715	715

Source: Authors' calculations
Notes: Significant at † p<0.1, * p<0.05, ** p<0.01, ***p<0.001; t-values in parentheses

of this would have resulted from the direct impact and the remaining from the spillover effects.

Similarly, a 10 percent increase in public school enrollment per capita results in a 6 percent increase in single-unit firm births. About 33 percent of the increase in new firm formation results from the direct impact and 67 percent from the indirect impact of human capital. The significant total impact of the population growth rate on new firm formation is 0.082 and almost all of that impact is comprised of spillover effects. Thus, for a 1 unit change in the population growth rate, single-unit firm births are expected to increase by more than 8 percent ceteris paribus.

Total effects of the establishment size ratio and the unemployment rate are both negative and statistically significant. Thus, for a 10 percent increase in the size of existing firms, new firm formation decreases by 6.6 percent and for a 10 percent increase in the rate of unemployment, new firm formation decreases by 3.1 percent. In addition, in the case of the establishment size ratio, both the direct and indirect impacts influence

Table 3: Global Moran's I statistics

Year	lsub	lpopden	lpubenrpc	lfincappc	lestratiol	luempr	popgr	perincgr
1999	0.515***	0.764***	-0.024	0.095†	0.232**	0.396***	0.314***	0.341***
2000	0.504***	0.765***	-0.072	0.075	0.261***	0.484***	0.356***	0.390***
2001	0.522***	0.764***	-0.067	0.079†	0.254***	0.360***	0.351***	0.178*
2002	0.522***	0.765***	-0.098	0.106†	0.244**	0.287***	0.302***	0.143*
2003	0.521***	0.765***	-0.118	0.137*	0.242**	0.412***	0.244**	0.217**
2004	0.524***	0.765***	-0.105	0.146*	0.216**	0.559***	0.289***	-0.003
2005	0.522***	0.764***	-0.091	0.118**	0.219**	0.610***	0.205**	0.169*
2006	0.541***	0.764***	-0.093	0.144**	0.242**	0.547***	0.055	0.206**
2007	0.524***	0.764***	-0.047	0.139**	0.245**	0.503***	0.051	0.024
2008	0.510***	0.764***	-0.097	0.141**	0.189**	0.569***	0.157*	0.021
2009	0.540***	0.763***	-0.078	0.052	0.207**	0.513***	0.147*	0.365***

Source: Authors' calculations
Notes: Significant at † p<0.1, * p<0.05, ** p<0.01, ***p<0.001

Table 4: Spatial panel models

	Fixed effects SAR	Fixed effects SDM
lpopden	0.781**	0.945**
	(2.77)	(2.98)
lpubenrpc	0.200**	0.146*
	(3.16)	(2.25)
lfincappc	-0.001	0.019
	(-0.04)	(0.83)
lestratiol	-0.245***	-0.260***
	(-5.06)	(-5.37)
luempr	-0.138***	-0.036
	(-5.04)	(-0.75)
popgr	-0.001	-0.006
	(0.16)	(-0.71)
perincgr	0.003†	0.002
	(1.67)	(1.02)
Lagged lsub (ρ)	0.532***	0.497***
	(15.65)	(13.40)
W*lpopden		0.668
		(1.33)
W*lpubenrpc		0.160
		(1.35)
W*lfincappc		-0.016
		(-0.33)
W*lestratiol		-0.075
		(-0.73)
W*luempr		-0.117*
		(-1.97)
W*popgr		0.046**
		(3.20)
W*perincgr		0.002
		(0.60)
Log-likelihood	536.345	547.447
AIC	-1054.689	-1062.894
Observations	715	715

Source: Authors' calculations
Notes: Significant at † p<0.1, * p<0.05, ** p<0.01, ***p<0.001; t-values in parentheses.

single-unit firm births, while in the case of the unemployment rate; only the spillover effect is significantly associated with single-unit firm births.

Finally, there was no significant relationship or spillover effect associated with the availability of local financial capital and personal income growth rates with respect to new firm formation.

5 Conclusion

Entrepreneurial ventures are important for the US economy, and this paper examined the association between new firm formation and its determinants as well as the spillover effects in New England at the county level from 1999 through 2009 using both non-spatial and spatial panel data models. Based on the SDM, it was found that population density had the largest, positive impact on single-unit firm births both within a county and among its neighbors and that the spatial spillover was larger than the comparable direct effect on a county. This suggests that agglomeration and urbanization are conducive to new firm formation and that rural areas are less favorable for starting new businesses. Human capital – formal education, professional and managerial skills, information training, and

Table 5: Estimated direct, indirect, and total effects

	Direct	Indirect	Total
lpopden	1.109***	2.111**	3.220***
	(4.05)	(2.62)	(3.56)
lpubenrpc	0.184*	0.416*	0.600*
	(2.44)	(1.97)	(2.41)
lfincappc	0.019	-0.010	0.009
	(0.69)	(-0.10)	(0.08)
lestratiol	-0.290***	-0.372*	-0.662**
	(-5.88)	(-2.01)	(-3.18)
luempr	-0.048	-0.264***	-0.312***
	(-1.04)	(-3.97)	(-4.25)
popgr	0.002	0.080**	0.082**
	(0.26)	(3.19)	(2.76)
perincgr	0.002	0.004	0.006
	(1.00)	(0.77)	(1.14)

Source: Authors' calculations
Notes: Significant at † $p<0.1$, * $p<0.05$, ** $p<0.01$, ***$p<0.001$; t-values in parentheses.

innovative abilities – is equally crucial for creating new ventures. A region with a high level of human capital will not only foster new firms within its boundary, but will also influence new firm formation in the neighboring areas. In addition, population growth is important in creating new start-ups both locally as well as in the nearby areas. This could be attributed to the fact that as the number of individuals increases, so does the demand for services and the potential entrepreneurs. A variety of earlier research findings support the results that population density, human capital, and population growth influence new firm formation (for example Fritsch 1992, Audretsch, Fritsch 1994, Reynolds et al. 1994, Armington, Acs 2002).

On the contrary, individuals are more likely to avoid the risk and uncertainties associated with new businesses and instead join existing firms that provide alternative employment and income-generation opportunities when such opportunities are available. Thus, as alternative establishment size increases, new firm formation decreases and such trends produce significant negative spillovers in neighboring areas. Similarly, as the rate of unemployment increases, single-unit firm births decrease. With increasing unemployment, individuals might migrate to other regions seeking opportunities or could rely on government welfare instead of starting opportunity or necessity based entrepreneurial ventures. Some earlier studies have found a significant negative association between new firm formation and establishment size as well as between firm births and unemployment (for example Armington, Acs 2002, Sutaria, Hicks 2004). Finally and unexpectedly, this study did not find any significant association between the availability of local financial capital or personal income growth with single-unit firm births.

A region endowed with various determinants of entrepreneurial ventures will not only influence itself, but its neighboring regions. Thus, rather than merely promoting policies to attract entrepreneurial ventures for economic growth and development, local/regional policymakers need to understand the nature of spatial externalities associated with new firm formation and should focus on how to benefit from them.

This study calibrated (non)spatial models using 65 contiguous counties and dropped two island counties. Future research should use other types of weighting schemes, such as distance- and nearest neighbor-based weight matrices, for the estimation purpose. However, it is hypothesized that the results would be similar. Moreover, as the focus was only on New England, future work should examine other regions of the US and may want to examine more explicitly the temporal considerations. While this study used the aggregate number of single-unit firm births, by disaggregating new firm formation by various industry sectors and calibrating sector-based panel models new insights related to economic structure might be provided.

Acknowledgement

The authors would like to thank Roger R. Stough for the data on new firm formation. They are also grateful to the editors and anonymous reviewer for the constructive feedback.

References

Acs ZJ, Armington C (2004) The impact of geographic differences in human capital on service firm formation rates. *Journal of Urban Economics* 56: 244–278. CrossRef.

Acs ZJ, Mueller P (2008) Employment effects of business dynamics: Mice, gazelles and elephants. *Small Business Economics* 30: 85–100. CrossRef.

Acs ZJ, Szerb L, Autio E (2015) Global entrepreneurship index 2016. The Global Entrepreneurship and Development Institute, Washington, DC. https://www.research-gate.net/publication/284727510_Global_Entrepreneurship_Index_2016. CrossRef.

Anselin L (1988) *Spatial econometrics: Methods and models.* Kluwer, Dordrecht, The Netherlands. CrossRef.

Anyadike-Danes M, O'Reilly M (2005) Watch that space! The county hierarchy in firm births and deaths in the UK, 1980-1999. *Small Business Economics* 25: 273–292. CrossRef.

Armington C, Acs ZJ (2002) The determinants of regional variation in new firm formation. *Regional Studies* 36: 33–45. CrossRef.

Audretsch DB, Fritsch M (1994) The geography of firm births in Germany. *Regional Studies* 28: 359–365. CrossRef.

Bailey TC, Gatrell AC (1995) *Interactive spatial data analysis.* Pearson, Essex, UK

Baltagi BH (2005) *Econometric analysis of panel data.* John Wiley & Sons, West Sussex, UK

Belotti F, Hughes G, Mortari AP (2016) Xsmle: Stata module for spatial panel data models estimation. https://ideas.repec.org/c/boc/bocode/s457610.html

Bosma N, Schutjens V (2011) Understanding regional variation in entrepreneurial activity and entrepreneurial attitude in Europe. *Annals of Regional Science* 47: 711–742. CrossRef.

Cheng S, Li H (2010) The effects of unemployment on new firm formation revisited: Does space matter? *Regional Science Policy & Practice* 2: 97–120

Dahl MS, Sorenson O (2012) Home sweet home: Entrepreneurs' location choices and the performance of their ventures. *Management Science* 58: 1059–1071. CrossRef.

Davidsson P, Honig B (2003) The role of social and human capital among nascent entrepreneurs. *Journal of Business Venturing* 18: 301–331. CrossRef.

Davidsson P, Lindmark L, Olofsson C (1994) New firm formation and regional development in Sweden. *Regional Studies* 28: 395–410. CrossRef.

Delfmann H, Koster S, McCann P, van Dijk J (2014) Population change and new firm formation in urban and rural regions. *Regional Studies* 48: 1034–1050. CrossRef.

Delgado M, Porter ME, Stern S (2010) Clusters and entrepreneurship. *Journal of Economic Geography* 10: 495–518. CrossRef.

Elhorst JP (2003) Specification and estimation of spatial panel data models. *International Regional Science Review* 26: 244–268. CrossRef.

Elhorst JP (2014) Spatial panel models. In: Fischer MM, Nijkamp P (eds), *Handbook of Regional Science*. Springer-Verlag, Heidelberg, Germany, 1637–1652. CrossRef.

Ellison G, Glaeser EL (1999) The geographic concentration of industry: Does natural advantage explain agglomeration? *American Economic Review* 89: 311–316. CrossRef.

Fairlie RW, Morelix A, Reedy EJ, Russell J (2016) The Kauffman index: Startup activity national trends. Ewing Marion Kauffman Foundation, Kansas City, MO, US, http://www.kauffman.org/~/media/kauffman_org/microsites/kauffman_index/-startup_activity_2016/kauffman_index_startup_activity_national_trends_2016.pdf

Fritsch M (1992) Regional differences in new firm formation: Evidence from West Germany. *Regional Studies* 26: 233–241. CrossRef.

Fritsch M, Falck O (2002) New firm formation by industry over space and time: A multi-level analysis. Working Paper No. 11, Freiberg University of Mining and Technology, Freiberg, Germany. http://www.wiwi.uni-jena.de/uiw/publications/pub_1999_2003/fritsch_falck_2002.pdf

Garvin DA (1983) Spin-offs and the new firm formation process. *California Management Review* 25: 3–20. CrossRef.

Guesnier B (1994) Regional variations in new firm formation in France. *Regional Studies* 28: 347–358. CrossRef.

Guzman J, Stern S (2015) Where is silicon valley? *Science* 347: 606–609

Kangasharju A (2000) Regional variations in firm formation: Panel and cross-section data evidence from Finland. *Papers in Regional Science* 79: 355–373. CrossRef.

Kim PH, Aldrich HE, Keister LA (2006) Access (not) denied: The impact of financial, human, and cultural capital on entrepreneurial entry in the United States. *Small Business Economics* 27: 5–22. CrossRef.

Krugman P (1991) Increasing returns and economic geography. *Journal of Political Economy* 99: 483–499. CrossRef.

Lee SY, Florida R, Acs ZJ (2004) Creativity and entrepreneurship: A regional analysis of new firm formation. *Regional Studies* 38: 879–891. CrossRef.

LeSage J, Pace RK (2009) *Introduction to spatial econometrics*. CRC Press, Boca Raton, FL, US. CrossRef.

Michelacci C, Silva O (2007) Why so many local entrepreneurs. *Review of Economics and Statistics* 89: 615–633. CrossRef.

Morelix A, Reedy EJ, Fairlie RW, Russell J (2016) The Kauffman index: Startup activity state trends. Ewing Marion Kauffman Foundation, Kansas City, MO, US. http://www.kauffman.org/~/media/kauffman_org/microsites/kauffman_index/-startup_activity_2016/kauffman_index_startup_activity_state_trends_2016.pdf

NBER (2009) US business cycle expansions and contractions. http://www.nber.org/-cycles/cyclesmain.html

Parajuli J, Haynes KE (2017) An exploratory analysis of new firm formation in New England. In: Lombard J, Stern E, Clarke G (eds), *Applied Spatial Modelling and Planning*. Routledge, Abingdon, UK, 17–32

Renski H (2009) New firm entry, survival, and growth in the United States. *Journal of the American Planning Association* 75: 60–77. CrossRef.

Reynolds PD, Miller B, Maki WR (1995) Explaining regional variation in business births and deaths: U.S. 1976-88. *Small Business Economics* 7: 389–407. CrossRef.

Reynolds PD, Storey DJ, Westhead P (1994) Cross-national comparisons of the variation in new firm formation rates. *Regional Studies* 28: 443–456. CrossRef.

Ritsila J, Tervo H (2002) Effects of unemployment on new firm formation: Micro-level panel data evidence from Finland. *Small Business Economics* 19: 31–40. CrossRef.

Robinson MJ, Cottrell TJ (2007) Investment patterns of informal investors in the Alberta private equity market. *Journal of Small Business Management* 45: 47–67. CrossRef.

Robinson PB, Sexton EA (1994) The effect of education and experience on self-employment success. *Journal of Business Venturing* 9: 141–156. CrossRef.

Schramm CJ (2004) Building entrepreneurial economies. *Foreign Affairs* 83: 104–115. CrossRef.

Storey DJ (1991) The birth of new firms: Does unemployment matter? A review of the evidence. *Small Business Economics* 3: 167–178. CrossRef.

Sutaria V, Hicks DA (2004) New firm formation: Dynamics and determinants. *Annals of Regional Science* 38: 241–262. CrossRef.

REGION   The Journal of ERSA

Powered by WU

Volume 4, Number 3, 2017, 77–86
DOI: 10.18335/region.v4i3.169

journal homepage: region.ersa.org

Urban Concentration and Spatial Allocation of Rents from natural resources. A Zipf's Curve Approach

Tomaz Ponce Dentinho[1]

[1] University of Azores, Azores, Portugal

Received: 17 October 2016/Accepted: 18 May 2017

Abstract. This paper aims at demonstrating how countries' dependency on natural resources plays a crucial role in urban concentration. The Zipf curve elasticity is estimated for a group of countries and related to a set of indicators of unilateral transferences. Results show that in comparison to others, countries with higher urban concentration explained by higher Zipf curve elasticity have a higher percentage of income coming from natural resources and education expenditures whereas public spending in health and net outflow of foreign direct investment seem to have spatial redistribution effects. Summing up, there are signs that the spatial allocation of property rights over natural resources and related rents influences urban concentration.

Key words: Urban concentration; Zipf Curve; Natural Resources; Rents

1 Introduction

Globally, more people live in urban areas than in rural areas and the world's fastest growing cities are located in Africa and Asia (United Nations 2014), these being increasingly connected to the complex constellation of the "New Urban World" (Kourtit, Nijkamp 2013). Notwithstanding this, urban concentration in the developing world is not necessarily a good thing and neither is it unmanageable. On the one hand, urban concentration can generate congestion, environmental disturbances and social problems that are difficult to address with reduced resources. On the other hand, urban concentration does not happen only due to global and undifferentiated factors, but may relate to manageable causes such as unilateral transferences between regions.

The 'New Urban World' is certainly interacting through competition, collaboration, exploitation and help. Actually, unilateral transferences between regions can occur when the rents from natural resources, distributed across the territory, go to the regions and places where their owners receive them. Permanent governmental transferences happen when taxes collected across the territory go to capital cities and to border areas where public services tend to be relatively more concentrated. Migrant remittances persist throughout time between immigrant places and emigrant localities. This is part of the migrant strategy that transfers a portion of their income to the areas where their families live. Finally, investment flows may lead also to spatial distribution of income. All of these unilateral and quite enduring transferences create persistent multiplier effects that accumulate in an uneven concentration of production and expenditure, employment and population, tradable and non-tradable activities.

Unilateral transferences between regions and the multiplier income effects associated with them explain why the spatial distribution of production may not be the same as the spatial distribution of expenditure. Therefore, it is not accurate to look at local and regional development and to the concomitant effects of urban concentration and rural desertification without taking into account unilateral transferences between places and regions.

In fact, the spatial allocation of rents of natural resources depends on the spatial distribution of property rights over natural resources and not on the territorial distribution of those resources. Due to the spatial distribution of property rights and the distribution of territorial resources being different, it is quite likely that permanent unilateral transferences occur and that dependent and exploited regions are created and maintained. Dependent regions are those, usually in the centre or at the territorial borders, who receive permanent transferences to obtain and secure the rents of territorial property rights. Exploited regions are those deprived from the rents of their territory (Dentinho 2012, 2017). The isolated estate of Von Thünen (1826) is a crucial reference if one wants to understand this, given that the author highlighted the creation of land rents, leaving the rent distribution implicit in the model. In the Von Thünen model, land rents go from territorial managers located in peripheral rings to the land owners located in the city centre; there the received rents generate income multiplier effects as thought by François Quesnay (1758). In the end, land ownership and rent distribution constitute crucial elements for urban concentration, regional development and, with free migration.

In extreme cases, one whole country can be concentrated into just one major city receiving the rents from a territory with much smaller localities. But in theory and in reality the hierarchy of cities is quite resilient as it is showed by Gibrat's Law (1931) and by the Zipf law (1949), which states that the second largest city is half the size of the biggest, the third largest city is a third the size of the biggest, and so on. As said by Gabaix (1999) this means that the probability of the size of a city being greater than some limit S is proportional to $1/S$: P (size> S)= C/S^{μ}; where $\mu = 1$ and $C =$ Constant.

There are many applications of Zipf's estimates focusing on the population of cities, dimension of companies, webpage popularity, impact of tornados and earthquakes as well as a few other phenomena (Pinto et al. 2012). In an application to the Chinese cities (Anderson, Ying 2005) it is concluded that cities tend to stay in the same position in the ranking and that the lognormal distribution explains the ranking profile better than the Pareto distribution. Jiang et al. (2015) tested the stability of the Pareto coefficient for truncated series of cities in China. Black, Henderson (2003) work on United States Cities found out that there is a concentration in service cities. Bosker et al. (2008) looked at the evolution of German cities from 1925 until 1999 and proved that, besides the enormous shocks caused by the economic crises of the thirties, world war II, the cold war and the fall of the Berlin Wall, there are increasing returns on scale for city growth. In an application to South Africa (Morudu 2016) it was suggested that the Zipf curve could be used to estimate the population of cities for a determined year where census data is not available.

It is also common to find in the literature theoretical analysis of the Zipf curve. Cristelli et al. (2012) demonstrate that truncated series of city population influences the estimates of Zipf coefficients. Along with the work of Anderson, Ying (2005), Benguigui, Blumenfeld-Lieberthal (2007) argue that the Zipf curve can be concave, linear or convex depending on the country. Peng (2010)Peng (2010) proves that the shape of the Zipf curve relates to the development of the network of cities in China. Cordoba (2008) shows that the profile of the Zipf curve comes from the regularity of the growth process across cities. Many authors test the validity of different distributions to explain the population size of the cities (Loannides, Overman 2003, Nitsch 2005, Newman 2005, Giesen et al. 2010, Gómez-Déniz et al. 2014, Gómez-Déniz, Calderín-Ojeda 2015, Shujuan 2016, Luckstead, Devadoss 2017).

Finally, there are many attempts to explain the regularity of the hierarchy of cities. Ades, Glaeser (1995) found that political factors do influence urban concentration and that dictatorships occur in central cities that are, on average, 50% larger than democratic countries of similar size. Krugman (1996) suggests that nature is also hierarchical in river basins and that cities rooted in natural capital have also a string hierarchy. Eaton,

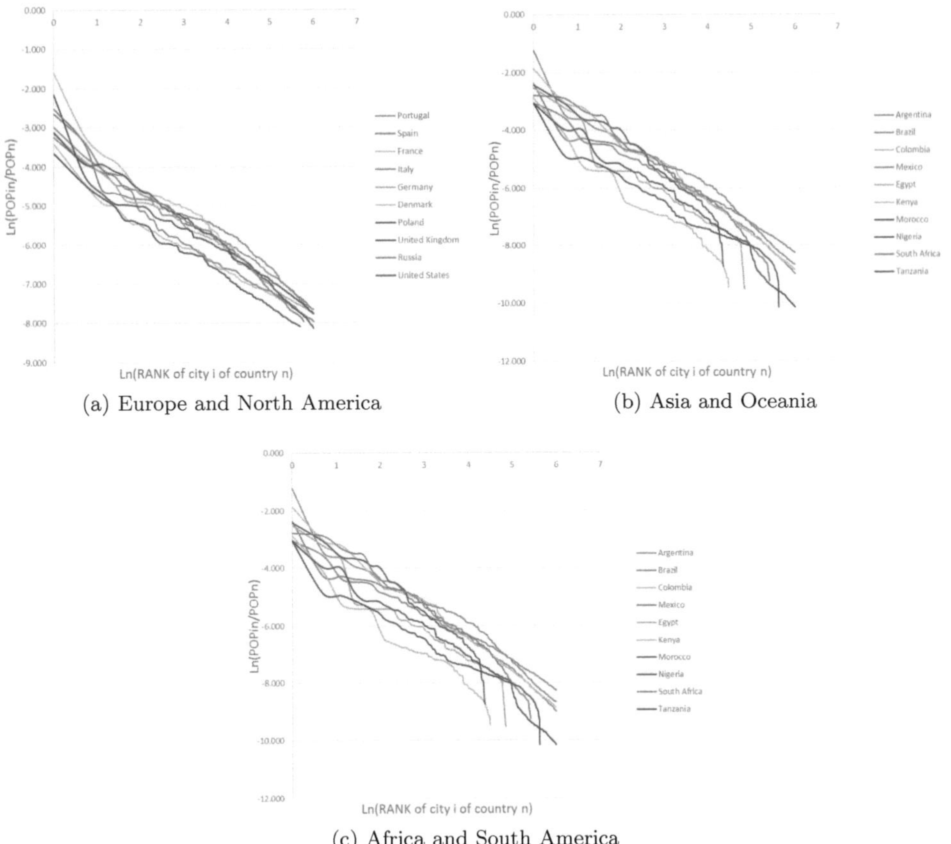

(a) Europe and North America

(b) Asia and Oceania

(c) Africa and South America

Figure 1: Zipf 's curve by Country

Eckstein (1997) relate the hierarchy to intercity migration. Gabaix (1999) connects the Zipf law with relative city growth and points out that parameter $\mu = 1$ does not change much with the age of the city network. Axtell, Florida (2001) reconcile the tension between centripetal and centrifugal forces. Duranton (2002) links the city hierarchy with a set of indicators related to innovation. Córdoba (2003) shows that the Zipf law happens when there is a similar growth path between cities. Giesen, Suedekum (2014) find that older cities tend to be larger than new ones. There is interesting literature linking urban concentration to economic growth (Bertinelli, Strobl 2007) where there is an optimal level of urban concentration that can be influenced by policy makers (Henderson 2003, Brülhart, Sbergami 2009). Kourtit, Nijkamp (2013) report that recently major cities, beyond being the engine for growth, show a rapid population rise while smaller ones shrink and can even fall below a critical sustainable population level. To my knowledge, there is not an analysis relating urban concentration to the distribution of rents from natural resources and other unilateral transfers although they very much reveal the institutional context of the territory that Ades, Glaeser (1995) tried to relate to the hierarchy of cities.

The aim of this paper is to look into urban concentration to test the hypothesis that the spatial allocation of rents from natural resources and other unilateral transferences do have a role in urban concentration. Section 2 presents the estimates of the Zipf elasticity for various countries. Section 3 links the estimated elasticity with the features of those countries and to unilateral transferences. Finally in Section 4 the discussion is based on the relation between spatial allocation of property rights and urban concentration.

2   Zipf's Law and the level of Urban Concentration

Data of city population by country was obtained from the site http://worldpopulation-review.com/countries/. The population of each city (Pop_i) was divided by the total

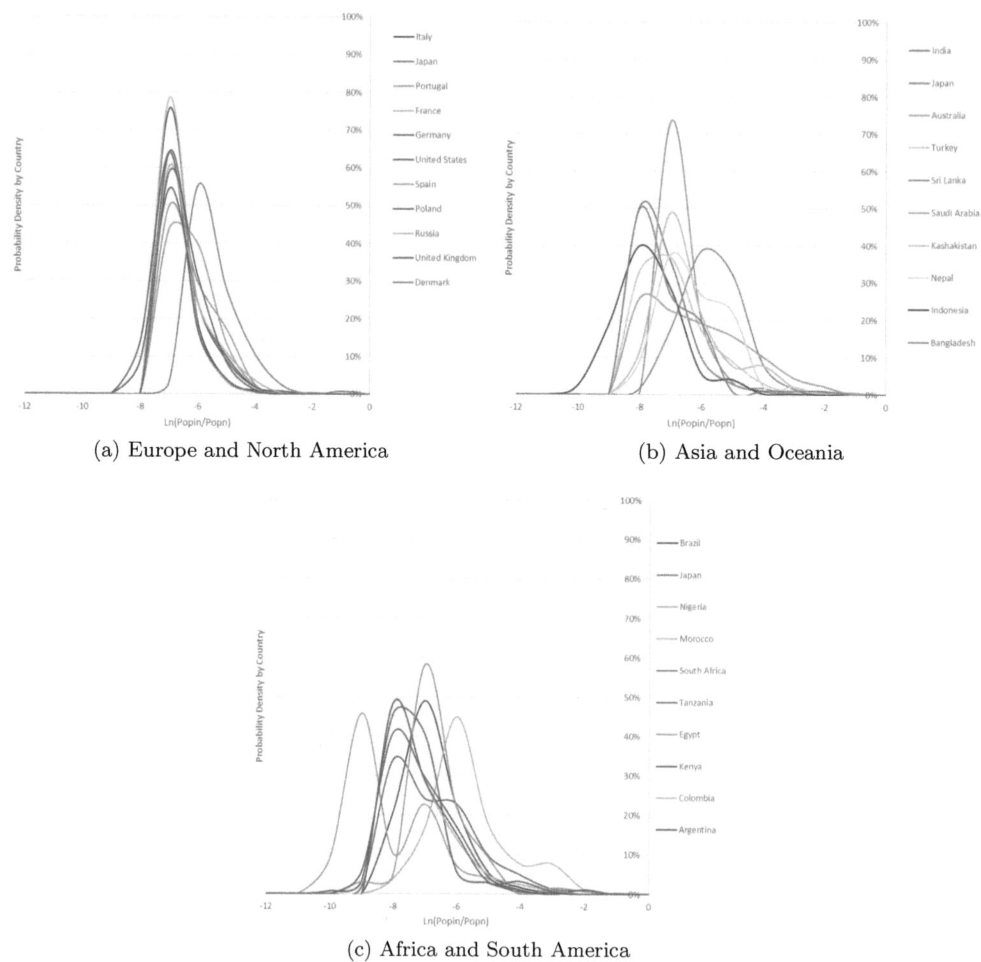

Figure 2: Kernel Density of the Logarithm of the Relative Size of the Cities by Country

population of the country (Pop) obtaining the weight of each city in the total population of the country. Then the coefficient of the Zipf curves by Country (μ) (Figure 1) was estimated regressing the logarithm of the weight of the city population with the logarithm of the rank order of the city (Equation 1).

$$\ln\left(\frac{Pop_i}{Pop}\right) = C - \mu r_i \qquad \text{for } n \text{ countries} \tag{1}$$

The Zipf curves for European and North American countries show, with the exception of Russia, lower slopes than in other parts of the world. Nevertheless, there are countries, like the United Kingdom or Denmark, where the major city reduces the importance of the following ones. In other countries, a set of major cities reduces the weight of those who are next in the hierarchy, this being the case of Russia and Spain. Finally, the middle part of the curves do not show a very monotonous profile, which may indicate the existence of unilateral transferences also involving middle ranked cities, with this appearing to be more relevant in the United States and Italy. The Zipf curves for Asian and Oceania countries show tails in the distribution of cities indicating that parts of the countries are very depopulated due to mountain areas (Pakistan and Nepal), ocean archipelagos (Japan and Indonesia) or by long lasting conflicts (Sri Lanka). On the other hand, research rich countries have higher concentrations of their resource rents in major cities (Saudi Arabia, Kazakhstan). The Zipf curves for Africa and South American countries also show tails associated to remote areas, mainly in African countries (Kenya, Morocco, Egypt, Nigeria, South Africa and Tanzania), and also in countries from South America (Argentina, Brazil, Colombia and Mexico) with a larger concentration of population in major towns.

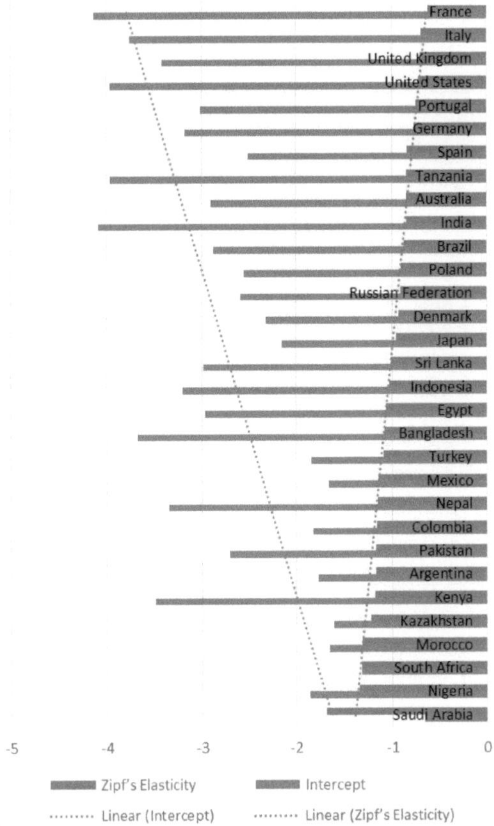

Figure 3: Zipf 's elasticity and intercept by country

Figure 2 shows the kernel densities of the logarithm of the relative size of the cities by country. Looking closer it is possible to identify various groups of countries. The countries in Europe and North America present very similar Pareto type distributions with more cities in the lower ranks of the distribution. For smaller countries close to bigger ones, like Denmark and somehow Portugal, there is a shift to smaller cities in the distribution. The distributions for countries in Asia, Oceania, Africa and South America are quite different from each other. Some Asian countries like India, Bangladesh and Australia behave like European and North American countries. A second group of countries do not have a mode in the cities with lower size; this happens with countries that have some remote and small cities like Brazil, the United States, Japan, Morocco, South Africa, Tanzania, Sri Lanka, Kazakhstan, Pakistan, Nepal, Poland and Indonesia. Finally, there are countries with two modes in the distribution of city sizes showing that the first cities emptied the second ones; this is the case of Nigeria, Turkey, Egypt, Kenya, Colombia, Mexico and Argentina.

The estimates of the Zipf curves by country are presented in Figure 3. As expected the intercept (C) increases when the Zipf coefficient (μ) decreases. Countries that do not match this expectable rule are the ones that have a reduced sample of cities: Tanzania, India, Bangladesh, Nepal, Kenya and Saudi Arabia.

Results in Figure 2 show that, although the value expected for the Zipf coefficient in the literature $(\mu = 1)$ is the average estimate, there are quite significant differences between more concentrated countries like Saudi Arabia $(\mu = -1.698)$ and more decentralized countries such as France $(\mu = -0.634)$.

If people can migrate from less affluent to more affluent places, the expected value of the Zipf elasticity is around 1, as proved by (Gabaix 1999). For values of the Zipf elasticity higher than 1 there is a concentration of the population in the bigger cities whereas for values lower than that threshold there is a distribution of the population in the smaller cities. This paper attempts to find out if the spatial allocation of rents from natural resources and from other unilateral regional transferences (private and public)

Table 1: Estimated Zipf curves coefficients and data on unilateral transferences (World Bank 2010)

Country name	Number of cities	Intercept	Zipf's elasticity	Total natural resources rents[1]	Public health expenditure[1]	Adjusted savings: Education expenditure[1]	FDI, net outflows[1]	Workers' remittances[1]
Saudi Arabia	89	-0.671***	-1.698***	53.73	2.7	7.186	0.867	0.05
Nigeria	400	-1.868***	-1.352***	32.56	1.92	0.850	0.465	5.1
South Africa	223	-1.327***	-1.326***	4.62	3.94	5.434	-0.044	0.31
Morocco	78	-1.661***	-1.317***	2.61	1.97	5.201	0.639	7.07
Kazakhstan	192	-1.614***	-1.230***	27.60	2.55	4.413	5.294	0.2
Kenya	88	-3.482***	-1.182***	1.33	2.11	5.916	0.005	5.52
Argentina	400	-1.778***	-1.178***	6.07	4.42	6.010	0.262	0.17
Pakistan	400	-2.703***	-1.173***	3.92	0.84	1.565	0.027	5.48
Colombia	400	-1.833***	-1.165***	7.86	5.52	3.907	2.272	1.41
Nepal	45	-3.341***	-1.162***	3.39	1.83	4.202	0.000	21.66
Mexico	400	-1.664***	-1.147***	7.29	3.09	4.798	1.310	2.13
Turkey	400	-1.846***	-1.099***	0.45	5.07	2.644	0.200	0.12
Bangladesh	98	-3.673***	-1.089***	3.28	1.17	1.811	0.000	10.81
Egypt	127	-2.968***	-1.073***	10.13	1.74	4.411	0.537	3.53
Indonesia	385	-3.202***	-1.037***	5.95	1.28	4.328	0.376	0.98
Sri Lanka	62	-2.984***	-1.017***	0.50	1.32	1.744	0.086	8.38
Japan	514	-2.149***	-0.962***	0.03	7.83	3.185	1043	0.03
Denmark	130	-2.317***	-0.937***	2.13	9.71	7.278	1.06	0.2
Russian Fed.	319	-2.591***	-0.914***	19.90	3.15	3.544	3.531	0.35
Poland	400	-2.557***	-0.907***	0.98	5.42	4.869	1.177	1.62
Brazil	400	-2.876***	-0.882***	5.30	4.24	5.162	0.541	0.19
India	200	-4.086***	-0.857***	4.04	1.18	3.082	0.781	3.21
Australia	400	-2.900***	-0.852***	8.31	5.93	4.536	2.167	0.43
Tanzania	275	-3.956***	-0.852***	6.78	4.05	2.393	0.000	0.11
Spain	400	-2.513***	-0.842***	0.06	6.95	4.210	2.710	0.76
Germany	400	-3.175***	-0.771***	0.12	8.97	4.394	3.392	0.35
Portugal	355	-3.013***	-0.759***	0.33	7.50	4.937	-3.211	1.56
USA	295	-3.954***	-0.730***	1.00	9.49	4.789	2.432	0.04
UK	400	-3.413***	-0.712***	1.49	8.08	5.054	1.320	0.33
Italy	400	-3.755***	-0.699***	0.17	7.4	4.411	1.595	0.33
France	400	-4.127***	-0.634***	0.07	9.25	5.053	3.311	0.61

Notes: [1]In percent of GNI

has a role in the urban concentration profile represented by the Zipf coefficient.

3   Zipf's Law and the level of Urban Concentration

To answer this question the positive value of the Zipf elasticity for each country is regressed against different variables that relate to unilateral income transferences (Data in Table 1):

1. The Total natural resources rents as a percentage of gross national income;

2. Public heath expenditure as a percentage of gross national income.

3. Adjusted savings: education expenditure as a percentage of gross national income.

4. Net outflows of foreign direct investment as a percentage of gross national income;

5. Workers remittances also as a percentage of gross national income;

The gross national income per capita was included in the model and provided significant results as indicated by Pinto et al. (2012). Nevertheless, there were problems of colinearity with the public health expenditure and it is more informative for the present exercise

Table 2: Correlation between dependent and independent variables

	Zipf's elasticity	Total natural resources rents	Public health expenditure	Adjusted savings: Education expenditure[2]	FDI, net outflows	Workers' remittances
Zipf's elasticity	1.00	-0.65	0.64	-0.05	0.18	-0.26
Total natural resources rents	-0.65	1.00	-0.35	0.08	0.19	-0.10
Public health expenditure	0.64	-0.35	1.00	0.38	0.28	-0.51
Adjusted savings: Education expenditure (% of GNI)	-0.05	0.08	0.38	1.00	0.10	-0.30
FDI, net outflows	0.18	0.19	0.28	0.10	1.00	-0.32
Workers' remittances	-0.26	-0.10	-0.51	-0.30	-0.32	1.00

Notes: [2]In percent of GNI

Table 3: Linear regression to explain the Zipf curve elasticity by country

	Model 1		Model 2		Model 3		Model 4		Model 5	
	Coef.	Sig.	Coef.	Sig.	Coef.	Sig.	Coef.	Sig.	Coef.	Sig.
Adj R^2		0.406		0.591		0.628		0.634		0.629
F		21.51		22.67		17.88		14.02		11.19
Intercept	0.923	0.000	1.121	0.000	1.014	0.000	1.017	0.000	0.967	0.000
Total natural resources rents[3]	0.013	0.000	0.010	0.001	0.009	0.002	0.010	0.001	0.010	0.001
Public Health expenditure[3]			-0.038	0.001	-0.048	0.000	-0.042	0.001	-0.037	0.010
Adjusted savings: Education expenditure[3]					0.037	0.062	0.035	0.079	0.036	0.074
FDI nct outflows[3]							-0.023	0.234	-0.021	0.280
Workers' remittances[3]									0.008	0.428

Notes: [3]In percent of GNI

to relate urban concentration with the spatial distribution of public spending than with the income level of the country. Table 2 presents the correlation between dependent and independent variables that indicates the strong positive correlation between the Zipf elasticity and the total natural resources rents and the strong negative correlation between the Zipf elasticity and the public health expenditures also slightly correlated with Workers' remittances.

Table 3 presents the estimated parameters of linear models that relate the urban concentration by country assessed by the Zipf elasticity with a set of unilateral transferences by country. Results are quite interesting:

First, the Percentage on the GNI of the Total Natural Resource Rents has a positive, significant and consistent relation with the Zipf city elasticity by country. Each percent point of the Total natural resources rents on the GDP increases the Zipf city elasticity by around 0.010. In other words, assuming that natural resources are distributed across the territory, bigger cities seem to own the property rights over natural resources across the territory and, through the multiplier effects of those rents, it increases their weight in the country population. That is why countries like Saudi Arabia, Nigeria and Kazakhstan – with higher percentage of the rents of natural resources on the total GNI – attract more population to the bigger city.

Second, the percentage of public health expenditure in the gross national income has a spatial distributive effect that is consistent across the various regressions with a quite robust coefficient that varies around 0.038. Interestingly the percentage of the "Adjusted savings: Education expenditure" in the gross national income has an urban concentration effect of the same scale on the distributive effect of public health spending.

Third, although not significant, countries that are net exporters of foreign direct investment tend to have less urban concentration, indicating somehow that investment that goes outside goes also inside the country.

Finally, the Percentage on the GNI of the Workers Remittances has no robust effect in the urban concentration of the country. Furthermore as shown in Table 2, this is very much correlated with public health expenditures limiting the capacity of the results of Model 5. The attempt was to know if there was an indication that migrants in other countries tend either to secure population in smaller cities by sending remittances to their families that reside in those areas, or to invest their savings in more urbanized areas. A more profound analysis of differences between countries could be analyzed.

4 Discussion

The hypothesis tested in this exercise is quite simple: the spatial allocation of property rights over territorial resources has strong effects on the spatial profile of the urban network through the multiplier effects of income associated with rents from natural resources that goes from the places where those resources are located to the places of residence of their owners. The test relates the urban concentration of each country, assessed by the elasticity of the respective Zipf curve, with the percentage of income coming from the rents of natural resources.

Results confirm what Ades, Glaeser (1995) said: Institutions, namely those created by the spatial distribution of property rights over natural resources and by the geographical allocation of public spending, do have a role in the urban concentration throughout space. Furthermore, since huge amounts of rents from natural resources come from land, it is obvious, also from the research presented in this essay, that the main driver of major cities is Real Estate as justified by Castells (2012). To some extend we confirm the old intuition of the Von Thünen model that assumed that land rents go from territorial managers located in peripheral rings to the landowners located in the city centre where rents generate income multiplier effects as envisaged by Quesnay (1758). Regarding the Duranton (2002) argument, namely that urban concentration and innovation go with each other; the present exercise raises the question whether public spending in education that seems to have strong effects on urban concentration stimulates such processes. Even more when urban concentration becomes the engine for growth as noted by Kourtit, Nijkamp (2013).

Furthermore, the analysis of data in point 2 has connections with the contributions of Loannides, Overman (2003), Nitsch (2005), Newman (2005), Giesen et al. (2010), Gómez-Déniz et al. (2014), Gómez-Déniz, Calderín-Ojeda (2015), Shujuan (2016), Luckstead, Devadoss (2017), that tried to find the best distributions to fit better the frequency of cities by size. Actually, although deserving further attention in future works, point 2 shows that Pareto distributions seem to fit most countries of the sample, Log normal distributions are better for countries with remote and small cities and a combination of distributions are the outcome of situations when first cities empty second ones.

Finally, this study confirms that truncated data may lead to strange results as it is demonstrated by Jiang et al. (2015) and Cristelli et al. (2012), as for countries with less number of recorded cities, the Zipf elasticity and Intercept do not seem to be interrelated (see Figure 3).

5 Conclusion

The motivation of this paper is to understand what are the effects in urban concentration of the spatial distribution of rents from natural resources and other unilateral transferences. The methodology used assessed the relation between the Zipf curve elasticity by country and indicators of unilateral transferences by country such as the percentage of the rents from natural resources on the national product, the percentage of education and health expenditures on the national product, the percentages of the net FDI outflows on the national product and the percentage of workers' remittances on the national product.

Results show that the ownership over natural resources and the spatial distribution of its rents are decisive factors for urban concentration and regional development. Furthermore, when resource rich countries do not consider this, they miss adopting adequate policies of spatial allocation of unilateral transferences. Even education policy has a concentration effect. In future work the location of the cities that are more distant from the estimated Zipf curve requires further attention to look into the factors of spatial justice.

References

Ades A, Glaeser E (1995) Trade and circuses: Explaining urban giants. *Quarterly Journal of Economics* 110: 195–228. CrossRef.

Anderson GT, Ying G (2005) The size distribution of Chinese cities. *Regional Science and Urban Economics* 35[2005]: 756–776. CrossRef.

Axtell R, Florida R (2001) Emergent cities: A microeconomic explanation of Zipf's law. Paper presents at the Society for Computational Economics, Yale University

Benguigui L, Blumenfeld-Lieberthal E (2007) Beyond the power law – A new approach to analyze city size distributions. *Computers, Environment and Urban Systems* 31: 648–666. CrossRef.

Bertinelli L, Strobl E (2007) Urbanisation, urban concentration and economic development. *Urban Studies* 44[13]: 2499–2510. CrossRef.

Black D, Henderson V (2003) Urban evolution in the USA. *Journal of Economic Geography* 4: 343–372. CrossRef.

Bosker M, Brakman S, Garretsen H, Schramm M (2008) A century of shocks: The evolution of the German city size distribution 1925-1999. *Regional Science and Urban Economics* 38: 330–347. CrossRef.

Brülhart M, Sbergami F (2009) Agglomeration and growth: Cross-country evidence. *Journal of Urban Economics* 65: 48–63. CrossRef.

Castells M (2012) *Networks of Outrage and Hope. Social Movements in the Internet Age.* Polity Press, Cambridge, MA

Cordoba J (2008) On the distribution of city sizes. *Journal of Urban Economics* 63: 177–197

Córdoba JC (2003) On the distribution of city sizes. working paper, Rice University

Cristelli M, Batty M, Pietronero L (2012) There is more than a Power law in Zipf. *Scientific Reports* 2[1]. CrossRef.

Dentinho TP (2012) New challenges for sustainable growth. In: Capello R, Dentinho TP (eds), *Networks, Space and Competitiveness. Evolving Challenges for Sustainable Growth.* Edward Elgar, Cheltenham, 276–290. CrossRef.

Dentinho TP (2017) Regional development and migration in the lower basin of the Zambezi river. The importance of property rights. *Socio-Economic Planning Sciences* 58: 87–102. CrossRef.

Duranton G (2002) City size distribution as a consequence of the growth process. Department of Geography and Environment, London School of Economics

Eaton J, Eckstein Z (1997) Cities and growth: theory and evidence from France and Japan. *Regional Science and Urban Economics* 27: 443–474. CrossRef.

Gabaix X (1999) Zipf's law for cities: An explanation. *The Quarterly Journal of Economics* 114[3]: 739–767. CrossRef.

Gibrat R (1931) Les inégalités economiques. Librairie du Receuil Sirey, Paris, France

Giesen K, Suedekum J (2014) City age and city size. *European Economic Review* 71: 93–208. CrossRef.

Giesen K, Zimmermann A, Suedekum J (2010) The size distribution across all cities – Double Pareto lognormal strikes. *Journal of Urban Economics* 68: 129–137. CrossRef.

Gómez-Déniz E, Calderín-Ojeda E (2015) On the use of the Pareto ArcTan distribution for describing city size in Australia and New Zealand. *Physica A: Statistical Mechanics and its Applications* 436: 821–832. CrossRef.

Gómez-Déniz E, Sordo MA, Calderín-Ojeda E (2014) The Log-Lindley distribution as an alternative to the beta regression model with applications in insurance. *Insurance: Mathematics and Economics* 54: 49–57. CrossRef.

Henderson JV (2003) The urbanization process and economic growth: The so-what question. *Journal of Economic Growth* 8: 47–71. CrossRef.

Jiang B, Yin J, Liu Q (2015) Zipf's law for all the natural cities around the world. *International Journal of Geographical Information Science* 29[3]: 498–522. CrossRef.

Kourtit K, Nijkamp P (2013) The "New Urban World" – the challenge of cities in decline. *Romanian Journal of Regional Science (Special Issue on the New Urban World)* 7: 10–28

Krugman P (1996) Confronting the mystery of urban hierarchy. *Journal of the Japanese and the International Economies* 10: 399–418. CrossRef.

Loannides YM, Overman HG (2003) Zipf's law for cities: an empirical examination. *Regional Science and Urban Economics* 33: 127–137. CrossRef.

Luckstead J, Devadoss S (2017) Pareto tails and lognormal body of US cities size distribution. *Physica A: Statistical Mechanics and its Applications* 465[Supplement C]: 573–578. CrossRef.

Morudu HD (2016) Developing annual population and gross domestic product estimates for local municipality development models in South Africa: Applications of Zipf's rule from 2001 to 2013. *South African Geographical Journal* 98[2]: 367–385. CrossRef.

Newman MEJ (2005) Power laws, Pareto distributions and Zipf's law. *Contemporary Physics* 46[5]: 323–351. CrossRef.

Nitsch V (2005) Zipf zipped. *Journal of Urban Economics* 57: 86–100. CrossRef.

Peng G (2010) Zipf's law for Chinese cities: Rolling sample regressions. *Physica A: Statistical Mechanics and its Applications* 389[18]: 3804–3813. CrossRef.

Pinto CMA, Lopes AML, Machado JAT (2012) A review of power laws in real life phenomena. *Commun Nonlinear Sci Numer Simulat* 17: 3558–3578. CrossRef.

Quesnay F (1758) O Quadro Económico. Fundação Calouste Gulbenkian, Lisboa

Shujuan L (2016) Rank-size distributions of Chinese cities: macro and micro patterns. *Chinese Geographical Science* 26[5]: 577–588. CrossRef.

United Nations (2014) World Urbanization Prospects: The 2014 Revision, Highlights. (ST/ESA/SER.A/352) Department of Economic and Social Affairs, Population Division

Von Thünen J (1826) *Der Isolierte Staat in Bezienhung auf Landwirtschaft und Na-tionalökonomie.* Pergamon Press, Oxford. Translated to English by C.M. Wartenberg as "Von Thünen's Isolated State", 1966

World Bank (2010) World Bank Open Data. https://data.worldbank.org/

Zipf GK (1949) *Human Behavior and the Principle of Least Effort.* Addison-Wesley, Cambridge, MA

Volume 4, Number 1, 2017, 129–146
DOI: 10.18335/region.v4i1.146

journal homepage: region.ersa.org

Regional Public Stock Reductions in Spain: Estimations from a Multiregional Spatial Vector Autorregressive Model

Miguel A Márquez[1], Julian Ramajo[2], Geoffrey J D Hewings[3]

[1] University of Extremadura, Badajoz, Spain (email: mmarquez@unex.es)
[2] University of Extremadura, Badajoz, Spain (email: ramajo@unex.es)
[3] University of Illinois Urbana-Champaign, Urbana-Champaign, IL, USA (email: hewings@illinois.edu)

Received: 21 July 2016/Accepted: 12 May 2017

Abstract. The estimation of the impact of public investment on regional economic growth requires consideration of the spatio-temporal dynamics among the state variables of each region. According to recent data, public investment in Spain has fallen in recent years, and in some regions the reduction has been so severe that public investment has not been able to replenish depreciated capital. Recent austerity policies in Spain that feature temporary decreases in the accumulation of regional public capital should thus be evaluated in terms of their impact on the economy as a whole and on specific regions together with the spillover effects from one region to the rest of the regional system. This paper uses a multiregional integrated specification to model interdependencies across regions; our results indicate that while global decreases in public investment have a homogeneously negative effect on the output of all Spanish regions, these regions portray heterogeneous responses from localized public capital stock reductions over the simulation period considered.

Key words: Regional investment; Public capital stock; Spillovers; Multiregional; Spatial econometrics; Vector autoregressions; Spain

1 Introduction

The international financial and economic crisis has had a major impact on European national budgets with European governments now increasingly trying to rebalance budgets, in most cases, by considering substantial expenditure cuts to eliminate budget deficits. The regional impacts of these budget adjustments are unlikely to be spatially blind generating the possibility that they will exacerbate existing disparities in welfare. The impact of austerity measures on public capital stock needs to be evaluated carefully; restrictive fiscal measures will require the consideration of new strategies on the one hand, and on the other hand, the impacts that spending reductions will have on policies to stimulate economic growth. National governments need to consider how best to rationalize public investment, and new tools are necessary to guide and prioritize these investments. Most analysts agree that unless policies are refocused to take up the new challenges, GDP could potentially fall across many European countries. At the regional level, in the face of declining resources, nations will be forced to prioritize how and where they invest public funds across regional areas. In this context, it is necessary to develop and implement quantitative approaches to guide infrastructure development and this paper tries to make a contribution to the provision of strategic information. For example, from a welfare perspective, across the board cuts (i.e. public expenditures are reduced by a similar percentage in all regions) may have a different total impact from reductions that are targeted to specific programs or in specific regions – even though the total volume of expenditure cuts might be the same in both cases. The complexities of the spatial allocation and the manner in which spatial spillover effects move across the region system require formal analysis of the kind proposed in this paper[1].

It is well known that the empirical analysis of the aggregate effects of regional public capital provision requires spillover effects to be considered (see, for example, Boarnet 1998, Moreno, López-Bazo 2007). These spillover effects could play a key role in regional economic performance, since they can be inferred as externalities that could lead to increasing returns to scale. Indeed, public capital accumulated in one region can create additional growth potentials in other regions. In this paper, growth spillovers are understood to characterize a situation in which some of the growth in a region may be traced to the public investment in neighboring regions. Following Capello (2009), the transmission channels of the influences from changes in the capital stock in a single regional economy to the growth of neighboring regional economies (and vice versa) will be via trade linkages and market relationships. Further, it is expected that trade linkages will transmit either positive or negative effects.

In the literature, one can appeal to input-output based analyses such as the hypothetical extraction method of Dietzenbacher et al. (1993). More complete evaluations could be accomplished with a multiregional computable general equilibrium model, adopting a similar strategy but with the added benefit of being able to trace some of the economy-wide impacts of fiscal re-allocations and differential tax rates (see McGregor, Swales 2003). A third alternative, adopted in this paper, is to use a multiregional integrated spatial vector autoregressive model (see Ramajo et al. 2017) to capture both the short-run and longer-run impacts of significant changes in fiscal policy. None of these approaches by themselves would encompass all of the necessary perspectives to address the problems at hand, but together they offer a rich source of information for policy analysts. The present paper promotes the third approach as a complement to the other two (rather than as a substitute) with a particular focus on the evaluation of austerity measures.

According to a recent research (Serrano Martínez et al. 2017), public investment in Spain has fallen almost 60% since 2009 and in some regions the reduction has been so severe that it has not been able to replenish depreciated capital. As such, it would be very interesting to simulate the effects of a reduction in the public stock of infrastructures. This paper specifies a 'global' approach to assess how output in every Spanish region is affected by a reduction in the public capital stock of another specific Spanish region. Specifically, a multiregional integrated spatial vector autoregressive (MultiREG-SpVAR) model is applied that allows the investigation of spatio-temporal interdependencies across regions[2]. This model is used to assess the magnitude of both intra-regional (domestic) and inter-regional (spillover) effects of public infrastructure for the regions of Spain. Domestic effects are understood to be the effects derived from public capital installed in the region itself, while the spillover effects are those derived from public capital installed outside the region.

The rest of the paper is organized as follows. Section 2 briefly reviews some issues about both the domestic impact of public capital on regional economic growth and the

---

[1]Even here the full welfare effects will not be estimated; to provide a more complete accounting, embedding this type of analysis within a multiregional computable general equilibrium model would be necessary.

[2]The used model draws on the methodological contribution developed in Ramajo et al. (2017). The MultiREG-SpVAR model extends the traditional VAR models applied in the economics literature (see Kamps 2005) to assess the effects of public capital at aggregate national level. Thus, the proposed approach encompasses both the VAR methodology, that specifies the single-region temporal dynamics (see Márquez et al. 2011), the bi-regional VAR approach (see Márquez et al. 2010a), and the uni-regional Spatial VAR approach (Márquez et al. 2015), combining different region-specific VAR models in a global specification in which the state variables of each region are related to the state variables of the rest of the regions.

spillovers effects of this type of capital, providing the intuition behind the empirical findings. Section 3 exposes the econometric background behind the MultiREG-SpVAR specification. Section 4 describes the Spanish regional system, and presents the database. The empirical application in Section 5 estimates the domestic and spillover effects of public capital in the Spanish regional system, and a discussion of the main implications of the empirical results are provided. Finally, Section 6 provides some summary remarks.

2   Theoretical background

The effect of public-sector capital on economic growth has been a recurring issue in economics. Initiated the seminal article by Ratner (1983) more than three decades ago, this literature was further stimulated by Aschauer (1989), who hypothesized and tested the role of public infrastructure investment on productivity and produced the result that it had a substantial impact. Nevertheless, the posterior evidence was not homogeneous. To name only a few works, Lynde, Richmond (1992) and Morrison, Schwartz (1996) argued that public capital investments fosters economic growth, while the empirical work by Tatom (1991) and Holtz-Eakin (1994) among others found that public capital formation is not a robust determinant of private output; other authors like Seitz (1993) and Devarajan et al. (1996) found negative effects of public capital on economic growth.

There is a substantial literature in regional economics on the impact of public expenditure on regional economic growth (see, among others, Munnell 1990, Garcia-Mila et al. 1996, Sturm et al. 1998, Destefanis, Sena 2005). More recently, there is an emerging consensus in the literature about the positive impacts of public infrastructure on per-capita income and productivity in the private sector (see, for example, Henderson, Kumbhakar 2006, Cohen, Morrison Paul 2007, Heintz 2010), although the effects are not as large as Aschauer (1989)Aschauer (1989) suggested.

The review of the extensive literature by Romp, De Haan (2007) highlights different approaches used to estimate the effects of public capital on regional economic growth[3]: production functions, cost functions and VAR/VECM models. In a survey of the literature measuring the impact of public investment expenditure, De la Fuente (2010) focuses on studies estimating aggregate production functions or growth equations, concluding that the contribution of public infrastructure investment to productivity growth is significant. Within the cost function approach, the pioneering work of (Deno 1988) stimulated studies at the regional level (e.g. Seitz, Licht 1995, Morrison, Schwartz 1996); while the data requirements for this type of approach are greater than in the case of the production-function approach, the main advantage is that the cost-function approach is more flexible than the production-function approach.

Finally, among the main methods, the use of the VAR approach to test the significance of the dynamic effects of public capital on economic growth presents some advantages (Kamps 2005). Whereas other approaches assume a causal relationship running from the inputs to economic output, the VAR approach does not impose any causal links between the variables a priori[4]. The VAR approach, although atheoretical in nature, allows for the existence of indirect links between the variables under investigation. In addition, it provides the opportunity to test the number of long-run (cointegrating) relationships. Moreover, if the number of long-run (cointegrating) relationships are tested and estimated consistently, the vector error correction (VEC) models would produce consistent estimates of the impulse response functions. With respect to the empirical literature where the VAR methodology has been used to simulate the effects of unexpected changes in the public capital on macroeconomic variables, it is possible to find different contributions at both country and regional levels. Recently, for example, Hunt (2012) worked with a set of OECD countries, Deliktas et al. (2009) analyzed seven regions of Turkey and Roca-Sagalés, Sala (2006) investigated the effects of public capital using the VAR approach for seventeen Spanish regions. Much of the previous empirical work appears to posit the existence of cross-sectional independence, which is unlikely to be the case.

---

[3]Considering different perspectives, these authors systematized previous research about the role of public capital in economic growth.

[4]Therefore, we will provide report results estimates according to which endogeneity of regressors (particularly public capital) is not a problem.

Although the approach used in the present paper shares the same starting point with previous empirical work using the VAR approach, the present approach relates more closely in spirit to recent work in regional economic growth through its preoccupation with the problem of spatio-temporal dynamics (e.g. Márquez et al. 2010b). Clearly, the processes of regional economic growth intrinsically embrace space and time interactions. Even though the effects of public capital formation considering spatio-temporal interactions at the regional level have received increasing attention over recent years (for example, see Pereira, Roca-Sagalés 2003), past research on the impact of public capital on regional growth has mainly ignored two relevant challenges. First, it has not considered the estimation of the spillover effects of a reference region's public capital on the economic growth of any other region of the country. Secondly, there has been no attempt to integrate, in some fashion, the state variables of each region with the state variables of the rest of the regions to provide a global perspective that allows for the investigation of interdependencies across regions. Consequently, the resulting parameter estimates and statistical inference of the empirical work produced to date could be open to criticism. Tackling these two problems simultaneously will allow the quantification of the contribution to overall regional economic growth of the provision of public capital in a determined region, making available an important tool to assist in formulating economic policies.

To deal with these open questions, the approach used in the present paper is the confluence of the recent empirical literature on the effects of public capital using VAR models (consistent with the argument that the analysis of these effects requires the consideration of dynamic feedbacks among the different variables) with the new developments in macroeconometric modeling following the Global VAR approach proposed by Pesaran et al. (2004) and Dees et al. (2007). The multiregional integrated approach (Ramajo et al. 2017) will contemplate both the spatial and temporal growth output effects derived from public infrastructure at the regional level.

At the aggregate level, it is not easy to disentangle the effects of public expenditure on regional growth; it is especially difficult to identify the channels through which they operate. The economics literature (see among others Gramlich 1994, Romp, De Haan 2007) highlights different channels through which public investments influence economic growth. The first channel makes reference to the direct increased flow of output due to the accumulation or the stock of public capital over time. Other channels are connected to the effects derived from the interactions between public and private capital; namely, the direct effects on productivity of private production inputs, the crowding-out effect on private spending through financial mechanisms, and the complementary effect from private investment. Following Baxter, King (1993), the aforementioned channels could generate both short-run and long-run effects. These traditional effects operate at the same time as other effects emphasized by Agénor, Moreno-Dodson (2006): indirect effects on the productivity of workers, effects related to adjustment costs in both private capital formation and its mobility, effects connected to the creation of production facilities that encourage economic activities, effects derived from enhancing the durability of private capital, and effects resulting from the positive outcomes on growth coming from improvements in health and education. Hence, there are a variety of ways in which public capital could affect economic growth.

It is important to highlight that the presence of strong spatio-temporal dynamic interaction effects can alter the standard predictions about the macroeconomic implications of regional public investment. The shifts in public capital could lead to potential multiplier effects that induce dynamic responses on regional growth. In turn, these dynamic responses within a single regional economy can influence the growth of neighboring regional economies (Cheshire, Carbonaro 1996). Although different works provide arguments that consider spatial spillovers from public infrastructures (Holtz-Eakin, Schwartz 1995, Álvarez et al. 2006, Yu et al. 2013)(see among others, Holtz-Eakin and Schwartz, 1995; Alvarez et al., 2006; Yu et al., 2013), regional trade linkages occupy a relevant place among the different transmission channels of the effects of regional public capital expenditure on the growth of the regions integrating the regional economic system (Capello 2009). Following the methodological approaches presented in Márquez et al. (2010a), a distinction can be made between growth spillovers sent from a region to its trade-related neighboring regions (push-out effects) and growth spillovers received for a region from its trade-related neighboring regions (push-in effects). From a theoretical perspective, push-in and push-out effects could exert positive or negative influences on the growth of regional economies (Young 1991, Chung, Hewings 2015). Nevertheless, and according to the recent literature (see Melitz, Ottaviano 2008), one could expect that regional growth spillovers transmitted through trade linkages would have a positive effect on the growth of other regional economies in the short run; but the impact in the long-run may be ambiguous. Effectively, these growth spillovers could stimulate regional growth through, among other ways, increases in productivity derived from competitive pressures from trade, from learning-through-trade, and from enhanced access (lower cost, more reliable service etc.) to inputs, outputs and intermediates. Alternatively, trade can displace regional production and regional factor productions, leading to a negative effect on growth. Taken all together, it is clear that the empirical outcomes derived from the effects of regional public capital on the growth of trade-related regional economies can be mixed. All of these growth spillovers must be addressed in advocating and developing an alternative to current approaches to measuring and understanding what are the regional effects of public investment.

3   The Multiregional Spatial Vector Autoregressive (MultiREG-SpVAR) model[5]

To capture both the domestic and the spillover effects of public capital among the Spanish regions, a multiregional integrated spatial vector autoregressive model has been built following the Global VAR macroeconometric modeling approach proposed by Pesaran et al. (2004) and Dees et al. (2007).

In similar fashion to Global VAR models, our MultiREG-SpVAR specification provides a multi-location framework that allows the investigation of interdependencies across regions and is composed of individual models formulated by corresponding spatial VAR specifications (namely VAR models augmented by spatially-lagged variables) that are combined in a consistent manner. Each region is linked with the others in the regional system under study by including spatial lags in the econometric specification. In this way, all regions are potentially affected by developments in the other regions of the system. In this paper, the spatial lags have been constructed using spatial weights that are based on region-region trade flows as explained in Section 4.

Consider N regions, indexed by $i = 1, 2, \ldots, N$, then the Spatial VAR (SpVAR) model for each region i at time t $(t = 1, 2, \ldots, T)$ is formulated as follows:

$$
\begin{aligned}
\boldsymbol{x}_{it} = {} & \boldsymbol{\Lambda}_{0i} + \boldsymbol{\Lambda}_{1i} t + \boldsymbol{\Gamma}_{1i} \boldsymbol{x}_{i,t-1} + \ldots + \boldsymbol{\Gamma}_{p_i i} \boldsymbol{x}_{i,t-p_i} + \\
& \boldsymbol{\Phi}_{0i} \boldsymbol{x}_{it}^* + \boldsymbol{\Phi}_{0i} \boldsymbol{x}_{it}^* + \boldsymbol{\Phi}_{1i} \boldsymbol{x}_{it-1}^* + \ldots + \boldsymbol{\Phi}_{q_i i} \boldsymbol{x}_{it-q_i}^* + u_{it}
\end{aligned}
\tag{1}
$$

where $\boldsymbol{x}_{it}$ is the vector of internal state variables, $\boldsymbol{x}_{it}^*$ is a vector of external spatially-lagged variables that summarizes the state of the economy in the other regions (their components, $x_{g,it}^* = \sum_{j=1}^{N} w_{ij} x_{g,jt}$, are a weighted average of x_g in all regions except the ith, since, by convention, $x_{ii} = 0$), $\boldsymbol{t}$ is a vector of deterministic time trends, $\boldsymbol{\Lambda}_{jt}$ $(j = 0, 1)$, $\boldsymbol{\Gamma}_{ji}$ $(j = 1, 2, \ldots, p)$ and $\boldsymbol{\Phi}_{ji}$ $(j = 0, 1, 2, \ldots, q)$ are matrices of coefficients to be estimated, and u_{it} is a vector of disturbances assumed to be serially uncorrelated with a zero mean and a non-singular covariance matrix, $\boldsymbol{\Sigma}_{ii}$.

The first step in building the MultiREG-SpVAR model, each regional SpVAR model is estimated individually and then the individual models are stacked to yield a 'global' compact specification in terms of a vector containing all the endogenous variables of the regional system, $\boldsymbol{x}_t = (\boldsymbol{x}_{1t}', \boldsymbol{x}_{2t}', \ldots, \boldsymbol{x}_{Nt}')'$:

$$
\boldsymbol{x}_t = \boldsymbol{\Psi}_0 + \boldsymbol{\Psi}_1 t + \boldsymbol{F}_1 \boldsymbol{x}_{t-1} + \ldots + \boldsymbol{F}_r \boldsymbol{x}_{t-r} + \boldsymbol{e}_t
\tag{2}
$$

---

[5]This section draws on Ramajo et al. (2017), where a more detailed technical explanation of the underlying econometric modeling approach is made.

for appropriate matrices $\boldsymbol{\Psi}_j$ $(j = 0, 1)$ and $\boldsymbol{F}_k$ $(k = 0, 1, \ldots, r)$, with $r = \max(p_i, q_i)$, where there are no restrictions on the covariance matrix $\Sigma_e = Cov(e_t)$. This expression is the basis for the analysis of the dynamic properties of the multiregional mode.

Although the model allows consideration of the regional interdependencies and heterogeneity in the underlying dynamic process, analyzing within the regional system the response of every region to a temporary shock in a state variable of one specific region (for more details, see Ramajo et al. 2017), the model does not allow the quantification of the relevance of different channels for transmission of spillovers.

4 The Spanish regional system and the database

The database used consists of yearly time series over the period 1964-2003 for the Spanish Autonomous Communities[6]. The analysis of this specific period is the interest of the paper. The paper explores the space-time dimensions of this evolutionary period, and the Multireg-SpVAR model is appropriate to accomplish this. The Autonomous Communities of Spain have achieved the status of self-governed territories, sharing governance with the Spanish central government within their respective territories. Given the transfer of important economic responsibilities from the central government to the regional executives, the NUTS2 level of disaggregation in Spain is the most interesting level from a political economy perspective. Currently, almost one third (about 31%) of the regional investments are carried out by the autonomous communities, almost a quarter (about 24%) by the central government, with local corporations and other public entities accounting for the remaining 45%. Thus, both central government and regional authorities are able to decide how public expenditures are allocated.

For each region, the macroeconomic variables that compose the vector $\boldsymbol{x}_{it}$ are the following: gross value added, GVA, measured at basic prices in thousands of year 2000 constant euros; total employment (E), in thousands of employed persons; and private (KPR) and public (KPU) net capital stocks[7], in thousands of year 2000 constant euros. The regional series for GVA and E have been drawn from the $BD.MORES$ database (Bustos et al. 2008) and the time series for KPR and KPU have been taken from the $Fundación$ $BBVA$-$Ivie$ database (Mas et al. 2009)[8]. Some summary statistics of these variables for the seventeen Spanish regions are shown in Table 1 (for reasons of comparability, the figures in this table are percentage shares; however, all the calculations in the paper have been made with the original data in logarithmic terms).

With respect to the vector of non-domestic variables $\boldsymbol{x}_{it}^*$, in our application, these have been built using trade-based weights w_{ij} in order to capture the economic interaction of region j with the ith region's economy and not only the geographic interaction. These weights were computed using data on interregional trade in Spain drawn from the C-$Intereg$ database (Llano et al. 2008, 2010). Initially, mean trade shares ($\bar{s}_{ij}$) were computed as the proportion of region j in the total trade (exports plus imports) of region i over the period 2004-2007 (measured in millions of euros)[9]. Thereafter, a binary trade-based spatial weight matrix was built defining non-normalized weights as and finally a row-standardized weights matrix was defined as

---

[6]This corresponds with a NUTS2 level of disaggregation in Eurostat nomenclature of statistical territorial units.

[7]The regional public capital stock comprises productive public capital owned by the local, regional, and national administrations, including transport infrastructure (roads, ports, airports, and railways), water and sewage facilities, and urban structures. As indicated by a referee, the analysis would benefit from a distinction between transport public infrastructures and the rest of productive infrastructures.

[8]The estimates of capital stock for the Spanish economy meet the methodological recommendations of the OCDE and converge with the procedure followed by the Bureau of Labor Statistics (BLS) and the EU KLEMS project. All the details about methodological aspects and the construction and revision of the database along time can be found in Mas et al. (2011).

[9]The out-of-sample period 2004-2007 was used to avoid endogeneity problems with the in-sample values of the state variables. The interregional trade flows data for Spain show a robust empirical regularity for the Spanish trade pattern (see Llano et al. 2010), demonstrating the existence for each Spanish region of stable relationships in terms of clients and suppliers. In essence, regional trade patterns do not change much over time.

Table 1: Summary statistics of the database (measured by the percentage of share)

	GVA	E	KPR	KPU
AND	13.8	15	13.6	14.9
ARA	3.1	3.2	3.5	4.4
AST	2.2	2.2	2.5	3.1
BAL	2.4	2.4	2.7	1.7
CAN	4.1	4.1	4.5	4.3
CANT	1.3	1.3	1.3	1.5
CAT	18.8	17.8	18.4	14
CLM	3.4	4	3.8	4.9
CYL	5.5	5.7	6.2	8.1
EXT	1.7	2	2	2.5
GAL	5.1	5.7	5.2	6.4
MAD	17.7	15.8	15.6	13.7
MUR	2.5	2.8	2.3	2.3
NAV	1.7	1.7	1.8	1.9
PV	6.2	5.5	6.4	6
RIO	0.8	0.8	0.8	0.9
VAL	9.7	10.3	9.4	9.3
SPAIN	**100**	**100**	**100**	**100**

Source: Own elaboration from BD.MORES and Fundación BBVA-Ivie databases.
Regional Abbreviations: Andalusia (AND), Aragón (ARA), Asturias (AST), Balearic Islands (BAL), Canary Islands (CAN), Cantabria (CANT), Catalonia (CAT), Castile-La Mancha (CLM), Castile and León (CYL), Extremadura (EXT), Galicia (GAL), Madrid (MAD), Murcia (MUR), Navarre (NAV), Basque Country (PV), La Rioja (RIO) and the Valencian Community (VAL).

$$w_{ij}^* = \begin{cases} 0 & \text{if } i = j \\ 1 & \text{if } \bar{s}_{ij} \geq 0.01 \\ 0 & \text{if } \bar{s}_{ij} < 0.01 \end{cases} \tag{3}$$

and finally a w row-standardized weights matrix was defined as $w_{ij} = w_{ij}^*/\sum_j w_{ij}^*$.

Thus, only trade-neighbors of region i those regions j that have a mean trade share above 10% of the total trade were used. This criterion is based on the idea that only 'relevant trader regions' have non-negligible spatio-temporal effects on their neighbors; the remaining regions were assumed to be less important and thus have negligible individual impacts. The 10% critical cut-off point yields a set of 3 to 5 (not necessarily contiguous) neighbors. To check the robustness of our results, two other values (5% and 15%) were adopted, and the results were qualitatively similar to those presented in this paper, and thus were omitted for the sake of brevity.

5 Empirical application: effects of public capital in the Spanish regional system

The issue of the effects of public capital formation on economic development is currently at the center of the policy debate in many European countries. The policies available to states are limited because, given existing resources, it is not possible to maintain the current levels of public investment. Due to economic and budget pressures, nations have to prioritize where and how they allocate public expenditure.

This section focuses on the estimation of both domestic and spillover effects of public capital innovations on regional outputs in Spain. The effects derived from a hypothetical reduction of public capital in the Spanish regional system are identified in order to determine the key regions that generate, sustain and improve the productive capacity of the regional economic system. The detection of these 'key regions' would contribute to enhancing the set of strategic information necessary to ensure the most efficient allocation of regional public investment in the context of economically interrelated regions and in prioritizing the provision of public resources.

Next, the estimation results of the MultiREG-SpVAR for the Spanish regional system are presented. Due to the very large number of regressions, as well as preliminary or intermediate results involved in the estimation, only the main estimation and specification test results are presented (see Ramajo et al., 2015, for details). In summary, given that all the conditions for the Global VAR approach are accomplished, the estimation of the MultiREG-SpVAR is justified, and the dynamic properties of the model can be investigated[10].

Thus, the purpose is to simulate the response of the system to either a unitary (one standard error) shock in one internal variable in one specific region, or a unitary global shock (a GVA-weighted average of variable/regional specific unit shocks across all the regions in the system) in the whole regional system. Given the existence of trade links between regions that are incorporated in the model, other regions in the system will be (more or less) affected from the disturbance, providing relevant information about the degree of interregional spillovers in the Spanish regional system.

In this application, both the domestic and spillover effects of one-time innovations in the public capital installed in one region are estimated, as are the effects of a global shock to public capital in the country on the output growth of the regions of Spain. Given the actual economic situation of the Spanish economy, characterized by a sizeable reduction in the government's current and infrastructure expenditure, negative shocks to public capital are simulated as either area-wide or individual shocks scenarios: a) a negative global shock to total public capital in Spain; and b) a negative unit shock to public capital in each region.

Tables 2 and 3 show detailed estimated effects in the first and the fifth years. In these tables, the last row shows the effects of a global shock, not originating in a particular region but common to the Spanish economy as a whole (it is defined as a GVA-weighted average of shocks to the public capital in all 17 regions in Spain); the remaining rows display the region-specific shocks, where the shaded cells document the own-response of output to a domestic public capital shock, and the non-shaded elements record the spillover effects in the different regions of Spain. As can be seen in Tables 2 and 3, the responses of output to a negative unit shock in public capital have more heterogeneous responses (positive and negative effects) initially than after five years (where negative responses clearly prevail).

Starting from the first shock scenario (a negative global shock to total public capital in Spain), the effects on output of a common global negative shock to the public capital in the Spanish economy as a whole are contained in the last row of Tables 2 and 3. It should be noted that the term global is used in a way that departs from the empirical definition applied in other empirical research. In this paper, the term global shock makes reference to an overall shock for the Spanish regional system, including all of the dynamic feedbacks among the trade-related regions.

While a common global negative shock to the Spanish economy as a whole has initially mixed effects on the regions (positive and negative, see Table 2), after 5 years the shock has similar (negative) impacts (see Table 3). The strongest negative effect from this initial (negative) global shock can be found in Castile La Mancha (-2.49%), closely followed by the Basque Country (-2.37%). The weakest negative effects are found in La Rioja (-0.64%), Extremadura (-0.65%) and Cantabria (-0.93%).

Generally, from Table 3, the GVA-weighted average shock shows responses of GVA that are similar to the ranking in the share of national GVA (the greater the share, the more negative the impact; see Figure 1). Some exceptions are the regions that have the largest negative effects, Castile-La Mancha (ninth position within the Spanish ranking considering its share in national GVA) and the Basque Country (fifth position in GVA shares). For Castile-La Mancha, the reason could be the lack of agglomeration derived

---

[10]The dynamic analysis presented in this section follows the Generalized Impulse Response (GIR) approach proposed by Koop et al. (1996), and developed further in Pesaran, Shin (1998) for VAR models. This approach generalizes the traditional Orthogonalized Impulse Response method of Sims (1980), being invariant to the ordering of the variables in the SpVAR models, which makes the GIR functions a very useful tool to analyze the propagation of shocks across regions.

Table 2: Estimated contemporaneous responses of output to a negative unit shock in public capital

							Response (%) in:									
Shock in:	AND	ARA	AST	BAL	CAN	CANT	CAT	CLM	CYL	EXT	GAL	MAD	MUR	NAV	PV	RIO	VAL
AND	-0.21	-0.05	-0.04	-0.21	0.31	0.06	-0.1	0	-0.09	0.15	0.15	0.07	-0.06	0.05	-0.05	0.04	0.06
ARA	-0.01	0.07	-0.15	0.05	0.62	0.09	0.05	-0.01	0.04	0.27	0.25	0.02	0.17	0.05	-0.15	0.09	0.16
AST	0.01	-0.05	-0.05	-0.02	0.11	-0.16	-0.09	0.24	0.03	-0.04	0.1	-0.18	-0.04	0.17	-0.22	0.01	-0.09
BAL	-0.02	0.14	0.28	0.07	-0.16	0.1	0.02	0.08	0.05	0.16	-0.02	0.09	-0.08	-0.1	0.28	0.36	-0.05
CAN	0.02	-0.03	-0.14	-0.28	-0.02	-0.11	-0.06	0.11	0.05	0.29	-0.09	-0.1	0.09	-0.2	-0.17	0.04	-0.09
CANT	-0.23	-0.22	0.05	-0.1	0.15	-0.14	-0.31	-0.05	0.02	0.11	0.06	-0.18	-0.17	-0.13	-0.08	0	-0.21
CAT	0.03	0.01	-0.12	0	-0.09	-0.1	0.09	-0.06	0	0.04	-0.02	-0.14	0.16	0.04	-0.19	-0.23	-0.02
CLM	0.14	0.13	0.02	0.26	0.06	-0.16	-0.03	-0.09	0.24	0.18	-0.09	-0.02	0.33	-0.29	0.08	-0.17	0.02
CYL	0.13	0.16	0.01	0.11	0.29	-0.02	0.04	0.19	0.18	0.18	0.16	0	0.11	0.03	-0.18	0.15	0.12
EXT	0.04	0	0.1	0.36	0.28	0.14	-0.02	-0.03	0.06	-0.04	0.11	-0.08	-0.08	-0.01	0.06	0.08	-0.03
GAL	0.01	0.06	-0.15	-0.17	0.24	0.07	0.1	-0.1	0.03	0.05	-0.02	0.12	0.1	-0.12	-0.04	-0.1	-0.18
MAD	-0.08	0.15	-0.14	-0.06	-0.14	0.05	0.08	-0.21	-0.1	-0.05	-0.11	0.09	0.15	0.18	-0.13	0.09	0.16
MUR	-0.23	0.02	-0.02	-0.13	0.21	0.06	-0.26	-0.21	-0.01	0.46	0.06	-0.39	-0.24	-0.43	-0.38	0.1	-0.13
NAV	-0.08	-0.01	-0.19	-0.06	0.51	0.1	-0.09	-0.12	-0.02	0.21	0.2	-0.19	-0.2	-0.09	-0.2	0.14	0.06
PV	-0.13	0.13	-0.06	-0.15	-0.15	0.19	0.09	-0.12	-0.05	-0.05	-0.07	-0.1	-0.09	-0.15	-0.3	-0.17	-0.13
RIO	-0.11	-0.1	0.2	0.18	-0.01	0	-0.02	-0.17	-0.13	0.13	-0.02	0.16	-0.02	-0.12	0.16	0.01	-0.04
VAL	-0.08	-0.12	-0.16	-0.22	0.01	-0.1	0.11	-0.1	-0.2	-0.16	-0.16	0.19	0.03	0.07	0.05	-0.21	-0.11
GLO	-0.23	0.14	-0.33	-0.28	0.17	0.03	0.08	-0.32	-0.16	0.21	-0.04	0	0.2	0.04	-0.41	-0.02	0.07

Notes: Numbers reported are median estimates of initial responses (impact) of GVA to one standard error negative shock to public capital in the region row or one standard error negative global shock to public capital. The bootstrapping method provides the impact on median bootstrap estimates (see the supplement A of Dees et al. 2007).

Table 3: Estimated responses of output to a negative unit shock in public capital after five years

Shock in:	\multicolumn{17}{c}{Response (%) in:}

Shock in:	AND	ARA	AST	BAL	CAN	CANT	CAT	CLM	CYL	EXT	GAL	MAD	MUR	NAV	PV	RIO	VAL
AND	-0.53	-0.08	-0.21	-0.81	0.25	0.33	-0.43	-0.64	-0.41	-0.19	-0.08	-0.07	-0.17	0.02	-0.26	0.3	0.17
ARA	-0.87	-0.38	-0.63	-0.69	0	-0.15	-0.94	-1	-0.48	-0.31	-0.28	-0.77	-0.7	-0.62	-0.89	-0.05	-0.44
AST	-0.45	-0.42	-0.44	-0.34	-0.55	-0.63	-0.7	-0.29	-0.19	-0.29	-0.34	-0.79	-0.6	-0.48	-0.83	-0.19	-0.66
BAL	-0.42	-0.19	-0.02	-0.03	-0.51	-0.29	-0.5	-0.37	-0.15	-0.11	-0.24	-0.43	-0.53	-0.54	-0.08	0.15	-0.53
CAN	0.11	0.12	-0.12	-0.24	0.13	0.11	0.11	0.19	0.04	0.36	-0.05	0.15	0.23	0.17	0.07	0.14	0.11
CANT	-1.27	-1	-0.79	-0.79	-0.81	-0.99	-1.61	-1.4	-0.61	-0.65	-0.71	-1.34	-1.24	-1.16	-1.36	-0.41	-1.12
CAT	-1.08	-1.08	-1.16	-0.73	-1.53	-1.29	-1.37	-1.26	-0.56	-0.37	-1.01	-1.67	-1.2	-1.45	-1.85	-1.01	-1.51
CLM	0.04	-0.02	-0.06	0.26	-0.11	-0.37	-0.11	-0.37	0.15	-0.03	-0.14	-0.21	0.06	-0.38	-0.03	-0.22	-0.26
CYL	-0.32	0.11	-0.03	-0.37	0.18	0.19	-0.4	-0.51	-0.08	-0.21	0.09	-0.22	-0.28	-0.13	-0.27	0.34	0.11
EXT	0.47	0.31	0.46	0.78	0.74	0.31	0.52	0.5	0.27	-0.05	0.42	0.38	0.28	0.45	0.64	0.14	0.22
GAL	-0.23	-0.06	-0.31	-0.37	0.05	0.09	-0.13	-0.28	-0.12	-0.1	-0.06	-0.07	-0.09	-0.13	-0.2	-0.14	-0.35
MAD	-0.64	-0.39	-0.61	-0.47	-0.93	-0.39	-0.64	-0.91	-0.37	-0.16	-0.58	-0.7	-0.62	-0.65	-0.84	-0.13	-0.6
MUR	-0.86	-0.52	-0.65	-0.52	-0.46	-0.41	-1.03	-1	-0.48	-0.31	-0.51	-1.16	-0.88	-0.92	-1.12	-0.17	-0.76
NAV	-0.68	-0.33	-0.55	-0.59	0.16	-0.06	-0.78	-0.89	-0.41	-0.43	-0.15	-0.74	-0.72	-0.44	-0.78	0.11	-0.24
PV	0.19	0.42	0.26	-0.04	0.01	0.62	0.44	0.3	0.16	0.17	0.18	0.25	0.29	0.28	0.48	0	0.13
RIO	0.24	0.28	0.6	0.41	0.56	0.38	0.52	0.27	0.05	0.13	0.37	0.73	0.5	0.48	0.78	0.11	0.51
VAL	-0.52	-0.2	-0.36	-0.73	-0.24	0.02	-0.31	-0.59	-0.32	-0.28	-0.23	-0.06	-0.24	-0.19	-0.28	-0.19	-0.17
GLO	-2.09	-1.17	-1.67	-1.83	-1.78	-0.93	-2.2	-2.49	-1.12	-0.65	-1.39	-2.06	-1.79	-1.76	-2.37	-0.64	-1.72

Notes: Numbers reported are median estimates of responses of GVA to one standard error negative shock to public capital in the region row or one standard error negative global shock to public capital. The bootstrapping method provides the impact on median bootstrap estimates (see the supplement A of Dees et al. 2007).

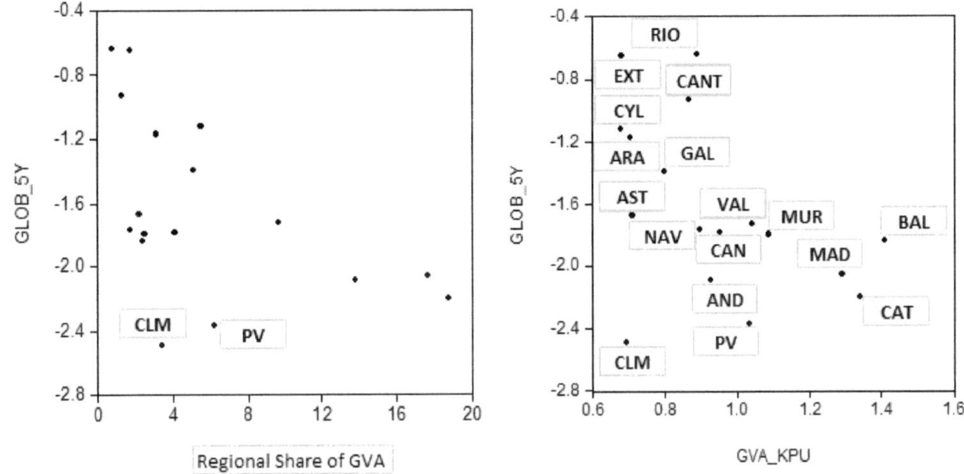

Figure 1: Effects after 5 years of a global negative shock (GLOB_5Y) vs. regional shares of national GVA and the regional ratios GVA/public capital (GVA_KPU)

from the low density that characterizes this region while in the case of the Basque Country, the explanation may lie in its economic and institutional differences from the rest of Spain.

On the other hand, Figure 1 also shows a negative correlation between the economic impact of a negative shock to public capital and the ratio of GVA to public capital. It seems that a negative global shock to public capital will induce higher negative response on GVA when the GVA/Public Capital ratio increases. This negative correlation seems to have little effect on the region Castile-La Mancha, since this region has an existing low ratio and it presents the lowest effect.

Overall, the estimation results suggest that a negative global shock will have a negative effect on the output of every region in Spain. However, global shocks can hide the detection of locations where the spillovers originate. Further, operating only with a global shock does not allow isolation of the effects from a specific region of interest. Consequently, the second shock scenario (a negative unit shock to public capital in each region) is needed in order to identify the regions where further reduction in public capital would have a greater negative impact, a lower negative impact, or even positive effects. Estimations of the domestic and the spillover output effects (from a region on the rest of the system) of one standard error negative shock to public capital in every Spanish region are provided in Tables 2 and 3. These results are new in the literature, since previous studies have only been able to reveal a part of the complex spatio-temporal feedbacks across regions; none of these studies has identified the spatio-temporal interdependencies between the state variables of all the regions.

From the estimates contained in Tables 2 and 3, the domestic and the spillover effects display positive and negative signs. Although negative effects prevail, the existence of positive effects opens a new dimension for the analysis of public investment. As seen in Table 3, for three of the seventeen regions, the domestic effects after five years are positive. Reduced funding for public capital accumulation in the Basque Country, Canary Islands and La Rioja will affect positively their regional economic growth. The underlying explanation might be in the fact that, while public capital formation will raise output directly in these regions (public and private capital are direct substitutes), the existence of a negative effect on the marginal productivity of private capital and employment could counterbalance the positive effects. This way, if increases in public capital imply negative effects on private capital (the direct substitution effects prevails for these regions), regional policy makers would have to implement measures in these regions that favor decreases in public capital. Among the negative domestic effects, Catalonia is the region with the lowest value; it is the most sensitive regional economy to a negative unit shock in public

Table 4: Regional Effects after 5 years

Regions	Domestic Effects	Mean Outward Effects (Weighted Average by GVA)	Mean Inward Effects (Weighted Average by GVA)	Mean Outward Effects / Domestic Effects	Mean Inward Effects / Domestic Effects
AND	-0,53	-0,18	-0,94	0,35	1,78
ARA	-0,38	-0,69	-0,11	1,82	0,28
AST	-0,44	-0,58	-0,10	1,32	0,24
BAL	-0,03	-0,38	-0,14	12,69	4,65
CAN	0,13	0,10	-0,15	0,77	-1,18
CANT	-0,99	-1,21	-0,02	1,22	0,02
CAT	-1,37	-1,30	-1,19	0,95	0,87
CLM	-0,37	-0,09	-0,29	0,25	0,79
CYL	-0,08	-0,19	-0,21	2,43	2,59
EXT	-0,05	0,44	-0,05	-8,80	1,02
GAL	-0,06	-0,16	-0,19	2,68	3,13
MAD	-0,70	-0,62	-1,16	0,89	1,65
MUR	-0,88	-0,86	-0,14	0,98	0,16
NAV	-0,44	-0,57	-0,10	1,29	0,22
PV	0,48	0,25	-0,50	0,52	-1,05
RIO	0,11	0,48	-0,01	4,32	-0,11
VAL	-0,17	-0,29	-0,56	1,72	3,28

Notes: Numbers reported are estimates of responses of GVA to one standard error negative shock to public capital in the region row or one standard error negative global shock to public capital.

capital.

With respect to the spillover effects shown in Table 3, it is also possible to find positive and negative effects. From the responses, it is important to highlight the existence of asymmetric shocks, ones that affect a pair of regions in a dissimilar way[11]. For example, a negative unit shock in the Valencian Community has negative effects on Andalusia, while a negative shock in Andalusia has a positive effect on Valencian Community. Another example is the case of the estimated effects between Catalonia and the Basque Country. For explanation, and in line with the applied methodology, it is not possible to rely on the nature of trade between these regions since the results are derived from a complicated process involving the tracing of paths of influence throughout the system.

Any attempt to analyze these spillovers will require the calculation of the average effects generated "from a region to the rest" (outward effects) and "from the rest to a region" (inward effects). The outward (inward) mean effects are computed from Table 3 by rows (columns) as weighted averages based on the regional shares of national GVA. The results are shown in Table 4. From columns 5 and 6 of this table, the estimation results show some evidence of the relative contribution of spillover effects on domestic effects. Ten of the Spanish regions (59%) have outward effects that are smaller than the corresponding domestic (internal) effects. In turn, for nine of the seventeen regions (53%), inward effects of public capital installed outside each region are more relevant than the domestic effects of public capital installed in the region.

The lowest negative outward effects can be found in Catalonia and Cantabria. Conversely, the highest positive effects (push-out growth spillovers) emanate from La Rioja, Extremadura and the Basque Country. Considering the range of values obtained by the domestic effects (X-axis) and the outward effects (Y-axis), different categories of regions can be depicted. Table 5 provides a taxonomy of the Spanish regional economies, highlighting the way in which reductions in public capital operate; different clusters of

---

[11]Chung, Hewings (2015) found similar complex typologies of interactions in an application in the Midwest state economies of the US.

Table 5: Regional taxonomy: Domestic Effects versus Mean Outward Effects

Mean Outward Effects	-1.37	-0.75	-0.13	0.48
0.47			CLM	CAN, EXT, PV, RIO
-0.11				
-0.7			AND, ARA, AST, VAL, MAD, NAV	BA, CL, GA
-1.3	CANT, CAT, MUR			

Domestic Effects

Table 6: Regional taxonomy: Domestic Effects versus Mean Inward Effects

Mean Inward Effects	-1.37	-0.75	-0.13	0.48
-0.01	CANT, MUR		CLM, AST, NAV, ARA	CAN, EXT, RIO, GA, CL, BA
-0.40				
-0.79			VAL	PV
-1.19	CAT		MAD, AND	

Domestic Effects

regions are observed And the classification of Table 5 generates some unexpected findings. For instance, negative shocks in the public capital of Cantabria, Catalonia and Murcia have more serious implications than others since they will produce important negative effects not only on their own regions but their corresponding trade-related regions. On the other hand, Canary Islands, Extremadura, the Basque Country and La Rioja are regions where the impact of austerity measures on public investment will produce lower negative effects than in the rest of regions.

Finally, Table 6 presents another taxonomy of the Spanish regional economies in view of the range of values obtained by the domestic effects (X-axis) and the inward effects (Y-axis). The different categories of regions recognize the importance of regional economic size in the generation of these effects, since all the regions, except the five largest regional economies (Catalonia, Madrid, Andalusia, Valencian Community and the Basque Country), have push-in effects above the mean. However, the larger regional economies are more sensitive to the negative shocks in public capital in the rest of regions.

The foregoing analysis suggests that a global reduction in the level of public capital stock will generate important implications for regional growth, and it is crucial, in designing regional growth-promoting strategies, to account for the variety of spatio-temporal effects through which regional public investment affect the rest of the regional economies.

5.1 Policy implications

From the economic literature, it would be expected that public investment in core regions would produce positive effects on regional growth due to the higher efficiency of investment in these type of regions (e.g. Caminal 2004), suggesting that regional public capital expenditure should be channeled to more developed regions (Blažek, Maceškova 2010). For the Spanish case, De la Fuente (2004, p. 502) recommends investing "... a lot more in some of the richest regions and considerably less in some of the poorest ones." Nevertheless, the uneven distribution of public investment, favoring only developed regions, could produce negative results in terms of regional equity.

In view of the previous results, some policy implications can be suggested that will have implications for regional growth strategies. Taking account of the current public financial difficulties, the results suggest that decisions about the allocation of regional public investments can affect regional economic growth. The detected effects of public capital on regional growth indicate that some regions act as key generators of economic activity within the Spanish regional economic system.

From a policy standpoint, this new approach can provide some important insights. First at all, a negative global shock to public capital in Spain (first scenario) would not be a prudent development, since all the regions will suffer a decrease in regional growth. Secondly (second scenario), a key policy lesson also is that regional economic policy should not underestimate the benefits of maintaining levels of public capital in some regions: when the contribution to regional economic growth may be compromised in terms of system-wide effects (rather than just in a single region), it would be necessary to maintain public investments in these key regions. On the other hand, there are some options for reductions in public capital in the regions where public capital resources are going to be underused in terms of their contribution to regional economic growth. However, data on the effective utilization of existing capital stock are not available.

On the other hand, some important findings can be highlighted with respect to the reciprocal contributions between Catalonia and the rest of the Spanish regions. First, negative shocks in public capital of the rest of the Spanish regions produces negative effects (above the mean) in Catalonia. Thus, Catalonia is within the group of Spanish regions that are more sensitive to the negative shocks in public capital of the rest of the Spanish regions, and this indicates a higher dependence of Catalonia on the rest of Spain. Secondly and at the same time, negative shocks in the public capital of Catalonia have more serious implications than negative shocks in other regions. The conclusion is that our analysis of reductions in public capital in the Spanish regional economic system indicates that Catalonia occupies the first place among the most sensitive regional economies in Spain; Catalonia belongs to the group with lower spillover effects, and it is the region with the lowest inward effect.

6   Final remarks and conclusions

Public capital is shown to be a significant determinant of regional output growth. People, private capital and other regional factors are mobile across regions, and trade will connect regions, generating variations in the responses to public capital provision both in the short- and long-run. Nevertheless, neither of the dominant methods of analyzing the impact of public investments within a regional economic system considers the possibility that regional responses reflect in part the changes in public capital in other region(s). In this paper, an empirical framework is used that links the allocation of regional public investment with regional economic growth.

The aim of this research has been to implement a quantitative approach to guide and prioritize public investment within a closed regional economic system. The performance of the Spanish regions has been evaluated through the assessment of how output in every region within the country is affected by a reduction in the public capital stock of another specific region. This procedure can be considered as a simulation of the impact of austerity measures on public expenditure of the Spanish central and regional governments.

To accomplish this task, a multiregional integrated method has been used to investigate the regional growth effects of public capital in Spain. The specified MultiREG-SpVAR model facilitates addressing many of the econometric criticisms of the previous literature. In fact, the traditional VAR framework so often used in the empirical analysis excludes the presence of spatial feedbacks among the relevant variables of the regions.

The contribution to the literature is twofold. First, in contrast to existing studies that estimate 'local' VAR models, a 'global' VAR specification is used to test the effect of a reduction (although in other economic circumstances it could have been an increase) in the stock of public capital, accounting for heterogeneity, simultaneity and spatial autocorrelation. This econometric approach provides the opportunity to identify both domestic and spillover effects of a reduction in public capital on regional output growth. Secondly, the analysis moves beyond most existing cross-section studies by providing more information about the location where the spillover effects originate. These contributions allow identification of regions in which further public capital reduction (increase) would have a lower (greater) effect on the output.

In particular, the responses of regional outputs to a negative unit shock in regional public capital have been analyzed using two different scenarios: a) a negative global shock to public capital in Spain; and, b) a negative unit shock to public capital in each region. From the first scenario, the detected effects appear quite plausible; the results show that reduced funding for public capital accumulation will negatively affect the economic growth of all the regions. The conclusion is that global decreases in public investment have a homogeneously negative effect on the output of all the regions. From the second scenario, the domestic and the spillover effects display positive and negative signs. Although negative effects prevail, the existence of positive effects can guide regional public capital allocation, prioritizing regional investment.

The empirical analysis reveals the existence of different clusters of regions. From this taxonomy, some regions facing substantial cuts in public investment may be able to maintain a modest level of regional growth over time. On the other hand, the diminution of public capital in other regions will negatively affect the regional economic system. In other words, the Spanish regions portray heterogeneous responses from localized public capital reductions over the years considered. This means that there is a place for strategic, planning actions from policy-makers in Spain to improve the allocation of public resources: it may be possible to partially mitigate the impact of austerity measures on government spending through a more considered, spatially targeted strategy. However, such a strategy presents significant political challenges to a central government interested in balancing concerns with national growth and development with attention to regional equity.

Although the findings in this paper make an important contribution to the ongoing debate about which regional policies need to be promoted to raise and sustain Spanish regional economic growth, some cautionary remarks seems appropriate. First, the analysis was conducted at the regional level; it would be interesting to considerer a multilevel analysis, since, at a lower level of disaggregation, regional responses may be even more heterogeneous and with a concomitant increase in spillovers. Disaggregation of public capital into its main components might also reveal some greater variations. At the same time, some integration of this modeling approach inside a multiregional general equilibrium model might enhance the understanding of the full system-wide impacts, especially the ways in which reductions in public investment affect employment levels, consumption, production, and government revenues.

Acknowledgement

We thank the editor and two anonymous referees for their comments. The authors acknowledge financial support from the Spanish Ministry of Economy, Industry and Competitiveness (Grant ECO2016-78352-P).

References

Agénor PR, Moreno-Dodson B (2006) Public infrastructure and growth: New channels and policy implications. Policy research, working paper, no. 4064, world bank. CrossRef.

Álvarez A, Arias C, Orea L (2006) Econometric testing of spatial productivity spillovers from public capital. *Hacienda Pública Española* 178[3]: 9–21

Aschauer DA (1989) Is public expenditure productive? *Journal of Monetary Economics* 23[2]: 177–200. CrossRef.

Baxter M, King RG (1993) Fiscal policy in general equilibrium. *The American Economic Review* 83[3]: 315–334

Blažek J, Macešková M (2010) Regional analysis of public capital expenditure: To which regions is public capital expenditure channelled – to 'rich' or to 'poor' ones? *Regional Studies* 44[6]: 679–696. CrossRef.

Boarnet MG (1998) Spillovers and locational effects of public infrastructure. *Journal of Regional Science* 38: 381–400. CrossRef.

Bustos A, Cutanda A, Díaz A, Escribá FJ, Murgui MJ, Sanz MJ (2008) La BD.MORES en base 2000: nuevas estimaciones y variables. Working paper d-2008-02, dirección general de presupuestos, ministerio de economía y hacienda

Caminal R (2004) Personal redistribution and the regional allocation of public investment. *Regional Science and Urban Economics* 34[1]: 55–69. CrossRef.

Capello R (2009) Spatial spillovers and regional growth: a cognitive approach. *European Planning Studies* 17: 639–658. CrossRef.

Cheshire P, Carbonaro G (1996) Urban economic growth in Europe. *Urban Studies* 33: 1111–1128

Chung S, Hewings GJD (2015) Competitive and complementary relationship between regional economies: A study of the Great Lake States. *Spatial Economic Analysis* 10: 205–229. CrossRef.

Cohen J, Morrison Paul C (2007) The impacts of transportation infrastructure on property values: A higher-ordered spatial econometrics approach. *Journal of Regional Science* 47[3]: 457–478. CrossRef.

De la Fuente A (2004) Second-best redistribution through public investment: a characterization, an empirical test and an application to the case of Spain. *Regional Science and Urban Economics* 34: 489–503. CrossRef.

De la Fuente A (2010) Infrastructures and productivity: an updated survey. UFAE and IAE working paper 831.10, Unitat de Fonaments de l'Anàlisi Econòmica (UAB) and Institut d'Anàlisi Econòmica (CSIC)

Dees S, Di Mauro F, Pesaran MH, Smith LV (2007) Exploring the international linkages of the euro area: a global VAR analysis. *Journal of Applied Econometrics* 22: 1–38. CrossRef.

Deliktas E, Önder A, Karadag M (2009) The spillover effects of public capital on the Turkish private manufacturing industries in the geographical regions. *The Annals of Regional Science* 43[2]: 653–378. CrossRef.

Deno K (1988) The effects of public capital on U.S. manufacturing activity: 1970 to 1987. *Southern Economic Journal* 53: 400–411. CrossRef.

Destefanis S, Sena V (2005) Public capital and total factor productivity: New evidence from the Italian regions 1970-98. *Regional Studies* 39[5]: 603–617. CrossRef.

Devarajan S, Swaroop V, Zou HF (1996) The composition of public expenditure and economic growth. *Journal of Monetary Economics* 37: 313–344. CrossRef.

Dietzenbacher E, van der Linden JA, Steenge AE (1993) The regional extraction method: EC input-output comparisons. *Economic Systems Research* 5: 185–206. CrossRef.

Garcia-Mila T, McGuire TJ, Porter RH (1996) The effect of public capital in state-level production functions reconsidered. *The Review of Economics and Statistics* 78[1]: 177–180. CrossRef.

Gramlich EM (1994) Infrastructure investment: a review essay. *Journal of Economic Literature* 32[3]: 1176–1196

Heintz J (2010) The impact of public capital on the US private economy: new evidence and analysis. *International Review of Applied Economics* 24[5]: 619–632. CrossRef.

Henderson D, Kumbhakar S (2006) Public and private capital productivity puzzle: A nonparametric approach. *Southern Economic Journal* 73[1]: 219–232. CrossRef.

Holtz-Eakin D (1994) Public-sector capital and the productivity puzzle. *The Review of Economics and Statistics* 76[1]: 12–21. CrossRef.

Holtz-Eakin D, Schwartz A (1995) Spatial productivity spillovers from public infrastructure: Evidence from state highways. *International Tax and Public Finance* 2: 459–468. CrossRef.

Hunt C (2012) The interaction of public and private capital: a study of 20 OECD members. 44: 739–764. CrossRef.

Kamps C (2005) The dynamic effects of public capital: VAR evidence for 22 OECD countries. *International Tax and Public Finance* 12[4]: 533–558. CrossRef.

Koop G, Pesaran MH, Potter SM (1996) Impulse response analysis in nonlinear multivariate models. *Journal of Econometrics* 74: 119–147. CrossRef.

Llano C, Esteban A, Pérez J, Pulido A (2008) La base de datos C-intereg sobre el comercio interregional de bienes en España: método y primeros resultados (1995-2006). *Ekonomiaz* 69[3]: 245–269

Llano C, Esteban A, Pérez J, Pulido A (2010) Opening the interregional trade black box: The C-Intereg database for the Spanish economy (1995-2005). *International Regional Science Review* 33[3]: 302–337. CrossRef.

Lynde C, Richmond J (1992) The role of public capital in production. *Review of Economics and Statistics* 74: 37–44. CrossRef.

Mas M, Pérez F, Uriel E (2009) El stock y los servicios del capital en España y su distribución territorial. Fundación BBVA-Ivie

Mas M, Pérez F, Uriel E (2011) El stock y los servicios del capital en españa y su distribución territorial y sectorial (1964-2010). Technical report

McGregor PG, Swales JK (2003) The economics of devolution/decentralisation in the UK: Some questions and answers. Discussion paper in economics 03-13, University of Strathclyde, Glasgow (http://www.strath.ac.uk/media/departments/economics/researchdiscussionpapers/2003/media_34453_en.pdf)

Melitz MJ, Ottaviano GIP (2008) Market size, trade, and productivity. *Review of Economic Studies* 75: 295–316. CrossRef.

Moreno R, López-Bazo E (2007) Returns to local and transport infrastructure under regional spillovers. *International Regional Science Review* 30: 47–71. CrossRef.

Morrison P, Schwartz A (1996) State infrastructure and productive performance. *The American Economic Review* 86[5]: 1095–1111

Márquez MA, Ramajo J, Hewings GJD (2010a) Measuring the spillover effects of public capital: A bi-regional structural vector autoregressive analysis. *Letters in Spatial and Resource Sciences* 3: 111–125. CrossRef.

Márquez MA, Ramajo J, Hewings GJD (2010b) A spatio-temporal econometric model of regional growth in Spain. *Journal of Geographical Systems* 12: 207–226. CrossRef.

Márquez MA, Ramajo J, Hewings GJD (2011) Public capital and regional economic growth: a SVAR approach for the Spanish regions. *Investigaciones Regionales* 21: 199–223

Márquez MA, Ramajo J, Hewings GJD (2015) Regional growth and spatial spillovers: Evidence from an SpVAR for the Spanish regions. *Papers in Regional Science* 94: S1–S18. CrossRef.

Munnell A (1990) Why has productivity declined? Productivity and private investment. New England Economic Review, Federal Reserve Bank of Boston, January-February (https://www.bostonfed.org/-/media/Documents/neer/neer190a.pdf)

Pereira AM, Roca-Sagalés O (2003) Spillover effects of public capital formation: Evidence from the Spanish regions. *Journal of Urban Economics* 53: 238–256. CrossRef.

Pesaran MH, Schuermann T, Weiner SM (2004) Modelling regional interdependencies using a global error-correcting macroeconometric model. *Journal of Business and Economic Statistics* 22[2]: 129–162. CrossRef.

Pesaran MH, Shin Y (1998) Generalized impulse response analysis in linear multivariate models. *Economic Letters* 58: 17–29. CrossRef.

Ramajo J, Márquez MA, Hewings GJD (2017) Spatiotemporal analysis of regional systems: A multiregional spatial vector autoregressive model for Spain. *International Regional Science Review* 40: 75–96. CrossRef.

Ratner JB (1983) Government capital and the production unction for U.S. private output. *Economics Letters* 13: 213–217. CrossRef.

Roca-Sagalés O, Sala H (2006) Efectos Desbordamiento de la Inversión en Infraestructuras en las Regiones Españolas. *Investigaciones Regionales* 8: 143–161

Romp W, De Haan J (2007) Public capital and economic growth: A critical survey. *Perspektiven der Wirtschaftspolitik* 8: 6–52. CrossRef.

Seitz H (1993) A dual economic analysis of the benefits of the public road network. *The Annals of Regional Science* 27[3]: 223–239. CrossRef.

Seitz H, Licht G (1995) The impact of public infrastructure capital on regional manufacturing production cost. *Regional Studies* 29: 231–240. CrossRef.

Serrano Martínez L, Mas Ivars M, Pérez García F, Uriel Jiménez E (2017) Acumulación y productividad del capital en España y sus comunidades autónomas en el Siglo XXI. Fundación BBVA, Bilbao

Sims CA (1980) Macroeconomics and reality. *Econometrica* 48[1]: 1–48. CrossRef.

Sturm JE, Kuper GH, de Haan J (1998) Modelling government investment and economic growth on a macro level: a review. In: Brakman S, van Ees H, Kuipers SK (eds), *Market Behaviour and Macroeconomic Modelling*. MacMillan Press Ltd, London, 359–406. CrossRef.

Tatom J (1991) Public capital and private sector performance. *Federal Reserve Bank of St.Louis Review* 73: 3–15

Young A (1991) Learning by doing and the dynamic effects of international trade. *Quarterly Journal of Economics* 106: 369–405. CrossRef.

Yu N, de Jong M, Storm S, Mi J (2013) Spatial spillovers of transport infrastructure: evidence from Chinese regions. *Journal of Transport Geography* 28: 56–66. CrossRef.

The Journal of ERSA
Powered by WU

Volume 5, Number 1, 2018, 33–51
DOI: 10.18335/region.v5i1.160

journal homepage: region.ersa.org

Towards an Integrated Evaluation Approach for Cultural Urban Landscape Conservation/Regeneration

Francesca Nocca[1], Luigi Fusco Girard[1]

[1] University of Naples Federico II, Naples, Italy

Received: 11 September 2016/Accepted: 15 December 2017

Abstract. The contemporary economic crisis (and also ecological and social crisis) calls for a new model of urban development. The international debate is today focused on the necessity of a new paradigm (Hosagrahar et al., 2016) that will define sustainable development policies and programmes: this new paradigm moves the concept of development towards a more humanistic and ecological point of view. The recent international debate around Sustainable Development Goals (SDGs) is going to highlight the role of cultural heritage for sustainable development (United Nations 2016, 2015a). Cultural heritage can play a critical role in the achievement of the above mentioned new humanistic and ecological paradigm of sustainable cities. In this paper some indicators to evaluate cultural urban landscape conservation/regeneration projects are identified, starting from case studies. The purpose of the analysis of good practices is to support the elaboration of a multidimensional matrix that can produce empirical evidence about the impacts of cultural urban landscape conservation/regeneration. After a particular focus on the relationship between variation of landscape and variation of wellbeing, this paper will present a methodological proposal to evaluate cultural urban landscape conservation/regeneration projects.

Key words: Cultural Heritage conservation, landscape variation/wellbeing variation, multidimensional indicators

1 Introduction

The contemporary economic crisis (and also ecological and social crisis) calls for a new model of urban development. The international debate is today focused on the necessity of a new paradigm (Hosagrahar et al. 2016) that will define sustainable development policies and programmes: this new paradigm moves the concept of development towards a more humanistic and ecological point of view. The necessity to change towards this more humanistic (suggested in the Agenda 2030 of United Nations) and more ecological (Paris Cop21 and Agenda 2030) paradigm is deeply felt. It is characterized by the human scale of development and is inspired by the wisdom of nature. The 2030 Sustainable Development Agenda has been defined as a plan of action for people, planet and prosperity (United Nations 2015a), based on 17 Sustainable Development Goals (SDGs) and 169 targets coming out from the Millennium Development Goals (MDGs) (United Nations 2015b). Most of these can be achieved in the space of cities. All of the problems, for example problems related to climate change, energy, water, food or wellbeing, are localized in the cities and thus can be faced in these cities.

The international debate around Sustainable Development Goals (SDGs) recently is highlighting the role of cultural heritage for sustainable development (United Nations 2015a). Cultural heritage can play a key role in the achievement of the above-mentioned new humanistic and ecological paradigm of the sustainable city. Therefore, cultural resources should be integrated into the sustainable development of cities. "Cultural matters are integral parts of the lives we lead. If development can be seen as an enhancement of our living standards, then efforts geared to development can hardly ignore the world of culture" (Sen 2000).

Despite the important role that cultural heritage can have in sustainable development and the acknowledgment of its importance at the national level (and not only), it has been kept out of the sustainable development debate for too long. It should be included in the framework of sustainable development because it reflects the mutual adaptation between humans and their environment and the relationship between people and heart. Cultural heritage plays an irreplaceable role as the source of a sense of belonging and identity for communities (UNESCO 2013, European Commission 2014, CHCfE Consortium 2015). It also reveals and symbolizes how people relate to other communities and what they value to enhance and improve the quality of their life. Cultural heritage is an integral part of communities' life and it is involved in social, economic and environmental processes. It is an expression of the culture, identity and religious beliefs of societies.

For this reason, all actions aiming to protect and improve the environmental, social and economic wellbeing of communities should take into account cultural heritage, the opportunities that it offers and the threats it poses due to inappropriate use. Despite all of these considerations, Cultural Urban Landscape and, more generally Cultural Heritage (CH), is weakly considered in strategies for achieving sustainable development: it is explicitly mentioned only once in Goal 11 ("make cities and human settlements inclusive, safe, resilient and sustainable"), and particularly in target 11.4, regarding "strengthening efforts to protect and safeguard the world's cultural and natural heritage".

The analysis of the relationship between cultural heritage and sustainable development could represent a first step to recognizing the critical role of cultural heritage in the current debate. This relation is highlighted, for example, in the Historic Urban Landscape Approach (UNESCO 2011) and European Landscape Convention (European Commission 2014). Both documents recognize the contribution of high quality landscapes to urban productivity. Cultural heritage is increasingly considered as a source of local development thanks to its capacity to produce new employment, to stimulate the localization of creative activities, to increase inclusion and social cohesion (UNESCO 2013, European Commission 2014, CHCfE Consortium 2015).

The role of culture heritage to achieve a more inclusive, resilient, safe and sustainable city is going to be more and more recognized. Cultural heritage is here understood through a holistic and systemic interpretation of landscape. "Landscape can be interpreted as a complex indicator for the sustainability of a city or territory, of the quality of life, vitality of a place, and a community's sense of belonging" (Hosagrahar et al. 2016). This vision is fundamental to operationalize the project. Complexity is related to multidimensionality, heterogeneity and dynamism. It is linked to technical-scientific and humanistic knowledge, to the individual's perception and how it turns into a community perspective. The subjective perception is here transformed into a community and inter-subjective result through dialogic and participative processes. It is therefore an inter-subjective result.

The answer to the main question, that is if Cultural Urban Landscape can play a role in sustainable development, could be yes only if we are able to produce empirical evidence about the contribution of cultural heritage to improve the economic, social and environmental productivity of the city (Fusco Girard 2013). It is important to convince public, private and social actors about the convenience (economic, social, environmental benefits) of cultural heritage conservation/regeneration. In order to achieve this goal, empirical evidence needs to be produced. Current studies about empirical evidence are limited to some benefits, in particular the economic ones. However, as Dalmas et al. highlighted (Dalmas et al. 2015), the notion of cultural heritage is "inseparable from its multidimensional nature". For this reason, multidimensional impacts need to be considered. If we want to be convincing about the capacity of cultural heritage to implement the new urban paradigm (Hosagrahar et al. 2016), we have to produce empirical evidence about the multidimensional benefits. There needs to be improved knowledge about the relationship between quality landscape variation and wellbeing variation (it will analyze in the third paragraph). In this new perspective linking landscape and productivity, the complex landscape could be considered as an indicator of the health of a city/region (Fusco Girard 2013). In other words, the aim is to demonstrate the productivity of conservation projects, including how cultural urban landscape conservation/regeneration can contribute to increasing local productivity and also to improving the wellbeing of inhabitants. In this perspective, Cultural Urban Landscape represents a precious resource. This paper would be a first step towards this goal, proposing a specific set of indicators in order to support the demonstration that cultural heritage conservation is an investment and not a cost (because benefits overcome costs). The purpose is to deduce, starting from experiences, a more effective evaluation approach, that can make integrated conservation more effective in implementing human sustainable development strategies (Fusco Girard 2014b). Tools are fundamental, but more important is an understanding of which perspective we want to move towards: the risk is that cities are not being able to achieve the human scale in this evolutionary dynamic.

The most recent operative tool proposed for the impact assessment of different projects on Cultural Heritage (included HUL) is the Heritage Impact Assessment (ICOMOS 2011). This is a fundamental tool to understand the impacts of projects on the integrity and authenticity of cultural heritage (Pereira Roders et al. 2013). It provides a framework for assessing the impacts of urban transformations on the cultural value of properties. However, it has some remarkable limitations; for example, it does not include the economic and social dimensions of heritage conservation. It is based on expert judgement without considering community perceptions and intangible dimensions that are important factors of Historic Urban Landscape. It is not a multidimensional approach. It considers HUL conservation/regeneration as a mere cultural issue and not as a driver/vehicle for sustainable development. Furthermore, HIA is a tool for the assessment of impacts on Cultural Heritage; we also need tools for the assessment of impacts from Cultural Heritage conservation on city productivity and wellbeing. Therefore, it needs to go beyond HIA, integrating it with the evaluation of impacts from cultural heritage and not only impacts on it, in order to evaluate all multidimensional benefits of HUL conservation/regeneration through an effective approach. We need a systemic approach based on empirical evidence and not only on principles. The challenge is to elaborate an evaluation approach able to make the integrated conservation more effective to achieve human sustainable development. The above-mentioned new perspective of city humanization suggests the steering of this approach towards human and social impacts of cultural heritage conservation/regeneration. In other words, it should be focused on its capacity to produce employment (direct, indirect, induced), social capital (bonds, synergies, etc.), social cohesion, human wellbeing/health thanks to the new attractive atmosphere and also on the capacity of these impacts to implement new value creation chains in a virtuous and self-reproducing spiral in time. Some indicators to evaluate cultural urban landscape conservation/regeneration projects are identified in the following paragraphs, starting from case studies. The purpose of this analysis of good practices is to support the elaboration of a multidimensional matrix that can produce empirical evidence about impacts of cultural urban landscape conservation/regeneration.

After a particular focus on the relationship between variation of landscape and variation of wellbeing, this paper will present a methodological proposal to evaluate cultural urban landscape conservation/regeneration projects.

2 Multidimensional benefits of cultural landscape conservation

In this period in which cities are facing three important challenges (economic, social and environmental crisis), it is important to understand and demonstrate the role that cultural heritage could have in sustainable development. It is important to demonstrate the capacity of cultural heritage to increase the economic (EVoCH 2012), social and environmental productivity of cities. City productivity is related to the capacity of the city to produce new added values starting from its available resources (rate between output and input). They are not only referred to as the good economic performance of the city, but they include also social and environmental dimensions. Cultural heritage can be considered as an input in this production process that, through the lens of landscape, can contribute to the enhancement of cities economic, social and environmental performance. The capacity to produce multidimensional benefits depends on strategies, policies and actions adopted that, in turn, depend on different aspects (i.e. city size, intensity of bonds and relationships).

In order to pass from principles to their operationalization, we need tools. We need to evaluate investments in cultural heritage in an operative way, deducing indicators starting from empirical evidence: in this paper some indicators, extrapolated from case studies, are proposed in this perspective. Many more indicators can be proposed (Nocca 2017). As empirical evidence shows, culture can boost the economy (CHCfE Consortium 2015). It is able to produce income, employment and new businesses. It can foster entrepreneurship capacity and skills and be a source of creativity and innovation (Fusco Girard 2013). Culture is also linked to the social dimension because it is able, through broadening capacities and increasing opportunities, to face poverty. It can support marginalized people because cultural-based activities can, for example, provide people with opportunities.

The indicators are grouped into 6 categories (each of them divided into sub-categories) (Fusco Girard et al. 2015, Nocca et al. 2016):

- Tourisn and recreation

- Creative and cultural activities

- Environment and natural capital

- Community and social cohesion

- Real estate

- wellbeing

The set of indicators for each category has been extracted from 17 case studies of cities from all over the world – 9 in Europe, 3 in Africa, 3 in South America, 1 in North America and 1 in the Middle East (Fusco Girard et al. 2015). The first category is about tourism and recreation (Table 1). The indicators about this category are the most popular because the impacts related to the tourism sector are more immediate and obvious, especially in the short term (D'Auria 2009). It is a sector able to transform cultural values into economic ones. It produces new employment and new wealth in the short time. There are many good practices that empirically demonstrate the benefits in the tourism sector, in terms of hotels, restaurants, visitors, etc.

Tourism refers, in particular, to the instrumental value of cultural heritage, but the latter has also intrinsic and social value (Fusco Girard 1987). The first one can be a source of shared identity and a sense of belonging or meaning etc., in other words, of heritage community. It is not linked to the use or function that it serves; it bonds community to places "determining the spirit of a place and the source of pride that is of interest for future generations". Social value refers to the capacity of cultural heritage to be a catalyst of social links and relationships (that trigger new economic value). Relationships become bonds that are able to create new value chains, which increase city productivity through circular processes, synergies and symbiosis (Fusco Girard 2014a). All of the above values are able to increase (in a direct or indirect way) the comprehensive productivity and thus prosperity of a city.

Cultural heritage regeneration could have negative impacts, such as the museification and gentrification of historic centres (Glass 1964). Development/transformation generates some interferences with landscapes. Overdevelopment often represents a cost to landscapes. Without proper measures, regeneration/valorization actions can produce negative

Table 1: Tourism and recreation indicators

Sub-category	Indicator	Unit measure
Employment	N. of new jobs in touristic sector	n./year
Employment	% of employed population related to tourism sector	%
Employment	% of the total workforce employed in hotels	%
Employment	Average number of jobs in touristic activities (hotels, restaurants, shops)	n./year (or day, week, month)
Employment	Monthly salary	€/month
Employment	% of hotels' contribution to tourism sector income	%
Employment	% of hotels' contribution to tourism sector total revenues	%
Touristic Demand	N. of visitors per year (or per day)	n./year (or day)
Touristic Demand	Visitors' expenditure per day (or per year)	€/day (or year)
Touristic Demand	Average length of stay	nights/person
Touristic Demand	Occupancy rate of touristic units	%
Touristic Demand	Average growth rate of number of nights and guests	%
Touristic Demand	% of international tourists	%
Touristic Demand	N. of one-day trips	n. trips/year
Touristic Demand	% of crowding in restaurants during holidays	%
Touristic Demand	Average number of daily users in stores	n./day
Touristic Demand	Average daily expenditure of users in stores	€/day
Touristic Demand	Average number of daily users in restaurants	n./day
Touristic Demand	Average daily expenditure of users in restaurants	€/day
Touristic Demand	N. of airline passengers	n./years
Touristic Demand	N. of visitors to museums	n./day
Touristic Supply	% of fixed assets related to the tourism sector	%
Touristic Supply	Average annual growth in touristic units and rooms	%
Touristic Supply	Average growth of touristic sector	%
Touristic Supply	N of new touristic shops	n/year
Touristic Supply	N. of touristic residences in rural space	n. units/year
Touristic Supply	Growth of service and infrastructures	%
Touristic Supply	Growth of catering sector	%
Touristic Supply	N. of hotels	n.
Touristic Supply	N. of hotel rooms	n.
Touristic Supply	N. of hotel beds	n.
Touristic Supply	N. of new travel agencies	n.
Touristic Supply	N. of airlines operating at the airport	n.
Touristic Supply	N. of new public underground parking lots	n.
Touristic Supply	N. of commercial licenses	n.
Economic Vitality	Average of companies lifespan	%
Economic Vitality	% of buildings for industrial use	%
Economic Vitality	% of formal/informal activities	%
Production of Goods	N. of new industrial activities	n./year
Typical Productions	Employment distribution in production sector	%
Typical Productions	Annual growth rate of traditional production	%
Typical Productions	Average value of traditional production per hectare	€/ha
Typical Productions	Selling price of traditional products (without VAT)	€
Typical Productions	Net present value of economic activity	€
Typical Productions	Internal profit rate of economic activity	%
Typical Productions	N. of artisan units	n.

Source: Indicators deduced from reports about analyzed case studies (Actum 2011, Bigio 2010, Dalberg 2013, HR&A Advisors 2010, IUCN 2014, Labadi 2008, Landorf 2009, Loureço-Gomes 2009, Mendes Zancheti, Gabriel 2010, Ogilvie 2009, Orbasli 2010, Pais et al. 2014, Quartesan, Romis 2010, Roland et al. 2004, Throsby 2012, Torquati, Giacché 2013, Torquati et al. 2011, Trivelli, Nishimura 2010, World Bank 2015)

impacts, such as more footfall, more noise, increase in pollution and disturbances to the ecological balance of the place, but also the erosion of "intrinsic values". Sometimes this excessive increase can also produce a particular phenomenon, gentrification, meaning local communities and young people can no longer afford to buy/rent apartments because of rising prices. As has emerged from some case studies, many apartments remain unused for years, and the owners do not care about maintenance, leading to deterioration. Furthermore, the increase in property values produces "touch and go" tourism because of the high prices to stay in the area of the project. Therefore, gentrification (interpreted as expulsion of the most vulnerable part of the population both in economic terms and cultural ones) often represents a consequence of regeneration. In addition to removal of the lower classes, there is also a loss of authenticity of a place. They are transformed from places to live in to places to consume, mainly in the touristic sense.

Gentrification is often considered an inevitable consequence of urban regeneration processes. According to this point of view, modifying social composition allows the redistribution of economic benefits from having richer inhabitants that, having more money to spend, can contribute to revitalizing the economy of the neighbourhood. But, in this way, the problem of poverty or more generally of social issues are simply moved outside. It is the consequence of actions that consider only economic attractiveness. Social and cultural components need to be considered in regeneration strategies/policies in order to limit the negative impacts. Furthermore, choices have to come from bottom-up approaches, through community involvement. The economic impacts are generally interpreted only in the touristic demand perspective, but empirical evidence shows that there are other impacts. It is important to highlight that the contribution of cultural heritage to economic development does not end in the tourism economy.

Cultural Urban Landscape conservation/regeneration is able to produce impacts also in creative, cultural and innovative activities (Table 2). Cultural activities refer to activities that embody and convey cultural expressions. Besides the traditional arts sectors (performing arts, visual arts, cultural heritage, etc.), these activities also include services and goods such as film, music, books and press, DVD, video, television and radio, video games as well as new media. This category includes historic and artistic heritage (cultural heritage) and contents, as well as the information and communications industries (publishing, cinema, advertising, television and radio) where the integration of high tech is a common thread.

Productivity, competitiveness and attractiveness of cities and regions are improved through innovations (Florida 2002), based on local resources, that is on human and social capital. Indicators about use of ICT related to knowledge/use of cultural heritage did not emerge in the analyzed case studies. The ICT impacts on cultural heritage are considerable and therefore indicators are needed to monitor the benefits produced by them.

Another category of indicators include environmental and natural capital (Table 3). Most benefits in this category are indirect; they are expressed in terms of "avoided costs" (reduction of energy consumption, waste reduction, etc.).

The World Bank recognized the investments in cultural heritage as a good solution to reduce CO2 emissions and climate change: activities related to cultural heritage represent an intrinsically more sustainable model of land use, consumption and production that has been developed over time through a continuous adaptation between communities and their environments. Cultural heritage can help to face challenges related to climate change, for example, "through the protection and revitalisation of the huge amount of embedded energy in the historic building stock" (CHCfE Consortium 2015). Therefore, the indicators deduced from case studies should be integrated with indicators related to the avoided costs due to the improvement of health conditions. Most case studies are lacking in these indicators, demonstrating the lack of awareness regarding benefits that cultural heritage conservation/regeneration can produce for the environment. But the lack of data does not imply the absence of such benefits.

The indicators about the real estate category (Table 4) are, as for the tourism category, more known because the impacts are more immediate and obvious, especially in the short term. The real estate benefits are direct benefits for owners and, at the same time, they

Table 2: Creative and cultural activities indicators

Sub-category	Indicator	Unit measure
Creative Firms	N. of new handcraft shops	n./year
Creative Firms	N. of craft producers	n.
Creative Firms	N. of antique stores/second hand bookshops	n.
Cultural Demand	Visitors stay for temporary cultural events	%
Cultural Demand	N. of visitors for cultural reason	n./year
Cultural Demand	N. of participants in cultural events	n./year
Cultural Demand	N. of schoolchildren taking part in the cultural events	n/year
Cultural Demand	Perception of cultural benefits	qualitative
Cultural Demand	Visitors' Willingness to make a contribution to heritage restoration	%
Cultural Supply	N. of cultural events per year	n./year
Cultural Supply	% of growth of cultural events	%
Cultural Supply	N. of cultural institutions	n.
Cultural Supply	Growth of creative activities	%
Cultural Supply	Attraction of new investments in Cultural Heritage	€
Cultural Supply	N. archives	n.
Cultural Supply	N. libraries	n.
Cultural Supply	N. movie theatres	n.
Cultural Supply	N. art galleries	n.
Cultural Supply	N. museums	n.
Cultural Supply	N. theatres	n.
Cultural Supply	N. of cultural facilities	n.
Employment	N. of jobs created in the short term in cultural activities	n.
Employment	N. of artists taking part in cultural activities	n/year

Source: see Table 1

Table 3: Environment and natural capital indicators

Sub-category	Indicator	Unit measure
Ecosystem Preservation	Economic value of ecosystem services (regulating and maintenance)	€ Net Present Value
Ecosystem Preservation	Attraction of new investments in ecosystem preservation	€
Ecosystem Preservation	Avoided damages from ecosystem/land preservation	€
Ecosystem Preservation	Benefits from preservation of agricultural land (ecosystem services evaluation)	€
Green Areas & Facilities	Attraction of new investments for enhancement of green areas	€
Green Areas & Facilities	Avoided costs of traffic congestion for the community (due to the enhancement of public transport)	€/year
Green Areas & Facilities	Avoided cost of traffic congestion for the community (due to pedestrian and bicycle routes)	€/year
Pollution Reduction	Attraction of new investment in infrastructure to reduce pollution	€

Source: see Table 1

can turn into tax impacts for the public. Therefore, cultural heritage is able to generate tax revenue for public bodies. Heritage landscape conservation refers to both intangible and tangible assets. The valorization, regeneration and "re-use" of heritage relates to the fixed capital, but also to values and knowledge. In built environments there is a great potential for saving energy. The investments can pay back well during the life cycle of the goods. Energy saving can be achieved through investments in technologies (such as renewable energy systems, energy efficient lighting, cooling, heating) but also through territorial management and behavioural and lifestyle changes. Through the protection and revitalisation of the huge embedded energy in the historic building stock, cultural heritage can contribute to facing climate change challenges (CHCfE Consortium 2015). The amount of raw materials- water, etc. and embedded energy savings can be a useful indicator for assessing environmental benefits from cultural heritage re-use.

Cultural heritage can contribute to facing climate change thanks to some key features. An effective orientation and the physical characteristics, for example the walling's gauge, contribute to guarantee a lower temperature inside and outside the buildings, improving the general microclimatic condition.

Furthermore, heritage reuse can contribute to revitalizing local economies with jobs, new businesses, tax revenues and local spending, as well as providing a valuable wildlife habitat and recreational amenities. Through functional re-use, we are also able to regenerate values, keeping them in time. The adaptive re-use (Douglas 2006) produces multidimensional benefits: cultural benefits (conserving "alive" a symbol of community identity), economic benefits (in terms of increase in productivity), and environmental benefits (i.e. reduction of resource consumption) and social benefits (i.e. employment). Cultural heritage adaptive re-use, that realizes operationally the circular economy model (Angrisano et al. 2016), can ensure that cultural heritage continues to "live" for present and future generations through ensureing use-values in an indefinite lifespan, thus preserving its intrinsic value. On the contrary, abandonment and obsolescence threaten its existence.

Through conservation/regeneration, new use values are created consistent with the value independent from the use. This does not mean loss of identity of heritage, but it means "to give" the places new functions (adequate to community's dynamism and changing needs) through projects and strategies highlighting the relationships between cultural resources and city transformation policies. The functional reuse of cultural heritage is here considered as a way to valorize the identity of the territory. This is based on its history, values, specific knowledge, etc. It is also a pretext to stir up cultural values, the recognition of a common identity (not just local, but also widen), traditions and shared memory. The functional reuse is an entry point to regenerate cultural, community and collaborative values in the belief that the challenges to development can be overcome only together.

There is still a lack of evidence about the contribution of heritage to the social cohesion/inclusion (Table 5). Cultural heritage has positive impacts on social capital, revitalizing synergies, bonds and collaborative relationships. It is able to encourage associations, crowdfunding projects, and cooperation that contribute to local economic productivity. Therefore, the importance of evaluating this specific category needs to be stressed. Cultural heritage is able to build social capital and to contribute to social cohesion through providing a framework for participation and engagement and also fostering integration (CHCfE Consortium 2015). Cultural heritage expresses values and identity and organizes communities as well as their relationships through its powerful symbolic and aesthetic dimensions. The preservation of the diversity of cultural heritage, an equitable access to it and a fair sharing of its benefits can enhance the sense of belonging and place. Cultural heritage expresses and maintains the values and traditions of a city and its community, but its significance differ amongst communities and also among members of the same community. It links past, present and future but, at the same time, has the potential for generating conflicts. Diverse social groups could have different values and belief as well as different perceptions about what is relevant for their identity this can attribute different values to a heritage place. Coexistence of these differences can represent a problematic issue and sometimes can be the cause of actions that could have negative impacts on heritage values.

Table 4: Real estate (RE) economic indicators

Sub-category	Indicator	Unit measure
Employment	Growth of employment within RE development	%
RE Values	Average monthly rent	€
RE Values	Average market value	€
RE Values	Increase in private land value	€
RE Values	Increase in public land value (due to infrastructure development)	% and €
RE Values	% of Increase in property values	%/year
RE Values	Evolution of ownership and rental structures	%
RE Values	Volume of transactions in the RE market	€
RE Values	Number of office spaces	n.
RE Values	Price of properties	€/year
RE Values	N. of commercial units	n.
RE Values	Value of historic buildings	€/sqm
RE Values	Increase in value of surrounding buildings	€/sqm
RE Values	Rent values for commercial-use properties	€
RE Values	Rent values for residential properties	€
RE Values	Average value of property transactions	€
RE development	N. of new residential units	n.
RE development	Square feet of commercial development	Sq. feet
RE development	Property taxes gained from commercial development	€
RE development	Increase in municipal taxes	€/ year
RE development	N. of new construction activities and new permits	n.
RE development	Number of construction, restoration and adaptation	n.
RE development	works on historic buildings	n.
RE development	Re-functionalization of historic buildings	%
RE development	Housing vacancy rate	%
RE development	% of well-preserved buildings	%

Source: see Table 1

Table 5: Community and social cohesion indicators

Sub-category	Indicator	Unit measure
Social Care	Number of individuals receiving social care	n./inhab.
Social Cohesion	N. of volunteers	n./year
Social Cohesion	New funds to support activities of a non-profit organization	€/year
Social Cohesion	Perception of personal safety	qualitative
Social Cohesion	Number of association	n./10000 inhab.
Sharing/ Collaborative Economy	N. of new cooperative enterprises	n.
Sharing/ Collaborative Economy	N. of participants in crowdfunding initiatives	n.
Sharing/ Collaborative Economy	Amount of money crowdsourced through crowdfunding campaigns	€

Source: see Table 1

Conflicts and disagreements (in terms of values, interests and beliefs) can represent, if not well managed, an obstacle in the achievement of heritage outcomes to produce benefits for each involved stakeholder. Differences are inevitable, but they need to be acknowledged and respected in order to mitigate possible conflicts. A fundamental step of heritage management is to understand heritage values held by different groups within a society. Effective cultural heritage conservation can be achieved only through a wide community participation in choices and actions. It is necessary to ensure community participation in decision processes related to heritage conservation. This needs to facilitate dialogue and open the lines of communication to improve relationships. In the consensus building process, the identification of stakeholders and their different interests, values and identities play a key role. The interaction between community and expert knowledge is a prerequisite for implementing the UNESCO approach (UNESCO 2011). Collaborative processes are important to resolve differences in order to reach consensus and adopt decisions that can be effectively and sustainably implemented. Today, the increasingly multicultural society requires dialogue and reciprocity. Cultural heritage becomes a source of identity and can represent an entry point for cultural dialogue, mutual knowing and comparison.

Cultural heritage is subject to continuous changes and continuous hybridization processes that adapt throughout history (Fusco Girard et al. 2014): each building expresses the "graft" of new points of view, new styles, etc. in the historical tradition. It represents an "ingredient" for putting end to conflicts through a mutual knowledge of values. Therefore, cultural heritage can play a key role in promoting a more peaceful coexistence.

The last category of wellbeing indicators (Table 6) is analyzed in more detail in the following paragraph. There are some indicators that are currently not proposed and do not emerge from the case studies. Some indicators can be proposed to quantify benefits related to social cohesion (Fusco Girard et al. 2015):

- Community participation for common goods management;

- N. of crowdfunding projects launched;

- N. of crowdfunding projects completed;

- Average donation per person;

- N. of "rewards" allocated;

- N. of local companies involved;

- N. of banking and community foundations.

Some indicators about the social economy category can be proposed:

- N. of cultural urban landscape regeneration projects financed through municipal bonds;

- N. of released bonds;

- Areas of cultural urban landscape regenerated through municipal bond/crowdfunding project.

3 Multidimensional indicators of cultural landscape conservation

Tables 1 to 5 reflect the list of selected multidimensional indicators. Considering these multiple dimensions of cultural heritage, as also Dalmas et al. (2015) recognized, an "inclusive approach" is necessary. This concept recalls the notion of Social Complex Value (Fusco Girard 1987) that expresses the value of the asset without separating it from the community and the environmental context. In this perspective, the value is expressed through a set of multidimensional indicators.

As emerged from the analysis of the case studies, it is important to underline that indicators can be both objective and subjective, both quantitative and qualitative. This is

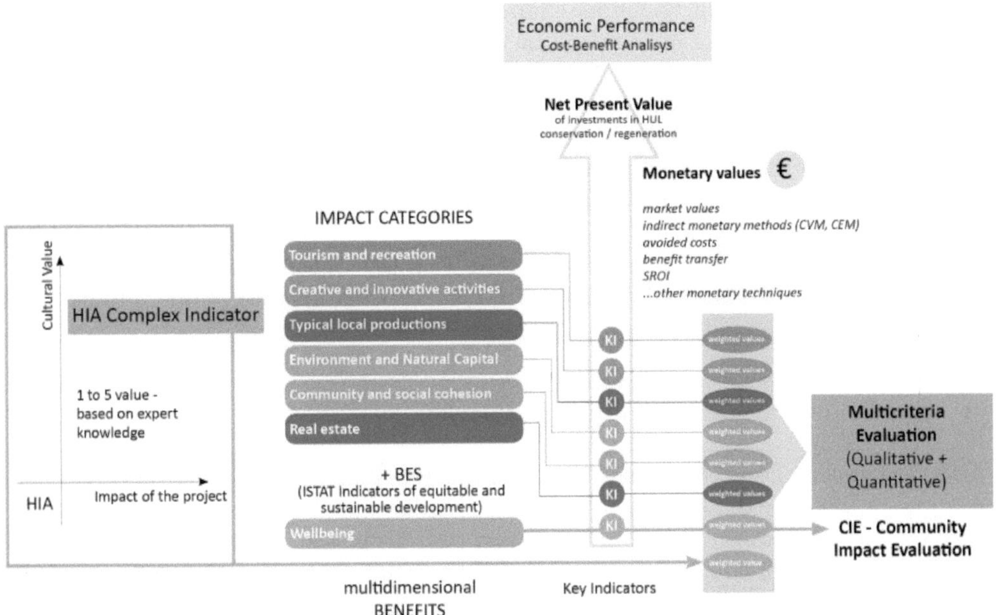

Source: Fusco Girard et al. (2015)

Figure 1: A methodological proposal for the assessing Cultural Urban Landscape

because the cultural urban landscape, just being a landscape, can be perceived in different ways from people who live within it. Our effort is to transform individual perception into a shared interpersonal perception.

Objective indicators are based on hard data, while subjective indicators refer to soft data. Subjective indicators are related to community perception of the landscape. Although they are not based on hard data, the subjective indicators can influence choices and have consequences for the economy and productivity of a city. Several community surveys and focus groups are necessary to support hard data about cultural heritage investments (Rypkema, Cheong 2011).

Once the matrix of the multidimensional indicators has been identified, it is important to understand how to use and "translate" them into operative terms. A first step towards an integrated approach is to evaluate these multidimensional indicators (related to impacts of investments in cultural heritage/landscape conservation/regeneration) as proposed in the methodological framework shown in Figure 1 (Fusco Girard et al. 2015).

This proposed approach considers the enhancement of the cultural value and the multidimensional benefits produced, taking into account all stakeholders' categories. The proposed assessment framework aims to be one step ahead of the Heritage Impact Assessment. It aims to integrate the assessment of integrity and authenticity of cultural heritage with the assessment of the multidimensional benefits produced by the projects. Therefore, in order to capture all impacts produced, indicators referring to all identified categories are considered. Key indicators are identified for each category. They depend on different aspects: scale of intervention, political context, socio-economic conditions, etc. They have to be identified on a case by case basis. The choice of the key indicators is based on both expert knowledge and the results of a participatory process of community involvement. Interviews and questionnaires allow understanding of through which indicators the different stakeholders perceive the project's impacts. Of course, it needs to be considered that the judgment is subjective and it can be influenced by external factors. A greater number of stakeholders increases the reliability of the results. The interaction between community and expert knowledge (Fusco Girard et al. 2013) is essential at this stage in order to identify shared and understandable indicators for (almost) everyone.

The proposed assessment framework has two significant outputs, represented by the Economic Performance and the Multicriteria Evaluation. Some key indicators can be monetized using different techniques (direct market pricing, avoided costs, contingent valuation, etc.), resulting in the monetary value produced by Cultural Landscape conservation/regeneration projects. This value should be compared to the investment and maintenance costs. This economic performance is only one of the outputs of the methodology. A multicriteria evaluation, based on heterogeneous values of key indicators can be structured using the identified impact categories. This process can integrate the Heritage Impact Assessment, providing a new comprehensive impact assessment. Considering the multidimensionality of the issue, it needs to hybridize different evaluation methods. The proposed assessment framework considers Cultural Urban Landscape "as a complex indicator for sustainability of the city or territory, of the quality of life, vitality of the place, and the community's sense of belonging" (Hosagrahar et al. 2016).

4 Landscape variation/wellbeing variation

In a period characterized by considerable unsustainability, the evaluation of wellbeing assumes a central role and human well-being can be recognized as the ultimate goal of sustainable development. According to this goal all public institutions should ensure wellbeing, both individual and collective. It is not only related to economic wealth, but also to the condition of ensuring social cohesion, human rights fulfilment, human needs fulfilment etc. In this perspective, understanding the linkage between the variation of landscape and the variation of wellbeing becomes a relevant issue. First and before evaluation, the concept of wellbeing needs to be defined. Wellbeing is a multidimensional concept that changes in the spatial and temporal dimension. It changes in time, place and culture. So it is difficult to define it in a univocal way.

Despite the health dimension, principally associated with medicine (that have always the same parameters), the wellbeing dimension involves dynamic characteristics. So, in order to define the wellbeing dimension, it is important to understand the context in which people live. The latter is important to define human wellbeing because different factors can interfere with each other and influence it.

Interesting considerations about the assessment of wellbeing and its dimensions are identified by the National Institute of Statistics (ISTAT) and analysed in the BES and URBES Reports (ISTAT 2015a,b). Equitable and Sustainable Wellbeing (BES) is an analysis of the aspects that contribute to the quality of life and it is articulated in 12 sectors (wellbeing dimensions) and 130 indicators. These reports (BES and UrBES) are part of the international debate on the topics "beyond GDP" and the "need for broader measures of progress to complement gross domestic product" (United Nation 2012). Their purpose is to produce a set of multidimensional indicators able to evaluate wellbeing. They achieve this by integrating the "traditional economic indicators" with indicators related to the quality of life that considers equity and sustainability issues in order to give a more complete point of view about society's development. The aim of ISTAT is to support the debate "beyond GDP", trying to bring together social, economic, environmental and good governance aspects (all of them are fundamental to achieve wellbeing). The wealth of the society has been for too long linked to increasing GDP. It represents an important economic indicator able to evaluate the wealth of a society; this linkage – between GDP (gross domestic product) and the wealth of society – is a common belief based principally on the idea of "economic growth". Nevertheless, GDP is not able to capture the multidimensional aspects of wellbeing. It does not represent human wellbeing (Stiglitz et al. 2009): instead it needs to go beyond the mere economic number. Economics should be only instrumental to the achievement of wellbeing. GDP is an oversimplified measure that leaves out many aspects that are not economically evaluable: it is not able to capture information about wellbeing, happiness and the level of life quality.

The above mentioned considerations and the shift towards the new paradigm (Hosagrahar et al. 2016) require an overcoming of this assumption. Therefore, in this perspective the need for new indicators emerges. The issue related to the evaluation of wellbeing assumes a central role in the current debate. It is important to evaluate wellbeing through multidimensional approaches, able to take into account for example aspects of subjective evaluation from citizens. In the ISTAT reports some indicators are identified. They (integrated with others) could be considered in the seventh category (wellbeing category) of the evaluation framework proposed in this paper. Due to the complexity of the notion of wellbeing and its subjectivity (wellbeing is perceived), it is difficult to identify general shared indicators.

In the common understanding wellbeing is associated with a good quality of life. It is a true assumption, but quality of life is not the only indicator of wellbeing. Wellbeing is associated with a comfortable, healthy, happy life and life quality affects this state. Life satisfaction is another indicators used (in combination with others) to assess wellbeing. The binomial "landscape-wellbeing" assumes a central role in the international debate related to sustainable development (Duxbury et al. 2016, Hosagrahar et al. 2016, ISTAT 2015a,b). Landscape is important for our wellbeing and this is intuitive: we unconsciously search for a place able to communicate to us a sense of harmony, balance, liveliness. At the same time, we usually get away from places that communicate untidiness.

An important factor of landscape is also its identity. A landscape is "good" if it is recognizable and it is "bad" if it has elements not recognizable as identities of that place, but rather seeming extraneous to it. Aesthetic value can contribute to wellbeing but, at the same time, it is the most subjective and personal value. Considering a landscape only as a source of aesthetic enjoyment is an oversimplification. It can also produce wellbeing or illness according to other aspects more complex and less immediately perceptible characteristics. The quality of landscape depends on aesthetic factors and also on aspects related to all landscape values. It is not only related to a visual perception (D'Auria, Monti 2013). In landscape the signs of the past are stratified, in a constantly changing way. The landscape keeps the signs of the evolution of the relationship between man, the environment and its history. This relation impacts on our wellbeing, "communicating" to us a sense of belonging, security, etc., contributing to individual and collective wellbeing. A good landscape produces a sense of wellbeing, a bad landscape produces illness. The landscape also affects our actions and our choices. A healthy landscape corresponds to attractiveness capacity, economic and social dynamics, etc., while an ill landscape corresponds to relocation and degradation, etc.

The economic dimension of the binomial landscape-wellbeing is also important. A good landscape has repercussion also on the economic field: a beautiful and interesting place, for example, attracts tourists, investors, etc. A good quality landscape is an attractor for localization of cultural services, art galleries, museums, theatres. Also the intangible landscapes (human and social) play a central role in local development, creating cooperative capacity, synergies and symbioses (Fusco Girard 2013). Empirical evidence shows that there is a relationship between landscape quality and goods and service demand/sale; in/for a good landscape, there is a higher willingness to pay.

If we are able to conserve Cultural Heritage, we build memory of ourselves and therefore we are able to conserve identity in the face of globalization changes. Conservation expresses the deliberate effort to fix memories in time, to avoid losing our identity. We can react to the risk of losing our identity (because of globalization) through Cultural Heritage. We fix the memory through Cultural Heritage that has been handed down and, in turn, we pass it on to future generations. For this reason, all actions aimed at protecting and improving the environmental, social and economic wellbeing of communities should take into account cultural heritage as well as the opportunities that it offers and threats due to an inappropriate use. Human participation in local cultural activities, such as music, dance and theatre, contributes to the improvements in wellbeing and quality of life (Duxbury et al. 2016). Community participation in cultural activities therefore fosters wellbeing.

There is not much empirical evidence about the contribution of cultural heritage to the achievement of wellbeing. This contribution is related both to the dimension of cultural heritage and identity, sense of belonging, etc. and to the mere functional dimension related to its use. Both of these are important to the achievement of sustainable development with particular reference to the wellbeing category. Cultural heritage contributes to bettering urban life in different ways. For example providing options for housing (through reuse etc.) to improve public spaces, etc. Below some wellbeing indicators (extracted from

Table 6: Wellbeing indicators associated to cultural heritage conservation

Sub-category	Indicator	Unit measure
Education and training	Young people who do not work and do not study	%
Work and life balance	Employment	%
Work and life balance	Non-attendance at work	%
Economic well-being	Available income	€
Housing quality	% of population living in homes without toilet	%
Social relationships	N. of volunteers in non-profit	N./10,000 inhab.
Social relationships	N. of non-profit institutions	N./10,000 inhab.
Social relationships	N. of social cooperatives	N./10,000 inhab.
Security	Murder	N./100,000 inhab.
Security	Theft in dwelling	N./100,000 inhab.
Security	Pickpocketing	N./100,000 inhab.
Security	Robberies	N./100,000 inhab.
Landscape & cultural heritage	Public libraries	N./100,000 inhab.
Landscape & cultural heritage	Museums	N./100,000 inhab.
Landscape & cultural heritage	Libraries users	N./100 inhab.
Landscape & cultural heritage	Museums visitors	N./100 inhab.
Landscape & cultural heritage	Green space	Sqm on 100 sqm
Environment	Drinking water drainage	% of water scattered on the fed volume of water
Environment	Urban air quality	Daily value for PM10
Environment	Urban green space	Green square meters per inhabitant
Environment	Protected natural areas	% of the municipal area
Environment	Urban gardens	Sqm per 100 inhab.
Research and innovation	Patents	Patent applications per million inhab.
Research and innovation	Productive specialization	Productive specialization in knowledge-intensive technological sectors for 100 emp. of local units
Quality of services	Cycle paths	km per 100 km^2
Quality of services	Pedestrian areas	smq per 100 inhab.

Source: Il Benessere Equo e Sostenibile nelle Città – Report ISTAT (ISTAT 2015b)

URBES indicators) are listed that could be considered for cultural heritage conservation projects.

An example is the case study of Skopje (Throsby 2012). The project aimed at the preservation of cultural heritage, the revitalization of the area and the promotion of participation of residents in the program design and implementation (2005). This produced an increase in the employment rate, for example the number of staffing in museums increased from 13 employees (pre-2005) to 50 employees (post-2005). The improvement of landscape increased the attractiveness of the city. It is "translated" in terms of increases in the number of visitors (economic benefits). In fact, the average number of visitors per year for three main museums/galleries in the Skopje old bazaar increased from 257,000 (pre-2005) to 414,000 (post-2005). Another social indicator able to show the capacity of cultural heritage to produce wellbeing is related to the increase in the average monthly wage/salary level that rose from 270 US\$ (pre-2005) to 515 US\$ (post-2005) for Managerial/administrative staff and from 185 US\$ (pre-2005) to 380 US\$ for service/selling staff (post-2005) (Throsby 2012).

Oaxaca De Juarez is another case study (Quartesan, Romis 2010) demonstrating the multidimensional benefits of cultural heritage conservation/regeneration. A significant indicator related to the conservation project of this city (year 2005) is the decrease of vecindades (units that hosts different families that share facilities such as lavatories, kitchens, etc.) from 75 (year 1997) to a number of 35 (2008) (Quartesan, Romis 2010).

The conservation project of the historic center of Salvador De Bahia is another significant example of the contribution of cultural heritage conservation to the increase of wellbeing and city productivity. In fact, after the conservation project, the median worker income increased from 609 Brazilean Reais (year 2000) up to 631 Brazilean Reais (year 2007) and the total unemployment rate decreased from 26.5% in the years 2001-2003 to 22.4% in the years 2005-2007 (Mendes Zancheti, Gabriel 2010).

The preservation project of Toronto produced an increase in the number of artists from 10.5 million (year 2004) to over 11.5 million (year 2006). In addition, the attendance at City-funded and City-operated cultural programs for youth (16-24) increased from 281,000 (year 2004) up to 593,000 (2006) (Ogilvie 2009).

After the nomination as European Capital of Culture 2008, Liverpool registered an increase in the number of employees in creative industry enterprises from 10,000 (year 2004) up to 10,987 (year 2008). It is also important to note the perception of the community. By the end of 2008, 85% of Liverpool's residents agreed that the city, after the nomination as European Capital of Culture, is a better place than before nomination with an improved quality of life (Garcia et al. 2008).

From case studies some data related to wellbeing has emerged: data related to job satisfaction, generalized trust, perceived access to services or satisfaction with relationships did not emerge. Like these case studies, there are many others demonstrating the benefits produced by cultural heritage conservation/regeneration, not only economic benefits, but multidimensional ones. They emerged also in the analysis of the case study of Pozzuoli (South of Italy) that is a forthcoming work (Nocca 2017).

5   Conclusions

This is a very important moment for urban policies because the international debate is focused on sustainable development and the "New Urban Agenda" has been approved at Habitat III, the United Nations Conference on Housing and Sustainable Urban Development, that was held in Quito, Ecuador, in October 2016 (United Nations 2016). It strengthened the idea that cultural heritage and landscape conservation /regeneration can play a key role in sustainable development.

Cultural heritage is interpreted as an essential component of the urban system, of the city as a living organism, and as Patrik Geddes anticipated in 1915 (Geddes 1915), of the city as a dynamic, complex and adaptive system reflecting the changes in society, turning with it, and adapting to new demands in a dynamic perspective. Therefore, the city as a living organism should emulate the behaviour of nature through organizing all processes according to circular economy processes in which nothing is wasted, but everything can be reused (Nocca 2017). In this way, each "product" becomes nutritious for the other and does not produce waste. In this perspective Cultural Heritage can be considered part of a circular productive process through maintenance, reuse and recycling.

The indicator matrix emerging from the present study represents a first step towards a new effective approach able to support the recognition of the key role of cultural heritage in sustainable development. As has emerged from the previous paragraphs, the cultural heritage approach requires an adaptation of evaluation methods. The challenge is to identify a more effective evaluation approach/method that contributes to make integrated conservation more effectively into sustainable human development strategies.

The above-mentioned perspective of city humanization through cultural heritage conservation/ regeneration suggests focusing on social and human impacts of conservation. The aim is to identify and evaluate the value of cultural heritage through quantitative and qualitative data, developing indicators and maps in order to demonstrate that cultural heritage can contribute to comprehensive local productivity.

As emerged from empirical evidence, Cultural Urban Landscape conservation can be an effective catalyst for stimulating local and regional economies (Licciardi 2012, Luxen 2010). The good practices demonstrate that it is able to contribute to city productivity. It is also able to produce economic impacts (Nypan 2005), but there is a need to demonstrate the multidimensional effects of investments. Economic parameters alone are not able to effectively evaluate the progress of societies, but they need to be integrated with social and environmental information and with indicators of inequality and sustainability.

Surely, the economic impacts of cultural heritage conservation/ regeneration need to be understood more in depth, especially because the society of today speaks the only language of economics. An economic matrix is absolutely necessary, but it is not sufficient. It is not able to capture the multidimensional benefits of cultural heritage conservation/regeneration. Hybrid evaluation methods (Fusco Girard 2014b,c) are therefore required in order to integrate the economic matrix with qualitative indicators, expressed by social (social matrix) and environmental components (ecological matrix) (Fusco Girard et al. 2015, Nocca, De Rosa 2015).

References

Actum (2011) Ecosystem services evaluation in the Škocjan Caves regional park. World Wide Fund for Nature, Rome

Angrisano M, Biancamano P, Bosone M, Carone P, Daldanise G, De Rosa F, Franciosa A, Gravagnuolo A, Iodice S, Nocca F, Onesti A, Panaro S, Ragozino S, Sannicandro V, Fusco Girard L (2016) Towards operationalizing UNESCO recommendations on historic urban landscape. *Aestimum* 69: 165–210. CrossRef.

Bigio AG (2010) The sustainability of urban heritage preservation. The case of Marrakesh. Discussion paper Idb-Dp-120, Inter-American Development

CHCfE Consortium (2015) Cultural heritage counts for Europe. Full report. http://blogs.encatc.org/culturalheritagecountsforeurope/outcomes/

Dalberg – Dalberg Global Development Advisors (2013) The economic value of Virunga national park. WWF International, Gland, Switzerland

Dalmas L, Noël J, Geronimi V (2015) Economic evaluation of urban heritage: An inclusive approach under a sustainability perspective. *Journal of Cultural Heritage.* CrossRef.

D'Auria A (2009) Urban cultural tourism: Creative approaches for heritage-based sustainable development. *International Journal of Sustainable Development* 12[2-4]: 275–289

D'Auria A, Monti B (2013) The guardianship of the landscapes between identification and assessment: Ischia and its lost identity. Proceedings of the international scientific conference on Society, Integration, and Education Location, Udine, Italy, June 27-28, 2013

Douglas J (2006) *Building Adaptation.* Butterworth Heinemann, Oxford. CrossRef.

Duxbury N, Hosagrahar J, Pascual J (2016) Agenda 21 for Culture United – why must culture be at the heart of sustainable urban development? Cities and Local Governments (UCLG)

European Commission (2014) Towards an integrated approach to cultural heritage for Europe. Communication from the Commission to the European Parliament, the Council, the European Economic and Social Committee and the Committee of the Regions. Brussels, 22.7.2014

EVoCH – Economic Value of Cultural Heritage (2012) Final conclusions EVoCH project. Valladolid, Junta de Castilla y León

Florida R (2002) *The Rise of the Creative Class: And How it's transforming work, leisure, community and everyday life.* Perseus Book Group, New York

Fusco Girard L (1987) *Risorse architettoniche e culturali: valutazioni e strategie di conservazione.* Franco Angeli, Milano

Fusco Girard L (2013) Toward a smart sustainable development of port cities/areas: the role of the historic urban landscape approach. *Sustainability* 5[10]: 4329–4348

Fusco Girard L (2014a) Creative cities: the challenge of humanization in the city development. *Bollettino del Centro Calza Bini* 13[1]: 9–33

Fusco Girard L (2014b) Presentation of theme 4: Community driven conservation and local empowerment. Proceedings of ICOMOS XVIII, general assembly and scientific symposium heritage and landscape as human values. Florence, Italy, November 10-14, 2014

Fusco Girard L (2014c) The role of cultural urban landscape towards a new urban economics: new structural assets for increasing economic productivity through hybrid processes. *Housing Policies and Urban Economics* 1[1]: 3–27

Fusco Girard L, Angrisano M, Bosone M, Gravagnuolo A, Nocca F (2015) Towards an economic impact assessment framework for historic urban landscape conservation and regeneration projects. *Bollettino Del Centro Calza Bini* 15[2]: 1–29

Fusco Girard L, Cerreta M, De Toro P (2013) Integrated assessment for sustainable choices. *Scienze Regionali* 13[1]: 111–142

Fusco Girard L, De Rosa F, Nocca F (2014) Verso il piano strategico di una città storica: Viterbo. *Bollettino del Dipartimento di Conservazione dei Beni Architettonici e Ambientali* 14[1]: 11–38

Garcia B, Melville R, Cox T (2008) IMPACTS 08 European Capital of Culture research programme. Creating an impact: Liverpool's experience as European Capital of Culture. University of Liverpool

Geddes P (1915) *Cities in evolution: an introduction to the town planning movement and to the study of civics.* Williams & Norgate, London

Glass R (1964) *London: aspects of change.* MacGibbon & Kee, London

Hosagrahar J, Soule J, Fusco Girard L, Potts A (2016) Cultural heritage, the UN sustainable development goals, and the new urban agenda. ICOMOS concept note for the United Nations Agenda 2030 and the third United Nations conference on housing and sustainable urban development (HABITAT III)

HR&A Advisors (2010) Conservation for the living city economic effects assessment, waterfront of Toronto. Technical memorandum

ICOMOS (2011) Guidance on heritage impact assessments for cultural world heritage properties. ICOMOS, Paris

ISTAT (2015a) BES. Il benessere equo e sostenibile in Italia. Report ISTAT 2015

ISTAT (2015b) URBES. Il benessere equo e sostenibile nelle città. Report ISTAT 2015

IUCN (2014) The benefits of natural world heritage. IUCN, Gland, Switzerland

Labadi S (2008) Evaluating the socio-economic impacts of selected regenerated heritage sites in Europe. European Cultural Foundation, Cultural Policy Research Award 2008

Landorf C (2009) Managing for sustainable tourism: A review of six cultural world heritage sites. *Journal of Sustainable Tourism* 17[1]: 53–70. CrossRef.

Licciardi G (2012) The economics of uniqueness: Investing in historic city cores and cultural heritage. Cultural heritage assets for sustainable development. World Bank, Washington, DC

Loureço-Gomes L (2009) Valoração económica de património cultural: Aplicação da técnica de escolhas discretas ao alto douro vinhateiro património da humanidade. PhD thesis in economic sciences, Universidade do Minho, Portugal

Luxen JL (2010) Heritage economics and conservation funding. Euromed Heritage Proceedings, Damascus, Syria, 6-8 June, 2010

Mendes Zancheti S, Gabriel J (2010) The sustainability of urban heritage preservation. The case of Salvador de Bahia. Discussion paper Idb-Dp-121, Inter-American Development

Nocca F (2017) Hybrid evaluation tools for operationalizing UNESCO historic urban landscape approach. Phd thesis

Nocca F, De Rosa F (2015) Sustainable development and urban conservation: the challenge of historic urban landscape. *Housing Policies and Urban Economics* 2[1]: 15–30

Nocca F, Gravagnuolo A, Angrisano M, Bosone M (2016) Towards an evaluation framework for the operationalization of Unesco historic urban landscape approach. Advanced Brainstorm Carrefour (ABC) The Science of the City. Naples, 21-23 March 2016

Nypan T (2005) Cultural heritage monuments and historic buildings as value generators in a post-industrial economy. With emphasis on exploring the role of the sector as economic driver. Directorate for Cultural Heritage, Norway

Ogilvie D (2009) Tourism Toronto annual report. Toronto convention and visitors association, http://www.seetorontonow.com

Orbasli A (2010) City of Bath world heritage site. Economic development appraisal, Oxford Brooks University, UK

Pais I, Peretti P, Spinelli C (2014) Crowdfunding. la via collaborativa all'imprenditorialità. EGEA, Milano

Pereira Roders A, Bond A, Teller J (2013) Determining effectiveness in heritage impact assessments. Proceedings of the 33rd annual conference of the International Association for Impact Assessment (IAIA13), Impact Assessment: The next generation, Calgary, Canada, 13-16 May 2013

Quartesan A, Romis M (2010) The sustainability of urban heritage preservation. The case of Oaxaca de Juarez. Discussion paper Idb-Dp-127, Inter-American Development

Roland M, Vilain E, Moussallam K (2004) Une année marquée par l'impact de Lille 2004. Bilan annuel de l'hôtellerie régionale – Comité Régional de Tourisme, Lille

Rypkema D, Cheong C (2011) Measurements and indicators of heritage as development. IICOMOS 17th general assembly, 2011-11-27 / 2011-12-02, Paris, France

Sen A (2000) Culture and development. World Bank Tokyo meeting. 13 December 2000

Stiglitz J, Sen A, Fitoussi J (2009) Rapport de la commission sur la mesure des performances économiques et du progrès social. http://www.stiglitz-sen-fitoussi.fr

Throsby D (2012) Investment in urban heritage. Economic impacts of cultural heritage projects in FYR Macedonia and Georgia. Urban development series, World Bank

Torquati B, Giacché G (2013) Paesaggio rurale storico italiano: analisi economica dei vigneti di Lamole in Toscana. In: Poli D (ed), *Agricoltura paesaggistica. Visioni, metodi, esperienze.* Firenze University Press, Firenze, Italy, 277–294

Torquati B, Giacchè G, Venanzi S (2011) The restoration and the development of the historical Italian wine-growing landscapes: Comparing the three case studies. Paper presented at 2nd International Conference on Landscape Economics, Padova, Italy, 4-6 July 2011

Trivelli P, Nishimura Y (2010) The sustainability of urban heritage preservation. The case of Valparaiso. Discussion paper Idb-Dp-122, Inter-American Development

UNESCO (2011) Recommendation on the historic urban landscape. UNESCO World Heritage Centre, Parigi

UNESCO (2013) Introducing cultural heritage into the sustainable development agenda. Hangzhou International Congress: Culture key to sustainable development. Panel discussion 3a-a. 15-17 May, 2013

United Nation (2012) Future we want – outcome document. United Nations Conference on Sustainable Development (Rio+20). Rio de Janeiro, Brazil. 20-22 June 2012

United Nations (2015a) Indicators and a monitoring framework for the sustainable development goals. Launching a data revolution. Report to the Secretary-General of the United Nations by the Leadership Council of the Sustainable Development Solutions Network, Sustainable Development Knowledge Platform, June 12, 2015

United Nations (2015b) The millennium development goals Report 2015. United Nations, New York, USA

United Nations (2016) Draft outcome document of the United Nations Conference on Housing and Sustainable Urban Development (Habitat III). Quito, Ecuador. October 17-20, 2016

World Bank (2015) Tanzania, Zanzibar urban services project appraisal document. http://www-wds.worldbank.org

Part C:

Spatial Mobility and Economic Disparity Effects

Volume 4, Number 3, 2017, 153–173
DOI: 10.18335/region.v4i3.145

journal homepage: region.ersa.org

Regional Spanish Tourism Competitiveness

Juan Carlos Martín[1], Cira Mendoza[1], Concepción Román[1]

[1] University of Las Palmas de Gran Canaria, Las Palmas, Spain

Received: 21 July 2016/Accepted: 18 May 2017

Abstract. The aim of this paper is to analyse the regional tourist competitiveness performance in Spain. We use the seven pillars of tourism from a very detailed and complete database carried out by the Spanish Government – MoniTUR 2010 as primary data. Thus, we calculate several regional tourist competitiveness indices using data envelopment analysis (DEA) to analyse the robustness of the results obtained in the ranking of the tourist competitiveness for the 17 Spanish Autonomous Communities. Our results are robust to the use of two different modelling strategies: (1) input and output variables selection; and (2) virtual and super efficiency DEA models. Madrid and La Rioja are found to be the most competitive regions; meanwhile other inland regions of Spain like Extremadura and Aragón are the least competitive. The position of each of the laggard Autonomous Communities should be analysed by their respective destination management organizations (DMOs) in order to envisage adequate corrective measures.

Key words: DEA; Regional tourist competitiveness; Destination management organizations; MoniTUR; Virtual Efficiency

1 Introduction

Tourism has become today one of the largest and fastest-growing economic sectors worldwide. It is an important driver of socio-economic progress as it stimulates economies and leads to the creation of jobs, incomes, investments and exports. Despite the obstacles faced during the impact of the unprecedented financial and economic crisis that hit the world in 2008, the sector has proven to be a consolidated industry which still maintains high levels of activity and has contributed to economic recovery. In 2014, tourism was responsible for generating a significant 9% world GDP (including direct, indirect and induced effect). International tourist arrivals worldwide reached 1,138 million in 2014, 51 million more than in 2013, and the UNWTO forecasts a growth between 3% and 4% in 2015 (UNWTO 2015). Despite the fall in the tourism activity in 2008 and 2009 due to the destructive effects of the financial crisis, Spanish tourism has proven to recover successfully from this observed unprecedented drawback. Spain attracted in the year 2014 for the first time in history a peak of 65.2 million international tourists, getting positioned as the third world's top tourist destination in international tourist arrivals and the second in international tourism receipts. In addition, the country ranked first among 141 countries in the Travel & Tourism Competitiveness Index 2015 published by the World Economic Forum. In fact, tourism is one of the main economic driving forces in the country, contributing directly 10.9% GDP, generating 12% of jobs and covering 276% of trade deficit (Ministerio de Industria, Energía y Turismo 2015). The most significant tourist segment in the country is sun and sand mass tourism. Cities and municipalities along the Mediterranean coast and the Balearics and the Canary Islands stand out as some of the world's sun and beach most favourite tourist destinations.

In order to be competitive, tourist destinations must persuade their potential tourists that they will obtain more benefit visiting their destination than any other else (Crouch 2011). Destination marketing plays a determinant role in this regard, assisting visitors with pre-visit information and after-arrival additional information; coordinating many constituent tourist sector elements; creating specific tourism planning laws; or helping to ensure the attractiveness of a set of events, programs and tourism facilities, among others. Nevertheless, when competences in tourism in a certain country are decentralized, regional governments cannot confer the same effort to tourism planning since the priorities and strategies for tourism might not be concordant. This is usually caused by the intrinsic and differential characteristics of territories. Thus, a regional analysis on tourist competitiveness within the Spanish territory is paramount in order to develop adequate destination marketing plans that enhance the image of the tourist Spanish brand.

Despite the favourable results of Spanish tourism, improvements in competitiveness from the regional perspective are needed in order to enhance the competitive position of the whole country and ensure a sustainable growth (Exceltur 2011b). Spain is divided into 17 regions at level II of the Nomenclature of Territorial Units for Statistics (referred as NUTS by the French acronym). These regions, also named Autonomous Communities, have regional governments that share governance with the Spanish central administration within their respective territories. In the field of tourism, the exclusive competence corresponds to the Autonomous Communities, so the medium and long term regional tourist competitive success depend largely on the regional tourist policies. Differences in tourist competitiveness among Spanish regions exist, mainly due to the existence of different territorial natural endowments. This dissimilarity makes the measurement and comparison of regional tourist competitiveness a complex and difficult task. Exceltur (2011b) reveals the existence of these differences on the base of climatic, scenic, cultural and sociodemographic characteristics that difficult the regional comparisons.

In this sense, the development of measurement techniques to benchmark regional tourist competitiveness becomes essential to boost the evolution of policies and private and public strategies that facilitate a differential gradual tourist repositioning. Alonso (2010) considers that the evaluation of competitiveness is a key aspect that allows destinations to facilitate, control and judge policies and strategies that quest for continuous improvements. The present research addresses this issue through the construction of a synthetic index to assess tourist competitiveness among the 17 Autonomous Communities in Spain. According to Cracolici et al. (2008), tourist areas endeavour to exploit their locational attractiveness by a smart use of input factors. Through Data Envelopment Analysis (DEA) methodology, multiple inputs and multiple outputs are combined to model multidimensional relationships among different regional competitiveness dimensions, and to compute several synthetic indices that measure the Spanish regional tourist competitiveness. Dealing with the seven tourism competitiveness pillars of MoniTUR 2010 report (Exceltur 2011b), the proposed approach uses DEA as a tool for multiple criteria decision making (MCDM). A further analysis of the robustness of the results obtained by different DEA methods is made and, furthermore, the paper will also analyse the potential differences observed among the Spanish regions highlighting the laggard regions.

The remainder of the paper is organized as follows: Section 2 offers some insights from the literature, section 3 describes the data section, section 4 details the methodology, section 5 presents and discusses the results, and finally section 6 offers some concluding remarks.

2 Literature review

The success of tourism destinations in world markets is determined by their competitiveness compared with other destination options (Dwyer et al. 2000). The concept of destination competitiveness can appear to be simple and easily understandable – it is the expression of qualitative and quantitative superiority of a territory over actual and potential competitors. Nevertheless, the complexity of the concept becomes apparent when we attempt not only to define it, but also to measure it. Numerous researchers have studied the concept of destination competitiveness, their models and determinants (Scott, Lodge 1985, Crouch, Ritchie 1999, Newall 1992, OECD 1994, Dwyer, Kim 2003, Dwyer et al. 2004, Enright, Newton 2004).

Enright, Newton (2004, p. 778) state that "a destination is competitive if it can attract and satisfy potential tourists and this competitiveness is determined both by tourism-specific factors and by a much wider range of factors that influence the tourism service providers". Similarly, Ritchie, Crouch (2003, p. 2), detailed that "what makes a tourism destination truly competitive is its ability to increase tourism expenditure, to increasingly attract visitors, while providing them with satisfying, memorable experiences, and to do so in a profitable way, while enhancing the well-being of destination residents and preserving the natural capital of the destination for future generations". These authors have developed since 1990s an extensive framework that has served as key reference for tourism destination management (Crouch, Ritchie 1994, 1995, 1999, 2005, Ritchie, Crouch 1993, 2000a,b, 2003, Crouch 2011). Their proposed model has as principal strength their capability to integrate all the significant factors that might symbolize destination's tourism competitiveness. They determine in their study that the attributes explaining destination competitiveness can be gathered into four major groups: (1) Core Resources and Attractors (physiography, culture and history, market ties, mix of activities, special events, entertainment and superstructure); (2) Supporting Factors and Resources (infrastructure, accessibility, facilitating resources, hospitality, enterprise); (3) Destination Management (resources stewardship, marketing, finance and venture capital, organization, human resource development, information/research, quality of service, visitor management); and (4) Qualifying Determinants (location, interdependencies, safety/security, awareness/image/brand, cost/value) and Destination Policy, Planning and Development. Crouch (2011) analysed the impact and magnitude of these factors affecting destination competitiveness, remarking that the Core Resources and Attractors were the most relevant. The weights of the factors and sub factors were also estimated in Crouch's study, finding that Accessibility, Physiography and Climate, Positioning/Branding, Quality of Service/Experience and Safety and Security were the most significant sub factors.

The research interest for tourism destination competitiveness that emerged in the 1990s also raised concerns for measuring it. There have been a growing number of studies that measure and assess destination competitiveness, and several evaluation methods have been reported like composite indicators based on linear aggregation models or other MCDM methods like DEA or TOPSIS (The Technique for Order of Preference by Similarity to Ideal Solution). Destination competitiveness can be assessed by using both quantitative and qualitative data. The use of hard data, such as income from tourism tourist arrivals, makes possible the quantitative evaluation of destination competitiveness performance. As Kozak, Rimmington (1999) state, qualitative performance of a destination is also useful, as it ultimately drives quantitative performance. These authors measure tourist destination competitiveness for international tourist destinations by using both quantitative and qualitative approaches. In fact, Jick (1979) advocates that both methods are complements instead of substitutes. Similarly, Mendola, Volo (2017) analyze ten of the most relevant papers on the tourism destination competitiveness (TDC) topic, admitting that qualitative performance measurement would rightfully complement quantitative measures to provide guidance in tourism policy making. However, the authors do not provide a protocol or good guidelines about how to proceed with this interesting idea, and to our knowledge, most of the papers are quantitative in nature although sometimes the databases contain some qualitative or soft data.

Regarding the unit of analysis for the destinations, it can be said that there are indeed different geographical references analysing tourist competitiveness at both regional/sub regional and national levels. For example, Kayar, Kozak (2010) measure destination competitiveness for 28 European countries applying the Travel & Tourism Competitiveness Index 2007 (TTCI). There exists also a balanced presence in literature of works in which Gooroochurn, Sugiyarto (2005) compute an aggregate index using confirmatory factor analysis to measure tourism competitiveness for over 200 countries. Dwyer, Kim (2003) built the Competitive Indicators of a Destination (CID) in order to determine the essential factors for the competitiveness of a destination. They determined the following elements: resource endowments (natural and cultural or heritage); resources created (tourist facilities, activities offered, etc.); support factors (general infrastructure, service quality, or accessibility of the destination); and destination management elements. The monitoring report on the relative tourist competitiveness of Spanish Autonomous Communities (MoniTUR) on its 2010 edition (Exceltur 2011b) analyzes their competitive and relative tourist position. It is composed by seven tourist competitive pillars, with 30 crucial areas of competitiveness and 79 final indicators. More detailed explanation of MoniTUR index may be found in the next section.

At regional and sub regional levels, Zhang et al. (2011) evaluate tourism destination competitiveness using TOPSIS and information entropy for sixteen cities in the Yangtze River Delta. The present study follows the theoretical and statistical approach of those of Cracolici, Nijkamp (2006), Cracolici et al. (2008) and Cracolici, Nijkamp (2009). These works employ DEA method in order to assess tourism competitiveness by analyzing the destination efficiency of Italian regions. Benito et al. (2014) also study the determinants of Spanish regions' tourism performance using DEA. At national level, Huang, Peng (2012) assess the competitiveness of tourism industries in nine Asian countries using Fuzzy Rasch model and TOPSIS. Abad, Kongmanwatana (2015) use DEA, super-efficiency DEA and the non-radial Nerlove-Luenberger super-efficiency DEA to compare the destination competitiveness ranking among 27 large and small countries in the European Union. Webster, Ivanov (2014) measure using a cross-section analysis the impact of competitiveness on tourism's contribution to economic growth for 131 countries.

3 MoniTUR and data

3.1 Monitoring report on the relative tourist competitiveness of Spanish Autonomous Communities (MoniTUR)

MoniTUR (Exceltur 2010, 2011b) is an index that measures the tourist relative competitiveness position of the 17 NUTS II (Autonomous Communities) in Spain. It is created by Exceltur in collaboration with Deloitte. Exceltur is a non-profit association formed by 25 of the most important companies throughout the Spanish tourism value chain and subsectors of central air, rail, sea and land transportation, lodging, travel agencies and tour operators, payment, car rental, tourist hospitals and bookings / GDS. Since 2002, these group leaders and heads of the Spanish tourism companies joined to promote a greater socio-economic recognition of what tourism, as a principal sector of Spanish economy, provides and represents and to contribute to achieve higher levels of competitiveness that consolidate a sustainable and rentable leadership and growth of tourism activity in Spain. According to Exceltur (2011b), tourism in Spain has still to face numerous challenges and opportunities with different accents and intensities according to the different Autonomous Communities. In this sense, MoniTUR 2010 is built as a benchmark to boost policy recommendations and private and public strategies in order to facilitate a gradual and differential tourist repositioning of global competitiveness and to rigorously identify the competitive risks and opportunities of each Spanish region.

MoniTUR 2010 (Exceltur 2011b) is the second and last published edition. It incorporates new areas, indicators and more accurate sources of information with respect to the previous MoniTUR 2009 edition. The MoniTUR 2010 report reveals the existence of four groups of Autonomous Communities that share structural similitudes. The first group is composed of the Community of Madrid, País Vasco and Catalonia, all with a high level of income and economic activity. A second group is distinguished by a higher specialization on littoral tourism, in which the Communities of Andalusia, the Canaries, the Balearics and Valencian Community, respectively, stand out. In fact, Catalonia, the Canaries, Balearics and Andalusia are, respectively, the main tourist Autonomous Communities. Together, they attracted 74.1% tourists who visited the country last year. The third group is comprised by mostly inland communities: Navarra, La Rioja, Castile-La Mancha

Table 1: MoniTUR 2010 global ranking

Autonomous Community	Ranking	Index. Average=100
Community of Madrid	1	114.2
Basque country	2	113.3
Catalonia	3	112.7
Andalusia	4	106.8
The Canaries	5	103.3
The Balearics	6	101.8
Valencian Community	7	101.4
Galicia	8	98.9
Navarre	9	98.8
La Rioja	10	98.7
Castile-La Mancha	11	97.8
Castile and Leon	12	97.5
Asturias	13	93.1
Murcia	14	93.0
Cantabria	15	92.1
Aragon	16	91.1
Extremadura	17	87.5

Source: Own elaboration

and Castile-and-León, together with Galicia which has coastline. Finally, a fourth group is comprised by three single-province Autonomous Communities: Murcia, Asturias and Cantabria, as well as Aragón and Extremadura which have more than one province. All of them are conditioned by a lagging tourist starting position, either by minor enhancement of their range of resources and attractions, their accessibility to markets, smaller business sector, or for their still incipient tourist planning and investments.

MoniTUR 2010 analyses 7 pillars of tourist competitiveness. The seven pillars analyses 30 determinant areas of competitiveness, which in turn are divided into 79 indicators. Table A.1 (in the appendix) shows the pillars, crucial areas for competitiveness, indicators and sub indicators that form the global index. Pillars and determinant areas are equally weighted in the index. The report identifies the competitive advantages and disadvantages for each region aggregating indicators and pillars using averages that obtain the global MoniTUR ranking (Table 1). It can be seen that the communities of Madrid, Basque Country, Catalonia, Andalusia and the Canaries were positioned as the top Autonomous Communities, respectively. The communities of Extremadura, Aragon, Cantabria, Murcia and Asturias were at the bottom of the ranking.

3.2 Data

The present study aims to analyse the tourism competitive position of Spanish NUTS II regions in Spain by composing a synthetic composite index. Data have been obtained from the MoniTUR report on its 2010 edition. MoniTUR 2010 obtained quantitative data from databases of both, public institutions, such as The National Institute of Statistics (INE), Turespaña or the Institute of Tourism Studies (IET), and from private associations, institutes and institutions, such as Google, La Caixa, Michelin guide or the Institute of Tourism Quality of Spain. In-depth information about data resources can be found at MoniTUR 2010 annexes (Exceltur 2011a).

In the present study, the 7 pillars were chosen to be the variables used to analyse regional Spanish competitiveness. A more disaggregated analysis was discarded as the number of units is too small. The variables correspond to the average aggregation of indicators characterising each pillar. Different methods based on the selection of input and output variables as well as DEA methods will be calculated in order to evaluate the robustness of the obtained synthetic competitiveness indicators. We will compare the results of two approaches according to the consideration of variables as follows:

Table 2: Descriptive Statistics

Variables/pillars	Mean	SD	Min	Region	Max	Region
Positive factors						
Structuring and diversification of tourist products	99.83	14.12	83.38	Cantabria	141.74	Catalonia
Talent attraction, training and efficiency of human resources	100.40	16.07	75.99	the Canaries	143.08	Basque Country
Political priority and tourism governance	99.86	8.91	87.17	Cantabria	116.46	La Rioja
Performance: social and economic outcomes	99.92	15.41	81.87	Cantabria	127.33	the Canaries
Unfavourable factors						
Vision of strategic marketing and commercial support	100.94	9.17	83.50	Andalusia	115.60	Extremadura
Transport accessibility and connectivity	99.23	17.12	52.15	Madrid	120.28	Extremadura
Tourist competitive regulation and other conditions	101.29	8.93	84.27	La Rioja	114.33	Murcia

Source: Own elaboration

(1) three input variables and four output variables; and (2) one fixed input variable and the seven pillars used as output variables[1]. For the first scenario, the first three pillars were linearly transformed to become inputs. In this way, unfavourable factors or inputs are formed by 'vision of strategic marketing and commercial support', 'transport accessibility and connectivity' and 'tourist competitive regulation and other conditions'. Conversely, the variables 'structuring and diversification of tourist products', 'talent attraction, training and efficiency of human resources', 'political priority and tourism governance' and 'performance: social and economic outcomes' constitute our set of positive factors.

Table 2 details the descriptive statistics of all the pillars included in the different models according to the original values that can be regarded as outputs (second scenario). It should be noted that with the transformation into inputs, the variables 'vision of strategic marketing and commercial support', 'transport accessibility and connectivity' and 'tourist competitive regulation and other conditions' will perform better for those regions with lower values. As it can be observed, severe differences are present in the minimum and maximum values of all the pillars. Cantabria has the worst aggregated MoniTUR index in the pillars 'structuring and diversification of tourist products', 'political priority and tourism governance' and 'performance: social and economic outcomes'. However, Catalonia is the region with the highest index value of 'structuring and diversification of tourism products'. The Basque Country seems to be the region succeeding at major talent attraction, training and efficiency of human resources. La Rioja boasts the maximum index values for political priority and tourism governance and 'tourist competitive regulation and other conditions'. In addition, the Canaries are noted for its performance of social and economic outcomes, despite that it is the region with the minimum value on 'talent attraction, training and efficiency of human resources'. This is an important drawback that should be corrected in the near future if the region wants to remain competitive because, as Assaf, Josiassen (2011) contend, 'it became clear during our interviews that the service level that tourists perceive is an important determinant. Some tourists simply would not even consider visiting a country that they perceive as having a poor level of

---

[1]This selection is based on the rule of thumb proposed by Cooper et al. (2000). The seven used variables could be considered outputs, as they contribute positively to the measure of competitiveness. But in order to have a more discrimination power and a less restrictive constraint regarding the size of the database, some of the variables were converted to inputs with a simple normalization process.

service mindedness. The tourism industry is a perfect context for the consideration of skills in services (p. 391).' The highlights of Madrid and Andalusia are 'transport and accessibility and connectivity' and 'vision of strategic marketing and commercial support', respectively. Contrarily, Extremadura exhibits, with great differences, the minimum values on these pillars. Finally, Murcia is the region with the worst performance on 'tourist competitive regulation and other conditions'.

4 Methodology

As said, our method is based on Data Envelopment Analysis (DEA). DEA was originally designed to measure the efficiency of a firm in a context of production economics. A firm is considered efficient if it produces the maximum output for a given level of input. Charnes et al. (1978) write the seminal paper that evaluates the performance of different DMUs – decision-making units. The DMUs are characterized by being empowered entities that have the capacity of decision about how to transform inputs into outputs. This was the origin of a discipline that measures the relative efficiency of each DMU when researchers have a sample of peer observations regarding the input and output quantities (Charnes, Cooper 1985). DEA is one of the most popular non-parametric methods to assess economic efficiency whose main advantage resides in that it is possible to use multiple inputs and outputs with no prior assumption about the subjacent technology between inputs and outputs. Moreover, the method can also be applied when the sample is small (Perrigot et al. 2009).

In conventional DEA, each data component is usually classified as either an input or resource or as an output or product depending on the nature of the firm under analysis. However, Ali, Seiford (1993) argue that DEA is also an interesting method in scenarios where researchers are interested in ranking units where the existence of a production function between inputs and outputs is not so obvious. The authors concur to follow a general guideline in which the input or output classification is based according to the analysis of whether it is better or not to have lower (inputs) or higher (outputs) values. It was already explained that in our case study all the pillars from MoniTUR have the consideration of outputs, but in order to analyze to what extent the results do not depend on the conversion of outputs to inputs, two scenarios are proposed.

Ali, Seiford (1993), Charnes et al. (1994), Coelli et al. (1998), Cooper et al. (2011) and Zhu (2014) are good references to cover the basic aspects of DEA models, DEA notation, formulation and geometric interpretation. Conventional DEA models can be divided in three different classes: variable returns to scale (VRS), constant returns to scale (CRS) and additive models. These models separate the DMUs into two different sets: (1) the efficient units that lie on the frontier of the envelopment surface; and (2) those who are inefficient because they show some slack when their position is compared with the obtained frontier.

The selection of a suitable DEA model that ranks the regional tourist competitiveness index in Spain is constrained by the characteristics of the available data, the sample size and the intrinsic nature of the issue under analysis. In particular, as in our case, if researchers are interested in obtaining a full rank of all the regions under analysis, then conventional DEA models might not be appropriate, and then some new refinement of DEA needs to be applied.

In DEA analysis, it is generally assumed that there are n production units to be evaluated, using amounts of m different inputs to produce quantities of s different outputs. Specifically, the oth production unit consumes x_{io} units of input i ($i = 1 \ldots m$) and produces y_{ro} units of output r ($r = 1 \ldots s$). The oth production unit can now be described more compactly with the vector (X_o, Y_o), which denote, respectively, the vectors of input and output values for DMU$_o$.

Next, it is necessary to determine a potential set of possible dominant or non-dominant comparisons for each production unit considered in the analysis. DEA usually considers the dominance of all the possible linear combinations of the n DMUs, i.e. $(\sum_k \lambda_k X_k, \sum_k \lambda_k Y_k)$, with the scalar restricted to be non-negative[2]. The production unit o is dominated, in

---

[2]Different envelopment surfaces may be obtained considering additional constraints about the scalars.

terms of inputs, if at least one linear combination of production units shows that some input can be decreased without making the rest of inputs and outputs worse off. If at least one linear combination of production units shows that some output can be increased without negatively affecting the rest of inputs and outputs[3], it is dominated in terms of outputs.

In our case, policy makers and DMO managers can affect the regional tourist competitiveness by planning and implementing policies that improve the performance for some of the indicators and sub indicators included in the MoniTUR. For example, it would not be difficult to implement a policy that increases the tourist product diversification contemplating and including more tourist segments. In this paper, and given the nature of the issue under analysis, the robustness of the results is going to be based on different DEA methods based on: (1) virtual constant and variable returns to scale with an output orientation model; and (2) super-efficiency DEA model.

Formally, the multiplier-DEA CRS output efficiency for the unit o is calculated through the following linear programming problem:

$$\min_{\nu,\mu} \frac{\sum_{i=1}^{m} \nu_i x_{io}}{\sum_{r=1}^{s} \mu_r y_{ro}} \tag{1}$$

$$s.t. \quad \frac{\sum_{i=1}^{m} \nu_i x_{ij}}{\sum_{r=1}^{s} \mu_r y_{rj}} \geq 1 \ (j = 1 \ldots n),$$

$$\text{where} \quad \nu_i, \mu_r \geq 0$$

The set of constraints requires that the same weights, when applied to all the countries, do not provide any region with efficiency lower than one. The solution to this minimization problem is not unique. Coelli (1996) shows that if there exists a solution (ν, μ) to the above problem, then there exists an infinite number of solutions because $(\phi\nu, \phi\mu)$ with $\phi \geq 0$ is also a solution to the problem. For this reason, the problem is reformulated in an equivalent linear programming program as follows:

$$\min_{\nu,\mu} \sum_{i=1}^{m} \nu_i x_{io} \tag{2}$$

$$s.t. \quad \sum_{i=1}^{m} \nu_i x_{ij} - \sum_{r=1}^{s} \mu_r y_{rj} \geq 0 \ (j = 1 \ldots n),$$

$$\sum_{r=1}^{s} \mu_r y_{ro} = 1$$

$$\text{where} \quad \nu_i, \mu_r \geq 0$$

A region o is in the frontier if and only if $\sum_{i=1}^{m} \nu_i x_{io} = 1$ in optimality. The constraint $\sum_{r=1}^{s} \mu_r y_{ro} = 1$ is known as a normalization constraint, and the weighted input and output are called virtual input and virtual output, respectively (Seiford, Thrall 1990). The efficiency ratio ranges from 1 to infinity, and each region under analysis obtains their optimal multipliers minimizing the self-efficiency, given the constraints.

As explained above, this method needs a major refinement as we are interested in ranking all the regions in Spain, and this is not possible for those that lie on the frontier. The discrimination power is even more acute in our case as we do not have a large sample size. For this reason, the analysis is constrained within the pillars of the database. Our database does not even satisfy the standard rule of thumb proposed by Cooper et al.

For example, variable returns to scale models (VRS) are obtained imposing that the sum of scalars is equal to one; and non-increasing return to scale models (NIRS) are characterized by the restriction of the sum of scalars being less or equal to one.

[3]This discussion is very close to the definition of Pareto-Koopmans efficiency. The unit o is considered fully efficient if and only if the performance of other DMUs does not provide evidence that some of the inputs or outputs of the unit o could have been improved without worsening off some of its other inputs or outputs. This definition of relative performance has its origin in Farrel (1957).

(2000): $n \geq \max(m \times s, 3(m + s))$, where n is the number of DMUs, m is the number of inputs and s in the number of outputs.

Ranking DEA methods have been analyzed and proposed in previous studies. There are different techniques and proposals based on: (1) cross-efficiency DEA models (Sexton et al. 1986, Doyle, Green 1994, Adler et al. 2002); (2) super-efficiency models (Andersen, Petersen 1993, Zhu 1996, Seiford, Zhu 1998); and (3) virtual efficiency models (Bazargan, Vasigh 2003, Martín, Román 2006, 2007, Barzegarinegad et al. 2014, Martín et al. 2017).

This paper uses two different approaches based on the super-efficiency DEA models and the virtual efficiency models. Super-efficiency DEA models are based on the evaluation of a DMU when this is not included in the reference set of the envelopment models. The super-efficiency models are thus calculated using the technological frontier constructed from the rest of the DMUs included in the analysis. Super-efficiency models are also very convenient to analyze the performance of the extreme efficient units.

On the other hand, the virtual efficiency models are based on the introduction of a virtual super-efficient region in the dataset. This method discriminates all the units as there is only one efficient region (this virtual champion). The efficient frontier, based on this model, therefore consists of only this virtual super-efficient region that has been constructed ad-hoc. The ranking is justified because the same virtual unit is used for all DMUs as the reference set.

The input and output vectors for this virtual super-efficient unit are:

$$X_\nu = \min_j \{X_j\}$$
$$Y_\nu = \max_j \{Y_j\}$$

where X_ν and Y_ν are the input and output vectors of the virtual super-efficient unit and X_j and Y_j are the input–output vectors of the jth region. In other words, the virtual region has the lowest input vector and the highest output vector of all the regions conserved in the analysis. Thus, the DEA model expressed by (2) is run with the inclusion of this new virtual unit and the efficiency scores are used to fully rank the Spanish regional tourist competitiveness. As expected by construction, the discrimination power of the method is maximum.

5 Results

Table 3 shows the results for the 17 Autonomous Communities of Spain under the two different scenarios considered regarding the selection of input and output variables and the three selected DEA models, the virtual efficient DEA model under constant and variable returns to scale and the super efficiency model under variable returns to scale. The first column shows the results of the virtual efficiency under constant returns to scale, and it can be seen that there are two regions that can be considered equally competitive: Madrid and La Rioja. An analysis of the table reveals that, according to this methodology, the five most competitive regions are Madrid, La Rioja, the Basque country, Galicia and Andalusia. In regard to the 5 least competitive regions (Aragon, Murcia, Extremadura, Cantabria and Castile and Leon) it can be seen that, with the exception of Murcia, the regions are not located in the Mediterranean coast.

This proposal seems to penalize some of the competitive regions according to the average figures from MoniTUR. In particular, the relative positions of the Balearic archipelago and the Valencian community shifts their ranking positions very much. The shift in position of La Rioja is also particularly relevant. According to MoniTUR, La Rioja occupies the tenth position, however, from our analysis it can now be considered one of the most competitive tourist regions in Spain with Madrid.

Looking at the tail of the distribution, it can be observed that the set of the four least competitive regions is not altered within both methods: MoniTUR and VDEA-CRS rankings. But, the relative position of the regions change. If we analyse now the ranking obtained by the model under variable returns to scale, it can be concluded that the most competitive regions in Spain are again Madrid and La Rioja, but there are now two

Table 3: DEA-MoniTUR index. Global ranking

Autonomous Community	Ranking	DEA Index
Community of Madrid	1	1.000
Basque country	3	1.037
Catalonia	6	1.089
Andalusia	5	1.080
The Canaries	7	1.165
The Balearics	12	1.353
Valencian Community	10	1.326
Galicia	4	1.068
Navarre	8	1.195
La Rioja	1	1.000
Castile-La Mancha	11	1.336
Castile and Leon	13	1.461
Asturias	9	1.217
Murcia	16	1.724
Cantabria	14	1.518
Aragon	17	1.732
Extremadura	15	1.635

Source: Own elaboration

additional communities that can be considered equally competitive: Catalonia and the Basque Country. The case of Catalonia is particularly relevant as it gains four positions in the ranking. Looking at the tail of the distribution, it can be seen that the position of the five laggard regions has changed but the set of the regions remains stable: Castile-León, Cantabria, Extremadura, Murcia and Aragón. The super-efficiency model in the first scenario that uses three pillars like inputs and the rest of the pillars as outputs is not very informative as there are six regions that belong to the set of extreme efficient units for which the linear program is unfeasible. Nevertheless, regarding the five least competitive regions, it can be observed that the set is also the same.

Analysing now the results for the second scenario, it can be seen that there is not any difference between the models based on virtual efficiency independently of what type of returns to scale is used. It is not a surprise that the most competitive regions according to these models are almost the same as those that exhibit an unfeasible solution for the first scenario under the super-efficiency model. It is less informative than other models as there are five competitive regions in Spain: Madrid, the Basque Country, Catalonia, Andalusia and La Rioja. Castile-La Mancha, Castile-León, Murcia, Aragón and Extremadura are the laggard regions in Spain with respect to tourist competitiveness. Finally, analysing the results obtained for the second scenario and the super-efficiency model, it can be seen that the model ranks all the Spanish regions, being the five most competitive: (1) Madrid; (2) Catalonia; (3) the Basque Country; (4) La Rioja; and (5) Andalusia. On the opposite side, the five least competitive regions are: (13) Castile-León; (14) Cantabria; (15) Murcia; (16) Extremadura; and (17) Aragón.

The position of Madrid is not surprising as it contains the capital city of the country, and its relative ranking in the seven pillars is always well positioned. In particular, Madrid shows the best performance in the pillar of transport accessibility and connectivity. Madrid has also the most impressive art museums in Spain, being the Prado, Reina Sofia and Thissen museums. On top of being some of the most important art museums in the world, they are located in an area where all of them can be easily reached by public transport from any neighbourhood of Madrid. Madrid has also three important World Heritage sites: El Escorial, Aranjuez and Alcalá de Henares. Ortega-Martínez, Such-Devesa (2013) find that Spanish National Tourist Organization (Turespaña) and Madrid websites that promote the tourism in Madrid do not use the denomination of World Heritage in promoting and communicating potential attractions in the community of Madrid. In the specific websites of the municipalities or even the main attractions, the World Heritage distinctive plays a more determinant role, although there are important differences between them. In 2014, the top ten visited places in Madrid were: (1) the Reina Sofia museum; (2) the Prado museum; (3) the Warner Bros Park; (4) the Amusement Park; (5) the Royal Palace; (6) the Thyssen museum; (7) the Real Madrid Santiago Bernabeu Tour; (8) the Zoo and Aquarium; (9) the lighted house; and (10) the Archaeological museum.

Another interesting result to highlight is that La Rioja shifts dramatically the position between different indices, the MoniTUR and all the indices proposed in this study. La Rioja always increases some positions from the tenth to the set of the most competitive regions in Spain. It can be seen that La Rioja shows the best performance in two out of the seven pillars: (1) the political priority and tourist governance; and (2) the tourist competitive regulation and other conditions. La Rioja is one of the inland communities in Spain that was more proactive in the past to boost tourist activities as a way to increase the value of its natural and cultural heritage (Vera, Marchena 1998, Ivars Baidal 2004). La Rioja also benefitted from the structural funds provided by the European Union, as a tool for stabilizing the rural population, that include concrete measures related to the promotion of tourism investment in rural areas through mainly agro-tourism, wine-tourism and rural tourism (Diéguez et al. 2014). In La Rioja, the importance of the protected denomination of origin (PDO) of "rioja wine" can be considered one of the most important causes that has fostered the development of wine tourism in this inland Spanish region, which has generated one of the most successful tourism products, creating important synergies with other resources such as gastronomy, monuments and cultural events (López-Guzmán, Sánchez Cañizares 2008). Cabello, Pascual Bellido (2015) contend that wine tourism has become the hallmark of the region for investments and support, both from the public and private sectors. The main Rioja wineries follow the Bordeaux wineries model, seeing in tourism a new opportunity to diversify its product, conditioning and opening not only the cellars but the vineyards to the tourist experience. The offer is enlarged with other activities such as accommodation, catering, education, training and spa, linking all of them to a broad concept of wine culture.

La Rioja competitiveness performance goes further beyond the definition provided by Ritchie, Crouch (2003, p. 2): "What makes a tourism destination truly competitive is its ability to increasingly attract visitors". It can be seen that this definition can be mainly approximated by the seventh pillar: 'the social and economic performance'. It is not strange that analysing the group of peers in which Extremadura should base the strategy in order to be more competitive, La Rioja plays a prominent role. In this regard, Extremadura can learn from the past experience of La Rioja in order to develop an adequate strategy with respect to other agricultural products that could become important icons for future agro-tourism development.

6 Conclusions

This paper presents a comparison of the MoniTUR index with six additional indices based on two different data scenarios and three methodological proposals, virtual efficiency with constant and variable returns to scale and super-efficiency. All these indices measure the Spanish regional tourist competitiveness for the year 2010. Our analysis is based on the seven pillars that conform the MoniTUR database. As it can be read in Exceltur (2011b), MoniTUR aims to provide an objective instrument that periodically assesses and compares the main transversal tourist competitiveness pillars among the seventeen Spanish Autonomous Communities.

Our results show that the proposed indices are quite robust regarding the sets of competitive and uncompetitive regions. It also seems that the indices based on DEA are particularly affecting the relative positions among three particular regions: the Balearic Islands, the Valencian Community and La Rioja. The two first regions are well-known tourist destinations where sun-and-sea tourism is one of the main segments that has been developed and attended. The beaches and good weather is one of the leading reasons why many tourists still spend holidays at destinations. Barros et al. (2011) and Benito et al. (2014) find that coastal regions are more competitive than inland regions using two-stage DEA models to analyse the regional tourist competitiveness in Spain and France. On the other hand, La Rioja developed a strategy to promote a greater cooperation between the private and public sector that took advantage of the wine PDO and positioned the region as the best place in Spain to enjoy an authentic experience of the culture of wine.

Our main contribution is that while MoniTUR measures tourist regional competitiveness in Spain with the average figures for the seven pillars included in the analysis, our method ranks the competitive performance using very different alternatives with pertinent robust results. It is not the purpose of this paper to elicit the best proposal but as the results are robust it can be concluded that the virtual efficiency CRS model for the first scenario and the super-efficiency model for the second scenario are two valid methods to analyse the Spanish tourist regional competitiveness. From here, this study can be used by all the main stakeholders that are part of Exceltur with a clear objective for highlighting areas for resource allocation and future investments that improve the relative regional competitiveness. Other stakeholders who can be benefitted from these results are those policy planners from the laggard regions.

On the other hand, an important venue for future research should be based on having a better understanding of the relevant attributes that determine the relative tourist regional competitiveness, with special emphasis in turning the focus of research more toward assessing the relative importance of these attributes (Crouch 2011).

Acknowledgement

This research was supported by a project "La calidad del servicio en la industria hotelera. ECO2011-23852" funded by the Ministry of Science and Innovation of the Spanish Government.

References

Abad A, Kongmanwatana P (2015) Comparison of destination competitiveness ranking in the European Union using a non-parametric approach. *Tourism Economics* 21[2]: 267–281. CrossRef.

Adler N, Friedman L, Sinuany-Stern Z (2002) Review of ranking methods in the data envelopment analysis context. *European Journal of Operational Research* 140: 249–265. CrossRef.

Ali A, Seiford LM (1993) The mathematical programming approach to efficiency analysis. In: Fried HO, Lovell CAK, Schmidt SS (eds), *The Measurement of Productive Efficiency: Techniques and Applications*. Oxford University Press, New York, 120–159. CrossRef.

Alonso V (2010) Factores críticos de éxito y evaluación de la competitividad de los destinos turístico. *Estudios y perspectivas en turismo* 19[2]: 201–220

Andersen P, Petersen NC (1993) A procedure for ranking efficient units in data envelopment analysis. *Management Science* 39: 1261–1294. CrossRef.

Assaf AG, Josiassen A (2011) Identifying and ranking the determinants of tourism performance: A global investigation. *Journal of Travel Research* 51[4]: 388–399. CrossRef.

Barros CP, Botti L, Peypoch N, Robinot E, Solonandrasana B, Assaf AG (2011) Performance of French destinations: Tourism attraction perspectives. *Tourism Management* 32: 141–146. CrossRef.

Barzegarinegad A, Jahanshahloo G, Rostamy-Malkhalifeh M (2014) A full ranking for decision making units using ideal and anti-ideal points in DEA. *The Scientific World Journal*. CrossRef.

Bazargan M, Vasigh B (2003) Size versus efficiency: A case study of US commercial airports. *Journal of Air Transport Management* 9: 187–193. CrossRef.

Benito B, Solana J, López P (2014) Determinants of spanish regions' tourism performance: A two-stage, double-bootstrap data envelopment analysis. *Tourism Economics* 20[5]: 987–1012. CrossRef.

Cabello SA, Pascual Bellido N (2015) La construcción del turismo en nuevos destinos: luces y sombras. El caso de La Rioja (España). Nóesis. *Revista de Ciencias Sociales y Humanidades* 24[47-1]: 30–48. CrossRef.

Charnes A, Cooper W, Lewin AY, Seiford LM (1994) *Data Envelopment Analysis. Theory, Methodology and Applications*. Kluwer Academic, Boston. CrossRef.

Charnes A, Cooper WW (1985) Preface to topics in data envelopment analysis. *Annals of Operations Research* 2[1]: 59–94. CrossRef.

Charnes A, Cooper WW, Rhodes E (1978) Measuring the efficiency of decision making units. *European Journal of Operational Research* 2[6]: 429–444. CrossRef.

Coelli T (1996) A guide to DEAP version 2.1: a data envelopment analysis (computer) program. CEPA Working Paper 96/08. Centre for Efficiency and Productivity Analysis. Armidale: University of New England

Coelli T, Rao DSP, Battese GE (1998) *An Introduction to Efficiency and Productivity Analysis*. Kluwer Academic, Boston. CrossRef.

Cooper W, Sieford L, Tone K (2000) *Data Envelopment Analysis. A Comprehensive Text with Models, Applications, Reference and DEA-Solver software*. Kluwer Academic Publishers, Norwell

Cooper WW, Seiford LM, Zhu J (2011) *Handbook on data envelopment analysis*. Springer Science & Business Media, New York. CrossRef.

Cracolici MF, Nijkamp P (2006) Competition among tourist destination: An application of data envelopment analysis to Italian provinces. In: Giaoutzi M, Nijkamp P (eds), *Tourism and Regional Development. New Pathways*. Ashgate, Aldershot, England, 133–152

Cracolici MF, Nijkamp P (2009) The attractiveness and competitiveness of tourist destinations: A study of Southern Italian regions. *Tourism Management* 30[3]: 336–344. CrossRef.

Cracolici MF, Nijkamp P, Rietveld P (2008) Assessment of tourism competitiveness by analysing destination efficiency. *Tourism Economics* 14[2]: 325–342. CrossRef.

Crouch GI (2011) Destination competitiveness: An analysis of determinant attributes. *Journal of Travel Research* 50[1]: 27–45. CrossRef.

Crouch GI, Ritchie JRB (1994) Destination competitiveness: Exploring foundations for a long-term research program. Proceedings of the Administrative Sciences Association of Canada 1994 annual conference, Halifax, Nova Scotia, 79-88

Crouch GI, Ritchie JRB (1995) Destination competitiveness and the role of the tourism enterprise. Proceedings of the Fourth Annual World Business Congress, Istanbul, Turkey, 43-48

Crouch GI, Ritchie JRB (1999) Tourism, competitiveness, and societal prosperity. *Journal of Business Research* 44: 137–152. CrossRef.

Crouch GI, Ritchie JRB (2005) Application of the analytic hierarchy process to tourism choice and decision making: A review and illustration applied to destination competitiveness. *Tourism Analysis* 10: 17–25. CrossRef.

Diéguez MI, Sinde AI, Gueimonde A (2014) Actividad empresarial y resultados percebidos más allá de la racionalidad económica: El caso del turismo rural. *PASOS. Revista de Turismo y Patrimonio Cultural* 12[1]: 79–93. CrossRef.

Doyle JR, Green R (1994) Efficiency and cross-efficiency in data envelopment analysis: Derivatives, meanings and uses. *Journal of the Operational Research Society* 45[5]: 567–578. CrossRef.

Dwyer L, Forsyth P, Rao P (2000) The price competitiveness of travel and tourism: A comparison of 19 destinations. *Tourism Management* 21[1]: 9–22. CrossRef.

Dwyer L, Kim C (2003) Destination competitiveness: Determinants and indicators. *Current Issues in Tourism* 6[5]: 369–414. CrossRef.

Dwyer L, Mellor R, Livaic Z, Edwards D, Kim C (2004) Attributes of destination competitiveness: A factor analysis. *Tourism Analysis* 9[1-2]: 91–10. CrossRef.

Enright MJ, Newton J (2004) Tourism destination competitiveness: A quantitative approach. *Tourism Management* 25[6]: 777–788. CrossRef.

Exceltur (2010) Monitur 2009. Monitor de competitividad turística relativa de las comunidades autónomas españolas. available at http://exceltur.org/wp-content/uploads/2014/10/MONITUR-2009_INFORME.pdf. (accessed 21st December 2015)

Exceltur (2011a) Monitur 2010. anexos. available at http://exceltur.org/wp-content/uploads/2014.old/10/MONITUR-2010_ANEXOS.pdf. (accessed 20th December 2015)

Exceltur (2011b) Monitur 2010. Monitor de competitividad turística relativa de las comunidades autónomas españolas. available at http://exceltur.org/wp-content/uploads/2014.old/10/MONITUR-2010_INFORME.pdf. (accessed 20th December 2015)

Farrel MJ (1957) The measurement of productive efficiency. *Journal of the Royal Statistical Society* A120: 253–290. CrossRef.

Gooroochurn N, Sugiyarto G (2005) Competitiveness indicators in the travel and tourism industry. *Tourism Economics* 11[1]: 25–43. CrossRef.

Huang JH, Peng KH (2012) Fuzzy Rasch model in TOPSIS: A new approach for generating fuzzy numbers to assess the competitiveness of the tourism industries in Asian countries. *Tourism Management* 33[2]: 456–465. CrossRef.

Ivars Baidal JA (2004) Regional tourism planning in Spain: Evolution and perspectives. *Annals of Tourism Research* 31[2]: 313–333. CrossRef.

Jick TD (1979) Mixing qualitative and quantitative methods: Triangulation in action. *Administrative science quarterly* 24[4]: 602–611. CrossRef.

Kayar cH, Kozak N (2010) Measuring destination competitiveness: An application of the travel and tourism competitiveness index (2007). *Journal of Hospitality Marketing & Management* 19[3]: 203–216. CrossRef.

Kozak M, Rimmington M (1999) Measuring tourist destination competitiveness: Conceptual considerations and empirical findings. *International Journal of Hospitality Management* 18[3]: 273–283. CrossRef.

López-Guzmán TJ, Sánchez Cañizares SM (2008) La creación de productos turísticos utilizando rutas enológicas. *PASOS. Revista de Turismo y Patrimonio Cultural* 6[2]: 159–171. CrossRef.

Martín JC, Mendoza C, Román C (2017) A DEA travel-tourism competitiveness index. *Social Indicators Research* 130[3]: 937–957. CrossRef.

Martín JC, Román C (2006) A benchmarking analysis of Spanish commercial airports. A comparison between SMOP and DEA ranking methods. *Networks and Spatial Economics* 6[2]: 111–134. CrossRef.

Martín JC, Román C (2007) Political opportunists and mavericks? A typology of Spanish airports. *International Journal of Transport Economics* 34[2]: 245–269

Mendola D, Volo S (2017) Building composite indicators in tourism studies: Measurements and applications in tourism destination competitiveness. *Tourism Management* 59: 541–553. CrossRef.

Ministerio de Industria, Energía y Turismo (2015) Balance año turístico 2014. available at http://www.minetur.gob.es/es-es/gabineteprensa/notasprensa/2015/documents/-150121dossier%20balance%20tur%C3%ADstico%202014.pdf. (accessed 3rd November 2015)

Newall JE (1992) The challenge of competitiveness. *Business quarterly* 56[4]: 94–100

OECD (1994) The world competitiveness report. World Economic Forum and IMD International, Lausanne, Switzerland

Ortega-Martínez E, Such-Devesa MJ (2013) Comunicación y conocimiento del patrimonio mundial de la Comunidad de Madrid. *Cuadernos de turismo* 31: 263–288

Perrigot R, Cliquet G, Piot-Lepetit I (2009) Plural form chain and efficiency: Insights from French hotel chains and DEA methodology. *European Management Journal* 27: 268–280. CrossRef.

Ritchie JRB, Crouch GI (1993) Competitiveness in international tourism: A framework for understanding and analysis. Proceedings of the 43rd Congress of the Association Internationale d'Experts Scientifique du Tourisme, San Carlos de Bariloche, Argentina, 23-71

Ritchie JRB, Crouch GI (2000a) Are destination stars born or made: Must a competitive destination have star genes? Proceedings of the 31st Annual Travel and Tourism Research Association Conference, Burbank, CA, 306-315

Ritchie JRB, Crouch GI (2000b) The competitive destination: A sustainability perspective. *Tourism Management* 21: 1–7

Ritchie JRB, Crouch GI (2003) *The competitive destination: A sustainable tourism perspective.* CABI, Wallingford. CrossRef.

Scott BR, Lodge GC (1985) *U.S. competitiveness in the World Economy.* Harvard Business School Press, Boston

Seiford LM, Thrall RM (1990) Recent developments in data envelopment analysis: The mathematical programming approach to frontier analysis. *Journal of Econometrics* 46: 7–38. CrossRef.

Seiford LM, Zhu J (1998) Stability regions for maintaining efficiency in data envelopment analysis. *European Journal of Operational Research* 108: 127–139. CrossRef.

Sexton TR, Silkman RH, Hogan AJ (1986) Data envelopment analysis: Critique and extensions. In: Silkman RH (ed), *Measuring Efficiency: An Assessment of Data Envelopment Analysis.* Jossey-Bass, San Francisco, 73–105

UNWTO – World Tourism Organization (2015) Tourism highlights. 2015 edition. available at http://www.e-unwto.org/doi/pdf/10.18111/9789284416899. (accessed 30th October 2015)

Vera F, Marchena M (1998) Efectos del turismo en las estructuras regionales periféricas. Una aproximación analítica. *Millars* 21: 109–144

Webster C, Ivanov S (2014) Transforming competitiveness into economic benefits: Does tourism stimulate economic growth in more competitive destinations? *Tourism Management* 40: 137–140. CrossRef.

Zhang H, Gu CL, Gu LW, Zhang Y (2011) The evaluation of tourism destination competitiveness by TOPSIS & information entropy – A case in the Yangtze river delta of China. *Tourism Management* 32[2]: 443–451. CrossRef.

Zhu J (1996) Robustness of the efficient DMUs in data envelopment analysis. *European Journal of Operational Research* 90: 451–460. CrossRef.

Zhu J (2014) *Quantitative models for performance evaluation and benchmarking: Data envelopment analysis with spreadsheets.* Springer, New York

A Appendix

Table A.1: MoniTUR 2010 tourism competitive pillars, crucial areas, indicators and sub indicators

Pillars	Crucial areas for competitiveness	Indicators	Sub indicators
1. Vision of strategic marketing and commercial support	1.1 Marketing strategies	1.1.a Strategic focus and consistency of institutional Tourism Marketing Plan 1.1.b Perceived efficiency of marketing strategy and institutional promotion	
	1.2 Budget allocations for marketing and promotion	1.2 Budget allocations for marketing and promotion	
	1.3 Online marketing strategy	1.3.a Commercial vocation of institutional tourism website 1.3.b Language accessibility of tourism institutional website 1.3.c Marketing on search engines	1.3.c.1 Website average position on search engines 1.3.c.2 Results of active marketing strategies on search engines
		1.3.d Marketing on social networks and related media	1.3.d.1 Social networks positioning 1.3.d.2 Proactive capacity on multimedia tools
	1.4 Institutional marketing management	1.4 Institutional marketing management	
2. Transport accessibility and connectivity	2.1 Air connectivity and accessibility 2.2 Rail accessibility and connectivity 2.3 Overland accessibility and	2.1.a Flight proficiency 2.1.b Air connectivity 2.2.a Sufficiency of high-end trains 2.2.b Rail connectivity 2.3 Overland connectivity	

Continued on next page

Table A.1 – continued from previous page

Pillars	Crucial areas for competitiveness	Indicators	Sub indicators
	connectivity		
3. Tourist competitive regulation and other conditions	3.1 Territory protection 3.2 Urban density on destinations 3.3 Attractiveness of public spaces 3.4 Environmental Commitment	3.1 Territory protection 3.2.a Land occupancy on tourism destinations 3.2.b Congestion level of tourism destinations 3.3 Attractiveness of public spaces 3.4.a Waste treatment 3.4.b Water purification 3.4.c Environmental manage of beaches 3.4.d Participation and/or membership to programs for environmental commitment	
	3.5 Other support services	3.5.a Provision of health services 3.5.b Security levels	3.5.a.1 Provision of health services. Doctors 3.5.a.2 Provision of health services. Beds
4. Structuring and diversification of tourist products	4.1 Integral management of the supply by product clubs	4.1.a Clubs of products developed by Autonomous Communities 4.1.b Clubs of products developed together with other entities	
	4.2 Diversification of products supply	4.2.a Beach tourism 4.2.b Cultural tourism 4.2.c Meeting tourism	4.2.a.1 Enhancement of beaches with equipment 4.2.a.2 Beaches with certified quality 4.2.b.1 Real heritage 4.2.b.2 Assets of cultural interest 4.2.b.3 Number of visitors to museums 4.2.c.1 Capacity for meetings

Continued on next page

Table A.1 – continued from previous page

Pillars	Crucial areas for competitiveness	Indicators	Sub indicators
		4.2.d Nature tourism	4.2.c.2 Number of meeting attendees 4.2.d.1 Enhancement of natural parks 4.2.d.2 Development of greenways 4.2.d.3 Endowment of approved trails
		4.2.e Golf tourism 4.2.f Cruise tourism 4.2.g Nautical tourism 4.2.h Snow tourism 4.2.i Spa tourism 4.2.j Language tourism	4.2.j.1 Accredited Spanish teaching centres 4.2.j.2 Spanish students
		4.2.k Gastronomic tourism 4.2.l Rural tourism	4.2.l.1 Provision of accommodation beds 4.2.l.2 Effective accommodation demand
		4.2.m Wine tourism	4.2.m.1 Provision of wineries in wine tours 4.2.m.2 Visitors in wineries in wine tours
		4.2.n Shopping tourism	4.2.n.1 Opening hours 4.2.n.2 Commercial provisioning
	4.3 Qualification of the lodging and restaurants supply	4.3.a Commitment for formal offer 4.3.b Presence of upscale hotels 4.3.c Quality of restoration	
5. Talent attraction,	5.1 Workers productivity	5.1 Workers productivity	

Continued on next page

Table A.1 – continued from previous page

Pillars	Crucial areas for competitiveness	Indicators	Sub indicators
training and efficiency of human resources	5.2 Human capital endowment of tourist workers 5.3 Employment stability 5.4 Quality of the training system	5.2 Human capital endowment of tourist workers 5.3 Employment stability 5.4.a Attractiveness of tourist university supply 5.4.b Quality of vocational training 5.4.c Support to lifelong learning	
6. Political priority and tourism governance	6.1 Political priority 6.2 Strategic vision 6.3 Tracking of economic performance and commitment to innovation 6.4 Institutionalization of cooperation with the private sector 6.5 Effectiveness of management of tourism competences 6.6 Inter-administrative coordination	6.1.a Position of tourism in the organization level 6.1.b Budgetary effort 6.1.c Inter-councils coordination 6.2 Strategic vision 6.3.a Monitoring of the economic impact of tourism 6.3.b Encouraging innovation 6.4 Institutionalization of cooperation with the private sector 6.5.a Agility of the administrative management 6.5.b Adaptation of tourist rules/laws 6.6 Inter-administrative coordination	
7. Performance: social and economic outcomes	7.1 Total tourism revenues 7.2 Tourism model efficiency	7.1 Total tourism revenues 7.2.a Tourist revenues range of accommodation place 7.2.b Hotel profitability (RevPAR)	

Continued on next page

Table A.1 – continued from previous page

Pillars	Crucial areas for competitiveness	Indicators	Sub indicators
	7.3 Seasonality 7.4 Market positioning 7.5 Social contribution	7.3 Seasonality 7.4.a Average expenditure of tourists 7.4.b Tourist satisfaction 7.5.a Tourism revenues per inhabitant 7.5.b Tourism employment	

Source: Own elaboration

Volume 4, Number 3, 2017, 1–17
DOI: 10.18335/region.v4i3.142

journal homepage: region.ersa.org

Territory and Sustainable Tourism Development: A Space-Time Analysis on European Regions

João Romão[1] João Guerreiro[2] Paulo M. M. Rodrigues[3]

[1] University of Algarve, Faro, Portugal (email: jfromao@ualg.pt)
[2] University of Algarve, Faro, Portugal (email: jguerreiro@ualg.pt)
[3] Bank of Portugal and Universidade Nova de Lisboa, Lisbon, Portugal (email: pmrodrigues@bportugal.pt)

Received: 8 July 2016/Accepted: 26 April 2017

Abstract. In the long run, tourism competitiveness depends on the sustainable use of territorial assets: the differentiation of destinations depends on the integration of cultural and natural resources into the tourism supply, but also on their preservation over time. Using advanced spatial econometric techniques this work analyses the relationships between regional tourism competitiveness, the dynamics of tourism demand and investment, as well as the existence of natural resources and cultural assets in the European context. Despite the close relationship between tourism activities and the characteristics of the territories, the application of methods of spatial analysis in tourism studies is still scarce and the results of this work clearly show their potential for this field of research. Among the main findings of this paper, it was observed that natural resources do not have the expected positive impacts on regional tourism competitiveness and that European regions with more abundant natural resources are often developing unsustainable forms of mass tourism with low value added and little benefits for the host communities. The existence of spatial correlation effects suggests that positive spillovers arising from tourism dynamics in neighbourhood regions prevail over potential negative effects related to the competition between destinations. Policy and managerial implications of these results are discussed and further research questions are proposed.

Key words: Cultural heritage; Natural resources; Endogenous resources; Spatial autocorrelation; Spatial econometrics; Competitiveness; Sustainability

1 Introduction

As one of the fastest growing sectors in the contemporary global economy, tourism activities face unprecedented levels of competition. However, it is not only a competition between product and service providers, but also between destinations and, consequently, between territories. On the other hand, as tourism attractiveness often relies on territorial natural and cultural endowments, questions related to the sustainable use of these resources assume greater importance as tourism is achieving higher relevance at the international level. This is expressed by the number of tourists worldwide and also by their socio-economic and environmental impacts.

The purpose of this work is to provide a comprehensive analysis of the importance of local resources – both cultural and natural – for regional tourism competitiveness, measured in terms of the gross value added by the tourism sector, at the European level.

Our analysis is framed by the concepts of competitiveness and sustainability in tourism. We assume the definition of competitiveness proposed by Ritchie, Crouch (2003), which establishes a clear link to the socio-economic benefits for the local communities and the sustainable use of sensitive territorial resources. Section 2.1 offers a brief literature review for this conceptual framework focusing on the relations between competitiveness and sustainability in tourism.

As our study aims to identify the impacts of tourism on regional socio-economic dynamics, the territorial level of analysis is not exactly the destination, but rather the regional level (NUTS 2, according to the definitions of Eurostat, which is the territorial level typically used for the application of regional policies, while the NUTS 1 level corresponds to the major socio-economic regions and NUTS 3 to small regions). Although these regions normally include more than one tourism destination, they are institutionally relevant in order to address policy questions related to the integration of tourism dynamics into broader resource management or economic development policies. A synthesis of tourism competitiveness studies focused on this territorial level is presented in Section 2.1. In particular, Cucculelli, Goffi (2016) and Cuccia et al. (2016) have analysed similar problems related to natural and cultural resources.

Assuming tourism as a place oriented activity, where territories interact with each other, the possible existence of spatial effects among the regions under analysis is also of interest for the purposes of our study. Despite the close connection between tourism and the territorial characteristics, very few studies have applied spatial econometric methods to the field of tourism as described in Section 2.3. For the purpose of our study, the analysis of the relations between tourism dynamics and cultural assets in Italian regions proposed by Patuelli et al. (2013) or the study of the impacts of natural and cultural endowment on regional tourism demand at the European level developed by Romão (2015) are relevant examples.

Considering that competitiveness implies the creation of high value added and the sustainable use of natural and cultural resources, our paper applies spatial analysis techniques in order to identify different spatial patters in tourism dynamics (Section 3). This analysis is combined with an econometric overall explanation, with the estimation of a general trend within European regions (Section 4). As the work focuses on a large group of regions and considers a period of eight years, a spatial panel data model has been chosen in order to deal with cross-sectional and time series characteristics of the data, while allowing for the identification and quantification of potential spatial effects.

Although limited data availability constrains a comprehensive analysis of all questions related to regional tourism competitiveness, the available information and the methodologies applied in this study contribute to the understanding of the relations over time between attractive and sensitive territorial resources, tourism dynamics and tourism competitiveness at the European regional level. This work provides an innovative analysis of the spatial effects between tourism demand, tourism infrastructures, regional tourism competitiveness and the sustainable use of natural and cultural resources in European regions with relevant results arising from the exploratory spatial analysis and the regression model. A discussion of their policy implications will be presented in the concluding section and issues for further research will be highlighted.

2 Competitiveness, Sustainability and Spatial Econometrics in Tourism

2.1 Tourism competitiveness and sustainable use of resources

The concepts of competitiveness and sustainability emerged in the literature during the 1980s. Michael Porter's analysis (Porter 1985, 2003) regarding the achievement of a competitive advantage at the firm level had clear implications on economic policy formulations at the regional and national levels. On the other hand, the concept of sustainability was introduced after the publication of the document "Our Common Future" (World Commission on Environment and Development 1987), establishing the principles of sustainable development and taking into consideration its multiple dimensions (economic, social or environmental).

These concepts have been applied to tourism studies during the subsequent years and a good synthesis has been provided in a short note by Poon (1994), by applying some of the generic strategic formulations proposed by Porter and defining a strategy of cost leadership (related to mass tourism, with low value added and high negative externalities) or differentiation (related to the creation of unique experiences, with high value added and low negative externalities, which are understood as corresponding to the concept of sustainability).

This idea would be questioned by Butler (1999) who claims that sustainability and the principles of sustainable development should also be applied to mass tourism development processes, while concerns related to the excessive use of resources are also relevant for small scale forms of tourism in sensitive natural areas. Of particular importance for our work was the distinction proposed by this author between the impacts of tourism on sustainable development and the sustainable use of territorial resources for tourism activities (which is the perspective adopted in our analysis). This conceptualization was supported by Jafari (2001) when defining the "Knowledge Based Platform" for tourism studies who pointed out that principles of sustainability should be addressed at policy and managerial levels in all types of tourism destinations. Both authors emphasised the human dimension of sustainability and the importance of the socio-economic benefits of tourism for the host communities.

During that period, other authors stressed the importance of the uniqueness of local resources for destination differentiation along with the perception and satisfaction achieved by tourists (e.g. Kozak 1999, Buhalis 2000) while bringing attention to the sensitiveness of natural resources and the necessary limits to be imposed to their usage (Buhalis 1999, Hassan 2000). This "environmental paradox", as later defined by Williams, Ponsford (2009), implies that the production of tourism experiences depends on the exploitation of local resources, which – at the same time – must be preserved.

Synthetizing these contributions, a definition of tourism competitiveness commonly accepted in the literature was provided by Ritchie, Crouch (2003) stating that "what makes a tourism destination truly competitive is its ability to increase tourism expenditure, to increasingly attract visitors, while providing them with satisfying, memorable experiences, and to do so in a profitable way, while enhancing the well-being of destination residents and preserving the natural capital of the destination for future generations". This definition stresses the importance of growth, economic impacts, consumer satisfaction, benefits for the host community and the preservation of resources over time. Our analysis is particularly focused on the regional economic impacts and the sustainable use of resources.

Following this definition, the authors developed a comprehensive model of destination competiveness while other systematic approaches were proposed in subsequent years (e.g. Vanhove 2005, Mazanek et al. 2007). In particular, Celant (2007) focused his analysis at the regional level, while Weaver (2006), Wall, Mathieson (2006) or Sharpley (2009) offered a more clear focus on the problems of sustainability. Tsai et al. (2009) as well as Park, Jang (2014) offer detailed overviews of these formulations. Systematic approaches combining tourism competitiveness with the principles of sustainable development were proposed as policy guidelines by international institutions like UNESCO (2000, 2005), the European Commission (2007), UNWTO (2007) or the World Economic Forum (2008).

2.2　The region as the territorial level of analysis

Although some of the studies on competitiveness previously mentioned are related to empirical applications focused on particular destinations, most of them aim at international comparisons, which has lead to the creation of country rankings based on composite indicators. One example with large international recognition is the Travel and Tourism Competitiveness Index developed by the World Economic Forum (2008), which uses a very large set of quantitative indicators. Based on this index, several authors applied different methodologies in order to refine the analysis of particular aspects of tourism competitiveness: Mazanek et al. (2007) selected a particular group of indicators in order to provide an explanatory model for tourism competitiveness; Navickas, Malakauskaite (2009) oriented the use of these indicators to questions related with innovation; Webster, Ivanov (2014) analysed the relation between this index and the contribution of tourism for economic growth; Martín et al. (2017) proposed a definition of a benchmark position and country profiles regarding tourism competitiveness.

Despite the abundant number of studies on tourism competiveness at the country level, comparative analyses between regions of different countries are relatively scarce, probably due to the difficulties in obtaining relevant and comparable data. Camisón, Forés (2015) focused on the firm level and analysed how regional competitiveness influences the performance of tourism companies. Cracolici, Nijkamp (2008) related the attractiveness of Southern Italian (NUTS 2) regions with tourist satisfaction as a proxy for regional competitiveness. Closer to the purposes of our study, and focusing on a larger number of Italian NUTS 2 regions, Cuccia et al. (2016) observed that cultural and environmental regional endowment positively affect the performance of destinations, but the existence of UNESCO sites does not imply similar benefits. With a different territorial focus (centred on the destination) Cucculelli, Goffi (2016) observed that factors related to the sustainable use of resources exert positive impacts on the performance of Italian certified destinations.

Considering NUTS 2 regions as the territorial level of analysis, our study aims at offering a comprehensive overview of the relations between tourism performance and natural and cultural endowment in order to achieve policy implications both in terms of tourism development and resource management, which are addressed at a relevant institutional level for strategic orientations.

2.3 Spatial econometrics in tourism

Due to the large increment of geo-referenced statistical information recently available and the development of easy-to-use software tools, spatial econometric methodologies are only currently becoming of widespread use even though they started to be developed in the mid 20th century (Florax, Vlist 2003, Anselin 2010). In particular, our work is based on a panel data approach. This allows for the development of complex analyses of economic processes and their spatial effects while taking into consideration more information, increasing the variation and reducing the collinearity between variables resulting in more efficient estimations (Elhorst 2003, 2014).

A limited number of panel data models have been used in tourism studies, mostly over the last 10 years, as summarized by Song et al. (2012). Moreover, despite the close relationship between tourism and territory, only a few works applied spatial panel data models in tourism: Marrocu, Paci (2013) analysed the determinants of tourism flows between 107 Italian locations; Yang, Fik (2014) examined spatial spillovers and spatial heterogeneity in order to explain the variability in tourism growth across 342 cities in China; Kang et al. (2014) analysed the territorial impacts of national tourism policies in South Korea; Ma et al. (2015) focused on the spatial correlation between tourism and urban economic growth in 272 Chinese regions; Majewska (2015) applied techniques of exploratory spatial data analysis to study the inter-regional agglomeration effects in tourism activities in Poland.

Closer to the purpose of our work, Patuelli et al. (2013) examined the importance of world heritage sites on internal tourism flows in Italy, finding positive impacts on the regions where the sites are located followed by negative impacts on tourism flows in the surrounding regions, suggesting the existence of a strong competitive effect. In particular, the results obtained by Romão (2015) in a spatial analysis of the impact of natural and cultural assets on tourism demand in European regions (identifying a positive correlation between the regional endowment on natural and cultural resources and the volume of tourism demand) can be compared with those presented in this paper.

3   Data, methodologies and results

This section includes a presentation of the data and variables under analysis, a preliminary panel regression estimating the impacts of the factors considered on regional tourism competitiveness, an exploratory spatial analysis aiming at the identification of possible spatial effects and, finally, an econometric regression including spatial effects and offering an overall explanatory framework.

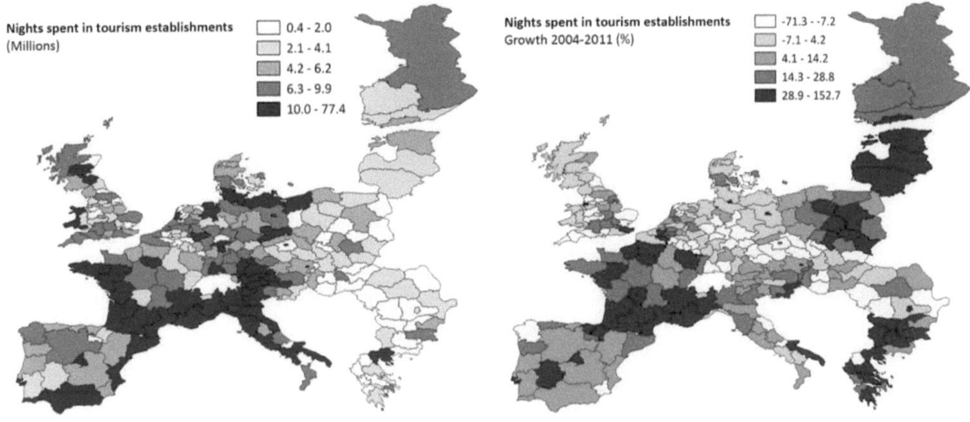

Figure 1: Regional tourism demand

3.1 Data and Variables: Tourism Dynamics, Culture and Nature

The territorial level considered in the present study is the NUTS 2 level according to the definitions of the Eurostat for the European regions. This regional scale is appropriate for the purposes of this study as it allows us to obtain relevant and comparable data and to discuss and address policy recommendations at an adequate institutional level. 237 regions (excluding islands) from Austria, Belgium, Bulgaria, the Czech Republic, Denmark, Estonia, Finland, France, Germany, Greece, Hungary, Italy, Latvia, Lithuania, Luxemburg, the Netherlands, Poland, Portugal, Romania, Slovakia, Slovenia, Spain and the United Kingdom have been considered. Other European regions have not been included due to the lack of statistical information. The source for the geographical representation of the data in the following Figures is GISCO – Eurostat (European Commission) for the administrative boundaries of European regions, while the information related to tourism dynamics, cultural assets and natural resources has been added to that source. The maps used in this section (Figures 1 and 2) were produced with QGIS 2.4, while those used in the following section (Figure 3) were produced with GeoDa 1.6.7.

Tourism competitiveness (the dependent variable considered in the spatial panel data model to be developed below) is measured based on available Eurostat data and taking into consideration the gross value added (at current prices) by tourism activities (including wholesale and retail trade; transport; accommodation and food service activities; information and communication services) in each region. This corresponds to a broad definition of tourism services and assumes the increasing importance of information and communication technologies (ICT) for tourism. Some missing data detected for a small number of regions were computed according to the existing information, considering the registered trends immediately before and/or after the missing information.

The explanatory variables considered in the model to be presented include tourism demand (measured by the nights spent at tourism accommodation establishments, according to Eurostat, as a proxy for regional tourism attractiveness) and investment in tourism (gross fixed capital formation in the sector, also based on Eurostat data, as a proxy for the tourism related infrastructures). Natural resources are measured taking into consideration the territory of each region classified by the European Union within the Natura 2000 network (according to a harmonized set of rules and criteria, with the information available at the European Commission – DG Environment), while cultural assets are measured considering the number of World Heritage sites classified by UNESCO at the regional level (also following an international classification based on universal criteria). The evolution between 2004 and 2011 is considered for all these variables.

The information for the most recent year (2011) regarding the geographical distribution of tourism demand in European regions measured by the nights spent in accommodation establishments (hotels, holiday and other short-stay accommodation, camping grounds, recreational vehicle parks and trailer parks) is represented in the map on the left hand

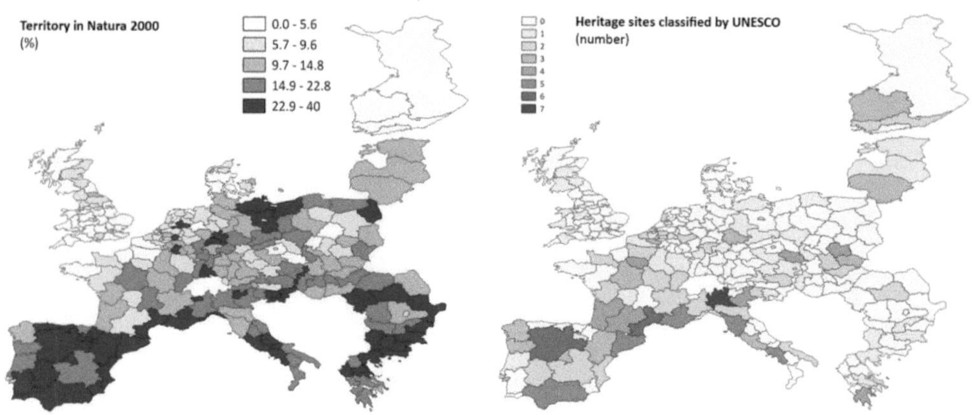

Figure 2: Natural and cultural resources

side of Figure 1, while the growth rates for this indicator between 2004 and 2011 are shown in the right hand side (the classes were created based on quintiles). The spatial pattern identified in Figure 1 reveals the importance of the Southern European regions, but the map on the right hand side of the same Figure reveals a clear shift in tourism demand with a large amount of regions located in the Eastern side of Europe (mostly Baltic, Bulgarian and Greek regions) among those with the highest growth rates registered between 2004 and 2011. However, it should be noticed that these high growth rates are also related to the low scores observed for these regions in the initial period.

The natural resources of each region have been measured taking into consideration the percentage of its territory included in Natura 2000, as a proxy for regional biodiversity. Although these protected areas are not necessarily tourism attractions, they reveal the potential attractiveness of natural resources for tourism demand in each region. In this analysis natural resources are not seen as tourism products, neither is it required that they are perceived as such (or even as protected areas) by tourists: they allow us to assess the sensitiveness and importance of regional ecosystems. The map presented on the left hand side of Figure 2 represents this information for 2011, showing the importance of Southern European regions for the biodiversity in Europe.

Finally, the number of sites classified as World Heritage by UNESCO in each region was assumed as a proxy for its cultural heritage (in a few cases, the same site is distributed along different regions and one site per region has been considered). Despite the existence of other important cultural elements (from tangible, like non-classified monuments or museums, to intangible, like local lifestyles, and including cultural events and festivals) extremely relevant for tourism attractiveness, it is not possible to have comparable quantitative information at the regional level for an international analysis. The map on the right hand side of Figure 2 represents cultural heritage as measured by the number by UNESCO sites again revealing the importance of the Southern European regions. In the same sense as it was seen for the natural resources, our analysis does not imply the utilization of these assets as tourism products or the perception of their historical importance by tourists: they represent a proxy for the richness of cultural heritage in each region.

3.2 Panel data model without spatial effects

As the purpose of this work is to analyse the effects of tourism demand, investment, natural resources and cultural assets on the regional tourism competitiveness in a large number of European regions over 8 years, a panel data model is an adequate tool. For the purposes of estimation of the models, logarithms are applied to the dependent variable (GVA in the tourism sector – "logGVA") and to some of the independent variables (such as the number of nights spent in tourism accommodation establishments – "logNIT" – and gross fixed capital formation in the tourism sector – "logINV"), in order to reduce

Table 1: Panel data model parameter estimates (individual effects; no spatial effects)

Parameters	Estimate	Std. Error	t-value
logNIT	0.146***	0.019	6.761
logINV	0.049***	0.010	4.823
NAT	-0.003***	0.001	-2.343
HERIT	0.031***	0.013	2.396

Notes: ***, **, * indicates statistical significance at a 1%, 5% and 10% significance level

the dispersion of the data. Absolute values are considered for the number of heritage sites ("HERIT") and percentages for the portion of the territory included in Natura 2000 ("NAT"). No spatial effects are considered in a first stage and the model is specified as:

$$\text{logGVA}_{it} = \beta_0 + \beta_1 \text{logNIT}_{it} + \beta_2 \text{logINV}_{it} + \beta_3 \text{HERIT}_{it} + \beta_4 \text{NAT}_{it} + u_{it} \qquad (1)$$

where the index i refers to the ith region, t is an index for the time period and u is an independent and identically distributed error term.

Although the number of periods under analysis is relatively small (8 years), the coss-sectionally augmented Im, Pesaran and Shin (IPS) test for panel unit roots (Pesaran 2007) has been applied (using the plm package in R; see Croissant et al. 2016) confirming the stationarity of the data under different test specifications allowing for individual intercepts or trends among the data, defining the number of lags of the test regression according to the Akaike Information Criteria and specifying the maximum number of lags as 2 or 4. The test statistics obtained were, respectively, -51.632 and -61.873, corresponding both to a p-value below 2.2e-16), confirming the stationarity of the data. A variance inflation test (VIF) was also computed (using the package car in R) and all the scores obtained (logNIT = 1.715; logINV = 1.807, NAT = 1.060; HERIT = 1,333) were clearly below the threshold of 5 suggested by O'Brien (2007), revealing the absence of problems of multicollinearity.

In order to choose between a fixed or a random effects model, a Hausman test has been computed with the plm package in R and its result (p-value < 2.2e-16) suggested that a fixed effects model should be preferred (methodologies and techniques are described in Croissant, Millo 2008). Nevertheless, as discussed by Clark, Liner (2015), the Hausman test has important limitations for a final decision regarding the choice of a specific model, which should be grounded on theoretical assumptions about the observations. In our case – and considering the close link between the specific characteristics of the territories and tourism dynamics, it seems plausible to assume that individual regional features have specific impacts on tourism activities, also justifying the option for a fixed effects model. Thus, a panel data model with fixed effects has been estimated.

The estimation results are presented in Table 1, revealing a positive (and statistically relevant) relation between tourism GVA and all the independent variables, except for natural resources. It is possible to confirm the expected positive correlation between the existence of classified heritage sites and tourism competitiveness. It is noticeable that the variables related to tourism dynamics (demand and investment) exert a higher impact on tourism competitiveness than the impact generated by the existence of cultural assets.

The result related to the negative impact of natural resources on tourism competitiveness requires a more careful interpretation: it could be argued that this negative correlation is the expectable consequence of the fact that natural resources are measured taking into consideration the proportion of protected areas in each region (since the related conservation measures that are implied generally impose restrictions on tourism activities). Nevertheless, as observed in the previous section, these regions are mostly located in Southern Europe, which are generally places with high levels of tourism demand. In fact, a positive relation between tourism demand and the portion of the territory included in Natura 2000 had been found in a previous study on the same regions and for a similar period (Romão 2015).

Table 2: Moran I tests for spatial autocorrelation

	logGVA		logNIG		logINV		HERIT		NAT	
	2004	2011	2004	2011	2004	2011	2004	2011	2004	2011
Test Results	8.869	9.105	10.34	11.74	6.586	9.498	6.728	8.695	16.76	18.69

Thus richer natural resources are correlated to higher levels of demand but to relatively low value added. In other words, despite the apparent potential of these regions to create a differentiated tourism supply, based on their rich biodiversity within the European context, they seem to develop tourism products and services oriented to mass consumption normally with relevant negative consequences in terms of the protection of sensitive environmental resources. Therefore, a strategy of cost leadership (implying a massive use of resources with low economic impact) seems to prevail over a differentiation strategy based on the uniqueness of the places (oriented to the provision of unique experiences with protection of sensitive resources and oriented to high value added products and services).

Despite the high statistical relevance of all parameter estimates of this model, the R-squared (0,048) and the Adjusted R-squared (0,042) obtained from this regression are relatively low. Although the R-squared statistic may have important limitations when applied to time series, the results suggest that the estimation can be significantly improved. Also, the computation (with the plm package for R) of a test (Pesaran CD) for cross-sectional dependence (Pesaran et al. 2008) has lead to results (test statistic of 54.592) suggesting evidence in favour of the existence of such characteristics in the panel under analysis, opening the possibility for the existence of spatial effects.

Finally, as suggested by Clark, Liner (2015), different specifications of the model have been computed in order to confirm the stability of the results. As can be seen from Table A.1 (Appendix) the signs of the estimates for all parameters are the same independently of the type of model (fixed effects, random effects or pooling), although some differences can be observed regarding the statistical relevance of the estimates. On the other hand, a second set of models has been computed (Table A.2 in Appendix) replacing the variables that had been logarithmized (GVA, gross fixed capital formation in the tourism sector, and nights spent in accommodation establishments), which were, instead, divided by the number of residents in each region (values per habitant were obtained) in order to consider the possible effects of the dimension of the region. As can be observed the results show exactly the same signs for all estimates, but with a much lower statistical significance.

3.3 Exploratory Spatial Data Analysis: Territorial Resources and Tourism Competitiveness

In order to identify the possible existence of spatial effects, several preliminary tests were computed by using indicators of spatial autocorrelation (Anselin 2005). This methodology requires the creation of a spatial weights matrix, defining the spatial impacts of each region on its neighbours (Anselin 2005). In this case, a neighbour is defined according to the rook contiguity criteria (two regions are considered neighbours if they share a common border) and it is also assumed that spatial impacts occur, not only for immediate neighbours, but also for the "neighbours of neighbours" (second level contiguity). Additionally, it is also assumed that the impact on immediate neighbours is double than the impact on second order neighbours and that all regions have the same potential to generate spillover effects (implying that the spatial weights matrix is row normalized). The results obtained suggest that this impact matrix offers useful insights for the estimation of spatial effects.

Moran I tests for spatial autocorrelation (Anselin 2005) provide a measure for global spatial correlation between neighbours. Table 2 shows the test results obtained (using Geoda 1.6.0) for all variables included in the model and considers the first and last year of the observations. The existence of spatial correlation is suggested by the test results obtained (a pseudo significance level is computed through a random permutation procedure, recalculated 99 times in order to generate a reference distribution).

Local indicators of spatial autocorrelation have also been computed (with Geoda

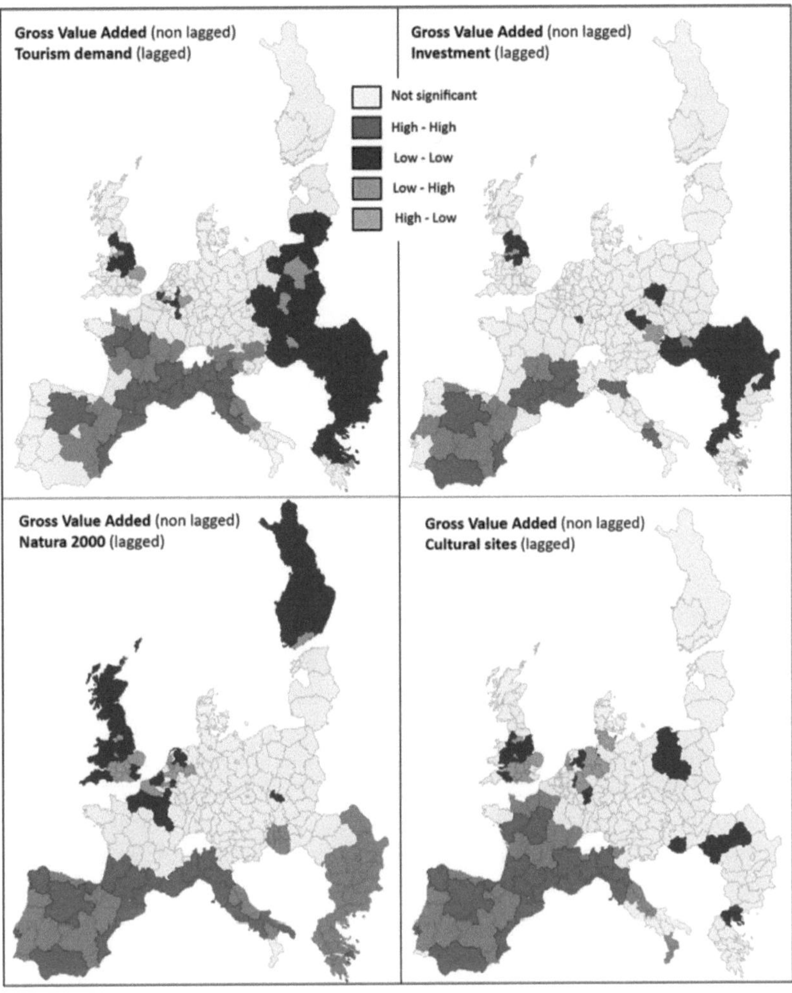

Figure 3: Local Indicators of Spatial Autocorrelation – Bivariate Analysis

1.6.0 and following the methodologies proposed by Anselin 2005) in order to generate a bivariate analysis based on the local Moran I indicators, relating a non-lagged variable (the dependent variable – GVA in tourism) with spatially lagged variables (each of the four independent variables – tourism demand, investment in tourism, natural resources and cultural resources). The maps in Figure 3 represent these spatial relations, considering a 95% significance level. Dark colours represent clusters of positively correlated regions (dark red for high values in both variables and dark blue for low values in both variables) and light colours represent negative correlation (light red for high values of the non-lagged variable and low values for the lagged variable, and light blue for the inverse situation).

The first map (top-left) reveals a cluster of high values for tourism GVA and high tourism demand in southern western regions (dark red), while clusters of low values for both variables are located in the east side of Europe (dark blue). Nevertheless, the existence of a large number of southern regions (mostly in Spain, France and Italy) where low value added in tourism is spatially correlated with high tourism demand (light blue) is also noticeable, suggesting that tourism is possibly based on low value added products and services. A very similar pattern is observed for the second map (top-right), revealing that a large number of regions from Southern Europe (mostly concentrated in Spain) register high levels of investment in tourism while achieving relatively low levels of GVA.

The combination of these results (high tourism demand and high investments in the tourism sector) suggests a high mobilization of regional resources for tourism. However they generate a relatively low value added, which can be related to a low productivity in the utilization of these resources (nevertheless, it should be noted that this study does not address the specific question of productivity and does not provide a measure for the relation between the output of tourism activities and the necessary inputs for their provision). This tendency is even more marked when we observe the relation between GVA and natural resources (down-left) or cultural heritage (down-right). In the second case (cultural heritage), we can observe that for a large number of regions from Portugal, Spain, France and Italy low gross value added is correlated with a high number of cultural sites classified by UNESCO. On the other hand, when natural resources are taken into consideration, this tendency is also observable for Greek and Bulgarian regions (although it does not happen in France, suggesting that higher value added is achieved with nature oriented tourism in French regions).

Generally, these observations confirm the results obtained from the panel data model previously estimated: the negative correlation between natural resources and the GVA generated by tourism activities is not related to a low level of tourism demand in protected areas, but to the supply of massive, low value added tourism products and services in these regions. Even if some of them (located in coastal areas) register high levels of tourism GVA, a large number of territories (mostly those without direct connection to the sea) do not achieve good performance in terms of GVA despite the high tourism demand.

3.4 Spatial Econometric Analysis

The final step of this work is the computation of a spatial regression model by adding the spatial effects explicitly to the panel data model presented in (1). The existence of a spatially lagged endogenous variable (included as one more explanatory variable and capturing potential endogenous interaction effects) and spatial effects in the error term (a spatial multiplier that captures un-modelled spatial effects expressed in the interaction among the error terms) will be tested before estimation. In a general form, a space-time panel data model with spatial effects among the dependent variables and the error term can be specified as:

$$
\begin{aligned}
Y_{it} &= \rho(WY)_{it} + X'_{it}\beta + u_{it}, & &\text{(2)}\\
u_{it} &= \lambda(Wu)_{it} + \epsilon_{it}, & i &= 1,\ldots,N \text{ and } t = 1,\ldots,T
\end{aligned}
$$

where

- Y_{it} represents the log of tourism GVA in region i at time t.

- X_{it} corresponds to a 4x1 vector of independent variables for region i at time t, namely:

    - the number of nights in tourism establishments;
    - the gross fixed capital formation in tourism;
    - the percentage of the territory classified in Natura 2000;
    - and the number of sites classified as World Heritage by UNESCO.

- W is a nonnegative $N \times N$ matrix of known constants describing the spatial impacts; the element w_{ij} indicates the intensity of the relationship between cross sectional units i and j and the diagonal elements are set to zero because no region can be its own neighbour;

- WY represents the endogenous interaction effects among the dependent variables;

- Wu shows the interaction effects among the disturbance terms of the different units;

- ρ is the spatial autoregressive coefficient;

- λ the spatial autocorrelation coefficient;

- i is an index for the regions and t is an index for the time period.

Table 3: Parameter estimates of the spatial lag and spatial error model with fixed effects

Parameter	Estimate	Std.Error	t-value
Intercept	-0.330***	0.028	3.843
logNIT	0.252***	0.014	17.787
logINV	0.655***	0.013	50.138
NAT	-0.019***	0.001	-14.940
HERIT	-0.005	0.008	-0.675
Spatial autoregressive coefficient (ρ)	0.402***	0.040	10.067
Spatial autocorrelation coefficient (λ)	0.109***	0.028	3.843

Notes: Note: ***, **, * indicates statistical significance at a 1%, 5% and 10% significance level.

The tests for the existence of spatial effects (Baltagi et al. 2003, 2007) were performed using the splm package in R (Milo, Piras 2012), aiming to identify whether the potential spatial effects are related to regional effects within the dependent variable (a spatial lag model, with $\lambda = 0$) and/or more general effects identified in the spatial distribution of the error terms (spatial error model, with $\rho = 0$). The score of 1469.973 obtained for the LM (Lagrange Multiplier) test implies the rejection of the null hypothesis of no random effects and no spatial autocorrelation (H_0: $\lambda = \rho = 0$) and suggests the existence of spatial effects related to the dependent variable and/or the spatial correlation among the error terms (alternative hypothesis is that at least one component is not zero). In fact, the Moran I test computed in the previous section had already shown the existence of spatial effects (implying $\rho \neq 0$).

The Baltagi, Song and Koh's SLM1 marginal test evaluates the inexistence of autoregressive spatial effects (H_0: $\rho = 0$), assuming that no spatial effects exist in the error term ($\lambda = 0$); the score of 0.0187 with a p-value of 0.9851 implies non-rejection of the null hypothesis. Conversely, Baltagi, Song and Koh's SLM2 marginal test, tests the null hypothesis of no spatial effects in the error term (H_0: $\lambda = 0$) assuming no autoregressive spatial effects ($\rho = 0$); the score of 0.00847 with a p-value of 0.9933 also implies non-rejection of the null hypothesis. Thus, the inexistence of one type of spatial effects also implies the inexistence of the other. Finally, applying Baltagi, Song and Koh's conditional test, LMλ, for no regional effects expressed in the error term (H_0: $\lambda = 0$), independently of the value of ρ, a score of 37.1293 was obtained leading to the rejection of the null hypothesis. Thus, it is possible to conclude for the existence of spatial autocorrelation effects in the error term.

The existence of both types of spatial effects leads to the computation of a general spatial Cliff-Ord type model (Cliff, Ord 1981), including a spatially lagged dependent variable and a spatially autocorrelated error term. Finally, the results obtained for a spatial Hausmann test lead us to opt for a fixed effects model.

This spatial lag and spatial error model [with: Y =logGVA and X =(logNIT, log INV, NAT, HERIT)] is defined according to expression (2) previously presented, considering fixed individual effects and requiring a specification of the disturbances assuming that spatial autocorrelation applies to both the individual effects and the error term (with the transformation proposed by Kapoor et al. 2007, for the disturbance term following a first order spatial autoregressive process – "kkp" type). Table 3 presents the results obtained based on maximum likelihood estimation:

Although the computation of the R-square statistic is not possible in a spatial context, other results (also with important limitations, as discussed by Elhorst 2014) reveal a relevant increase in the adjustment regarding the model without spatial effects. The computation of a squared correlation coefficient between actual and fitted values (proposed by Elhorst 2014) has led to a result of 0.833 (0.320 for the model without spatial effects previously presented), while the computation of a Pseudo R-squared based on the quotient between the variance of the estimations and the variance of the actual values (proposed by Anselin, Lozano-Gracia 2008) has led to a result of 0.883 (0.830 for the model without spatial effects). Even if the measures of goodness of fit have important limitations in both cases, the model with spatial effects clearly performs better than the model without spatial effects.

Comparing the estimated parameters with those obtained from the model without spatial effects, the same type of relations (expressed in the sign of the correlations) between the dependent variable and the independent variables were identified although the impact of cultural assets loses statistical significance when spatial effects are included. This model confirms the expected positive correlation between tourism GVA, tourism demand and investment in the tourism sector, but in this case the impact of investment is higher than the impact of tourism demand. Possibly, a part of the regional dynamics (linked to tourism demand) is now captured by spatial effects associated to the lagged variable (tourism GVA), while the impact of cultural assets can eventually be captured by unmodelled spatial effects related to the error term. The model also confirms the negative correlation between regional natural resources and tourism GVA previously observed, which is the most important result arising from this analysis.

The existence of spatial effects among regions is also clear. The spatial effects identified in the space-time model reveal the existence of spillover effects (expressed in the positive value of the spatial autoregressive coefficient, showing that tourism dynamics in one region has positive consequences on the contiguous regions) and also unmodelled effects (expressed in the positive value of the spatial autocorrelation coefficient). Although it is clear that a major part of these effects are captured by the spatial distribution of the dependent variable (with a much larger estimated parameter), the existence of spatial effects in the distribution of the error terms suggests that other type of variables can be included in further works in order to increase the explanatory power of the model.

4 Discussion and Concluding Remarks

A first important conclusion of this study is the confirmation of the useful contribution of spatial analysis in tourism studies with a clear impact on the goodness of fit of the econometric model and the identification of spatial patterns in tourism activities and its determinants. It was possible to conclude from our exploratory spatial analysis that the impacts of the determinants of competitiveness taken into consideration differ across the territorial units despite the existence of a general trend identified by the econometric model. This is the first contribution of this work, leading from a policy point of view to the idea that the implementation of guidelines to improve tourism competitiveness must take into account the specific territorial conditions.

The results of this spatial analysis also imply that contemporary regional tourism dynamics is related, not only to regional resources and conditions, but also to the dynamics observed in neighbouring regions. This also has clear implications for tourism policies suggesting that local resource management, promotional strategies, transport systems or accommodation provision can be more efficiently planned if there is some collaboration among clusters of regions with similar characteristics. In fact, this type of complementarity between regions is possible to observe in many parts of Europe, even belonging to different countries as can be observed in e.g. mountain areas like the Alps (Switzerland and Italy) or the Pyrenees (Spain and France) or along major rivers (like the Danube).

The analysis of the determinants of regional competitiveness developed through the computation of a spatial panel data model confirmed the expected positive correlations between GVA generated by tourism activities, regional tourism demand and investment in the tourism sector. Nevertheless, the results also showed a negative relation between tourism GVA and the existence of natural resources. Although this negative correlation could be linked to the type of data used in the model (suggesting that it could be related to protective measures implemented in these areas), it was also possible to observe that regions with more protected areas are located in Southern European areas with high levels of tourism demand where mass tourism prevails.

A second contribution of this work for the existing literature is the identification of this negative correlation between the existence of rich natural resources and tourism competitiveness in European regions, which was only possible through the combined analysis of the econometric model (providing an overall general explanation) and the exploratory spatial analysis (identifying different spatial patterns and highlighting the role of Southern European territories in this context). In fact, the indicators of spatial autocorrelation used for the exploratory spatial analysis revealed the existence of a large number of regions from Southern Europe where abundant natural resources coexist with high levels of tourism demand and low value added in the tourism sector. Thus, the results suggest that massive tourism related to natural resources tends to generate less positive impacts on the regional GVA, despite its potential negative impacts on ecosystems and landscapes.

This analysis reveals an unsustainable process of tourism development for these regions apparently following a cost leadership competitive strategy based on low prices. Instead, taking into consideration their richness in terms of natural and cultural assets, a strategy of differentiation aiming at the provision of unique experiences based on the specific territorial resources could lead to a more sustainable form of tourism development. This would reinforce the linkage with other local economic activities with larger impacts on regional development and higher protection of sensitive resources. In fact, good practices related to this kind of utilization of natural resources for the creation of high value tourism products and services can already be found in many natural parks all over the world including Europe, while countries like Australia or New Zealand tend to give very high importance to these services within their tourism activities.

Finally, it is important to notice that the increasing amount of geo-referenced information related to tourism opens new opportunities for the application of spatial analysis techniques in order to identify spatial patterns of tourism development. Questions related to the effective usage of natural or cultural resources as tourism products or a more detailed analysis of tourism infrastructures can be integrated into similar models in the future, along with the consideration of other determinants of tourism competitiveness (marketing, management, planning, etc.). Another possible development of this work relates to the scale of analysis, given that NUTS 2 regions can include different tourism destinations within the same territory. The NUTS 3 level can be more appropriate for this purpose when comparable relevant statistical information is available.

References

Anselin L (2005) Exploring spatial data with GeoDa^{TM}: A workbook. Center for Spatially Integrated Social Science, Santa Barbara http://la1.rcc.uchicago.edu/media/-geoda_files/docs/geodaworkbook.pdf

Anselin L (2010) Thirty years of spatial econometrics. *Papers in Regional Science* 89: 3–25. CrossRef.

Anselin L, Lozano-Gracia N (2008) Errors in variables and spatial effects in hedonic house price models of ambient air quality. *Empirical Economics* 34: 5–34. CrossRef.

Baltagi S, Jung B, Koh W (2003) Testing panel data regression models with spatial error correlation. *Journal of Econometrics* 117: 123–150. CrossRef.

Baltagi S, Jung B, Koh W (2007) Testing for serial correlation, spatial autocorrelation and random effects using panel data. *Journal of Econometrics* 140[1]: 5–51. CrossRef.

Buhalis D (1999) Limits of tourism development in peripheral destinations: problems and challenges. *Tourism Management* 20: 183–185

Buhalis D (2000) Marketing the competitive destination of the future. *Tourism Management* 21: 97–116. CrossRef.

Butler R (1999) Sustainable tourism: A state-of-the-art review. *Tourism Geographies* 1[1]: 7–25. CrossRef.

Camisón C, Forés B (2015) Is tourism firm competitiveness driven by different internal or external specific factors? New empirical evidence from Spain. *Tourism Management* 48: 477–499

Celant A (2007) *Global Tourism and Regional Competitiveness*. Patron, Bologna

Clark T, Liner D (2015) Should I use fixed or random effects? *Political Science Research and Methods* 3[2]: 399–408. CrossRef.

Cliff A, Ord J (1981) *Spatial Processes, Models and Applications*. Pion, London

Cracolici M, Nijkamp P (2008) The attractiveness and competitiveness of tourist destinations: A study of southern Italian regions. *Tourism Management* 30: 336–344. CrossRef.

Croissant Y, Millo G (2008) Panel data econometrics in R: The plm package. *Journal of Statistical Software* 27[2]: 1–43. CrossRef.

Croissant Y, Millo G, Tappe K, Toomet O, Kleiber C, Zeileis A, Henningsen A, Andronic L, Schoenfelder N (2016) Package "plm". CRAN, https://cran.r-project.org/web/-packages/plm/plm.pdf

Cuccia T, Guccio G, Rizzo I (2016) The effects of UNESCO world heritage list inscription on tourism destinations performance in Italian regions. *Economic Modelling* 53: 494–508. CrossRef.

Cucculelli M, Goffi G (2016) Does sustainability enhance tourism destination competitiveness? Evidence from Italian destinations of excellence. *Journal of Cleaner Production* 111: 370–382. CrossRef.

Elhorst J (2003) Specification and estimation of spatial panel data models. *International Regional Science Review* 26: 223–243. CrossRef.

Elhorst J (2014) *Spatial Econometrics: From Cross-Sectional Data to Spatial Panels*. Springer, New York

European Commission (2007) Agenda for a sustainable and competitive European tourism. European Commission, Luxembourg. http://eur-lex.europa.eu/legal-content/-EN/TXT/?uri=celex:52007DC0621

Florax R, Vlist A (2003) Spatial econometric data analysis: Moving beyond traditional models. *International Regional Science Review* 26[3]: 23–243. CrossRef.

Hassan S (2000) Determinants of market competitiveness in an environmentally sustainable tourism industry. *Journal of Travel Research* 38[3]: 239–245. CrossRef.

Jafari J (2001) The scientification of tourism. In: Smith V, Brent M (eds), *Hosts and Guests Revisited: Tourism Issues of the 21st Century*. Cognizant Communication Corporation, New York

Kang S, Kim J, Nicholls S (2014) National tourism policy and spatial patterns of domestic tourism in South Korea. *Journal of Travel Research* 53[6]: 791–804. CrossRef.

Kapoor M, Kelejian HH, Prucha IR (2007) Panel data model with spatially correlated error components. *Journal of Econometrics* 140[1]: 97–130. CrossRef.

Kozak M (1999) Destination competitiveness measurement: Analysis of effective factors and indicators. European Regional Science Association Conference Papers, Dublin, http://www-sre.wu-wien.ac.at/ersa/ersaconfs/ersa99/Papers/a289.pdf

Ma T, Hong T, Zhang H (2015) Tourism spatial spillover effects and urban economic growth. *Journal of Business Research* 68[1]: 74–80. CrossRef.

Majewska J (2015) Inter-regional agglomeration effects in tourism in Poland. *Tourism Geographies* 17[3]: 408–436. CrossRef.

Marrocu E, Paci R (2013) Different tourists to different destinations – evidence from spatial interaction models. *Tourism Management* 39: 71–83. CrossRef

Martín J, Mendoza C, Román C (2017) A DEA travel-tourism competitiveness index. *Social Indicators Research* 130[3]: 1–21. CrossRef.

Mazanek J, Wober K, Zins A (2007) Tourism destination competitiveness: From definition to explanation? *Journal of Travel Research* 46: 86–95. CrossRef.

Milo G, Piras G (2012) splm: Spatial panel data models in R. *Journal of Statistical Software* 47[1]: 1–38. CrossRef.

Navickas V, Malakauskaite A (2009) The possibilities for the identification and evaluation of tourism sector competitiveness factors. *Engineering Economic* 1[61]: 37–44

O'Brien R (2007) A caution regarding rules of thumb for variance inflation factors. *Quality and Quantity* 41[5]: 673–690. CrossRef.

Park J, Jang S (2014) An extended gravity model: Applying destination competitiveness. *Journal of Travel & Tourism Marketing* 31[7]: 799–816

Patuelli R, Mussoni M, Candela G (2013) The effects of world heritage sites on domestic tourism: A spatial interaction model for Italy. *Journal of Geographical Systems* 15: 369–402. CrossRef.

Pesaran MH (2007) A simple panel unit root test in the presence of cross-section dependence. *Journal of Applied Econometrics* 22[2]: 265–312. CrossRef.

Pesaran MH, Ullah A, Yamagata T (2008) A bias-adjusted LM test of error cross-section independence. *The Econometrics Journal* 11[1]: 105–127. CrossRef.

Poon A (1994) The 'new tourism' revolution. *Tourism Management* 15[2]: 91–92. CrossRef.

Porter M (1985) *Competitive advantage – creating and sustaining superior performance*. The Free Press, New York

Porter M (2003) The economic performance of regions. *Regional Studies* 37[6/7]: 549–578. CrossRef.

Ritchie J, Crouch G (2003) *The competitive destination: A sustainable tourism perspective.* CABI International, Oxfordshire. CrossRef.

Romão J (2015) Culture or nature: A space-time analysis on the determinants of tourism demand in European regions. Discussion papers spatial and organisational dynamics 14, http://www.cieo.pt/discussionpapers/discussionpapers14.pdf, Research Centre for Spatial and Organizational Dynamics, Faro

Sharpley R (2009) *Tourism Development and the Environment: Beyond Sustainability?* London

Song H, Dwyer L, Cao Z (2012) Tourism economics research: A review and assessment. *Annals of Tourism Research* 39[3]: 1653–1682. CrossRef.

Tsai H, Song H, Wong K (2009) Tourism and hotel competitiveness. *Journal of Travel and Tourism Marketing* 26[5]: 522–546. CrossRef.

UNESCO (2000) *Sustainable Tourism and the Environment.* UNESCO, Paris

UNESCO (2005) *World Heritage Centre – Sustainable Tourism Programme.* UNESCO, Paris

UNWTO (2007) *Practical Guide to Tourism Destination Management.* UNWTO, Madrid

Vanhove N (2005) *The Economics of Tourism Destinations.* Elsevier, Oxford. CrossRef.

Wall G, Mathieson A (2006) *Tourism: Change, Impacts and Opportunities.* Pearson, Essex

Weaver D (2006) *Sustainable tourism: Theory and practice.* Elsevier, Oxford. CrossRef.

Webster C, Ivanov S (2014) Transforming competitiveness into economic benefits: Does tourism stimulate economic growth in more competitive destinations? *Tourism Management* 40: 137–140. CrossRef.

Williams P, Ponsford I (2009) Confronting tourism's environmental paradox: Transitioning for sustainable tourism. *Futures* 41: 396–404. CrossRef.

World Commission on Environment and Development (1987) *Our Common Future.* Oxford University Press, New York

World Economic Forum (2008) *The Travel and Tourism Competitiveness Report 2008.* World Economic Forum, Geneva

Yang Y, Fik T (2014) Spatial effects in regional tourism growth. *Annals of Tourism Research* 46: 144–162. CrossRef.

A Appendix

Table A.1: Panel estimations

	Fixed Effects Est.	Random effects Est.	Pooling effects Est.
Intercept		2.978***	0.686***
NAT	-0.003*	-0.007***	-0.021***
HERIT	0.031*	0.062	0.003
logINV	0.049***	0.130***	0.686***
logNIG	0.146***	0.316***	0.236***
Adj. R2	-0.090	0.236	0.802

In this case, logarithms were applied to the variables Tourism Gross Value Added (dependent variable), Gross Fixed Capital Formation in tourism (logINV) and nights spent in tourism accommodation establishments (logNIG).

Table A.2: Alternative panel estimations

	Fixed Effects Est.	Random effects Est.	Pooling effects Est.
Intercept		4180.750***	2800.108***
NAT	-1.094	-6.397	-83.236***
HERIT	25.354	69.189	62.367
INVpc	0.071	0.196***	3.677***
NIGpc	100.813***	127.257***	61.196***
Adj. R2	-0.120	0.052	0.553

In this case, the values for the variables Tourism Gross Value Added (dependent variable), Gross Fixed Capital Formation in tourism (INVpc), and nights spent in tourism accommodation establishments (NIGpc), were divided by the number of residents (per capita), in order to consider the dimension of the regions. Nevertheless, the results obtained were much less significant.

REGION

The Journal of ERSA
Powered by WU

Volume 4, Number 3, 2017, 175–200
DOI: 10.18335/region.v4i3.171

journal homepage: region.ersa.org

Spatial mismatch, wages and unemployment in metropolitan areas in Brazil

Ana Maria Bonomi Barufi[1], Eduardo Amaral Haddad[1]

[1] University of São Paulo, São Paulo, Brazil

Received: 25 October 2016/Accepted: 9 August 2017

Abstract. The spatial mismatch hypothesis states that a lack of connection to job opportunities may affect an individual's prospects in the labour market, especially for low-skilled workers. This phenomenon is especially observed in large urban areas, in which low-skilled minorities tend to live far away from jobs and face geographical barriers to finding and keeping jobs. This paper aims to investigate whether this negative relationship between spatial mismatch and labour market outcomes is valid in Brazil after controlling for individual characteristics. Our conclusions indicate that there is no clear relation between different measures of accessibility to jobs and the probability of being unemployed. However, for wages there is a clear correlation, which is stronger in larger metropolitan areas than in the country and has a more detrimental effect for low-skilled workers. This paper contributes to the literature by investigating the spatial mismatch in urban labour markets in Brazil. For the empirical literature in the country, this is an original contribution, as the comparison of intra-urban labour market dynamics of different urban areas provide a more comprehensive perspective of the role city size may play in local labour markets. Given the exploratory nature of this work, our results still rely on strong identification hypotheses to avoid potential bias related to simultaneous location decisions of workers and firms within the city. Even if these conditions do not hold, the results are still meaningful as they provide a better understanding of the conditional distribution of wages and the unemployment rate in the biggest metropolitan areas of Brazil.

JEL classification: R32, J64, J31

Key words: spatial mismatch, labour market, metropolitan areas.

1 Introduction

The spatial landscape of labour market opportunities varies significantly within an urban area. On average, the number of job openings and the wage level tend to decline as distance to the urban centre increases, which is usually modelled as a monocentric city. However, this relationship varies according to specific characteristics of each city, related to geography, amenities' distribution, sector composition and specialisation, transportation policies, the number of business centres (polycentric or monocentric city), among other factors (Capello 2007). Another important source of heterogeneity in the urban shape comes from the locational choices of firms in different sectors (McCann 2013), based on their cost-benefit analysis coming from the interaction between land and transportation costs, and the potential benefits that may arise from a more central location.

In some cases, jobs with better pay in the service sector can be concentrated near the centre, as they benefit more from knowledge spillovers that generate agglomeration externalities (Partridge et al. 2009). On the other hand, manufacturers started moving to the outskirts of the bigger cities in order to avoid high rents, effect that is widely acknowledged in the literature, together with additional impacts on the housing market (Lucas Jr, Rossi-Hansberg 2002). Furthermore, this relationship is said to be stronger for larger and denser areas, because congestion costs and the size of the urban sprawl lead to a higher cost of living in central areas. In this context, the spatial mismatch relates the structure of cities to unemployment and poverty (Gobillon, Selod 2013).

The urbanisation process in Brazil was fast in the second half of the twentieth century, as the urbanisation rate went from less than 50% to more than 80% in forty years. More than 90% of the GDP is created in cities (Da Mata et al. 2007). However, this process was not accompanied by a similar rise in the country's GDP per capita (Chauvin et al. 2016). Urban areas with less than 100,000 inhabitants made up 23% of the Brazilian population in 2010, while in the US, they housed 33% of the population.

Local labour markets are formed by the interaction of firms and workers with heterogeneous skills in various geographical locations, given the strong connection between housing and labour markets. Geographical location gives market power to firms over potential workers, especially over those residing close to them. In their model, Brueckner et al. (2002) define two different spaces (skills spaces and urban spaces), and in equilibrium low-skilled workers will be distant from firms in both of these spaces, providing a rationale for socioeconomic ghettos (Zenou 2009), consistent with the spatial mismatch hypothesis (Kain 1968). The main underlying mechanism of this model is the monopsonistic power of firms in the surroundings close to them, which depends on the elasticity of the firm's labour pool (which itself is negatively related to the costs of commuting and acquiring skills). Brueckner et al. (2002) show that workers will be separated in space by skill type, and firms set wages that exploit this separation in space. Low-skilled workers will then live far away from their jobs.

There are at least two main dimensions through which this intra-urban equilibrium in the labour market can be evaluated: unemployment and wages. According to Zenou (1999), urban efficiency wages may lead to involuntary unemployment, as they are set above the competitive equilibrium wage in order to induce workers not to shirk. Moreover, individuals living far away from jobs have poor information about job opportunities, which decreases their probability of finding a job. As a result, spatial mismatch is observed in large urban areas in which low-skilled minorities live far away from jobs and face geographical barriers to finding and keeping jobs. In addition to the spatial dimension, there is also a social separation faced by low-skilled workers and minorities (Zenou 2013), which reduces their chances of finding a job.

Based on this theoretical perspective, this paper provides a two-fold analysis of the relationship between spatial mismatch and labour market outcomes in large metropolitan areas in Brazil. This effect is calculated through the relationship between the average wage or the probability of being unemployed and distance to jobs (measured as the commuting time from home to work or the distance to the main business centre). This paper therefore contributes to the literature by investigating the spatial mismatch in urban labour markets in Brazil. For the empirical literature in the country, this is an original contribution, as the comparison intra-urban labour market dynamics of different urban areas provide a more comprehensive perspective of the role city size may play in local labour markets.

Moreover, it shows empirically that in the Brazilian case the spatial mismatch is more relevant in relation to individual wages, while the probability of being unemployed is not as regularly distributed in space. The latter result is an interesting contribution to the literature and may indicate that the probability of unemployment may not be the best measure to attest the effect of the spatial mismatch in the labour market. According to the literature, duration of unemployment may be a better fit for this role, a variable that is not available in the database considered in this study.

There is also an emphasis on how the spatial mismatch can be more harmful to low-skilled workers, a result that is in accordance to previous findings in the literature. In sum, city size and the capacity that individuals have to adapt and find job opportunities are relevant aspects to be considered to understand intra-urban labour market dynamics

The paper is structured as follows. Section 2 provides a brief literature review of spatial mismatch and local labour markets focusing on social interactions within the city. In Section 3, we describe the econometric strategy and the database, while in Section 4 we analyse the results. Concluding remarks follow in Section 5.

2 Spatial mismatch and labour market equilibrium

The intra-urban spatial distribution of economic agents and production inputs has been modelled as the result of location decisions made by workers and firms (Roback 1982). A wide range of factors, among whose there are agglomeration economies, may be included in different models, as indicated by the New Economic Geography and Urban Economics literatures (Fujita, Thisse 2012, Krugman 1995, Ottaviano 2004). The locational problem is usually analysed by evaluating how local prices (rents and wages) relate to the distance from the present location to the Central Business District (CBD) of the city (Lucas Jr, Rossi-Hansberg 2002). Distance to multiple tiers of the urban hierarchy within a city can also be relevant for this analysis (Partridge et al. 2009).

The concept of spatial mismatch dates back to the mid-1960s (Kain 1992). This concept appears as a possible partial explanation to racial conflicts and riots in the United States, with the identification of ghettos and unequal labour market outcomes. Low rates of employment and low wages for Afro-American workers could be related to limitations on residential choice and the distribution of jobs around the city. Among other dimensions, education, housing and employment reflect and reinforce the spatial mismatch in cities. There has been significant discussion on whether this hypothesis does explain inequalities in the city, given the variety of analytical methods, spatial mismatch measures and data aggregation levels.

More than that, there was considerable uncertainty about the magnitude of the effects of spatial mismatch in urban areas (Holzer 1991). Recently, Kain (2004) showed that the public education system of the United States reinforced the spatial mismatch, given that racial segregation resulted in the concentration of Black children in low-achieving schools. More recent developments combine the concept of spatial mismatch with the analysis of local prices within a city and the embedded location decisions of workers and firms. Spatial mismatch in the labour market means that people face spatial frictions when accessing jobs in metropolitan areas (Houston 2005a). This phenomenon relates to the way in which low-skilled minorities are affected by distance to job locations (Zenou 2009). The resulting distributions arise from the equilibria in the labour and the housing markets, which are simultaneously determined by the different decisions made by firms and workers.

The spatial mismatch hypothesis argues that low-skilled minorities face poor labour market outcomes because they are disconnected from job opportunities within the city (Gobillon et al. 2007). Even nowadays, this concept is still commonly used to investigate the case of afro-descendent population or other minorities in US cities, who often live far away from low-skilled jobs that are available in the suburbs of American cities (see for instance Ihlanfeldt 2006, Zenou 2009, Andersson et al. 2014).

The range of mechanisms underlying the theoretical frameworks that generate spatial mismatches are related either to the labour market itself or to the factors that potentially explain why minorities are physically disconnected from jobs (Gobillon, Selod 2013). According to Gobillon et al. (2007), these mechanisms can be analysed separately for workers and firms. From the workers' perspective, they are the following:

(i) long commuting may lead a worker to refuse a job opportunity after carrying out a cost-benefit analysis;

(ii) search efficiency may decrease with distance to jobs;

(iii) search intensity may also be affected by distance to jobs; and

(iv) high search costs may cause workers to restrict their search to a limited area.

From the firms' perspective, the main mechanisms are:

(v) stigma or prejudice may make firms discriminate against workers who live in certain locations;

(vi) employers may pay lower wages or refuse to hire workers who commute for long distances, as the commuting may decrease their productivity; and

(vii) employers may have a prejudice against specific workers because of the expected preferences of their customers.

As mentioned above, the spatial mismatch hypothesis is usually considered in the specific case of low-skilled minorities living in urban areas. However, the concept of 'spatial mismatch' in general terms is broadly used to investigate the disparity between locations of jobs and individuals that lead in an endogenous way to different levels of unemployment and wages across a city.

Among some of the theoretical models devoted to describing spatial mismatches in the urban environment, Zenou (2000) develops a model with endogenous city formation mechanisms that result in jobs concentrating in the CBD, employed individuals residing in the vicinity of the city centre, and the unemployed being further away from jobs. Urban unemployment will then be reinforced in the outskirts of the city, because the further away an individual is from jobs (which are concentrated in the CBD), the harder it is for her to find a job. Within a similar setting generated from a model based on a monocentric city combined with an efficiency wage mechanism and high reallocation costs, wages are expected to decrease with distance to the centre, as demonstrated by Zenou (2006).

It is important to note that the modelling of metropolitan labour markets can be significantly different for low-skilled and high-skilled workers, given the more limited distance that low-income individuals can commute. Thus, low-skilled workers will face a segmented urban labour market, while for high-skilled workers space is less restrictive. Unemployment for low-skilled workers will be associated with the lack of jobs in the areas close to their residence, while high-skilled workers will search for jobs in a wider spatial scale (Morrison 2005). Therefore, for high-skilled individuals, urban landscape is expected to have a smaller impact on their labour market outcomes. These two mechanisms can co-exist within the city to generate the observed distribution of unemployment rates.

One additional remark is that the literature of spatial mismatch is intrinsically related to spatial spillovers, social networks and proximity in different dimensions (Topa, Zenou 2015). Accessibility to jobs captures these effects just in a partial way, as it differentiates individuals by their reach to opportunities, and an interesting extension of research in this area should encompass these neighbouring relations in a more direct way.

Despite the large amount of empirical literature, Houston (2005b) argues that there is no clear consensus on the importance of the spatial mismatch in the explanation of labour market outcomes. Andersson et al. (2014) consider the duration of unemployment as a labour market outcome to measure the effects of spatial mismatch. They use a matched employer–employee database, and build person-specific measures of job accessibility with an empirical model of transport modal choice and network travel-time, finding that better job accessibility helps to decrease the duration of joblessness for lower-paid workers. Moreover, under-privileged groups are more affected by the lack of accessibility. The same dependent variable is employed by Rogers (1997), whose results indicate that unemployment duration in the Pittsburgh labour market area is influenced by residential location relative to employment opportunities, especially for less-educated individuals. According to Johnson (2006), the efficiency of job search is largely related to job accessibility. Then, 40% of the racial disparities in search duration is explained by spatial search-related variables.

The total number of jobs available in each region of the city and the impedance for reaching those regions can be used to define accessibility to jobs in a specific location. The impedance measure is usually defined either by the Euclidean distance or by commuting time between residential location and jobs, which may be derived from transport availability in each area of the city. The latter approach is followed by Vieira, Haddad (2015) for the São Paulo Metropolitan area, and they find indications that accessibility and income are strongly and positively related in the city. Di Paolo et al. (2016) find that car availability is relevant for job–education mismatch and that public transportation has an effect on better matching in the labour market for each schooling level.

Åslund et al. (2010) calculate the accessibility measure by considering the number of jobs and people of working age within a 5 kilometres-radius of the individual's residential location. They consider the exogenous allocation of refugees in Sweden ten years earlier and build an instrument that is based on how accessible jobs are to immigrants in their arrival year, and find a positive correlation between local job proximity and individual outcomes.

Job accessibility, demand and supply in the Chicago metropolitan area are used by Hu (2014) to find that socioeconomic restructuring (an increase in poverty and a reduction in relevant job opportunities) negatively affects poor job seekers, while spatial transformation (when jobs and job seekers move to the outskirts of the city) has a positive effect on their job prospects. The latter effect is caused by poorer individuals following jobs to suburban areas. With a similar empirical strategy, Hu, Giuliano (2014)'s results indicate that there is no relationship between spatial accessibility and the unequal employment status of the poor in the Los Angeles metropolitan area.

According to Tyndall (2015), public transportation has a causal and negative effect on neighbourhood unemployment rates, particularly for groups who are more dependent on this transport mode. The author explores a natural experiment from Hurricane Sandy, which exogenously reduced access to public transport in some neighbourhoods in New York City.

The empirical literature on spatial mismatch can be subdivided into two main strands: the first aims to understand the causes, while the second discusses the consequences of a spatial mismatch (Gobillon, Selod 2013). Houston (2005b) states that the consequences of a spatial mismatch are usually evaluated through an analysis of (i) residential segregation, (ii) comparisons of commuting times, (iii) comparisons of earnings, and (iv) measures of job proximity. Accordingly, Ihlanfeldt (2006) highlights the fact that the effects of spatial mismatch have been investigated on lower earnings, longer commutes and higher unemployment, especially in the case of black workers in the United States. Usually, employment and earnings equations include measures of local job opportunities, with a strategy based on a gravity model with a distance-decay function to take account of being further away from job opportunities.

Among the main econometric problems arising from this strategy there is the fact that residential location and the measurement of job opportunities are potentially endogenous (Ihlanfeldt 2006). Such endogeneity may appear through self-selection of more or less productive workers to specific areas, by the potential reverse causality of job opportunities and the probability of being unemployed, or through the simultaneous location decisions of firms and workers in a general equilibrium setting. One can deal with the simultaneity issue by including historical or geographical instruments that influenced the location of transportation infrastructure within a city without directly determining the location of workers and firms. This approach is explored by Haddad, Barufi (2017) for São Paulo Metropolitan Region with river shore access as an instrument, but is not replicable for the whole country as such detailed geographical information is not available yet in a larger scale.

Our identification strategy will be based in more restrictive hypotheses. In the short run, prices in the labour market are assumed to be close to the equilibrium level, and workers and firms are relatively immobile (Gibb et al. 2014). This endogeneity issue is then expected to be less relevant in the case of labour market outcomes. In addition, the measurement of local job opportunities can be indirect (using the assumption that there is a geographical centre in the city or by considering commuting time as a possible measure of the distance to jobs). The specific location of job opportunities is not included in the analysis, meaning that this endogeneity issue can be less relevant. In this study, we will assume that these aspects are able to soften such concerns. In any case, the potential direction of an endogeneity bias will be discussed in the following sections.

Usual measures of spatial mismatch may be problematic (Houston 2005b). On the one hand, long commutes may be a sign of either high mobility (highly paid workers) or a spatial mismatch between workers and jobs. On the other hand, different groups have specific propensities to commute, which means that studies usually measure commuting patterns of employed individuals, while spatial mismatch is generally concerned with the unemployed, who may behave differently. Houston (2005b) also suggests that job accessibility should take into account not only distance but also the amount of competition for the accessible jobs. Finally, total travel burden should take into account time, pecuniary costs and inconvenience (Bruzelius 1979). Commuting time, cost or distance are therefore, by themselves, incomplete measures. However, data availability restricts this analysis to such incomplete measures. We acknowledge this limitation and try to assess its potential impact in our results.

In summary, the empirical literature finds some mixed results, especially regarding the relationship between different measures of spatial mismatch and the unemployment rate. However, an increase in accessibility to jobs seems to improve labour market outcomes, especially for low-skilled minorities for whom the spatial mismatch is more relevant. There are significant empirical issues related to the estimation of this effect, whose consequences will be further discussed.

The next section presents our empirical strategy, which deals with comparisons of earnings and measures of job proximity (items (iii) and (iv) discussed above and listed by Houston (2005b)). In addition, we focus on the probability, for each economically active individual, of being unemployed, according to her residential location. To compare earnings, the unavailability of data means that we measure wages from a residential location perspective instead of a workplace basis, even if the latter would be a more appropriate approach (Houston 2005b).

3 Empirical strategy and data

The empirical strategy developed here is based on the estimation of the relationship between different measures of distance to jobs and labour market outcomes (earnings and the probability of being unemployed). All dependent variables are residence-based, due to data availability. Such strategy aims at exploring different dimensions of the spatial mismatch hypothesis in Brazilian metropolitan areas.

Estimations are conducted for individuals residing in a specific metropolitan area in order to capture the effect of each variable in relative terms within a specific urban structure. We assume that the wage equation can be written as follows:

$$w_i = \alpha + \beta X_i + \gamma_1 \text{inv\_dist}_r + \gamma_2 \text{inv\_dist}_r^2 + \epsilon_i \tag{1}$$

where w_i is the logarithm of the hourly wage measured for employed individuals who do not work at home, and X_i includes age, age squared, sector of activity, occupation, formalization status of the job, colour or race, education level, whether the individual is married, whether he or she has at least one child younger than fifteen living in the house, whether the house is owned by the family and whether the person is or is not the head of the household. In addition, inv_dist_r refers to the inverse of the Euclidean distance from the centroid of the weighting area to the main business centre[1]. This strategy is adopted since there is no data available to measure distance over each city's road infrastructure.

An alternative formulation for the reduced form presented in (1) is given by:

$$\begin{aligned} w_i &= \alpha + \beta X_i + \theta_1 \text{time\_commut\_6\_30}_i + \theta_2 \text{time\_commut\_31\_60}_i \\ &\quad + \theta_3 \text{time\_commut\_61\_120}_i + \theta_4 \text{time\_commut\_121\_more}_i + \epsilon_i \end{aligned} \tag{2}$$

In this case, instead of the inverse distance to the centre, commuting time from home to work is used to evaluate the relationship between wages/productivity and the urban

---

[1]Under the simplifying assumption of a monocentric city, we consider the inverse distance from the weighting area where the individual lives to the main business centre of the metropolitan area, to calculate an approximate measure of distance to jobs.

landscape[2]. All these models are estimated with a simple OLS. Another dimension of spatial mismatch is the heterogeneity in the unemployment rates within the urban area. This dimension will be assessed by estimating the probability of being unemployed for each economically active individual, given her relative location to the main centre of the city:

$$h_i = P[U_i = 1] = F[\beta X_i + \gamma_1 \text{inv\_dist}_r + \gamma_2 \text{inv\_dist}_r^2] \tag{3}$$

In this specification, U_i refers to the employment status (it equals 1 when a person is unemployed) and F is a logistic cumulative probability function. Here, X_i is the set of observed characteristics for the individual (age, age squared, colour or race, education level, whether the individual is married, whether he or she has at least one child younger than fifteen living in the house, whether the house is owned by the family and whether the person is or is not the head of the household). Finally, β is a vector of parameters, and inv_dist$_r$ is measured as before. An alternative formulation is the following:

$$
\begin{aligned}
h_i &= P[U_i = 1] \\
&= F[\beta X_i + \theta_1 \%\_\text{time\_commut\_6\_30}_r + \theta_2 \%\_\text{time\_commut\_31\_60}_r + \\
&\quad \theta_3 \%\_\text{time\_commut\_61\_more}_r]
\end{aligned} \tag{4}
$$

In this case, the spatial mismatch is approximated by the percentage of individuals in the neighbourhood whose time spent in commuting belongs to a particular time span.

In sum, two different measures of accessibility to jobs are considered here. Individuals in the Demographic Census are located in weighting areas, as it will be better explained below. Then, the first measure is based on the Euclidean distance of the centroid of the weighting area of residence to the business centre of each metropolitan area. This centre is equivalent to the geographic coordinates of the administrative centre of the municipality with the largest employment level of each metropolitan area.

The second accessibility measure is calculated through the commuting time spent from home to work. As a limitation, this variable is only available in categories (up to five minutes, from six to thirty minutes, thirty minutes to one hour, more than one hour to two hours, more than two hours). In the case of wage models, this variable is obtained through the individual's own reported commuting time. For the probability of unemployment, it is calculated by the percentage of workers who reside in each weighting area that are classified in each category and used in the regressions for the individuals living in that specific weighting area.

Apart from the whole database, these four models will be estimated for each metropolitan area and for three separate groups: (i) individuals who did not complete primary school[3], (ii) up to high school graduates without a college degree, and (iii) individuals who completed college education. In a country such as Brazil, inequality derived from the spatial mismatch can be more or less pronounced depending on the city size and the distance to the main concentration of job opportunities, and it may affect distinct skilled groups in different ways.

3.1 Database

The Brazilian Institute of Geography and Statistics (Instituto Brasileiro de Geografia e Estatística – IBGE) conducts a Demographic Census every ten years, with regional disaggregation at the municipal level (or at the census area level for bigger municipalities). The Demographic Census collects information on the main characteristics of individuals and households, providing details on the living conditions of the population in each municipality, and serving as a very important policy instrument in a country with a land area the size of Brazil. A shorter questionnaire applies to the whole population at the

---

[2]This impedance measure is the commuting time from home to work, calculated at the individual level for the wage equation or for the neighbourhood in the case of the estimation of unemployment probability. This second approach may be associated with a multicentric city structure. Census data only provides commuting time in categories, what represents an additional limitation of this analysis.

[3]Eight years of education.

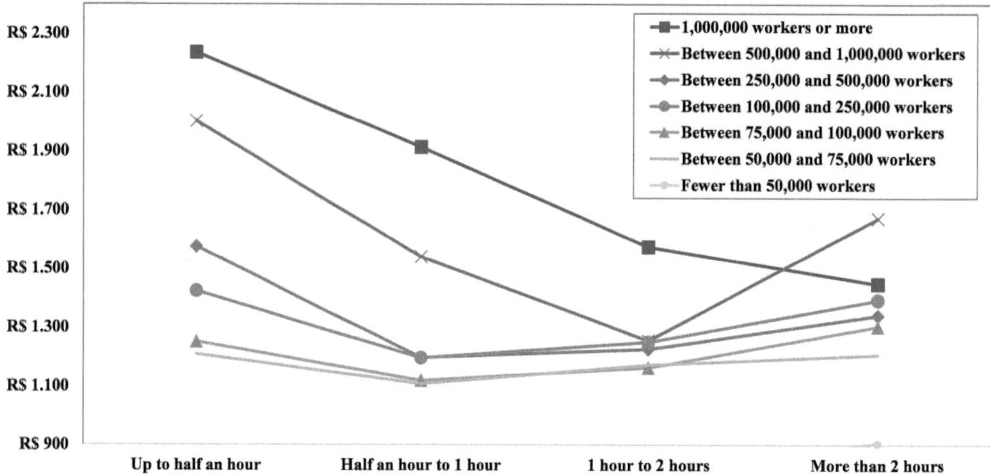

Source: IBGE

Figure 1: Average wage of workers according to their commuting time from home to work and the size of the municipality of residence, 2010

census tract level, while specific individual characteristics are investigated in a longer set of questions that are given to a sample and are representative at the weighting areas level (conglomerates of census tracts with at least 400 households). Microdata at the individual level are available for this sample. We will use weighting areas as our definition of neighbourhood.

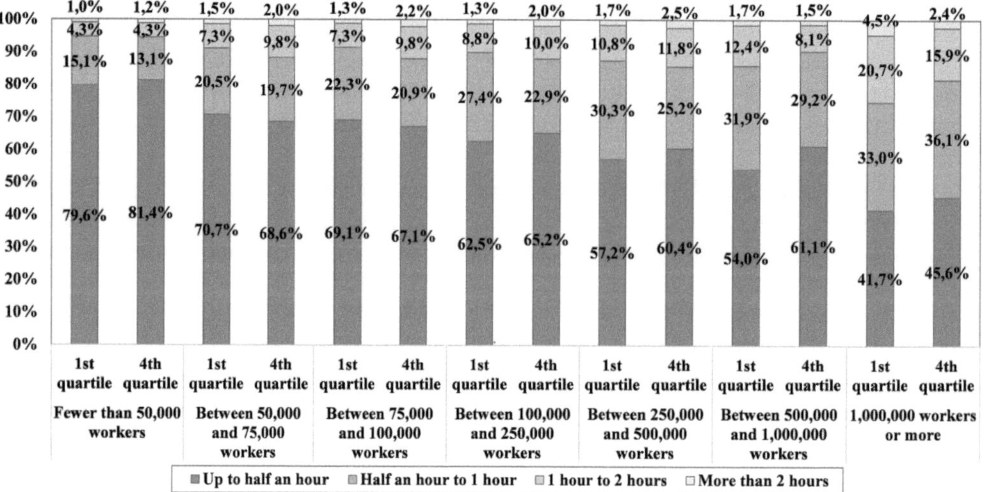

Source: IBGE

Figure 2: Distribution of workers who commute from home to work and belong to the 1st and the 4th quartile of the wage distribution, according to their commuting time and the size of the workforce in the municipality of residence, 2010

3.2 Descriptive statistics

The problem at hand is fundamentally related to metropolitan areas, as commuting costs and agglomeration economies become more relevant at a larger urban scale (Partridge et al. 2009). In fact, if one considers the average wage received by workers according to their commuting time from home to work, it is noticeable that the negative relationship between these two variables is clearer when cities with at least 500,000 workers are taken into account (Figure 1).

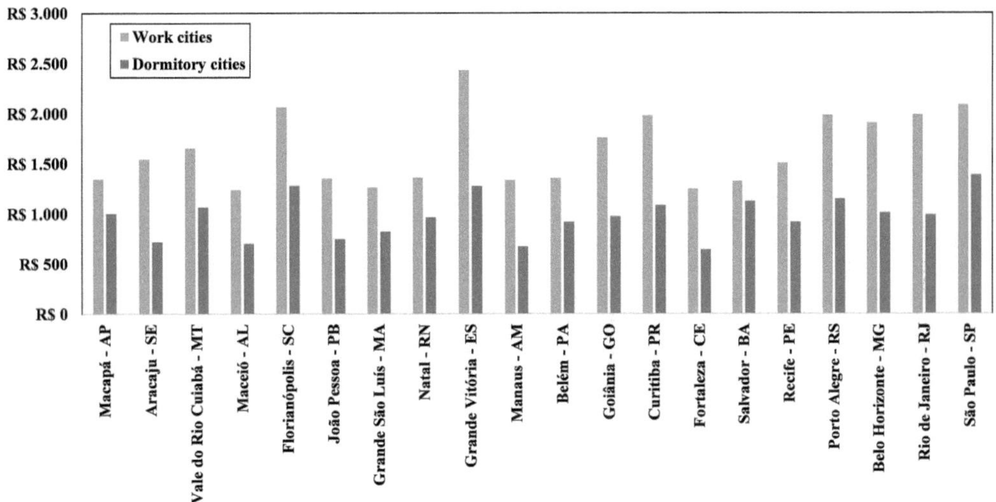

Source: IBGE

Figure 3: Average monthly wage for workers who live in work or dormitory cities inside each metropolitan area, (ordered by the size of working population), 2010

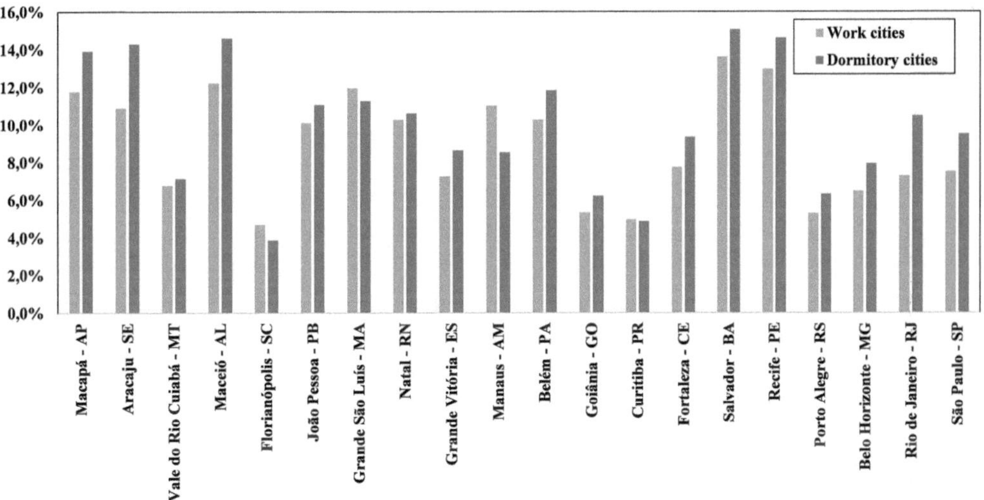

Source: IBGE

Figure 4: Average unemployment rate for people who live in work or dormitory cities inside each metropolitan area, (ordered by the size of working population), 2010

This difference between cities of different sizes is made clear in the analysis presented in Figure 2. In fact, the biggest differences in commuting times faced by workers in the richest (4th) and the poorest (1st) quartiles of the wage distribution in each municipality is seen in places with at least 500,000 workers. Furthermore, the decreasing relationship between wages and commuting time is stronger for those who commute for up to two hours.

For this reason, only 20 metropolitan areas containing state capitals were included in the study. In addition, only male workers aged 25 to 64 years old were kept in the database, in order to homogenise their decisions to participate in the labour market. For the wage regression, the database contained only workers who commuted to work and returned home every day.

It is also possible to show how wages and the unemployment rate vary according to the distance between the residential location of a worker and the centre of the city. Considering the daily commuting flows from home to work obtained from the Demographic

Table 1: Descriptive characteristics of each metropolitan area (ordered by the size of working age population), 2010

Metropolitan region	Macro region	Average hourly wage (R$ 2010)	Unemployment rate	Individuals commuting >1 hour (in %)	Working age population (men aged 25-64)
Macapá - AP	North	R$ 10.44	7.7%	5.3%	85,494
Aracaju - SE	Northeast	R$ 10.87	7.4%	10.7%	159,838
Vale do Rio Cuiabá - MT	Centre-West	R$ 13.58	4.3%	7.7%	160,638
Maceió - AL	Northeast	R$ 9.27	8.2%	13.3%	216,904
Florianópolis - SC	South	R$ 13.77	2.6%	6.6%	217,208
João Pessoa - PB	Northeast	R$ 9.72	6.5%	7.7%	230,930
Grande São Luís - MA	Northeast	R$ 10.96	7.5%	16.1%	244,017
Natal - RN	Northeast	R$ 9.85	7.1%	8.4%	258,207
Grande Vitória - ES	Southeast	R$ 11.94	4.9%	14.6%	353,561
Manaus - AM	North	R$ 11.19	7.1%	16.7%	378,496
Belém - PA	North	R$ 10.85	7.0%	14.4%	402,170
Goiânia - GO	Centre-West	R$ 12.32	3.4%	11.2%	415,541
Curitiba - PR	South	R$ 13.51	3.0%	13.1%	623,103
Fortaleza - CE	Northeast	R$ 9.41	5.6%	12.4%	666,504
Salvador - BA	Northeast	R$ 11.01	9.2%	20.0%	723,297
Recife - PE	Northeast	R$ 10.00	9.5%	17.2%	745,952
Porto Alegre - RS	South	R$ 12.38	3.7%	11.4%	807,268
Belo Horizonte - MG	Southeast	R$ 11.82	4.2%	18.7%	1,115,715
Rio de Janeiro - RJ	Southeast	R$ 12.92	5.8%	30.5%	2,402,075
São Paulo - SP	Southeast	R$ 15.37	5.7%	28.8%	3,953,270

Source: IBGE

Census of 2010, it is possible to define work and dormitory cities in each metropolitan area. The former are characterized by a higher inflow of people going there to work than an outflow of those who live there and go somewhere else to work, while the latter present a higher daily worker outflow than an inflow.

Figure 3 shows that average wages are much higher for people who live in work cities than for those who live in dormitory cities. However, in the case of the unemployment rate, there are mixed signs (Figure 4). In some metropolitan areas (Manaus, Grande São Luís, Florianópolis and Curitiba), dormitory cities show a lower unemployment rate than work cities. This pattern is unexpected under the hypothesis of a monocentric metropolitan area, but may be associated to the fact that these specific metropolitan areas are less dense than other more developed metropolitan areas in Brazil, for which the unemployment rate is larger in dormitory cities.

The econometric discussion outlined above explains the need to calculate the distance of each weighting area to the relevant business centre. This should be done on the basis of the main location of jobs around the city. In Brazil, however, there is no consolidated database covering all metropolitan areas and showing the location of jobs. Therefore, we consider a different approach, in which the centre of the metropolitan area is given by the administrative centre of the largest municipality (defined according to the number of employed individuals in 2010[4]).

Focusing more specifically on the models, the main descriptive characteristics are presented in Tables 1, 2 and 3, and Tables A.1, A.2 and A.3 in the Appendix. Table 1 indicates that the metropolitan areas considered in this study are significantly heterogeneous and should be treated separately, as each of them has a specific distribution of jobs and wages. Furthermore, areas with a bigger labour market have a higher average wage and a higher percentage of workers who commute for more than one hour to reach their jobs. This characteristic is clearer for metropolitan areas with more than a million male workers aged 25 to 64. For the unemployment rate, there seems to be more of a

---

[4]Data obtained from the Ministry of Labour and available at http://pdet.mte.gov.br/acesso-online-as-bases-de-dados.

Table 2: Percentage of workers who spend more than one hour commuting from home to work, according to the distance the worker lives from the centre, (ordered by the size of working population), 2010

	Distance from centre (in kilometer)							
	<2.5	2.5 to <5	5 to <10	10 to <20	20 to <30	30 to <40	40 to <50	50 or more
Macapá - AP	4.4%	4.9%	5.5%	6.3%		8.1%		4.0%
Aracaju - SE	7.0%	8.1%	11.4%	15.3%	15.9%			
Vale do Rio Cuiabá - MT	6.0%	5.0%	7.2%	10.2%	15.8%			8.7%
Maceió - AL	5.6%	6.9%	10.2%	20.4%	14.2%	11.9%		
Florianópolis - SC	3.5%	3.0%	5.2%	9.4%	12.5%	4.1%	4.9%	2.5%
João Pessoa - PB	6.7%	6.8%	8.0%	8.7%	6.0%	7.0%	10.7%	7.7%
Grande São Luís - MA	6.0%	11.2%	12.0%	23.2%	21.4%	14.5%		
Natal - RN	16.3%	13.4%	5.8%	5.4%	9.6%	8.3%	6.2%	
Grande Vitória - ES	7.4%	9.9%	16.9%	16.3%	22.2%	11.4%	6.1%	
Manaus - AM	10.6%	9.4%	12.0%	22.7%			20.0%	11.4%
Belém - PA	5.8%	6.7%	7.8%	19.4%	23.0%	11.2%	15.2%	
Goiânia - GO	3.6%	4.5%	6.6%	15.7%	21.2%	12.2%	11.5%	8.2%
Curitiba - PR	3.8%	4.2%	9.8%	16.5%	21.1%	6.9%	17.7%	8.7%
Fortaleza - CE	14.7%	13.2%	14.1%	12.6%	8.7%	8.0%	6.4%	5.3%
Salvador - BA	15.2%	13.8%	19.8%	29.4%	18.8%	9.0%	9.4%	10.7%
Recife - PE	7.4%	8.1%	13.1%	24.1%	20.1%	15.9%	7.2%	12.6%
Porto Alegre - RS	2.5%	5.1%	8.4%	15.7%	17.6%	7.8%	4.3%	4.7%
Belo Horizonte - MG	7.3%	10.9%	13.0%	24.6%	25.8%	17.5%	13.4%	6.3%
Rio de Janeiro - RJ	14.1%	13.5%	18.3%	28.1%	37.8%	39.7%	39.4%	22.8%
São Paulo - SP	23.9%	20.0%	21.1%	28.5%	34.7%	29.9%	21.5%	16.9%

Source: IBGE

regional aspect to the level observed in each metropolitan area, as regions located in the Northeast, for example, show a much higher level of unemployment than other regions.

There is a strong relationship between commuting time and distance to the centre, as can be seen in Table 2. In São Paulo and Rio de Janeiro, the largest metropolitan areas in Brazil, the percentage of individuals who commute for more than one hour is significantly higher for people who live more than 10km from the centre than for those living less than this distance away. However, this percentage decreases when the distance to the centre is greater than 30km in São Paulo or 40km in Rio de Janeiro. Since our objective is to investigate labour market characteristics related to the main business centre of each metropolitan area, we will focus on individuals living within a circle with a radius of 30km.

Table 3: Descriptive statistics by individual characteristics, 2010

	Unemp. Rate	Average hourly wage (R$ 2010)
Age		
25 to 34 years old	7.4%	9.75
35 to 44 years old	4.9%	12.31
45 to 54 years old	4.7%	15.48
55 to 64 years old	4.7%	19.06
Education level		
Less than 7 years of schooling	6.9%	6.62
8 to 10 years of schooling	6.3%	8.29
11 to 14 years of schooling	5.7%	11.21
15 years of schooling or more	3.0%	33.37

Continued on next page

Table 3 – continued from previous page

	Unemp. Rate	Average hourly wage (R$ 2010)
Colour		
White	4.8%	16.91
Black	6.8%	8.43
Yellow	5.1%	18.20
Brown	6.7%	8.84
Indigenous	6.4%	8.97
Marital status		
Single	7.7%	10.08
Married	3.7%	15.48
Children		
No children up to 15 years old	6.9%	13.07
Has at least one child up to 15 years old	4.1%	12.29
Home ownership		
Tenant	5.4%	11.39
Owned home	5.9%	13.21
Household position		
Another member of the household	8.0%	10.36
Head of the household	4.2%	14.33
Formality status		
Informal sector		9.46
Formal sector		13.93
Sector		
Agriculture		7.51
Manufacture and construction		9.59
Other industrial activities		14.26
Commerce		10.26
Services		10.53
Auxiliary services		17.83
Transport and communication		9.86
Health and social services		24.84
Education		17.85
Public sector		22.01
Other activities		15.79
Occupation		
Non-applicable		16.80
Leaders		30.45
Scientific, artistic or similar		30.88
Technical level		14.93
Administrative service		9.61
Commerce and service		7.14
Agriculture, livestock, extractive activities		4.14
Manufacture		7.26
Military		23.73
Commuting time to work		
Up to 5 minutes		13.66
6 to 30 minutes		13.47
31 minutes to 1 hour		12.68
More than 1 hour to 2 houres		11.27
More than 2 hours		11.15

Source: IBGE
Notes: The unemployment rate is calculated for the weighting area in which the individual resides

In Table 3, we can note that the wage level is higher for older individuals, those who are better educated, married people, those who are Indians, from Asiatic ancestry or white, those who are the head of a household, people employed in the formal sector and those who work in health and social services or leaders, scientists or artists. In addition, workers who commute for a longer time have a lower salary, on average. On the other hand, the unemployment rate is higher for younger individuals, those who are less educated, those who are black or brown, single people, people with no children, and those who are not heads of households.

The theory of spatial mismatch states that a lack of connection to job opportunities may affect an individual's prospects in the labour market, especially for low-skilled workers. Complementing the results presented in Table 3, Tables A.1, A.2 and A.3 provide wage levels and unemployment rates using different impedance measures. Distance to jobs can be calculated in many ways: (i) distance from the centroid of the weighting area to the business centre of the metropolitan area; (ii) individual commuting time from home to work; or (iii) percentage of workers in the weighting area whose commuting time falls within each time span. For the wage equation, we consider alternatively (i) and (ii) for employed individuals. On the other side, for the estimation of the probability of unemployment, (i) and (iii) are used, calculated at the weighting area level.

With these considerations in mind, Tables A.1, A.2 and A.3 show that wages seem to be higher near the centre of each metropolitan area, and that this effect is stronger in larger areas. However, for the unemployment rate, the expected positive relationship with distance to jobs is not clear. The main results will be presented in the next section.

4 Results

The first set of results refers to the estimation of wage equations that control for individual characteristics and uses two different measures of relative distance in the city: the distance to a unique centre (a monocentric city) and the distance to each worker's job (a multicentric city).

Table 4 shows that wages have a positive relationship with the inverse distance to the main centre of each metropolitan area (and, as a consequence, a negative relationship with distance itself). This effect is more significant for larger metropolitan areas, and it seems to be stronger for individuals with a higher education level. Therefore, wages are lower for individuals who live further away from the main business centre. However, this result demonstrates more of a correlation than a causal effect, especially because individuals are analysed with reference to their residential location. There may be inverse causality in this case, as an individual's choice of location may be affected by the wage previously received, and this can affect current labour market prospects and productivity.

Table 4: OLS regressions of the logarithm of the hourly wage, for all individuals and by education group

	Macapá - AP	Aracaju - SE	Vale do Rio Cuiabá - MT	Maceió - AL	Florianó- polis - SC	João Pessoa - PB	Grande São Luís - MA
All individuals							
Inverse of distance	0.244‡	0.935‡	1.323‡	0.439‡	0.281‡	0.004	0.122
Inverse of distance squared	-0.072	-0.855‡	-2.057‡	-0.064	-0.053	-0.004	-0.007
N	5,559	7,736	8,121	9,068	15,481	10,490	10,421
Adjusted R squared	0.429	0.463	0.364	0.455	0.421	0.44	0.354
Up to incomplete primary school							
Inverse of distance	0.349†	1.482‡	0.627	0.096	-0.308†	0.428‡	0.546‡
Inverse of distance squared	-0.126	-2.011‡	-0.878	0.234	0.213*	-0.118‡	-0.030‡
N	1,754	2,889	2,777	3,918	4,158	4,551	2,916
Adjusted R squared	0.134	0.121	0.088	0.103	0.081	0.116	0.081
Complete primary school to incomplete tertiary school							
Inverse of distance	0.215*	0.534*	0.902†	0.568‡	0.151*	0.008	-0.046
Inverse of distance squared	-0.058	-0.199	-1.604†	-0.244*	-0.033	-0.001	0.002

Continued on next page

Table 4 – continued from previous page

N	3,015	3,979	4,187	4,091	8,071	4,674	6,403
Adjusted R squared	0.321	0.32	0.2	0.276	0.23	0.243	0.197
Complete tertiary school							
Inverse of distance	0.246	1.458†	3.897‡	0.740‡	0.725‡	-1.237‡	-0.152
Inverse of distance squared	-0.083	-1.601†	-5.515‡	-0.257	-0.274‡	0.316‡	0.007
N	790	868	1,157	1,059	3,252	1,265	1,102
Adjusted R squared	0.293	0.283	0.196	0.296	0.3	0.298	0.237

	Natal - RN	Grande Vitória - ES	Manaus - AM	Belém - PA	Goiânia - GO	Curitiba - PR	Fortaleza - CE
All individuals							
Inverse of distance	-0.179	0.300‡	0.633‡	0.594‡	1.283‡	1.069‡	-0.355‡
Inverse of distance squared	-0.211	-0.344‡	-0.347‡	-0.258‡	-0.739‡	-0.302‡	0.224*
N	12,056	24,887	11,912	15,523	17,317	32,745	26,254
Adjusted R squared	0.46	0.431	0.34	0.374	0.361	0.389	0.408
Up to incomplete primary school							
Inverse of distance	0.365*	-0.143	1.001‡	0.461‡	1.252‡	0.764‡	-0.341†
Inverse of distance squared	-0.714†	0.253	-0.492‡	-0.214*	-0.812‡	-0.174‡	0.364*
N	4,512	7,780	3,541	4,933	6,466	10,605	9,248
Adjusted R squared	0.124	0.094	0.097	0.077	0.071	0.092	0.076
Complete primary school to incomplete tertiary school							
Inverse of distance	-0.613‡	0.202†	0.471‡	0.439‡	1.175‡	1.056‡	-0.023
Inverse of distance squared	0.278	-0.290†	-0.238‡	-0.148	-0.674‡	-0.293‡	-0.161
N	6,041	13,138	6,989	8,728	8,448	16,835	14,345
Adjusted R squared	0.268	0.216	0.182	0.19	0.215	0.19	0.213
Complete tertiary school							
Inverse of distance	0.334	1.460‡	0.445	1.134‡	1.255‡	1.038‡	-1.937‡
Inverse of distance squared	-1.546	-1.576‡	-0.333*	-0.646‡	-0.716‡	-0.295‡	1.361†
N	1,503	3,969	1,382	1,862	2,403	5,305	2,661
Adjusted R squared	0.268	0.283	0.216	0.256	0.249	0.254	0.269

	Recife - PE	Salvador - BA	Porto Alegre - RS	Belo Horizonte - MG	Rio de Janeiro - RJ	São Paulo - SP
All individuals						
Inverse of distance	0.758‡	0.538‡	1.251‡	1.267‡	0.617‡	1.399‡
Inverse of distance squared	-0.639‡	-0.202‡	-0.616‡	-0.681‡	-1.005‡	-1.107‡
N	33,635	25,865	35,715	47,034	79,277	154,088
Adjusted R squared	0.409	0.416	0.435	0.427	0.404	0.369
Up to incomplete primary school						
Inverse of distance	0.07	0.177	0.411*	0.362†	-0.013	1.359‡
Inverse of distance squared	-0.001	0.12	-0.118	0.045	0.036	-1.011‡
N	11,393	7,617	10,425	17,149	20,809	45,808
Adjusted R squared	0.093	0.088	0.091	0.079	0.073	0.08
Complete primary school to incomplete tertiary school						
Inverse of distance	0.607‡	0.379‡	1.234‡	1.101‡	1.066‡	1.650‡
Inverse of distance squared	-0.549‡	-0.112†	-0.575‡	-0.600‡	-1.686‡	-1.271‡
N	18,298	14,563	20,476	23,695	43,703	79,875
Adjusted R squared	0.203	0.217	0.233	0.216	0.186	0.18
Complete tertiary school						
Inverse of distance	1.776‡	1.202‡	1.392‡	1.821‡	1.165‡	0.705‡
Inverse of distance squared	-1.734‡	-0.552‡	-0.717‡	-1.079‡	-4.248‡	-0.641‡
N	3,944	3,685	4,814	6,190	14,765	28,405
Adjusted R squared	0.254	0.246	0.244	0.291	0.228	0.202

Source: Authors' calculations

Notes: Controls: age, age squared, colour or race, household head, with children up to 15 years old, married, sector of activity, occupation, existence of a formal contract. For the regressions with all individuals, the education attainment of the individual was included as an additional control. Significance levels: * $p<0.10$, † $p<0.05$, ‡ $p<0.01$. Only male individuals aged 25 to 64 years old living within a distance of 30km from the centre are considered in the analysis. Sampling weights are taken into account with Stata command pweight. Complete tables can be requested from the authors.

This issue may also be present when the spatial mismatch is captured by each individual's commuting time from home to work (Table 5). The estimated coefficients are then likely to be underestimating the real effect. Therefore, if this reverse causality issue is correctly dealt with, distance to jobs should be even more relevant in determining wage levels, as it would be possible to discount the effect of relocation by looking at job opportunities over the city.

In any case, Table 5 shows that the negative effect of commuting time on wages is significant for workers commuting for 30 minutes or more, and is higher the longer the time spent in this activity. For low-skilled workers in smaller metropolitan areas, wages are not significantly correlated to this measure of spatial mismatch. Moreover, for most metropolitan areas, workers who commute for two hours or more do not see any significant effect on their wages, which may result from the fact that there are only a few workers belonging to this group, and no clear wage pattern.

The second set of results refers to the probability of being unemployed. Coefficients are presented as odds-ratios, with values greater than one indicating a positive effect of the variable of interest on the probability of unemployment. Tables 6 and 7 present the estimated coefficients related to specific distance measures. Metropolitan areas are ranked from left to right according to the size of their labour market. There is an indication in Table 6 that the probability of unemployment is not significantly correlated with the inverse distance to the centre. This result is consistent for most metropolitan areas, and there is no specific pattern for groups with different levels of schooling. The same result is found when distance to jobs is measured by the time spent by workers in the neighbourhood commuting from home to work (Table 7). Once again, for most metropolitan areas this relationship is not significant, and it does not show any pattern regarding education level, labour market size, or the sign of the correlation itself in cases when it is in fact significant.

Table 5: OLS regressions of the logarithm of the hourly wage, for all individuals and by education group

	Macapá - AP	Aracaju - SE	Vale do Rio Cuiabá - MT	Maceió - AL	Florianó-polis - SC	João Pessoa - PB	Grande São Luís - MA
All individuals							
Workers commuting 6'-30'	-0.093‡	0.002	-0.038	-0.029	-0.008	0.021	-0.013
Workers commuting >30'-1 hour	-0.100†	-0.058	-0.137‡	-0.017	-0.040*	-0.015	-0.022
Workers commuting >1-2 hours	-0.194‡	-0.069	-0.216‡	-0.085†	-0.098‡	-0.043	-0.106†
Workers commuting >2 hours	0.086	0.121	-0.046	0.007	0.081	0.002	-0.048
N	5,559	7,736	8,121	9,068	15,481	10,828	10,680
Adjusted R squared	0.429	0.461	0.366	0.446	0.418	0.442	0.356
Up to incomplete primary school							
Workers commuting 6'-30'	-0.035	0.018	0.029	0.008	0.001	0.048	-0.028
Workers commuting >30'-1 hour	-0.017	0.015	-0.033	0.050	0.033	0.084	0.008
Workers commuting >1-2 hours	-0.089	0.017	-0.129*	0.038	0.032	0.048	-0.054
Workers commuting >2 hours	0.062	0.016	-0.085	0.034	-0.136	-0.003	-0.038
N	1,754	2,889	2,777	3,918	4,158	4,804	3,017
Adjusted R squared	0.130	0.114	0.090	0.097	0.080	0.123	0.079
Complete primary school to high school graduates without college degree							
Workers commuting 6'-30'	-0.109†	-0.016	-0.056	-0.056	-0.016	-0.018	-0.029
Workers commuting >30'-1 hour	-0.084	-0.110*	-0.176‡	-0.078	-0.042	-0.105†	-0.014
Workers commuting >1-2 hours	-0.214‡	-0.163†	-0.211‡	-0.192‡	-0.096†	-0.113*	-0.121†
Workers commuting >2 hours	0.009	0.069	0.153	0.039	0.069	0.080	-0.022
N	3,015	3,979	4,187	4,091	8,071	4,749	6,550
Adjusted R squared	0.320	0.320	0.206	0.271	0.230	0.246	0.199
College degree							
Workers commuting 6'-30'	-0.171†	0.099	-0.058	0.041	-0.020	-0.051	0.063
Workers commuting >30'-1 hour	-0.367‡	0.057	-0.186	0.087	-0.116†	-0.115	-0.129
Workers commuting >1-2 hours	-0.452†	0.028	-0.293	-0.037	-0.286‡	-0.252	-0.192
Workers commuting >2 hours	0.104	0.579	-0.259	0.181	0.444†	-0.232	-0.128
N	790	868	1,157	1,059	3,252	1,275	1,113

Continued on next page

Table 5 – continued from previous page

Adjusted R squared	0.301	0.279	0.181	0.263	0.287	0.285	0.241

	Natal - RN	Grande Vitória - ES	Manaus - AM	Belém - PA	Goiânia - GO	Curitiba - PR	Fortaleza - CE
All individuals							
Workers commuting 6'-30'	-0.014	-0.027	0.029	-0.044	-0.018	0.011	-0.013
Workers commuting >30'-1 hour	-0.095‡	-0.075‡	-0.042	-0.066†	-0.089‡	-0.033*	-0.024
Workers commuting >1-2 hours	-0.109‡	-0.153‡	-0.121‡	-0.132‡	-0.193‡	-0.123‡	-0.112‡
Workers commuting >2 hours	0.078	-0.069*	-0.039	-0.015	-0.050	-0.102‡	-0.086*
N	12,056	24,887	11,912	15,523	16,951	32,523	27,034
Adjusted R squared	0.458	0.433	0.340	0.369	0.355	0.379	0.408
Up to incomplete primary school							
Workers commuting 6'-30'	-0.035	-0.095‡	0.045	-0.001	-0.005	0.006	0.031
Workers commuting >30'-1 hour	-0.023	-0.083†	0.048	-0.021	-0.028	0.014	0.091‡
Workers commuting >1-2 hours	-0.013	-0.125‡	-0.032	-0.106*	-0.122†	-0.018	0.038
Workers commuting >2 hours	-0.063	-0.054	-0.018	-0.077	0.017	-0.119†	-0.083
N	4,512	7,780	3,541	4,933	6,284	10,494	9,662
Adjusted R squared	0.122	0.096	0.089	0.074	0.062	0.088	0.078
Complete primary school to high school graduates without college degree							
Workers commuting 6'-30'	-0.002	0.004	-0.013	-0.061	-0.017	-0.032	-0.032
Workers commuting >30'-1 hour	-0.083†	-0.044	-0.119†	-0.049	-0.091†	-0.065‡	-0.052*
Workers commuting >1-2 hours	-0.162‡	-0.118‡	-0.172‡	-0.095†	-0.239‡	-0.176‡	-0.143‡
Workers commuting >2 hours	0.168	-0.041	-0.036	0.045	-0.105	-0.137†	-0.034
N	6,041	13,138	6,989	8,728	8,284	16,737	14,691
Adjusted R squared	0.262	0.219	0.186	0.184	0.210	0.180	0.214
College degree							
Workers commuting 6'-30'	-0.053	-0.059	0.143	-0.054	-0.060	0.128†	-0.137
Workers commuting >30'-1 hour	-0.359‡	-0.189‡	0.058	-0.223†	-0.227‡	-0.003	-0.289‡
Workers commuting >1-2 hours	-0.305†	-0.373‡	-0.217*	-0.360‡	-0.178	-0.249‡	-0.612‡
Workers commuting >2 hours	0.218	-0.187	0.004	-0.061	-0.135	0.323†	-0.323
N	1,503	3,969	1,382	1,862	2,383	5,292	2,681
Adjusted R squared	0.281	0.287	0.222	0.247	0.240	0.241	0.270

	Recife - PE	Salvador - BA	Porto Alegre - RS	Belo Horizonte - MG	Rio de Janeiro - RJ	São Paulo - SP
All individuals						
Workers commuting 6'-30'	-0.016	0.040	0.005	-0.013	-0.011	-0.018
Workers commuting >30'-1 hour	0.010	0.051†	-0.009	-0.048‡	-0.002	-0.014
Workers commuting >1-2 hours	-0.051†	0.042	-0.044†	-0.125‡	-0.031†	-0.067‡
Workers commuting >2 hours	-0.022	0.085†	-0.062	-0.134‡	-0.049†	-0.095‡
N	33,852	27,923	42,000	48,518	83,302	154,584
Adjusted R squared	0.406	0.409	0.424	0.419	0.397	0.367
Up to incomplete primary school						
Workers commuting 6'-30'	-0.050	0.020	-0.037	-0.068†	-0.082‡	-0.046†
Workers commuting >30'-1 hour	0.001	0.067	0.004	-0.035	-0.025	-0.012
Workers commuting >1-2 hours	-0.026	0.022	-0.028	-0.091‡	-0.030	-0.041†
Workers commuting >2 hours	-0.063	0.091	-0.110†	-0.092†	0.005	-0.047†
N	11,485	8,451	13,073	17,989	22,455	45,652
Adjusted R squared	0.094	0.084	0.092	0.078	0.072	0.077
Complete primary school to high school graduates without college degree						
Workers commuting 6'-30'	-0.010	0.018	0.004	-0.010	-0.017	-0.022
Workers commuting >30'-1 hour	0.023	0.031	-0.034	-0.058†	0.002	-0.030*
Workers commuting >1-2 hours	-0.040	0.038	-0.053†	-0.144‡	-0.032	-0.081‡
Workers commuting >2 hours	0.046	0.055	-0.032	-0.182‡	-0.075‡	-0.110‡
N	18,418	15,722	23,617	24,277	45,919	80,089
Adjusted R squared	0.201	0.211	0.222	0.212	0.181	0.175
College degree						
Workers commuting 6'-30'	0.072	0.150*	0.078	0.064	0.108†	0.022
Workers commuting >30'-1 hour	0.060	0.052	0.054	-0.020	0.025	0.026

Continued on next page

Table 5 – continued from previous page

Workers commuting >1-2 hours	-0.086	0.058	-0.067	-0.131†	-0.011	-0.053*
Workers commuting >2 hours	-0.162	0.173	0.034	0.007	-0.049	-0.162‡
N	3,949	3,750	5,310	6,252	14,928	28,843
Adjusted R squared	0.245	0.236	0.229	0.257	0.228	0.204

Source: Authors' calculations

Notes: Controls: age, age squared, colour or race, household head, with children up to 15 years old, married, sector of activity, occupation, existence of a formal contract. For the regressions with all individuals, the education attainment of the individual was included as an additional control. Reference category: workers commuting for up to 5 minutes. Significance levels: * p<0.10, †p<0.05, ‡p<0.01. Only male individuals aged 25 to 64 years old living within a distance of 30km from the centre are considered in the analysis. Sampling weights are taken into account with Stata command pweight. Complete tables can be requested from the authors.

Table 6: Logit model for the probability of being unemployed, regressions with all individuals and by education groups

	Macapá - AP	Aracaju - SE	Vale do Rio Cuiabá - MT	Maceió - AL	Florianópolis - SC	João Pessoa - PB	Grande São Luís - MA
All individuals							
Inverse of distance	1.175	0.464	0.119	0.432	2.925†	1.410	1.713
Inverse of distance squared	0.944	6.556	31.848	1.390	0.455*	0.943	0.970
N	6,034	8,459	8,525	10,020	16,009	11,378	11,291
Pseudo R squared	0.055	0.064	0.038	0.053	0.051	0.067	0.061
Up to incomplete primary school							
Inverse of distance	0.322	0.192	0.003*	0.310	0.112	1.502	1.176
Inverse of distance squared	2.335	36.753	37,017.1*	1.407	4.366	0.912	0.992
N	1,917	3,223	2,952	4,448	4,320	5,083	3,186
Pseudo R squared	0.026	0.048	0.019	0.024	0.053	0.037	0.030
Complete primary school to incomplete tertiary school							
Inverse of distance	2.355	0.621	2.430	0.496	11.255	1.703	2.065*
Inverse of distance squared	0.584	2.704	0.058	1.339	0.138	0.889	0.960*
N	3,300	4,343	4,385	4,464	8,357	4,991	6,963
Pseudo R squared	0.064	0.047	0.038	0.056	0.062	0.068	0.061
Complete tertiary school							
Inverse of distance	0.531	98.561	0.620	1.195	2.783	0.172	1.181
Inverse of distance squared	1.648	0.061	37.412	0.749	0.484	1.852	0.992
N	817	893	1,188	1,108	3,332	1,304	1,142
Pseudo R squared	0.131	0.245	0.104	0.152	0.063	0.187	0.163

	Natal - RN	Grande Vitória - ES	Manaus - AM	Belém - PA	Goiânia - GO	Curitiba - PR	Fortaleza - CE
All individuals							
Inverse of distance	2.487	0.846	0.468	0.697	1.354	1.204	1.151
Inverse of distance squared	0.276	1.252	1.441	1.528	0.782	0.962	1.039
N	13,086	26,231	12,933	16,838	18,004	33,821	27,974
Pseudo R squared	0.053	0.035	0.035	0.038	0.030	0.026	0.046
Up to incomplete primary school							
Inverse of distance	2.789	0.124†	0.176*	0.257*	0.204	1.108	2.385
Inverse of distance squared	0.388	9.381*	2.620	3.555†	4.159	1.161	0.397
N	5,027	8,268	3,916	5,409	6,768	10,976	9,953
Pseudo R squared	0.038	0.026	0.016	0.021	0.030	0.022	0.026
Complete primary school to incomplete tertiary school							
Inverse of distance	1.332	1.989	0.734	1.010	4.190	3.190†	0.646
Inverse of distance squared	0.428	0.473	1.091	1.089	0.286*	0.706*	2.237
N	6,495	13,860	7,583	9,494	8,772	17,410	15,259
Pseudo R squared	0.050	0.031	0.033	0.038	0.032	0.026	0.051

Continued on next page

Table 6 – continued from previous page

Complete tertiary school

Inverse of distance	1662.660*	3.270	0.542	1.987	0.448	0.117†	1.921
Inverse of distance squared	0.000	0.399	1.265	0.770	1.824	1.817†	0.278
N	1,564	4,103	1,434	1,935	2,464	5,435	2,762
Pseudo R squared	0.134	0.082	0.084	0.060	0.055	0.041	0.096

	Recife - PE	Salvador - BA	Porto Alegre - RS	Belo Horizonte - MG	Rio de Janeiro - RJ	São Paulo - SP
All individuals						
Inverse of distance	0.430†	0.411‡	2.409*	1.007	0.736	1.253
Inverse of distance squared	1.629	1.604†	0.694	0.848	1.176	0.654
N	37,419	28,533	37,203	49,194	84,152	164,255
Pseudo R squared	0.057	0.053	0.027	0.031	0.042	0.032
Up to incomplete primary school						
Inverse of distance	0.536	0.550	13.921*	0.569	0.275*	6.053‡
Inverse of distance squared	1.459	1.201	0.132‡	1.180	4.335	0.183‡
N	13,098	8,711	10,940	18,033	22,383	49,540
Pseudo R squared	0.027	0.023	0.027	0.022	0.018	0.016
Complete primary school to incomplete tertiary school						
Inverse of distance	0.342†	0.393†	2.030	0.865	0.877	0.644
Inverse of distance squared	1.732	1.722†	0.800	1.476	0.965	0.894
N	20,214	15,990	21,323	24,813	46,498	85,260
Pseudo R squared	0.053	0.050	0.024	0.031	0.041	0.029
Complete tertiary school						
Inverse of distance	1.012	0.143	0.803	1.430	54.645*	0.669
Inverse of distance squared	0.979	2.427	1.170	0.388	0.000	1.614
N	4,107	3,832	4,940	6,348	15,271	29,455
Pseudo R squared	0.090	0.080	0.028	0.032	0.055	0.028

Source: Authors' calculations

Notes: Controls: age, age squared, colour or race, household head, with children up to 15 years old, married. For the regressions with all individuals, the education attainment of the individual was included as an additional control. Coefficients are presented as odds-ratios. Significance levels: * $p<0.10$, †$p<0.05$, ‡$p<0.01$. Only male individuals aged 25 to 64 years old living within a distance of 30km from the centre are considered in the analysis. Sampling weights are taken into account with Stata command pweight. Complete tables can be requested from the authors.

A few aspects can be highlighted in relation to these results. On the one hand, unemployment levels may vary throughout the city in an irregular way, with no specific pattern in either monocentric or multicentric cities. In a sense, this conclusion in the Brazilian case matches part of the literature, which finds no regular pattern for the spatial distribution of the unemployment rate.

However, the conclusion goes against recent theoretical predictions that distance to jobs can affect the probability that individuals belonging to low-skilled minorities find a position. If these theoretical predictions are valid, it might be that there are methodological issues driving this unexpected result. First, distance is not measured in relation to an individual, but relates only to her neighbourhood. In addition, we do not take into account the location of job offers and existing jobs. Our database locates individuals by their place of residence. Therefore, there may be difficulties in correctly identifying the centres in the city and in calculating the relative location of each potential worker. Moreover, when distance is measured as the commuting time for workers in the neighbourhood, this may not be the same as the commuting time a potential worker would spend if he or she were in work.

Table 7: Logit model for the probability of being unemployed, regressions with all individuals and by education groups

	Macapá - AP	Aracaju - SE	Vale do Rio Cuiabá - MT	Maceió - AL	Florianó-polis - SC	João Pessoa - PB	Grande São Luís - MA
All individuals							
% workers commuting 6'-30'	0.048†	0.664	-0.091	0.293	0.327	0.212	0.507
% workers commuting >30'-1 hour	0.105	0.288	2,219	0.175	0.049†	0.475	0.168†
% workers commuting >1 hour	0.516	0.929	2.128*	1,205	0.428	1,267	0.723
N	6,034	8,459	8,525	10,020	16,009	11,782	11,566
Adjusted R squared	0.056	0.063	0.040	0.053	0.054	0.064	0.061
Up to incomplete primary school							
% workers commuting 6'-30'	0.011*	3,231	-0.161	1,304	0.004†	0.151	1,532
% workers commuting >30'-1 hour	0.005*	0.995	5,118	1,424	0.021*	0.159	0.546
% workers commuting >1 hour	1,398	1,639	2,514	1,715	0.006‡	0.898	1,071
N	1,917	3,223	2,952	4,448	4,320	5,389	3,291
Adjusted R squared	0.026	0.046	0.019	0.025	0.059	0.035	0.030
Complete primary school to high school graduates without college degree							
% workers commuting 6'-30'	0.101	0.299	0.040	0.047†	2,798	0.799	0.291
% workers commuting >30'-1 hour	0.336	0.160	3,518	0.018†	0.078	3,474	0.081†
% workers commuting >1 hour	0.349	0.884	2,588	0.631	1,368	3,524	0.570†
N	3,300	4,343	4,385	4,464	8,357	5,079	7,122
Adjusted R squared	0.064	0.047	0.039	0.058	0.067	0.067	0.063
College degree							
% workers commuting 6'-30'	0	0.012	-0.301	0.337	0.210	0.000	2,668
% workers commuting >30'-1 hour	0.056	0.005	0.031	0.010	0.061	0.002	0.574
% workers commuting >1 hour	0.158	0.003†	0.240	26.935*	4,475	0.002	0.999
N	817	893	1,188	1,108	3,332	1,314	1,153
Adjusted R squared	0.139	0.260	0.102	0.177	0.064	0.162	0.164

	Natal - RN	Grande Vitória - ES	Manaus - AM	Belém - PA	Goiânia - GO	Curitiba - PR	Forta-leza - CE
All individuals							
% workers commuting 6'-30'	0.196*	3,722	0.322	0.869	0.274	1,508	8.937*
% workers commuting >30'-1 hour	0.111†	5,284	5,128	0.357	1,030	1,296	5,723
% workers commuting >1 hour	0.790	1.715*	0.847	2,357	0.756	1,576	4,325
N	13,086	26,231	12,933	16,838	17,626	33,594	28,821
Adjusted R squared	0.054	0.035	0.037	0.039	0.032	0.026	0.046
Up to incomplete primary school							
% workers commuting 6'-30'	0.126	1,701	0.493	36,757	0.210	0.816	2,237
% workers commuting >30'-1 hour	0.257	2,175	5,536	5,896	0.698	0.868	0.353
% workers commuting >1 hour	0.705	1,634	1,028	132.388*	1,024	1,929	3,518
N	5,027	8,268	3,916	5,409	6,579	10,862	10,416
Adjusted R squared	0.038	0.025	0.016	0.022	0.033	0.022	0.028
Complete primary school to high school graduates without college degree							
% workers commuting 6'-30'	0.155	13.582†	0.166	0.102	0.496	2,746	113.524‡
% workers commuting >30'-1 hour	0.038†	14.542†	4,042	0.074	1,371	2,788	110.358‡
% workers commuting >1 hour	0.711	2.230*	0.657	0.223	0.741	1,232	19.355†
N	6,495	13,860	7,583	9,494	8,604	17,310	15,623
Adjusted R squared	0.051	0.032	0.036	0.039	0.032	0.025	0.051
College degree							
% workers commuting 6'-30'	0.343	0.047	13,079	0.266	0.234	0.305	0.042
% workers commuting >30'-1 hour	0.493	1,331	901,885	0.139	10,454	0.064	4,959
% workers commuting >1 hour	0.524	0.180	1,656	0.878	0.071†	3,154	0.004
N	1,564	4,103	1,434	1,935	2,443	5,422	2,782
Adjusted R squared	0.128	0.086	0.086	0.059	0.065	0.038	0.102

Continued on next page

Table 7 – continued from previous page

	Recife - PE	Salvador - BA	Porto Alegre - RS	Belo Horizonte - MG	Rio de Janeiro - RJ	São Paulo - SP
All individuals						
% workers commuting 6'-30'	0.545	0.503	0.360	0.487	1,264	0.679
% workers commuting >30'-1 hour	0.982	0.264	0.433	0.901	0.909	0.771
% workers commuting >1 hour	1,370	1,047	0.376†	0.733	1,158	1,020
N	37,669	30,873	43,722	50,753	88,531	164,684
Adjusted R squared	0.057	0.051	0.024	0.031	0.042	0.032
Up to incomplete primary school						
% workers commuting 6'-30'	0.273	1,333	1,986	0.278	0.935	0.628
% workers commuting >30'-1 hour	0.609	0.358	1,593	1,120	0.696	0.779
% workers commuting >1 hour	0.699	2,183	1,376	0.738	1,321	0.981
N	13,207	9,678	13,696	18,924	24,195	49,331
Adjusted R squared	0.027	0.023	0.022	0.024	0.019	0.016
Complete primary school to high school graduates without college degree						
% workers commuting 6'-30'	0.670	0.404	0.067†	0.358	1,048	0.902
% workers commuting >30'-1 hour	1,243	0.249	0.111†	0.396	0.948	0.873
% workers commuting >1 hour	1,854	0.837	0.121‡	0.526	1,049	1,094
N	20,350	17,292	24,572	25,418	48,893	85,450
Adjusted R squared	0.053	0.048	0.023	0.031	0.042	0.029
College degree						
% workers commuting 6'-30'	6,864	0.015	17,634	12,783	0.689	0.337
% workers commuting >30'-1 hour	1,456	1,056	18,005	55,136	0.345	0.512
% workers commuting >1 hour	7,570	0.148	2,771	2,117	0.523	0.915
N	4,112	3,903	5,454	6,411	15,443	29,903
Adjusted R squared	0.091	0.080	0.024	0.030	0.058	0.029

Source: Authors' calculations
Notes: Controls: age, age squared, colour or race, household head, with children up to 15 years old, married. For the regressions with all individuals, the education attainment of the individual was included as an additional control. Coefficients are presented as odds-ratios. Significance levels: * $p<0.10$, †$p<0.05$, ‡$p<0.01$. Only male individuals aged 25 to 64 years old living within a distance of 30km from the centre are considered in the analysis. Sampling weights are taken into account with Stata command pweight. Complete tables can be requested from the authors.

As robustness checks, some additional results are provided in Table A.4, in the appendix[5]. We run the models for all individuals without dividing the database between metropolitan areas. Then, we also include in these models the control for the metropolitan area of residence. As it can be seen, the regression for the logarithm of the hourly wage against distance measures indicate that the farther away from the city centre the lower the wage received on average. A higher education attainment is associated to higher wages, which are also present in some of the largest metropolitan areas. However, when Model 2 is considered, the partial correlation of commuting distance and wages does not have the expected sign (longer commuting should be associated with lower wages). This is due to the fact that longer time periods are more common in larger urban areas, which are associated to more populated metropolitan areas. This is an indication that there are iterative effects of commuting distance and city size which should be controlled for (what is done in the estimations presented in Table 5).

For the models related to the probability of unemployment, the results indicate that a lower chance of unemployment is associated with longer commuting times in the weighting area (once again, an unexpected result). This is most likely caused by the fact that iterations between metropolitan areas and commuting times are not taken into account. In addition, the probability of unemployment is lower for more educated individuals. These considerations make our previous estimations preferable in relation to this additional exercise.

---

[5]We thank the contribution of an anonymous referee who suggested that we estimated these alternative models to enrich our analysis.

5 Final remarks

There is significant spatial mismatch in the labour market in Brazilian metropolitan areas. The influence of spatial location and distance to jobs on labour market outcomes is stronger for larger urban areas, and wages are more strongly related to distance to jobs and to distance to the centre than unemployment rates are. In addition, the difference in the commuting time for poor and rich workers is larger in labour markets with 500,000 workers or more.

The literature on spatial mismatch suggests that this phenomenon is predominantly urban and that it is more relevant for low-skilled minorities in larger urban areas for whom congestion costs are relatively more important. In addition, these minorities may face more limitations in their social interactions, with a significant impact on their ability to find a better match in the job market.

In this paper, we have attempted to investigate whether this negative relationship between spatial mismatch and labour market outcomes is valid in Brazil after controlling for individual characteristics. Our conclusions indicate that there is no clear relation between two different measures of accessibility to jobs and the probability of being unemployed. However, for wages there is a clear correlation, which is stronger in larger metropolitan areas.

These results indicate that in the Brazilian case, the spatial mismatch is more relevant to determine individual wages (in accordance to the relationship mentioned by Gobillon et al. 2007). On the other hand, the probability of unemployment may not be affected as much by it. This can be a result of the empirical strategy adopted here, in which commuting time spent by workers is used to calculate the potential commuting time an unemployed person would have spent in case she was employed. It may also be an indication that the spatial mismatch has a stronger effect than alternative measures of unbalance in the labour market, such as unemployment duration, as it was found in the literature (see for instance Rogers 1997). Finally, the adequate estimation strategy should allow for iterative effects between accessibility measures and metropolitan areas. This means that each metropolitan area has a particular dynamic in the labour market.

In any case, city size and skill level seem to be relevant aspects for the chances an individual has to perform well in the labour market. Intra-urban policies should aim to reduce inequalities in terms of accessibility. Since education attainment is strongly related to income, poorer neighbourhoods, which are also less served by public policies – and in the peripheries are usually far away from jobs – should be the main focus of transportation policies in the short run and education programs for middle and long run results.

This is intended to be an exploratory work. In this sense, we have explored correlations between labour market outcomes and measures of accessibility to jobs for Brazilian metropolitan areas. Our results depend on strong identification hypotheses to avoid bias related to simultaneous location decisions of workers and firms within the city (Ihlanfeldt 2006). If these conditions do not hold, our results may not represent a causal relationship, but will be meaningful in the sense of providing a better understanding of the conditional distribution of wages and the unemployment rate in the biggest metropolitan areas of Brazil.

The broader analysis of urban labour markets in Brazil provides an indication that there are relevant differences in the way workers and firms interact in space, and urban scale seems to be important to this relationship. Future work should investigate these issues more thoroughly. In this sense, different proximity dimensions could be included in the analysis, in order to investigate the factors that generate the spatial mismatch. However, this approach would require a more comprehensive database of the characteristics of Brazilian labour markets and the local interaction between individuals, which are not available yet.

Acknowledgement

Eduardo Amaral Haddad acknowledges financial support from CNPq.

References

Andersson F, Haltiwanger JC, Kutzbach MJ, Pollakowsky HO, Weinberg DH (2014) Job displacement and the duration of joblessness: The role of spatial mismatch. NBER working paper series, WP 20066. CrossRef.

Åslund O, Östh J, Zenou Y (2010) How important is access to jobs? Old question – improved answer. *Journal of Economic Geography* 10: 389–422. CrossRef.

Brueckner JK, Thisse JF, Zenou Y (2002) Local labor markets, job matching, and urban location. *International Economic Review* 43[1]: 155–171. CrossRef.

Bruzelius N (1979) *The Value of Travel Time.* Croom Helm, London

Capello R (2007) *Regional Economics.* Routledge Advanced Texts in Economics and Finance, Abingdon

Chauvin JP, Glaeser E, Ma Y, Tobio K (2016) What is the difference about urbanization in rich and poor countries? Cities in Brazil, China, India and the United States. *Journal of Urban Economics* 98: 17–49. CrossRef.

Da Mata D, Deichmann U, Henderson JV, Lall SV, Wang HG (2007) Determinants of city growth in Brazil. *Journal of Urban Economics* 62: 252–272. CrossRef.

Di Paolo A, Matas A, Raymond JL (2016) Job accessibility and job-education mismatch in the metropolitan area of Barcelona. *Papers in Regional Science* 96[S1]: S91–S112. CrossRef.

Fujita M, Thisse JF (2012) *Economics of Agglomeration: Cities, industrial location and regional growth* (2nd ed.). Cambridge University Press, Cambridge

Gibb K, Osland L, Pryce G (2014) Describing inequalities in access to employment and the associated geography of wellbeing. *Urban Studies* 51[3]: 596–613. CrossRef.

Gobillon L, Selod H (2013) Spatial mismatch, poverty, and vulnerable populations. In: Fischer MM, Nijkamp P (eds), *Handbook of Regional Science.* Springer, 93-107. CrossRef.

Gobillon L, Selod H, Zenou Y (2007) The mechanisms of spatial mismatch. *Urban Studies* 44[12]: 2401–2427. CrossRef.

Haddad EA, Barufi AMB (2017) From rivers to roads: Spatial mismatch and inequality of opportunity in urban labor markets of a megacity. *Habitat International* 68: 3–14. CrossRef.

Holzer HJ (1991) The spatial mismatch hypothesis: What has the evidence shown? *Urban Studies* 28[1]: 105–122. CrossRef.

Houston D (2005a) Employability, skills mismatch and spatial mismatch in metropolitan labour markets. *Urban Studies* 42[2]: 221–243. CrossRef.

Houston D (2005b) Methods to test the spatial mismatch hypothesis. *Economic Geography* 81[4]: 407–434. CrossRef.

Hu L (2014) Changing job access of the poor: Effects of spatial and socioeconomic transformations in Chicago. *Urban Studies* 51[4]: 675–692

Hu L, Giuliano G (2014) Poverty concentration, job access, and employment outcomes. *Journal of Urban Affairs* 39[1]: 1–16. CrossRef.

Ihlanfeldt KR (2006) A primer on spatial mismatch within urban labor markets. In: Arnott RJ, McMillen DP (eds), *A Companion to Urban Economics.* 404-417, Oxford. CrossRef.

Johnson RC (2006) Landing a job in urban space: The extent and effects of spatial mismatch. *Regional Science and Urban Economics* 36: 331–372. CrossRef.

Kain JF (1968) Housing segregation, negro employment, and metropolitan decentralization. *Quarterly Journal of Economics* 82: 32–59. CrossRef.

Kain JF (1992) The spatial mismatch hypothesis: Three decades later. *Housing Policy Debate* 3[2]: 371–459. CrossRef.

Kain JF (2004) A pioneer's perspective on the spatial mismatch literature. *Urban Studies* 41[1]: 7–32. CrossRef.

Krugman P (1995) *Development, Geography, and Economic Theory.* The MIT Press, Cambridge, Mass

Lucas Jr RE, Rossi-Hansberg E (2002) On the internal structure of cities. *Econometrica* 70[4]: 1445–1476. CrossRef.

McCann P (2013) *Modern Urban and Regional Economics* (2nd ed.). Oxford University Press, Oxford

Morrison PS (2005) Unemployment and urban labour markets. *Urban Studes* 42[1]: 2261–2288. CrossRef.

Ottaviano G (2004) Chapter 58 – Agglomeration and economic geography. In: Henderson JV, Thisse JF (eds), *Handbook of Regional and Urban Economics, Volume 4.* Elsevier, Amsterdam, 2563–2608

Partridge M, Rickman DS, Ali K, Rose-Olfert M (2009) Agglomeration spillovers and wage and housing cost gradients across the urban hierarchy. *Journal of International Economics* 78: 126–140. CrossRef.

Roback J (1982) Wages, rents and the quality of life. *Journal of Political Economy* 90[6]: 1257–1278. CrossRef.

Rogers CL (1997) Job search and unemployment duration: Implications for the spatial mismatch hypothesis. *Journal of Urban Economics* 42: 109–132. CrossRef.

Topa G, Zenou Y (2015) Neighborhood and network effects. In: Duranton G, Henderson JV, Strange WC (eds), *Handbook of Regional and Urban Economics, Volume 5A.* Elsevier, Amsterdam, 561–624. CrossRef.

Tyndall J (2015) Waiting for the R train: Public transportation and employment. *Urban Studies* 54[2]: 520–537. CrossRef.

Vieira R, Haddad EA (2015) An accessibility index for the metropolitan area of São Paulo. In: Kourtit K, Nijkamp P, Stough RR (eds), *The Rise of the City: Spatial Dynamics in the Urban Century.* Edward Elgar Publishing, Cheltenham, UK, 242–258. CrossRef.

Zenou Y (1999) Unemployment in cities. In: Huriot JM, Thisse JF (eds), *Economics of Cities.* Cambridge University Press, Cambridge, 343–389

Zenou Y (2000) Urban unemployment, agglomeration and transportation policies. *Journal of Public Economics* 77: 97–133. CrossRef.

Zenou Y (2006) Efficiency wages and unemployment in cities: The case of high-relocation costs. *Regional Science and Urban Economics* 36: 49–71. CrossRef.

Zenou Y (2009) *Urban Labor Economics* (1st ed.). Cambridge University Press, New York. CrossRef.

Zenou Y (2013) Spatial versus social mismatch. *Journal of Urban Economics* 74: 113–132. CrossRef.

A Appendix

Table A.1: Average hourly wage (in Brazilian real) in each weighting area by the distance to the main business centre, 2010.

	Distance from centre (in kilometer)							
	<2.5	2.5 to <5	5 to <10	10 to <20	20 to <30	30 to <40	40 to <50	50 or more
Macapá - AP	12.96	10.98	10.00	7.61		8.47		7.32
Aracaju - SE	11.80	14.75	9.08	9.07	5.29			
Vale do Rio Cuiabá - MT	13.95	24.74	11.97	8.83	8.03			6.57
Maceió - AL	19.11	6.60	10.14	6.53	5.28	4.90		
Florianópolis - SC	24.60	20.15	15.59	11.07	9.30	8.31	7.71	7.64
João Pessoa - PB	7.58	10.99	12.01	7.04	3.72	3.91	4.65	4.48
Grande São Luís - MA	8.79	14.08	13.28	9.52	5.33	4.58		
Natal - RN	5.60	6.14	11.04	13.95	4.62	5.64	5.24	5.24
Grande Vitória - ES	13.59	15.30	12.84	10.00	8.10	7.79	10.41	10.41
Manaus - AM	12.44	14.44	15.31	9.42			4.58	6.68
Belém - PA	20.14	13.85	11.42	8.44	6.19	5.32	5.73	5.73
Goiânia - GO	28.69	18.71	13.19	9.21	6.69	7.12	7.21	9.00
Curitiba - PR	28.58	31.99	14.51	9.45	9.10	6.62	7.38	6.68
Fortaleza - CE	6.13	7.67	12.46	10.37	6.73	4.44	3.84	4.19
Salvador - BA	12.63	23.79	9.69	8.68	10.41	7.32	8.89	7.62
Recife - PE	21.29	12.68	11.67	8.25	6.46	4.66	6.67	6.38
Porto Alegre - RS	26.99	31.46	17.78	10.09	9.15	8.65	9.05	8.41
Belo Horizonte - MG	34.98	19.37	14.90	9.85	7.50	8.90	6.88	7.79
Rio de Janeiro - RJ	7.74	15.58	17.51	14.84	11.77	8.91	8.08	8.25
São Paulo - SP	23.47	21.54	21.51	16.88	10.69	11.14	10.09	9.96

Source: IBGE

Table A.2: Average individual hourly wage (in Brazilian real) by commuting time from home to work, 2010.

	Up to 5 min.	6 min to $\frac{1}{2}$ hour	$>\frac{1}{2}$ to 1 hour	>1 to 2 hours	>2 hours
Macapá - AP	10.96	11.04	8.32	7.39	12.36
Aracaju - SE	11.72	12.16	9.27	7.85	16.58
Vale do Rio Cuiabá - MT	18.88	14.47	11.81	7.75	15.31
Maceió - AL	7.96	10.01	9.21	6.87	11.14
Florianópolis - SC	13.52	14.19	13.48	11.10	15.77
João Pessoa - PB	9.56	10.97	7.99	6.56	6.93
Grande São Luís - MA	11.16	12.48	10.49	7.76	10.94
Natal - RN	10.81	11.35	7.66	6.61	11.45
Grande Vitória - ES	14.40	13.23	11.05	8.31	10.10
Manaus - AM	10.01	13.60	10.38	7.82	8.81
Belém - PA	12.18	11.49	10.70	7.99	12.06
Goiânia - GO	17.91	13.44	9.99	7.42	14.08
Curitiba - PR	14.54	15.32	12.55	8.54	9.45
Fortaleza - CE	10.04	10.45	8.80	6.33	8.43
Salvador - BA	9.45	10.85	11.23	11.08	13.33
Recife - PE	10.58	10.17	10.50	8.36	8.29
Porto Alegre - RS	12.27	13.50	11.55	9.82	9.97
Belo Horizonte - MG	13.18	13.02	11.55	9.25	9.05
Rio de Janeiro - RJ	14.22	12.87	13.29	12.77	10.46
São Paulo - SP	17.53	16.79	15.83	13.15	11.95

Source: IBGE

Table A.3: Average unemployment rate in each weighting area by the distance to the main business centre, 2010

	Distance from centre (in kilometer)							
	<2.5	2.5 to <5	5 to <10	10 to <20	20 to <30	30 to <40	40 to <50	50 or more
Macapá - AP	8.4%	6.7%	6.6%	10.3%		12.4%		4.7%
Aracaju - SE	10.0%	6.6%	6.9%	9.5%	7.3%			
Vale do Rio Cuiabá - MT	4.1%	3.2%	4.4%	4.3%	7.7%			8.9%
Maceió - AL	5.4%	8.6%	7.5%	8.3%	13.0%	11.8%		
Florianópolis - SC	2.5%	3.8%	2.7%	1.8%	3.4%	3.9%	1.6%	1.9%
João Pessoa - PB	9.1%	5.3%	5.5%	6.8%	8.0%	8.0%	13.9%	8.8%
Grande São Luís - MA	7.7%	10.1%	7.2%	7.7%	6.0%	4.1%		
Natal - RN	7.3%	8.0%	7.4%	5.9%	8.7%	5.4%	8.6%	
Grande Vitória - ES	5.9%	4.5%	4.4%	4.9%	5.7%	4.9%	7.3%	
Manaus - AM	6.0%	8.2%	6.4%	7.7%			4.2%	6.9%
Belém - PA	6.8%	7.4%	5.3%	7.3%	7.6%	5.8%	8.1%	
Goiânia - GO	3.5%	3.2%	3.0%	3.6%	3.5%	4.4%	3.8%	5.8%
Curitiba - PR	3.4%	2.8%	3.0%	2.9%	3.4%	1.5%	2.2%	3.3%
Fortaleza - CE	5.2%	6.8%	5.4%	5.2%	6.7%	6.9%	5.1%	6.3%
Salvador - BA	8.6%	5.7%	8.2%	9.5%	9.3%	12.2%	12.9%	14.6%
Recife - PE	6.7%	7.9%	9.2%	9.7%	11.2%	11.6%	9.6%	11.9%
Porto Alegre - RS	3.7%	4.4%	4.0%	3.7%	3.9%	3.6%	3.1%	2.7%
Belo Horizonte - MG	2.7%	3.8%	4.7%	4.3%	4.1%	4.2%	4.7%	3.7%
Rio de Janeiro - RJ	6.0%	5.1%	5.1%	5.3%	6.0%	6.3%	6.7%	7.8%
São Paulo - SP	5.5%	5.2%	5.1%	5.9%	6.1%	5.5%	5.0%	4.1%

Source: IBGE

Table A.4: Regressions for the whole database

	Model 1 ln(hourly wage) OLS	Model 2 ln(hourly wage) OLS	Model 3 unemp. (P = 1) Logit	Model 4 unemp. (P = 1) Logit
Inverse of distance	1.177‡		1.024	
Inverse of distance squared	0.990‡		0.999	
Commuting time of workers in the weighting area				
% workers commuting 6' to 30'				0.547†
% workers commuting more than 30' to 1 hour				0.543†
% workers commuting more than 1 hour				0.876
Individual commuting time (Reference: up to 5')				
6' to 30'		0.994		
More than 30' to 1 hour		0.979‡		
More than 1 hour to 2 hours		0.930‡		
More than 2 hours		0.932‡		
Metropolitan area (Reference: Belém - PA, 402,170 men 25-64)				
Macapá - AP (85,494 men 25-64)	0.996	1.007	1.078	1.093
Aracaju - SE (159,838 men 25-64)	0.935‡	0.932‡	1.168‡	1.198‡
Vale do Rio Cuiabá - MT (160,638 men 25-64)	1.154‡	1.146‡	0.647‡	0.666‡
Maceió - AL (216,904 men 25-64)	0.842‡	0.842‡	1.323‡	1.334‡
Florianópolis - SC (217,208 men 25-64)	1.186‡	1.175‡	0.439‡	0.447‡
João Pessoa - PB (230,930 men 25-64)	0.811‡	0.826‡	0.995	1.026
Grande São Luís - MA (244,017 men 25-64)	0.997	0.987	1.134†	1.138†
Natal - RN (258,207 men 25-64)	0.878‡	0.872‡	1.150‡	1.171‡
Grande Vitória - ES (353,561 men 25-64)	1.107‡	1.102‡	0.804‡	0.800‡
Manaus - AM (378,496 men 25-64)	1.106‡	1.105‡	1.078	1.073
Goiânia - GO (415,541 men 25-64)	1.150‡	1.139‡	0.547‡	0.550‡
Curitiba - PR (623,103 men 25-64)	1.167‡	1.157‡	0.523‡	0.525‡
Fortaleza - CE (666,504 men 25-64)	0.875‡	0.869‡	0.874‡	0.878‡
Salvador - BA (723,297 men 25-64)	0.989	0.987	1.309‡	1.279‡
Recife - PE (745,952 men 25-64)	0.862‡	0.856‡	1.522‡	1.512‡
Porto Alegre - RS (807,268 men 25-64)	1.081‡	1.068‡	0.627‡	0.629‡
Belo Horizonte - MG (1,115,715 men 25-64)	1.105‡	1.097‡	0.679‡	0.665‡
Rio de Janeiro - RJ (2,402,075 men 25-64)	1.131‡	1.122‡	0.916†	0.865‡
São Paulo - SP (3,953,270 men 25-64)	1.236‡	1.225‡	1.006	0.947
Education attainment (Reference: up to incomplete primary school)				
Complete primary school to incomplete college	1.304‡	1.305‡	0.782‡	0.788‡
Complete college	2.576‡	2.588‡	0.426‡	0.440‡
N	583,184	583,184	621,359	621,359
Pseudo R squared			0.048	0.048
Adjusted R squared	0.406	0.405		

Source: Authors' calculations

Notes: Controls for Models 1 and 2: age, age squared, colour or race, household head, with children up to 15 years old, married, sector of activity, occupation, existence of a formal contract. Controls for Models 3 and 4: age, age squared, colour or race, household head, with children up to 15 years old, married. Coefficients are presented as odds-ratios. Significance levels: * p <0.10, †p <0.05, ‡p <0.01. Only male individuals aged 25 to 64 years old living within a distance of 30km from the centre are considered in the analysis. Sampling weights are taken into account with Stata command pweight. Complete tables are available under request to the authors.